BRAZEN

BRAZEN

MY UNORTHODOX JOURNEY
FROM LONG SLEEVES TO LINGERIE

JULIA HAART

CROWN

NEW YORK

Published in the United States by Crown, an imprint of Random House, a division of Penguin Random House LLC, New York.

CROWN and the Crown colophon are registered trademarks of Penguin Random House LLC.

All photos are courtesy of the author, except the following:
Photo insert page 7, middle: "Metropol Parasol" © Nathan Rupert

Hardback ISBN 978-0-593-23916-2
Ebook ISBN 978-0-593-23917-9

Printed in the United States of America on acid-free paper

crownpublishing.com

2 4 6 8 9 7 5 3 1

FIRST EDITION

Book design by Simon M. Sullivan

I would like to dedicate the book to my children,
Batsheva, Shlomo, Miriam, and Aron.
I would not be alive today without all of you!

AUTHOR'S NOTE

~

Dearest Reader,

I want to thank you for spending some hours with me and reading my book. I began writing *Brazen* in 2017, a smidge over four years after I left everyone and everything familiar behind and time traveled to the twenty-first century. It was a journey born of such unendurable misery that I had to flee or die. I walked into a world in which no one knew me. I had no past, no shared history. I was a zero. Now I pursue zeros of a very different kind for thousands of women around the world. I felt deep within my heart that this story could inspire others to change their lives, to go for their dreams, and to not wait for permission.

I want to be very clear. I love being a Jew. I am proud of my heritage and I do not believe that the way I was brought up has anything to do with Judaism. Like other religions all over the world, Judaism is about love and caring for one another and living for a purpose higher than your own self-interest. I think all religions are beautiful and have these moralistic concepts at their core. It is only when they are perverted by extremists who see any change to archaic laws as a direct defiance to God that something meant to improve the world and humankind becomes an intolerable prison.

Since my TV show, *My Unorthodox Life*, premiered, I've been blessed to have received tens of thousands of messages from people all over the world, sharing their own unorthodox lives, their own struggles and difficulties. Out of the tens of millions of people who watched the show, so many have written that they found the courage to make changes in their own lives, to leave whatever or whomever was causing them anguish, and to jump into the unknown. The reality is that if I can do it, then so can anyone, and that fact is both wonderful and terrible.

For those people who are truly suffering and just need a push to get up and improve their lives and the lives of those they love, I say that extreme change is possible at any age, and I hope this story gives them strength and faith in a better future. May they arm themselves with my struggles and face their own with bravery and grace.

For those people who are petrified of the unknown, this fact is dangerous. I am dangerous. I am a woman who left and not only survived but succeeded. My story doesn't fit the narrative of anyone who wants to use religion as an excuse to make women subservient to men. My very existence is a serious threat.

My Unorthodox Life is about my present defined by my past. *Brazen*, however, is my whole story as I remember it. This book takes you through my entire journey, and believe me, I mean the *entire* journey. I am as hard on myself and my choices as I am direct about everything that occurred. I stand before you, stark naked, without pretense or camouflage. I lay my heart and soul at your feet, dear reader. Sharing this book with the world is one of the most difficult things I've ever done. Part of me just wants to hide it away and leave it as a cathartic exercise for my eyes only. And yet I know I cannot. I feel my responsibility keenly. If my story can help people around the world find a better tomorrow, what is one woman's difficulty measured against so many others' joy?

To me, demanding change in archaic laws is the very definition of an act of love, as it comes from the desire for future generations to have more rights, more freedoms than we currently possess. Just as my children gave me the courage I needed to leave, the legion of people who have reached out to me with messages of change that they've made in their own lives after watching my show gives me the courage I need to share this book.

You see a smiling and confident Julia now. That joy and self-assurance was hard-won. It took me years to make peace with what was stolen from me, with the burning anger that was in my heart. Sometimes I feel as old as Methuselah, and sometimes I feel like an eight-year-old child, curious and excited by every new first, every extraordinary experience. I am an eternal student, always stretching my mind, challenging old ways of thinking to create new ideas, new possibilities. I urge you to do the same. Stop taking pride in what you already know. Find your inner child and become proud, once again, of how quickly you can learn and grasp new concepts. It is this trait, coupled with intense determination, that I attribute my success to, as well as the hand of God. I have had many miracles happen to me since the day I walked out the door. To me, they are proof positive that if your will is strong enough, and you have purity of purpose, God (or whatever else you would like to call a higher power) will help you succeed.

I am in no way overstating how severely the restrictions of the community I came from shackled my life. I wish I was! I wish I hadn't spent the first forty-two years of my life in utter misery. Within these pages, I have brought the sources for every word I say about my old world. It's important to me to share these with everyone, so I've put the sources on the book's website: brazenbook.com. I strongly suggest you peruse them. I've also include articles, references, and insights for those who want to delve deeper into the complex concepts you will find in this book.

So, I ask all my dear readers to truly feel my words. I am opening up the most intimate parts of my life to you. I hope my story gives you strength. I hope my story makes you stop and think. I hope you read it with the same love and attention with which it was written. I hope this book encourages other women and people to come out and share their truth and fight for a better future.

With love,
Julia Haart

BRAZEN

CHAPTER ONE

Our lineage is the ultimate prequel to our lives. To truly understand yourself, you must understand your history, the intricate thoughts and lives that brought yours into existence. My parents come from Russian "royalty." On my father's side, my grandfather, a decorated general in the Russian army during World War II, was a very influential Communist after the war. When my father was nineteen, he was named head of the Komsomol (the young-adult arm of the Communist Party).

My mother too had some helpful lineage. Her mother was a ballerina in the Bolshoi Ballet, and her dad was an inventor who created a chemical that restored old photos. Her family lived in Bender, Moldova, in the largest house in the center of the city. Sometimes Moldova was part of Romania, and sometimes it was part of the Soviet Union, and my grandfather managed, by some miraculous wrangling, to get a patent for his invention in a country that neither allowed personal business initiative nor recognized individual accomplishment. Yet, somehow, he did it. They both lived very privileged lives.

Lina, my mom, had one sister. My mother was considered "the smart sister" while her sister, Elena, was "the beautiful sister." In photos of them as young women they look almost identical, both extremely smart and lovely, but there it was. Throughout my life, whenever anyone would compliment my mom on her looks, she would look at them with disbelief and shake her head.

My mom took her role of "the smart sister" very seriously. In her entire education, from kindergarten all the way through her two PhDs, one in mathematics and one in philosophy, she never got anything less than an A. She even received a gold medal from the Soviet government, for never getting a single test answer wrong.

When she was nineteen, she met a very handsome and charming young man named Michael. My dad is charismatic and great with people. Everyone always loves him. He's the life of the party. On top of being brilliant, and an engineer (he and my mom both worked for IBM on the first PC computer), he's also a concert pianist and guitar player and a fantastic dancer.

My mom is quiet and thoughtful and very serious—his polar opposite in every way. She is intense and somber. She loved his liveliness and he fell for her indifference. She was the only woman who wasn't instantaneously charmed by him. She was tough and she challenged him and he loved it.

Within six months, they were inseparable. He was a committed and faithful Communist. She, however, had serious doubts. Eventually she would become more ideological and fundamentalist in her religion than my father ever was as a Party member, for it would be her faith that became the driving force in all our lives.

Due to my dad's high standing in the Komsomol, he was given the unique task of traveling around the country preaching the Communist gospel, with the hope that as a bright and vivacious young man, he would inspire others to strengthen their faith in the system. Brezhnev was running the country at that point, and travel was verboten except to the very connected, because they didn't want people seeing that the Communist reality was far from the Utopia Karl Marx had promised. My father, however, was deemed so completely committed that they were unconcerned with him being disillusioned and felt that his positivity and charm would keep the faithful strong. He, of course, was ecstatic, and invited his girlfriend to accompany him. Lina, always curious though already doubting the truth of Communism, eagerly joined him. But what ensued was not at all what the Party had in mind. What Lina and Michael found was a country in complete disarray, where most of the people they met were drunk until noon from the night before and living intolerable lives. My mother, already disillusioned because she had been fighting anti-Semitism her whole life in a country not known for being kind to its Jews, lost the last vestiges of faith in Communism. My father's faith, already broken during that fateful journey, crumbled completely under her irrefutable arguments.

My young parents were believers by nature and went looking for something to replace Communism. They found Judaism. Being Jewish had always hampered my mother, and she had felt its nagging presence since she was a child. She wanted to know more, to understand what it meant to be a Jew.

Of course, religion was illegal during that time, and the Gulag and prisons were full of people who had risked it all to practice their faith. Even reading a religious book could land you in jail, yet they embarked on a harrowing journey of learning about their heritage. Meetings of like-minded, curious Jews happened in basements in the dead of night. Any neighbor or stranger or even friend could be an informant. If one member of the group was caught, he could be tortured and reveal the names of all the other members. Learning about their Jewish heritage was fraught with danger and subterfuge. For two idealistic young people in their twenties, it was just what they needed: a cause to believe in and risk their lives for. It was what they had been taught was the supreme act of goodness: to find a reason for existence outside of yourself to devote your life to, even at the cost of your own. The Cause was what they had been fed their whole lives. They just changed causes.

Despite the risk, my mother even took it upon herself to observe the mikvah (ritual bath) to ensure I was born pure. Women are supposed to dunk themselves three times into a mix of rainwater and regular water seven days after their periods, to regain purity, but there was obviously no ritual Jewish bathhouse in Moscow. My mother, undeterred, found out that you could also dunk in an open body of water, and so, under cover of night, risking her life, she dunked herself in the Black Sea. For my mother, the more difficult the task the greater the reward.

Within a month of their trip across the country, when my mom was twenty-one and my dad twenty, they got married. Then two things occurred simultaneously: my father was "offered" (in the Soviet Union, the Party made "offers" you couldn't refuse) a very high-ranking position in the Communist Party—a post that would have put him at the center of Soviet power and under the watchful eye of the KGB—and my mother got pregnant.

Now living their double life—learning about Judaism on the down-low whilst my father was a top Communist—would be impossible. But it was an offer he literally couldn't refuse. So my mom went in front of the Communist Committee, seven months pregnant, and convinced them that if my dad got this new position, which would require extensive travel and time away from his family, she would end up killing herself and this unborn future Communist leader (yours truly) would be at risk. My mother is a force of nature, and these mere mortals were no match for her. They withdrew their offer, and my dad was allowed to continue his job as a research engineer while my mom worked on her first PhD.

But eventually living in the Soviet Union became too much, and so my birth and their desire for a better life for their baby were the catalysts for them to begin the strenuous process of emigration. The minute you applied for a visa you were an enemy of the state, because emigrating meant that you didn't believe in the Communist vision and were a capitalist pig. Those who tried to leave were called refuseniks, because most often people who applied never received permission to leave. The Soviets even came up with a tax that any émigré with a college degree had to pay, which was equivalent to five years of income, making it impossible for most people. My family, however, was one of the lucky ones. The United States had sponsored the Jackson-Vanik amendment, which basically meant that America traded grain for Jews. Due to the Soviet Union's rampant anti-Semitism, the United States had put an embargo on grain, and because the Soviet Union was in the midst of a hunger pandemic and grain shortage, that embargo made an impact. My family was literally traded for food.

They left with me, my dad's guitar, and a single American dollar bill that one of the members of their underground Jewish network had managed to acquire. It was 1974, and I was three years old. At this point, my parents had been learning English and Hebrew illegally for three years and were fluent. My mother still speaks with a British accent, because the illegal records she listened to in Moscow were all from the UK.

A U.S. nonprofit organization that dealt with Jewish refuseniks called the Hebrew Immigrant Aid Society (HIAS) sent us from Moscow to a processing center in Vienna. I don't remember my time in Vienna at all, although we spent six months there waiting to find out which country would take us in. From Vienna, we were sent to another processing center in Rome to await our fates.

My first happy memories are from Rome: the first time I ever saw or tasted a cherry, the first time I ate a pizza. To this day I can close my eyes and recall the scent of the cheese mingled with sauce. I had never seen or even heard of a tomato, so marinara sauce was like something from another planet. The memories of walking around Rome with my father (my mother never accompanied us on these walks, as she felt they were a waste of time), of eating pizza on the street, the sauce oozing through my fingers, are some of the happiest of my childhood. I understood nothing of our predicament or lack of a home. All I knew was that I had gone from a world filled with gray buildings and boiled potatoes to a magical place filled with colorful people and cherries and tomatoes.

Rome is also the first time I can remember hearing my parents argue, as they tried to decide what country they wanted to live in. My father wanted to live in Israel, but my mother thought that was risky. It was still, in her mind, a third-world country. And what would two engineers do there? My mother wanted to move to Australia, to get as far away from the Soviet Union as possible. He wanted Israel, she wanted Australia, and they got the United States.

That leads me to my name. My parents wanted to name me Berenika (we ended up naming our dog that instead), because in history, there was a Russian princess with that name who was known to be

Jewish. Permission to name me Berenika was denied by the Russian government, however, as the clerk who received the paperwork said my parents would be crippling me for life with such a patently Jewish name. Clearly, I owe this clerk big-time. My parents were at a loss, and I went nameless for a few months, and then, when most babies crawled, I started twirling. I would sit on my chubby behind and spin myself around and around, gurgling and cackling. They called me Yulia—from *volchok yula*, which means "spinning top" in Russian—until I was in my twenties and legally changed it myself to Julia, even though everyone I knew at the time called me Talia. For some reason, it didn't occur to me to change it legally to Talia when I got married. I just wanted to eradicate that last vestige of my shameful Russian-ness, which set me apart from the rest of my peers. I didn't want to be Yulia, so I changed the *Y* to a *J*.

There are other memories of Rome, like meeting the Pope and receiving his blessing. My parents received this honor because of my father's exquisite piano playing. His reputation reached the Pope himself, who had been so supportive of the Jewish refuseniks. My father was asked to perform for the Pope and brought along his only child, as he felt it was beneficial for a young child to stand in the presence of greatness. All I can remember from that day is all the drama, and the fact that everyone made such a fuss over a kind man with gentle eyes putting his hands on my head.

There was another brilliant pianist in the internment center, and her son was responsible for my realization that I loved all things fashion. He was five years old to my four, and he did odd jobs—little tasks that people would pay him for because he was so cute. He used all that money to buy me my very first handbag. (Italian leather!) My love affair with fashion began right then and there.

To leave the placement center you needed a community to sponsor you, and a branch of HIAS in Austin, Texas, decided to sponsor my family. I have the picture that was sent to Austin, and I can understand why they chose us. My mother is twenty-six, young and slim, with emerald eyes and long, jet-black hair that falls to her waist. She looks so lovely and serious with her solid glasses, like a hippie librarian. My father looks like a shorter version of Clark Gable: luxurious mustache and wavy hair, guitar slung across his body. I was decidedly plump, and until I turned six, everyone called me Blintzy, because I look like a stuffed blintz. I have my hand on my hips and my legs planted widely apart. We looked adorable and eminently adoptable. And of course, there was the fact IBM wanted my parents to work in their new PC development program at the Austin Research Laboratory.

Once we made it to Texas, we were put up in an apartment that was paid for by the Austin Jewish community and given some food and money to start us off. Within two years, my parents, both employed by IBM while my mom finished her PhD, returned every dollar that it had cost HIAS to sponsor them, and they continued donating to them for years.

We began living the American dream. And our first holiday season in Austin, NBC even did a story about us. We were an oddity. A Russian Jewish immigrant family living in Austin, Texas. This is ten years before perestroika, when Gorbachev would drive tens of thousands of Russians to America's shores. I wouldn't meet another Russian until I was fourteen years old and living in New York. Within three years, we moved from our first apartment to an attached house and then to our very own home on Rickey Drive. It was a lovely house at the end of a cul-de-sac. I loved that house so much. My parents even got me a dog that we named Berenika. (I always called her Nikka.) She was a mix between a German shepherd and a collie, and I was madly in love with her. When she was fully grown, she was so big that when I would come home from school, she would jump over me instead of on top of me. I thought she was absolutely perfect.

I was enrolled in elementary school, and when I was seven and in second grade, there was an important test to determine what kind of school you would get into. I had been in the country for less than three years and had just learned English, and I was so afraid my lack of an American education would mark me for the less educationally driven school. But I needn't have worried. I got one of the top scores in the state of Texas.

My score brought me to the attention of Jeremy Wilmington, a very prominent Texan entrepreneur who was involved with one of the most prestigious schools in Austin. He was a real WASP and looked like an actor in a movie. He told my parents that I was too brilliant to be in a regular public school and that they should try and get me into the private school. My parents were ecstatic. It was such an honor to be noticed by this brilliant and enormously wealthy man.

I remember the first time I went to the Wilmington home. It was palatial. They had a daughter my age named Kristin, who had this messy mat of red hair that, in all the years I knew her, she never once combed. She had a parrot named Barkley who would scream out words that would make a sailor blush. She loved Barkley. I found him absolutely terrifying. She also had a tree in the middle of her bedroom. An actual tree! Her room was cavernous, and smack dab in the middle of it was an actual tree with a trunk and branches, and up on top, a tree house. It was her reading tree house. We would climb up there with muffins and cookies that her maid had just taken out of the oven and sit in her tree house in the middle of her room and read. It became my favorite place on earth. Her whole life seemed like magic. It was a warm, happy, completely mad house. It was a bit like being Alice in Wonderland, where up was down and down was up.

Jeremy Wilmington was a giant. (OK, everyone over five-foot-seven looks like a giant from my perspective, but he really was super tall: six-foot-five.) He looked like a president. Perfect clothes, perfect diction, a full head of hair, like someone from a movie. And he was always smiling. Content and confident. Russians don't smile so much. Get a Russian drunk and he gets somber and serious. Think of all the great Russian writers . . . Tolstoy, Dostoevsky, Gogol. Everyone always gets killed or commits suicide. Happiness is for simpletons. My parents were not big on laughter or smiling, especially my mom.

At Kristin's house, there was laughter. They had maids and a nanny and a chauffeur and a gardener and a cook, and yet there was constant chaos. Happy, absurd chaos. Kristin's mom was the calmest human being I'd ever met. I understood why. The house was always complete bedlam. Kristin was something between a free spirit and a whirling dervish. There was ten acres of property attached to the house, and that first year when they came into our lives, they invited my family for Thanksgiving, where they served a turkey that Jeremy had hunted himself. I'd never even heard of someone hunting, and it just sounded like something out of a Wild West movie.

Jeremy thought that, with my incredible test score, it would be easy to get me into school. After all, I had beaten every other child in the state, and by that time, my parents were perfectly comfortable financially and had no issue paying the tuition. It seemed like a no-brainer. It turned out to be anything but.

After making excuses that they had no room for me, the principal finally had a private meeting with Jeremy and told him that they didn't want to take me because I was a Jew. At the time, the school had 400 students, and 399 of them were white Protestants and 1 was African American—not a single solitary Jew. Jeremy came to our home and regaled my parents with the entire story, and with his stentorian voice I heard every single word.

The principal told Jeremy that he had managed to keep all the Jews out and he wasn't going to make an exception with me, no matter how promising or intelligent I was. He thought Jeremy would understand, but he was wrong.

Jeremy couldn't believe that this school, which he thought so highly of, was openly anti-Semitic. He refused to back down and after much wrangling, a deal was struck. I would be given an IQ test, and if I tested at genius level, I would be allowed to go to private school. Let's just say that after that, the principal had no choice but to let me in.

What strikes me as odd in hindsight is that I never felt uncomfortable there. I was only eight years old, and I knew the whole drama of them not wanting me because I was Jewish. And yet I walked in there thinking "I'll show them," not "What if no one likes me?"

The most important part of the Wilford School, though, was my friendship with a girl named Patricia. I did not make friends easily;

I read the thesaurus and wrote poetry for fun. Not exactly your typical kid. Yet Patricia and I hit it off immediately. Her father was an artist, so writing poetry seemed perfectly normal to her. Her family had a weekend ranch on the outskirts of Austin, and I spent so much time there that they gifted me my own horse, who I named Windy. We would sit on her couch and watch Pippi Longstocking, my heroine. I thought it would be so wonderful to be in charge of your own life and have enough money to do what you wanted, and to travel the world with a monkey and a horse. She was also inordinately strong and could lift houses. She was the first strong, kick-ass, independent woman I'd ever come across. I prayed for red hair like Pippi's for years, because I associated red hair with strength and independence.

While I was leading this wonderful new American existence, another influence was seeping into our lives. My father comes from a deeply religious Chasidic, Lubavitch family. After World War II, some from the town fled to Israel and America and retained their religious identities, and others, like my father's parents, stayed and became irreligious Communists.

One major difference between the Lubavitch Chasidim and most fundamentalist Jewish religious sects is that the Lubavitch believe in proselytizing. Not in proselytizing to non-Jews, God forbid. In fact, converts are not encouraged. Being Jewish is so complicated, and considered such a privilege, that only those born of Jewish mothers have the right DNA to make it. People who try and convert are turned away three times, and only if they manage to stay the course will they be allowed to join the club. So, when I say that the Lubavitch community proselytizes, I don't mean to non-Jews. I mean to lost Jews. Jews, like my parents, who, due to war or some country's ideology, have lost their way.

Most religious Jews look down their noses at irreligious Jews and consider them members of the low-class, ignorant masses. If your family stayed religious throughout World War II and didn't throw the yarmulkes and tefillin into the bay when they first saw Lady Liberty, then you're religious royalty. Supposedly, the water surrounding Ellis Island is filled with the yarmulkes and tefillin of Jews who threw out the old to embrace the New World. America is called, in Yiddish, di goldene medina (the land of gold), and many traded in the land of milk and honey (Israel) for the land of gold.

If your family stayed religious, it's like having come over on the *Mayflower*. It's called yichus (lineage). It's pretty much the same concept as nobility. If you come from a duke or a duchess and your family has noble blood, people want to marry into your family, and your descendants are "blue bloods." In Judaism, if there's an illustrious rabbi or two in your background, you're Jewish nobility, and people who want their daughters or sons to be matched with a son or daughter of Jewish nobility had better pay a hefty price. Noble Jewish spouses don't come cheap.

There are other major issues with irreligious Jews. The concept of "you are what you eat" is taken very literally in Judaism. Kosher food makes you a Kosher Person. According to Judaism, unkosher food is to the soul what a peanut is to someone allergic to nuts. It's deadly. Just like when food gets caught in your throat, and you choke and can't breathe and can die, so too, unkosher food is toxic. It prevents you from receiving spiritual beneficence and goodness, as it clogs your spiritual soul. An irreligious Jew who eats unkosher food is damaged goods. It doesn't matter if it's due to ignorance, because their parents or grandparents were sinners who relinquished their religion. Their souls are filthy and clogged with unkosher substances that dirty the soul. Who wants to marry or befriend someone with a dirty soul?

Now, the Lubavitch look at irreligious Jews very differently. To them they are lost souls who, through no fault of their own, have been estranged from Judaism. There is this concept of a "tinok shenishbah," which refers to a Jewish child who has been taken into captivity. They claim that, just as a tinok shenishbah is not held responsible for not eating kosher, so too a person who is ignorant of Judaism through no fault of their own cannot be held responsible and therefore can and should be brought back to Judaism, and should be loved and respected as much as a Jew who has been religious since birth. Someone who becomes religious of their own volition as opposed to being born into an ultrareligious family is called a ba'al teshuva, which roughly translates to "person of repentance." There is a saying in Judaism that the place that a ba'al teshuva gets in heaven is even greater than that of a pious, righteous rabbi who was born religious, as the ba'al teshuva has a much harder road. All religious Jews believe this as well, in theory. In practice, however, snobbery and entitlement win the day, and the ba'alei teshuva are always "less than." This kind of thinking played a very crucial role in my life, as we were ba'alei teshuva. Most Jews who come back to Judaism spend an entire lifetime trying to be more pious and religious than their illustrious neighbors, as they have something to prove. It's analogous to the nouveau riche in Philadelphia in the early 1900s, trying to outsnob their old-money neighbors.

The Lubavitch therefore made it their mission in life to bring ignorant, lost Jewish souls back to the fold. They call it shlichus, which means "the sending," and they sent newly married Lubavitcher couples to the most far-flung places on earth to bring Jews "home." It's pretty much the same concept as missionaries, except their target is not the rest of humanity but only lost Jewish souls.

My father had a great-uncle, a rabbi whose name was Yisroel Leibov. He was extremely renowned in Lubavitch communities all over the world. He was a published scholar and founded Kfar Chabad in Paris (an enormous enclave and community of Lubavitch Jews that still thrives today) and Kfar Chabad in Israel. He had also done a great deed during the war, which gave him a lifetime of honor and respect. He had managed to smuggle the Lubavitcher rebbe's mother out of Poland and saved her life. The Lubavitcher rebbe is as close to Jesus as Jews get. Many Lubavitchers believe that although Rav Menachem Schneerson died and his body is buried in accordance to Jewish law, he will be resurrected. (A rav is a rabbi who is specially trained in providing guidance.) The rest of the religious Jewish world is very antagonistic toward the Lubavitch community for this reason. They feel that the Lubavitcher rebbe has been deified, and that their beliefs are more akin to Christianity than Judaism.

When we moved to Austin, Texas, the Lubavitcher rebbe was still alive, and when my great-great-uncle would visit him, he would be given a seat at the rebbe's right-hand side. It was the greatest imaginable honor accorded to any Lubavitch Jew. Think of it as sitting beside the Pope while millions of supplicants wait in line for days and days to kiss his hand. That's what it's like. So my great-great-uncle, when he heard we were in the United States, was determined to "save" our souls. He found my family almost immediately, and once he knew our location, he contacted the Chabad-Lubavitch rabbi of Austin, Texas. That one phone call was destined to change the course of my life completely. This rabbi was the single most influential person in the direction that our lives took. His name was Rabbi Feinstein, and he was a warm, friendly, kind, gentle man. It was literally impossible to dislike him. He was so incredibly charming and charismatic and, above all, sincere. You knew he believed everything he was saying. You knew instantaneously that he was not just spouting rhetoric for some ulterior motive. He practiced what he preached. He had eight children. (Lubavitchers don't believe in using birth control.) His children were fun and rambunctious and his wife was extremely well dressed and elegant, although constantly tired and harried. Raising eight children on her own, anything else was impossible.

My great-great-uncle traveled from Israel to personally introduce us to Rabbi Feinstein, and to appeal to my parents to learn more about their Jewish religion. My great-great-uncle had a long gray beard and very somber eyes. I remember him watching me and thinking that he was trying to peer into my soul. He made me uncomfortable. Where Rabbi Feinstein was all warmth and kindness, my great-great-uncle Yisroel Leibov was formed of harder stuff. He had been through hell and survived to build Jewish communities all over the world to spread God's word. He was a man on a mission. He found fertile ground on which to plant his seeds.

My mother was already trying to replace the ideology she had been born into. She had already risked her life for Judaism. She had already suffered as a Jew in Russia. She knew so little about the religion, but she was a sponge. Eager to learn more.

In his introduction to the Mishna (which is where the oral laws that govern all our lives are written), Rambam tells a story about a king who built a magnificent palace surrounded by a resplendent garden. One day, a tzaddik (a righteous Jew) sought respite there, against the cool stones of the palace walls. Unbeknownst to the king, the entire reason God allowed him to build this palace was for that tzaddik who would need to find shelter there. I am sure Rabbi Feinstein felt at that moment that the whole reason for his being sent to Austin, Texas, was for this very purpose. To be the one to bring back Rabbi Yisroel's lost relatives. So, we became his raison d'être.

We became close friends with Rabbi Feinstein's whole family, and we started spending more and more Saturdays with them having the traditional Shabbos meal. In the beginning, it wasn't even remotely onerous. The nice Shabbos meals with RF and his family didn't infringe on my life at all. It was just a fun thing to do on a Saturday, after I had watched my favorite TV shows. I liked *She-Ra* and *Wonder Woman* best, followed closely by *He-Man* and the hilarious *Get Smart*. For two years, the Chabad became part of my life in a very noncommittal way. My parents were still exploring other sects of Judaism. The community that had adopted them when they arrived were all Conservative Jews, who take the laws less seriously and are fully intertwined with the modern outside world, and so my parents spent time in the Conservative synagogue as well.

My only happy memories from my childhood are from those first years before my world was utterly transformed. There I sat, unknowing and unaware that this man, my great-great-uncle, would forever change the path of my life and lead me into a world of servitude and misery. A world of No. He came not long after our arrival, so I was only six at the time, but that day is burned into my mind forever. My mother inhaled it all. She was so happy to learn that she had married into such an illustrious Jewish family, and she was hungry for more. At the time, she was getting her PhD in philosophy, always searching for the truth, always wanting to understand the purpose of existence. This was a panacea against the madness that was the outside world. Everything had meaning. Everything had purpose. You were part of a master plan, and you mattered, and your actions mattered and suffering mattered. And not only that, there was a rule book, a clear path toward goodness and righteousness. There was a manual for living that had survived thousands of years and been passed down from father to son, from generation to generation. To my brilliant, logical mother, having a rule book created by the Being that created this world to begin with made perfect sense.

I remember, when I was sixteen, meeting someone who had grown up in Communist Russia. He was living with his family in Brighton Beach (a very Russian neighborhood in Brooklyn), and bemoaning having had to leave his beloved Russia. I was so curious, because my parents had always made Communism sound like hell on earth, what it was exactly that he missed about his past life. He looked at me with his sad eyes and told me that even though he had no money and very little food in the Soviet Union, at least he always knew what to do, because Communism made all your decisions for you. With freedom comes choice and confusion. Freedom is onerous, and there are no guidelines. You're left floundering alone.

Religion fixes that problem. Especially ultra-Orthodox Judaism. There is a rule for absolutely everything. You're not alone. You don't have to decide anything, because it's all been decided for you in the Torah, and if something isn't completely clear to you, all you have to do is ask a rabbi and he will decide for you. You never have to wonder what is the right thing to do, because it's not your choice anyway. There is a law about which shoe to put on first (the right shoe). There is a law for what to do from the time you wake up to the time you go to bed. Everything is fraught with purpose and meaning. Yes, you have to relinquish your freedom and control of your own life, but you are given something vast and powerful in return: Purpose. Meaning. Community. Righteousness.

The feeling of righteousness is the most powerful drug in the world. Do not ever underestimate the power of that emotion. It floods your entire being. It's a huge rush. You feel so much better than everyone else. So elevated. You look at others and feel so superior to them. Poor lost souls, they are walking around in a murky, ambivalent, meaningless existence, and I, I have the answers to all of life's questions. I am a Chosen One. I am the one who knows the purpose of existence. To feel superior to others, and to feel part of something great and powerful, is the biggest rush imaginable. I remember days when I was particularly good and had managed not to commit too many sins, and I felt totally high. Your body feels airy and light, and you feel connected to this higher power. You feel so strong and so much better than everyone else. It's that feeling of entitlement and righteousness that feeds people. Yes, it comes at the price of your freedom, but like any other drug, once you've tasted the high, you're willing to give up anything to feel it again.

Later, when I attended religious school, they would always say that children are the holy ones: look how beautifully children daven (pray), how holy children are before they're sullied by life and start committing sins. If a child can behave so piously, then surely an adult should be more religious and pious. It took me till I was almost forty to find the error in that thinking. It's not because a child is closer to God and more holy that they believe so easily. It's that the world is black and white to them. They're not just innocent, they're also ignorant and easily indoctrinated because they don't see shades of gray. Children need order. They need rules. They're not comfortable without boundaries and structure.

So when my family brought me to the Chabad house, I went comfortably and willingly along. I loved the warmth and the long Shabbos meals with singing and everyone gathered around the table. There was such a sense of camaraderie and friendship, and the rabbi's kids were so lovely to me. I wasn't super keen on all the rules, but they creep up on you so slowly that you don't even realize.

Rabbi Feinstein's first major victory came when he convinced my parents that I shouldn't go to a camp with non-Jews. This struck a chord with my parents because they had seen the Jewish communities in Russia eradicated in just a few decades. They thought it was eminently reasonable that my befriending and playing only with Jews would help the continuity of the Jewish people. So I ended up at a Jewish day camp.

I was so excited to go to camp. It sounded like a huge adventure, and it would mean getting out of my house, which, since my parents fought frequently about religion and the path our life should take, was something to look forward to. But that first day, I came home crying hysterically and told my parents in no uncertain terms that I never wanted to go back. Those monsters had fed us *dogs* for lunch. *Hot dogs!* What kind of horrible people ate *dog?* My parents were quite perturbed, as I was not prone to lying, and the tears streaming down my face showed that I had clearly been traumatized. My parents called the camp and, as you can imagine, much laughter ensued. I went back to camp the next day, greatly mollified, and enjoyed the rest of the summer.

But after that, things began to change at home. First, my mother decided she wanted a kosher kitchen. She believed you couldn't receive God's light or His message if your soul was clogged with unkosher food. My father fought against it vehemently due to the prohibitive cost. To have a kosher kitchen, you need three sets of dishes and three set of pots and pans and three ovens and three sinks, since meat and dairy cannot be cooked or eaten together. Therefore, you need a set of milchig (dairy) dishes and a set of fleishig (meat) dishes and a set of pareve dishes, which are neither milk nor meat. Then, of course, you must buy kosher food, which costs three times as much as regular food because it requires rabbinic supervision, which doesn't exactly come cheap and is something of a monopoly. They can charge extravagant prices because they have a captive clientele.

At this point, we weren't eating kosher outside of the home, so my father didn't see why we should have to spend $50,000 to keep kosher in the home. The arguments went on and on. My mother is nothing if not relentless, but my dad is an extremely stubborn Russian man, and he refused to budge. My mother calculated the precise figure that would be necessary for our kitchen to be turned into a kosher one. It was $51,225.

They were in the midst of their own personal Cold War when something happened that my father couldn't ignore. His boss at IBM realized that in the three years my father had been working for

IBM, he had never put in for overtime. My dad didn't know such a concept existed. He received the check for his overtime, and it was exactly the amount my mom had calculated would be necessary for the kosher kitchen: $51,225! The argument was settled. God Himself had sent a sign that a kosher kitchen was the way to go.

It took me years to realize it, but the concept of kosher is a powerful element of control. When you can't sit down and have a meal with someone, it separates you as effectively as a ghetto wall. It's funny, looking back at it now, how in my mind, the worlds of my childhood were divided. There was all the Jewish stuff—the Chabad house, kosher food, Shabbos, the rabbis—and then there was the other part of my life—the Wilford School, my non-Jewish friends, horseback riding with Patricia. I never questioned the dichotomy. In fact, I was too young to realize it existed at all.

The summer of my tenth birthday my mother got pregnant. Before I was born, she had been told that she would never be able to have children, but then she proved them all wrong when she got pregnant with me. Despite having eight miscarriages between me and my first sibling, she would eventually go on to have seven more children. So my days of being an only child were over, big-time. Her pregnancy happened when we started keeping a kosher home, so to her, it was further proof that God was pleased and that she was on the right path.

I was overjoyed when my first sibling, Chana, was born. I was completely obsessed with her, and I wouldn't let anyone touch or play with her. My mother was perfectly content with that, as just seven weeks after she gave birth to Chana, she was pregnant again.

That year, "tznius," a word that would come to rule over and haunt me for decades, entered our lives. Like my mother, I swallowed it willingly and fervently. It means "modesty," but it doesn't just mean modest clothes. It means being totally unseen and never being special or exceptional in any way. There is one story I remember so clearly that perfectly encapsulates the concept.

When I was in ninth grade, attending Bais Yaakov of Spring Valley, my class was sitting on the floor in school having a kumzitz—

a kind of campfire sing-along, minus the campfire and with religious songs. My friend Basya was a marvelous singer. Lost in the beauty of the melody, she sang her heart out, her voice rising above everyone else's. When the song ended, the principal, who had been sitting on a chair, a little bit removed from the singing but ever watchful, rose from her chair, her voice quivering with rage and horror, and chastised Basya for upstaging everyone. "How dare you raise your voice above all the other girls? If you are born with a beautiful voice, it's God's way of testing you to see if you'll be modest and never sing in public. You are an immodest, arrogant girl, and God will surely punish you for this terrible crime." I will never forget Basya's face. She was publicly humiliated and made to feel ashamed of her gift. She never once sang in front of a single person again as far as I know. That is the meaning of true tznius. Be invisible. Blend in. Do not stand out in any way.

Because it was tznius, my mother began covering her hair. According to Jewish law, a woman's hair is very sexual and should only be seen by her husband. So my mother cut off her beautiful black tresses and started wearing a kerchief from morning till night.

In the fall, school at the Wilford School went on as usual, but my life started becoming more complicated, as Rabbi Feinstein slowly introduced new strictures to our family. I was still wearing shorts and tank tops, but we no longer ate unkosher food in or outside of the home. It became difficult to hang out with my non-Jewish friends, since we lived in Texas, where pork barbecue is king. Since I couldn't even eat on plates that had had unkosher food on them, or even kosher food if it was cooked by a non-Jew or an irreligious Jew (as anyone who isn't Orthodox is not to be trusted and could sneak in some unkosher ingredient), it made eating at my friends' homes completely impossible. You have to have a religious Jewish person turning on the flame or the oven for even kosher food to still be considered kosher.

The message is clear: the outside world is the enemy and not to be trusted. The same law applies to irreligious Jews as well. If a non-Jew or an irreligious Jew (such as yours truly) touches a bottle of kosher wine, the wine becomes unkosher instantaneously. Even if a non-Jewish waiter opens a kosher bottle of wine at a restaurant, it is technically not kosher.

That winter, my mother stopped wearing pants and short-sleeved tops. She was totally covered head to toe: collarbone, ankles, knees, and elbows. These were the lines of demarcation, and anything exposing skin beyond those lines was a sin and would send you straight to hell. As she grew more pregnant with my brother, my world began to shrink. There were no more cartoons on Saturday. It wasn't Saturday anymore; it was Shabbos now. On Shabbos you don't use electricity. You cannot turn lights on or off, or change the setting of your air conditioning, or cook, or use your phone, or turn on your TV. It's a day of reflection, when you commune with God and family.

We began spending more and more time at Rabbi Feinstein's house, and he came to explain to my parents that in the eyes of God, my mom and dad weren't actually married. They'd only had a legal, non-Jewish ceremony, and they had not had a ketubah (marriage contract) signed and witnessed. Plus, a rabbi hadn't married them. My mother was horrified and set out to rectify the situation immediately. So, my parents got remarried. I still have photos from that day. My mother in a dumpy, shapeless maternity dress, pregnant with my brother Yitzchok, and with my sister Chana and I in attendance. I remember feeling so lucky; I was the only person I knew who got to be at their own parents' wedding.

I have always loved to dance. In fifth grade, when I was about ten years old, I became eligible to be a cheerleader, and I was dying to be on the squad. I figured it wasn't really dancing, so hopefully God wouldn't mind. I still remember the cheer that I tried out with: "Everyone's got the fever, and everyone's got the beat, it's all very easy if you move your hands and feet. Now step to the right and step to the left and move up and down. Now step to the front and then to the back and turn yourself around." I did all the accompanying moves really well, and I got in. I came home that day ecstatic and told my parents that I had made it into the squad. My parents explained that the cheerleading outfits weren't tznius, as they were way too short, and that dancing was prohibited in front of men, so it was out of the question. I felt so guilty that I hadn't realized that myself, and that I had even thought to try out. Something must be seriously wrong with me that I am so untznius, I thought to myself. I wrote it down in what I had taken to calling my "book of sins" and cried for hours, begging God to forgive me.

In fact, I kept a running written record of my sins and good deeds of every day. You're supposed to repent your sins on Yom Kippur, and show your good deeds, and hope they tip the scales of judgment in your favor. Being extremely logical and completely and utterly and without question believing that I was being judged and that life and death hung in the balance, I reasoned that there was no way I could repent my sins of the past year if I didn't remember them. I would therefore, before I went to sleep, every night from the time I was ten until I turned forty, write down all my sins and good deeds so I would know what to repent when Yom Kippur came along. Most people just read the general list of sins in synagogue. I would bring reams of paper—all the documented evidence of my horrible sins—and cry my heart out over every single one of them, for more than ten hours every Yom Kippur. My daughter Miriam found some of these notebooks last year and read a few of them and felt so bad for me, because my sins were so pathetic. They were along these lines: (1) Had a bad thought about Yosef [my husband] today. (2) Forgot to pray the evening prayer. (3) Had bad thoughts about my mother. I didn't act out. I kept my bad thoughts in the realm of the nebulous, too afraid to give voice to the daily inequities I suffered. To call my sins PG is a mild understatement.

In the summer, Yitzchok was born. We had the bris (formal ceremony of circumcision) in our house, with my mother cooking and making everything herself because there were no kosher caterers. She had given birth to Yitz only eight days before, and there she was, cooking for fifty people.

That summer, I wasn't allowed to go to camp, since I had siblings to watch over. My summer was spent changing diapers, but it never occurred to me to complain. It was a huge mitzvah (good deed) and my responsibility, and that was that. And then at the very end of the summer, my parents dropped a bomb. I was too old to be going to a mixed school with non-Jews, and it was time for me to be in a religious school. But most importantly, there were not enough religious Jews in Austin. So, we would be moving to Monsey, New York— a haven of ultra-Orthodox religious Jews.

Kosher food was not as prevalent as it is now, and there was none to be found in Austin. My mother had to cook everything at home because there were no kosher restaurants, no kosher bakeries, no kosher grocery. Kosher chicken and meat had to be shipped in frozen from New York. I stopped drinking milk because my parents started keeping a religious stringency called cholov Yisroel. A stringency is an additional barrier decreed by the rabbis in order to protect us from committing the actual sin. For example, the law says you're not allowed to write on Shabbos (Friday night sundown to Saturday night sundown). The chumrah (stringency) is that you're not allowed to even hold a pen. The thinking is, if you don't ever hold a pen, you will never come to the sin of writing. That is one kind of chumrah. The other, like cholov Yisroel, is meant as an additional restriction to make you even holier. To be holy, you had to drink kosher milk. To be superholy, you had to drink cholov Yisroel milk. "Cholov Yisroel" means that a rabbi had *watched* the cow being milked. Why? In case some non-Jew, wanting to trick people, substituted a non-kosher animal's milk and called it cow's milk. The only way to be sure is to have a rabbi watch that milk from its very extraction from a cow until it was packaged. As you can imagine, there was no cholov Yisroel milk in Austin, Texas, so it had to be shipped in, also frozen, from New York, and it would come with all these nasty pieces floating in it, and I refused to drink it. Till this day, I can't drink milk unless it's hidden in very strong coffee, and I eat my cereal dry. I couldn't eat bread unless my mom made it. We stopped going out to eat. It wasn't very fun, but I thought it was wonderful and right, because it was what God wanted, and who needs a doughnut if God says it will destroy your soul? No doughnut is that important.

They promised me that moving would be wonderful, because I could start going to kids' houses again, as everyone would be kosher, just like us. We could start eating out at restaurants because this special community had many kosher ones. I would no longer be the only girl required to cover her elbows and knees and ankles and wearing socks in the summer heat (which I had recently started doing), because everyone in Monsey dressed like that. I had just recently started keeping the laws of tznius, covering my whole body and no longer wearing shorts and T-shirts, and let me tell you, in 120-degree Austin summers, having to wear stockings (tights) and long-sleeved shirts and long skirts was torture. Of course, it was what God wanted, and I wanted God to like me and to let me into heaven, so I wanted to be very, very good.

I had very mixed feelings. On one hand, I loved Austin and my school. On the other hand, I couldn't deny that it would be nice to not be the only girl eating kosher and wearing long skirts and socks. I had to say goodbye to Austin. We left almost at the beginning of the year. They told me we couldn't take our dog with us, as the community we were moving to didn't have dogs, and so I gave Nikka to Kristin, because I knew she would take good care of her and Nikka would have plenty of space to run around and play in their wonderful property. It was the only time I cried during the whole transition: watching Kristin and Nikka and my whole life fade in the rearview mirror of my car. Nikka, who had loved me so dearly and so well, and who I loved with all my heart. I have a picture of myself and Nikka to this day. I am already covered from head to toe, and I'm eleven years old, and I look so happy with my arms around her. It's a bittersweet memory.

And so, my real life began. All these memories from my very young childhood, and everything pre-Monsey, were locked deep inside my mind, only taken out in times of severe pain and stress, when I couldn't control my thoughts and they wandered back to Rickey Drive and a different life.

CHAPTER TWO

The difference between Austin and Monsey was monumental. In Austin the houses were new, the streets were new, and the sidewalks were so clean that when it got very hot, for fun, we would cook eggs on them. Monsey was dirty and old and dilapidated. Nothing was new. There was garbage on the side of the road. The houses looked forlorn and gloomy. There wasn't a single irreligious Jew, and definitely not a single non-Jew, for miles around. I spent the entire ride through Monsey trying desperately not to cry.

Our house on Smolley Drive was significantly smaller than our Austin house, and our family was now five instead of three. It was a split ranch with four bedrooms, three upstairs and one downstairs. I had the bedroom downstairs, which made me very happy as it meant I had a modicum of privacy.

My parents had chosen not to become Lubavitch, regardless of our uncle's standing in the community, and chose to become ultra-Orthodox instead. So, they became Black Hatters, or yeshivishe people (which is what my parents called themselves). "Yeshivishe" literally means "coming from a yeshiva," which is a religious place of higher learning. To make it simple for the uninitiated, Chasidim's center of devotion is the synagogue, while for yeshivishe people, the center of devotion is the yeshiva.

Chasidus started relatively late in the Jewish world. It was begun by a rabbi called the Ba'al Shem Tov (One with the Good Name) in the eighteenth century, to help solve the prevailing religious issue of that time: assimilation. Prior to Chasidus, the yeshiva was the center of the Jewish world. This alienated a lot of Jews, as many in Eastern Europe were excruciatingly poor and had neither the time nor the money to be able to sit and learn Torah. There are many holy books in the ultra-Orthodox world. First there is the Torah, which is essentially our Bible (the five Books of Moses, the "Tanach" which stands for Torah, Neviim [the prophets] and Ksuvim, which are the Megilas [like the story of Esther and the story of Rus], and Ecclesiastes, etc., that non-Jews call "The Old Testament"). The Mishna is the compendium of the Jewish oral laws that govern our lives. It's written in a very succinct form, and so we have the Talmud as the commentary on the Mishna. The Babylonian Talmud and the Yerushalmi Talmud are the explanation of the oral Torah written by the rabbis when the Jews were exiled to Babylonia and other parts of the world. The Babylonian Talmud and the Yerushalmi Talmud are often known as the Gemara. (Women are still forbidden from studying the Talmud, Gemara, and Mishna, all the books that rule their existence.)

Since many men were illiterate and women weren't even given a rudimentary education, they were leaving the religion in droves. The Ba'al Shem Tov realized that someone needed to create a less cerebral attachment to God so as to appeal to the mass of illiterate or poverty-stricken Jews. He made it all about prayer and the synagogue. Whereas yeshivishe people served God through study, the Chasidim served God with song and extended, lengthy prayer. It was emotion versus intellect. Of course, today, the reality is very different. The only thing that really separates the two worlds are attire and minute details of custom. All the core concepts are the same, especially for women. This is why my parents chose to be yeshivishe. The focus on study and knowledge appealed to my intellectual parents.

People always ask about the differences in observance and custom between Chasidim and yeshivishe people/Black Hatters. To the uninitiated, Chasidim, with their long payos (sidelocks) and their shtreimels (the big fur hats) look less connected to the outside world than their black-hat compatriots. The reality, however, is that the same rules apply to both. Women are treated under the same exact principles, and whether you wear a pillbox hat on top of your sheitel (wig) or just a sheitel, the same concepts apply. Chasidish women wear very short sheitels and then a hat on top of that as well. Yeshivishe women are allowed to wear longer sheitels and they don't have to wear a hat on top of the sheitel. Whereas the short sheitel may look stranger to the outsider, both traditions stem from the same fundamentalist idea that women's bodies are responsible for men's thoughts.

For either group, a woman's hair is shameful and not to be seen by anyone other than her husband. The idea that women aren't allowed to study Talmud is exactly the same. Some Chasidic girls aren't even allowed to study from the Bible directly and instead learn from a text called *Tz'enah Ur'enah*, which is a man retelling and dumbing down stories from the Bible for the "simpler" minds of women.

The two main concepts—the laws of modesty and the role/place of women in life—are exactly the same for both groups. Once you assume that women are less intelligent than men and put on this earth for only one purpose, whatever stems from that assumption is wrong and painful. Women cannot get divorced without their husbands' permission. Women cannot study secular or even Talmudic works or go to college. Women get married off at seventeen to nineteen years of age, assuming their families can get a shidduch (match) for them. Their roles in life are all the same. All women's destinies are the same. All women are put on this earth to be wives and mothers. Your biology defines your destiny.

Why does a woman need to study the Talmud? It will take time away from her only purpose in life. It may also give her dangerous ideas and make it less likely that she will be obedient to her husband. An educated woman is a dangerous one in both those worlds.

I often get comments relating to how "normal" I looked when I was still in my black-hat community. My clothes may have looked more current than those of Chasidic women, and my wig may have fooled you into thinking it was my real hair, but I was still forced to wear a wig and to cover myself head to toe.

When I first arrived in Monsey, however, I went to neither a Chasidic school nor a yeshivishe one. I started sixth grade when I was eleven years old, at Adolph Schreiber Hebrew Academy of Rockland (ASHAR), which was Modern Orthodox.

For a fundamentalist, ultra-Orthodox Jew, Modern Orthodox Jews might as well be non-Jews. It's something akin to how Protestants and Catholics felt about one another a hundred years ago. But my parents and I were totally clueless about the different sects at this point. At ASHAR, I was still the only girl in my class who wore long-sleeved shirts and stockings and socks above my stockings. I had never met a JAP (Jewish American Princess) before. I hated it! Every second of it. I had never felt more different in my life. I had felt so much more comfortable with my goyish (non-Jewish) friends than I did with these JAPs. I still have a picture of what I wore to school that first day. I was very excited about my outfit and thought I looked super cool. Boy, was I wrong! I wore shiny purple Jordache sneakers and a plaid skirt that was red and green and black, and a purple blouse to match my purple sneakers. I looked like a color-blind elf had dressed me. They were all in matching twinsets made of soft cashmere and perfectly pleated wool skirts from Chanel. Because ASHAR was a Modern Orthodox school, there were both boys and girls in the school, but all the classes were separate. It had a perfectly decent level of academics for a regular school, but coming from my special classes where I was learning about logarithms, it was laughable.

I really enjoyed learning Hebrew, because it was the only challenging part of school, but the rest was super boring. The biggest problem with ASHAR was that the kids weren't religious enough for me or my parents. The girls talked to boys and wore pants. A lot of their houses didn't have the same level of kosherness that my parents had. The moms didn't cover their hair. I was back where I started, except surrounded by people who were supposed to be like me! It only made me feel even more alone. At least when I was the only girl wearing a skirt and eating cholov Yisroel in Austin, I knew I was the only religious Jew and that I should be proud to be different. Here it was so much harder, because they were supposedly religious Jews, just like me, but they seemed much closer to my non-Jewish friends than my family.

I changed schools and started seventh grade at Yeshiva of Spring Valley, which was a different animal altogether. It was only girls—and they all looked just like me. They only wore long sleeves and covered their collarbones and their knees and ankles. They never spoke to boys. Boys ceased to exist altogether. They wore long skirts, four inches past the knees, so that when they sat down, their knees would still be covered. They wore knee socks on top of their stockings, just like me. All their fathers were rabbis. There were only a few girls in my entire class besides me whose dads were working dads and not rabbis. I had finally made it. I was in an ultra-Orthodox yeshivishe school.

My father was employed by IBM in Westchester, and I was so embarrassed and ashamed that he had a job. I was determined that my husband would be a rabbi and my children would never have to be ashamed of their father.

There were basically no secular studies in this school. Prayer began every morning at eight-thirty, and religious studies continued until around three-thirty. From around three-thirty to five was for secular studies—only an hour and a half of our whole day. It was a total joke. But I didn't even care, as I was learning so much in the religious classes. I drank in every word. I prayed three times a day, and I recited from Tehillim (Psalms) for hours. Our Judaics teacher was named Morah Greenberg, and she had been very suspicious of me when I first came to class, because she knew I came from a family of ba'alei teshuva. But I became her favorite by year's end because I was so diligent and absorbed everything like a sponge. I was also the most tznius girl in class. My skirts were the longest, and I cut my hair really short, like a boy, because long hair was immodest.

I thrived at Yeshiva of Spring Valley. I could eat at other girls' houses. And my Shabbos and their Shabbos was exactly the same: the same Shabbos food, the same singing at the Shabbos table. Everyone I knew also had a bunch of younger siblings, too. The only difference was that there wasn't a ten-year difference between them and their next sibling, so everyone shared the chores, which made life much easier for them. I didn't have that luxury.

We were at the age when every girl in my class was having a bat mitzvah. This was not the Modern Orthodox version of a bat mitzvah; there were no DJs or dancing. But everyone did have a dinner with rabbis speaking about girls becoming women and having to be even more tznius. It was still an occasion.

I waited and waited for my parents to remember my bat mitzvah was coming up. Finally, during Passover, on the night of my birthday, my father looked at me, and said, "Hey, isn't it your birthday tonight? How old are you turning?" I tried so hard not to cry, but I know my voice betrayed my hurt as I said, "I'm twelve." My parents looked at each other and laughed about how they had completely forgotten. So, the day after Passover, they made me call my classmates to invite them to a bat mitzvah that Sunday at my house. It was outside on the porch, and my parents bought pizza. That was it for my bat mitzvah. There is a picture of me from that day, and my eyes look so sad that it hurts me now to look at it. Although I never complained to my parents, and I never cried, it hurt to have been forgotten. These things take on huge importance when you're young and all your friends and everyone you know is celebrated on that day, and you know you're just an afterthought. It hurt, but I hid it well.

In fact, the next week, I made a conscious decision to never let them see me cry ever again. That week had been particularly difficult. My mom was pregnant again and not feeling well. Yitzchok had just hit his terrible twos, and both he and Chana were constantly crying and screaming.

That Shabbos, as usual, my father came to my room at 6:00 A.M. to wake me up to take the kids downstairs and play with them so he and my mom could sleep late. I served everyone and fed Chana and Yitz. Then I cleaned up and put all the dishes in the sink. We don't wash dishes on Shabbos, as that's considered work, and you're not allowed to work on Shabbos. You can't pre-soak, so by the time I could wash them, everything would be rock hard and ten times more difficult to wash. After cleaning up lunch, I played with the kids and then put them down for a nap. After that, I would get to read a book (a Jewish one, of course). Then I would change the kids when they woke up, pray the afternoon prayer, and feed them dinner. I would clean that up and then set the table for shalosh seudos, the third meal of Shabbos, and then I would serve that and then clean up, adding more dishes to the sink. Finally, it would be time to put the kids to sleep, and Shabbos would be over.

That night, when Shabbos was over, I washed every single dish, and there were a lot of them. Then came cleaning the kitchen floor, which was the thing I hated most. It was linoleum, and everything stuck to it. Using a mop wasn't good enough. I had to get down on my hands and knees and wash it with a cloth. It was after 10:00 P.M. when I finished cleaning, and as I sat there on the floor, a feeling of happiness overcame me. I felt accomplished. I had only just turned twelve, and I had managed to get through the day without a single complaint to my parents and with a smile on my face. I felt quite sure that God was very happy with me.

Maybe God was happy with me, but my mother was not. She walked into the kitchen, and she looked at the spotless counters, the clean sinks, and saw that all the dishes had been not only washed but also dried and put away. She walked quietly around the entire room, looking into all the corners, checking under the table, and finally stopped by the oven. She told me to come over and pointed to a speck on the floor under the oven door. She looked at me with disappointment in her eyes. "You missed a spot," she told me. "Can't you ever do anything properly?" She looked at me, daring me to cry, to act out.

I was devastated. I just wanted one word of praise, one thank-you. She stood watching me, waiting for a reaction, for me to say something wrong or inappropriate, so she could censure me further. I felt the tears gathering behind my eyes, yet when I looked in her face, I realized that that would give her the power. That was the moment I made a decision that would stand me in good stead my whole life. Never let them see you cry.

I thought to myself, Anyone can truly hurt you, Julia. They can wound you and make you feel small and insignificant, but they cannot make you cry. Only you have the power to decide whether you cry. And so that became my motto: never let them see you cry.

Now, the more people who try to malign me, to attack me, to hand my accomplishments over to a man, and the angrier I get, the quieter and calmer I become. I don't just work well under pressure, I thrive on it. It is also only recently that I've let myself go and feel safe enough to cry in public. Before, crying felt like weakness. Now that I've made it, I'm strong enough and powerful enough to cry.

Seventh and eighth grades passed in a whirl. That summer I went to sleep-away camp. Of course, it was an ultrareligious all-girls camp this time. I wore stockings and long skirts and long-sleeved shirts while I played games in the scorching sun. We all did. But I loved camp. I had a new best friend, oddly enough also called Patricia, and we became inseparable. She went to the same school as me, and we had started being friends in class, but now, in camp, we became especially close.

Patricia and I lost contact after elementary school because she went to an all-girls high school in New Jersey, which, according to my parents, was not for us because they learned secular subjects there and some of the girls went to college after—which, in the super frum (religious) world I was growing up in, was like walking into the devil's own backyard. If you were frum, you did not, under any circumstance, go to college. I remember clearly, in my high school, some twelfth-grader decided she wanted to go to college. She made the mistake of asking for her school transcript. They responded forcefully and publicly. They locked the doors of the school (literally, not figuratively) and wouldn't allow her to come into the school. She was ostracized, and we had an entire school assembly about her. I remember thinking she was completely crazy. Why would anyone want to go to a place with so much sin? The whole point of our lives was to be good mothers and good wives. A girl didn't need college for that.

This is the type of high school I started in ninth grade. Bais Yaakov was the most religious girls' high school in all of Monsey, and was run by this militantly fundamentalist but brilliant woman named Rebitzen Solevetchik. A woman married to a rabbi is called a rebitzen, which is not to be confused with a female rabbi. In the ultra-Orthodox world, there is no such thing. Women are not obligated to pray three times a day in shul (synagogue) like men, because they're supposed to be at home having and taking care of babies. That's their sole purpose in life: to raise dutiful, righteous sons and support righteous husbands. So their only way into heaven is through a man.

We read a book in class about this famous rebitzen who was married to one of the gedolei hador (literally translated as "great ones of the generation"). The phrase refers to the most righteous and powerful rabbis and leaders of a generation. The book was all about what it takes to be a rebitzen to a gadol hador, and what attributes we need to develop within ourselves to merit such a blessing. Her book was a study in misery and deprivation. She gave birth in her home without ever crying out, because she didn't want to disturb her husband's learning. She cooked in hundred-degree heat and never asked for an air conditioner so her husband could be solely focused on learning and not on mundane matters such as her comfort. The highest level for a girl to aspire to was complete self-abnegation in the service of her husband. Suffer alone and do not bother him and never complain or ask for anything or disagree, because to do so would take away precious time he could be spending studying the holy books. This was the example set before us. The embodiment of goodness and purity and the only type of woman God could possibly love.

Another story that always stayed with me was about a woman who was arrested by a Germanic tribe. Her punishment was to be dragged through the streets, tied to a horse. She knew that as she would be dragged, her skirt would lift up and some man might see her knees, and so she grabbed two metal rods and stuck them through her skirt and through her body, effectively attaching the skirt to her legs by impaling herself. She did all of that so that some man, while watching this horrible punishment, wouldn't get turned on. These are just two of the myriad stories we were indoctrinated with every single day.

Though I'd had friends in middle school, high school was a different situation. I so badly wanted to belong at school, to be popular. I had major marks against me. I was a ba'alas teshuva—not born religious—so I would always be lesser than. Additionally, my parents and I came from Russia. I always found it so absurd that in Russia I was the outsider because they labeled me "Jew," and in Monsey I was the outsider because they labeled me "Russian." This was before the oligarchs and the uberwealthy Russians made being Russian super cool. I was Russian when Russians were just lost refugees who came to the United States without a dollar. My family wasn't wealthy yet, which would have been the only thing to cleanse the mark of our less-than-favorable beginnings.

There was this girl, Ahuva, who came from a very long and illustrious line of rabbis. She was vivacious and popular. She wouldn't invite me to her house, because her parents thought that, as a ba'alas teshuva, I would be a bad influence. After being in class together for two years, she finally relented and decided I was safe. I was so happy to be included. It was a snowy day, and you aren't allowed to drive on Shabbos, so I walked the hour to her house for a Shabbos party. As soon as I got there, her mother took me aside and grilled me for over an hour before I was allowed to go downstairs and join my class. Had I ever read a secular book? Did I (God forbid!) have a TV in my house? Had I ever eaten unkosher food? She made me feel more uncomfortable than I had ever felt being the only Jew in the Wilford School.

I finally went downstairs, already on the verge of tears and feeling very isolated and alone. They all looked up at me when I came into the basement, and there was that awful, awkward silence that occurs when you've just been the topic of conversation. I smiled and made some stupid joke about surviving the KGB, and everyone laughed, and the party went on. But Ahuva was so awful to me. She made fun of my parents' Russian accents and asked me how I spoke Hebrew so well when I was brought up in—*ewwwwww*—Russia. They made fun of my clothes, which were definitely not "Monsey fashionable." These girls were a different type of snobby than the girls in ASHAR. They didn't wear Chanel or Gucci, as it was deemed inappropriate to be fashionable, but they wore clothes from Jewish clothing stores that charged just as much as Chanel and Dior. I left Ahuva's house feeling lonelier than I had ever felt in my life and spent the whole freezing walk home praying to God that I would be frum enough, tznius enough, that God would grant me friends, and that I would finally find my place in the world.

It still hurts to think about how utterly vulnerable I allowed myself to be, how much the opinions of these girls mattered to me. Many years later, while I was still religious and living in Monsey, one of my former classmates came down with leukemia, and her rabbi told her that she must have harmed someone for God to punish her like that, and she should search her heart to find out who she had hurt in her life. She called me. I was the one person she could think of who she had ever harmed. I have to say that I was really shocked to receive her call, because compared to many of the girls in my high school, she had been an angel to me. That says a lot. Of course, I immediately told her that I absolutely forgave her and that I had no bad feelings in my heart toward her. Still, it says a lot about my high school experience that she thought that the reason she had leukemia was because of how horribly she had treated me in high school.

That year I did find the two friends who would see me through all of high school and beyond: Sorah Greenberg and Tova Finestein. Sorah and Tova couldn't have been more different, but we became quite the threesome. Sorah was really the one I was closest to, and Sorah's family became closer to me than even my own. She came from a family of eight children, but she wasn't the oldest. She had one older sister and an older brother. Her mother was utterly scatterbrained, and her father was an angel. At least that's how I saw it back then, and her house was a complete disaster. Sorah had curly hair (which has since been tamed and flattened under a wig since she was nineteen), but when we were in high school, it was this wild mess of curls. She was just so nice. She never gossiped, and she always thought everyone was wonderful. She was as gentle and calm and kind as her father, and as disorganized as her mom.

Her father came from a very wealthy family, and although he was a rabbi, they had a lot of money because he had inherited extensive real estate holdings from his family. Sorah's house was palatial in comparison to mine. It had ten bedrooms, a gargantuan kitchen, and a whole separate kitchen just for Passover! This was the height of luxury, because it meant you could just close off your regular kitchen during the Pesach (Passover) holidays, and you didn't have to spend a month cleaning and kashering your kitchen (making it kosher) for Passover. This is a huge undertaking, as even a crumb of wheat or leavened bread, or a cookie or a cracker, can render your entire kitchen not kosher for Passover, and then your soul will be karais, or separated from the rest of the Jewish people for all eternity, even after death. Karais is the Jewish version of excommunication— a heavy price to pay for a cracker crumb. It took a full month of non-stop labor to kasher a kitchen for Pesach. It was pure, unadulterated torture. I literally cleaned the sockets in the kitchen walls with a toothbrush, just to give you an idea of how complicated it was. Fuck spring cleaning. It's a joke compared to what we did every single March.

So to have a whole kitchen that was only used once a year for eight days, that never had to be cleaned or kashered for Pesach, was the ultimate in religious luxury. Her Pesach kitchen was vastly bigger than my regular one. She also had a nanny and two cleaning ladies—a staff! Her house, however, was complete bedlam.

Our home was a tenth of the size of hers, and we had just as many babies floating around, but you could eat off our floors (thanks to yours truly), and it was always spotless. I did laundry every morning before leaving for school, and folded it and put it away when I got home, so all the kids always had clean clothes. At Sorah's house, even with all the maids, somehow the laundry was a never-ending pile. There were mountains of laundry sprouting up here and there constantly. There wasn't a single chair or cushion without something on it. And whereas, in my family, we were all giant goody-goodies, and the only thing my siblings did that could be qualified as bad was cry a lot, her siblings were hellions. They were always getting into trouble for being chutzpadik (talking back or being rude) in class, and they were always skipping school, or not doing their homework, or some other shenanigans. Back then, I had no pity for Sorah's mother. She was literally the most disorganized human being I have ever met. There was never anything to eat, as she would forget to shop. I once made the mistake of taking a piece of cheese out of the fridge, only to find a clump of mold growing on it. Undeterred, Sorah just cut away the moldy part and proceeded to eat the cheese. She saw my aghast look and just shrugged. "If you're picky in this house," she said, "you'll just starve."

Her mother used to drop us off at Pathmark (the neighborhood grocery store) and send us in with a grocery list to do the food shopping, and then forget to pick us up. She would come two hours late and mumble something about having to nurse the baby. She was always nursing some baby or other. Back then, I had been taught that our only purpose in life was to be wives and mothers, and so I judged her for not doing it perfectly. I feel terrible about that now. Who knows what struggles she faced with all those children? Maybe she had had dreams of a different life for herself one day, and the chaos was a result of her unhappiness. I will never know.

I remember the first time I spent Shabbos at Sorah's house, and her brother Naftali, who was eight years old, wanted the challah (traditional bread served on Shabbos) that was at the other side of the table. He didn't ask anyone to pass it. He didn't get up and go around the enormous table and take some himself. He stood up on the table itself and walked around the coleslaw and the hummus and the matbucha, with his shoes on, squatted down to reach a piece of challah, and then nonchalantly walked back across the table and plopped back into his seat. I was completely aghast. He walked on the table. During the Shabbos meal. And no one said a single word. No one even reacted. I tried to imagine someone in my house getting up on the table, and my very active imagination failed me. Impossible.

Despite the chaos in Sorah's house, I loved being there more than anything. That was because of her dad, Rabbi Greenberg. I'd never met such a kind, loving, and patient man. He never yelled. He never complained. When his food was two hours late and tasted like shoe, he smiled and said, "Delicious." Of course, he never served food or cleaned the house himself, but that wouldn't have even occurred to him, or me for that matter. Men didn't clean. Period. But in my house, my father would not be pleased if supper was late or if I hadn't finished folding laundry by the time he came home. Sorah's father never seemed to mind.

One day I was at her house, after we had just learned the concept of "nashim daytan kalos"—that women's minds are light. Basically, it means that women have inferior, lighter minds. Their minds are unable to hold heavy concepts and focus on in-depth Torah tomes, which is why it's their job to have babies and take care of their families' physical needs, because they are incapable of being the rabbis themselves. I was feeling very sad and confused. I didn't think my mind was inferior to a man's mind, and it hurt me to know that God had said it was. I must have looked despondent, because Rabbi Greenberg asked me why I was upset. The fact that he had noticed was a testament to his kindness, because he was a rabbi, and I, a mere slip of a teenage girl, was generally beyond notice.

I told him what we had learned and why it had upset me. He thought about what I said and told me that there is another way to interpret those words. He said that a woman is able to multitask more easily than a man because her mind is light, that it can flit from one topic to another with greater ease. He changed something that seemed to denigrate women to say the opposite: that a woman is superior to a man in this regard. He smiled his warm smile and walked away, not knowing that I would treasure those words for years to come.

Of course, his words, however kind, didn't really answer my question, as that sentence is used to explain why women aren't allowed to study the Talmud or Mishna, which governed every minuscule aspect of our lives. There are many places in the Mishna and Gemara that refer to this. For example, in the Babylonian Talmud, Tractate Sotah 21b, it says that "anyone who teaches his daughter Torah is teaching her promiscuity." The Jerusalem Talmud, Sotah 3:4, "The wisdom of a woman is only in her spinning rod," as it is written (in Exodus 35:25): "All wise women spin with their hands." The Talmud continues, "May the words of the Torah be burned and not be delivered to women." Women weren't allowed to study the very books that imprisoned them in a web of modesty laws. We had to rely on men to translate books, written by men, that told women who and how to be.

From the day a child is old enough to pray until the day they die, there are sets of prayers that are required. The first set of prayers is said in the morning. You start off saying "Modeh Ani Lefanecha," thanking God for waking us up and giving us life. The set of prayers, however, differs for men and women. Every single morning of a boy's or a man's life, he starts his day off saying "Baruch Ata Hashem sheloh Asani Eesha," which means "Thank you God for not making me a woman." A woman says "Baruch Ata Hashem sh'asani kirzono," which means "Thank you God for making me as you desired. Thank you God for not making me a slave." So a woman is somewhere between a man and a slave. Now my world explains this horrific blessing by saying that what men are really thanking God for, when they say "Thanks for not making me a woman," is giving them extra mitzvos (positive commandments), like learning Torah, becoming rabbis, going to synagogue, being leaders, and so forth, that women don't have. We were taught that the reason that women weren't commanded to do any of those things was due solely to God's infinite kindness, because all God wanted from us was to be wives and mothers and so He didn't want to burden us with additional commandments. Again, our biology defining our destiny. (Abudarham, Third Gate, Blessings on Commandments: "The reason women are exempt from time-bound positive commandments *is that a woman is subjugated to her husband for the fulfillment of his needs.* If she were obligated to perform time-bound commandments, it might happen that just when she is performing the commandment her husband will command her to do his bidding. If she were to fulfill the command of the Creator and ignore [her husband's] command, woe to her from her husband! And if she were to fulfill his command and ignore that of the Creator, woe to her from her Creator! Therefore, the Creator exempted her from his commandments, so that she can be at peace with her husband.")

I probably don't even need to explain how egregious and abysmal this thinking is, but I will, regardless, as to me it's the fundamental flaw in the laws that govern the extreme, ultra-Orthodox community I come from. The largest flaw, obviously, is that not all women were put on this earth to have children and not all men were put on this earth to be leaders. Some men want to be caregivers and stay-at-home dads and aren't intellectual or remotely interested in being in the limelight. Some women are just not meant to be mothers, through their own choice, or due to the fact that they are physically, mentally, or emotionally unable to have children. Determining people's roles based solely on their biology is absurd. It has been proven throughout the secular, modern world that many women excel at being the CEO and many men excel at being the primary caregiver. This rigid and fundamental demarcation between what God supposedly wants from *every* man and what God supposedly wants from *every* woman is torture to anyone who is an outlier or unique and unusual in any way.

The second flaw in this prayer is that, according to the explanation, women aren't *commanded* to learn Torah or Mishna or Talmud. If you take it at its meaning, it should therefore mean that women are *permitted* to study those books, but just not commanded to do so. Nothing can be further from the truth. Not only were we taught that we weren't commanded to study the laws that governed our lives, we were told that we were *forbidden* from doing so. As early as elementary school, we girls were fed stories about women who had

broken that rule and had ended up committing suicide. Nashim Daytan Kalos (women's minds are light), combined with this prayer, put
every single woman in a lower position than every single man by law.

The penultimate disastrous effect of this prayer is that it forces a
woman into the background by definition, as it's her husband who is
commanded to fulfill all of these special mitzvos: going to synagogue,
leading the traditions at the Shabbos table and at the yom tov table,
dealing with the schools, and more. He is the forward-facing one by
the very word of God. What woman has the utter audacity to argue
with what God wants from her?

The very last effect of this prayer (which encapsulates this kind of
thinking) is that if the ultimate purpose of life (learning Torah) is
done through the man, then a woman's very existence is to be subservient to the man, as it is only he who is commanded to study Torah,
which is the entire purpose of life. Women are necessary for only
two reasons, to remove all responsibility from a man so that he can
be solely occupied with Torah study, and to propagate the Jewish
race. The worst sin, therefore, that a woman can commit, is to be a
distraction to men based on her looks, voice, personality, attire, or
attitude. Her purpose is to make Torah learning easier for a man,
not more difficult, which engenders all the tortuous laws of tznius.
These laws are certainly not found in the Bible, but are created by
men, transcribed and memorialized by men, and denied any access
to women.

This is precisely why women can't sing in public, dance in public,
or live on their own, must be covered head to toe, and are married off
as teenagers. If your only roles in life are to help a man achieve greatness and to perpetuate the Jewish race, the best way, logically, to do
so is to make yourself as invisible as possible so that you never take
a man's attention away from his Torah learning.

The comical part is that, supposedly, God didn't give us these
commandments to study Torah and go to shul, etc., so we could be
freed up to have babies and raise them. What no one seems to mention in this prayer is that we were far from freed up. There is a prayer,

"Aishes Chayil mi Yimtzah," that talks about what a righteous woman is, and that every single family sings every single Shabbos. Well, in the prayer, it talks about a woman going to the field and doing the work so that her husband won't have to have any physical or monetary responsibilities to his wife and children. So let's see. A woman has to be pregnant every year if God blesses her, while she also raises a multitude of children *and* is responsible for making money and supporting the family. Since she's not allowed to work in any position that's forward facing or outside of the community, and since she's not allowed to go to a normal college, she is forced into menial jobs that pay minimum wage and ensure that she needs to put in hundreds upon hundreds of hours of work just to keep her family fed. And that's a kindness? While all the man has to do is study Torah all day and is forgiven from any responsibility relating to hearth and home? Are you kidding me? Does this make any sense whatsoever? So while Rabbi Greenberg's answer was there to make me feel better, in the end it was all a farce and as far from the reality of my existence as Jupiter.

There was another person who was to have great influence on my life. The Horowitzes lived in our neighborhood and Rabbi Horowitz was probably my mother's only equal in terms of intellect that I have ever met. He was brilliant and had published several books. Of their children, the youngest, Yechiel, was the most unusual. He was a voracious reader of secular literature, a huge military buff, and could tell you about every single battle. He had even read Confucius and Sun Tzu. He was truly unique.

Though I was trying harder to be ultrareligious, I still had a nagging curiosity about things outside our community, and he was the only person I could talk to about the secular world. And of course I thought he was handsome—though, looking at pictures now, he definitely was not. He had huge ears that stuck out the side of his head and a nice, pronounced nose. But in my eyes, he was gorgeous.

In our world, the only time you saw a member of the opposite sex was at the Shabbos table. And this was if your parents had over friends who had kids around your age. You never actually got to talk to them directly, but at least, in a room full of people, you could stare longingly at one another.

After our families had Shabbos together, Yechiel started coming over to my house to "borrow" things. Then he befriended my father. He even did chores around my house and helped with the kids. Anything to have some time around me. The way he would look at me. Oh my God! At night I would stare at myself, standing naked in front of the mirror, wondering what he saw when he looked at me. I wondered what it would be like if he were my husband, and how he would touch me.

For a full year, we did nothing but stare at each other and try to find excuses for our families to be together. Then, on my fifteenth birthday, which my family had forgotten again, he came to my house to return something he had borrowed and made a detour to my room in the basement. On his way out, he signaled me to go to my room. I ran downstairs. Sitting on my bed was a tiny, insignificant matchbox, and inside, a note. A few words that I hugged to myself and read over and over again. "Take a walk to Bais Yaakov, and go around to the forest behind it." That's all that was written. How daring! How risky! And at my high school, that bastion of religious indoctrination. It didn't even occur to me to resist. I was too thrilled. Just the thought of getting to spend a few minutes alone with Yechiel was enough to make me delirious with excitement.

I dressed and redressed a thousand times. I can still remember, to this day, what I wore that night. It was an outfit I had bought myself with babysitting money—a long cream-colored skirt and this ethereally soft cashmere sweater that had swirls of pearl and sky blue and dollops of peach. I felt so pretty. I told my mother I was going for a walk. She didn't even bother looking up. I was shaking with excitement and trepidation. The guilt would come later. Right now, all I could think of was how adventurous this felt.

The forest behind my school was small but totally secluded and away from everything. I made my way through the trees and there he was, in a white shirt and black pants, as always—the mandatory uniform of a yeshiva boy. His sleeves were rolled up, and I could see the sinewy muscles on his arms. His whole face lit up when he saw me. It was only then I realized that he must have been worried that a good little girl like me might not show up.

We walked awkwardly up to one another. Of course, we didn't touch. Not even to shake hands. Touching was so verboten that it didn't even occur to me. I was already breaking every rule to just be there with him. He told me to close my eyes, and I complied without a thought. And then, he said, "OK, open them now." I opened my eyes and . . . fireworks! Literal fireworks. The sky lit up with them! He had set up a whole fireworks display, just for me. It was the best birthday ever. I stood there stunned. No one had ever done anything like this for me. If I had adored him before, I was in love now. We didn't even talk, but he saw that I was so pleased. I had already been gone for thirty minutes, and soon I would be missed. I headed home, but I had no doubt that one day soon, in just a few short years when I turned eighteen, we would be married.

After that, whenever we could, we would meet in the forest be-hind Bais Yaakov and just sit and talk. We never touched. We didn't even sit close to one another. I was too afraid. We would talk about our families, how difficult life was, and how we couldn't wait to start a family of our own. He never asked to marry me. It was just a given. We even imagined the furniture in our future house. He asked if I would be OK with having a TV, and I was properly horrified. He laughed and called me his little rebitzen. I thought he was perfect.

And then tenth grade began, which was a huge turning point in my life. I became even more religious, more extreme in my views. Until tenth grade, I was still illicitly reading some secular fiction. I would walk to the Finkelstein Memorial Library and take out books and hide them everywhere around the house. I found Nero Wolfe and Rex Stout. All my understanding of love and courtship came from the Regency England romance novels of Barbara Cartland and Philippa Carr. I read Agatha Christie. Dorothy Sayers. I related to them so well. Women being hidden away until they were on the marriage market was a normal Wednesday for me. Young girls having to be so careful of their precious reputations that one false move and their family and their match would be in ruins and the chances of all younger siblings for a good match destroyed? Sound like the 1800s to you? It was normal life to me.

But in tenth grade, I stopped even those small literary forays into the secular world, albeit a secular world that no longer existed. I began praying in earnest three times a day. Not just going through the motions and saying the words but really pouring out my heart to God. I would spend a good three or four hours a day in prayer. Before I went to sleep at night, I would read Psalms. Between that, and homework, and watching my siblings and doing laundry and cleaning the house, there was no time for nonsense.

I became so pious that the school noticed. I was given special attention, as I seemed to be having a positive influence on the class. I became more popular as the girls who had stayed away because of my questionable lineage became more comfortable with me.

Even then, in my most religious year, my love for fashion continued unabated. I taught myself how to sew, learning from books and from the Vogue patterns I could buy from a frum fabric store. I didn't have a sewing machine, as my parents couldn't comprehend why I cared so much about fashion and my appearance. So I taught myself how to make patterns and to sew by hand.

I remember the first dress I ever made. It was the eighties, and peplums were a big deal. I found this stunning pattern for a drop-peplum dress. It would be the first dress I ever sewed in its entirety. I "tzniafied" the pattern, adding a high collar and long sleeves and no décolleté. I used taffeta, which is notoriously difficult to sew, as it shows every single stitch, and if you mess up, it's not fixable. My friend Henya, in twelfth grade, was about to be married. She hadn't even managed to finish high school before her shidduch was done and she was to become a wife. I wore my first creation, in silver taffeta, to her wedding. I brought along a needle and thread in case a seam unraveled, and sure enough, during one of the interminable going-around-in-a-circle "dances," something caught on my peplum and took half of it clear off! I ran to the bathroom, praying no one had noticed, and sat on the toilet to fix my dress. It certainly wasn't perfect, but I didn't mind. I'd created it with my own two hands, and it gave me great joy.

My love of fashion got me into some absurd situations that year. Sorah and I used to share clothes. The only problem with that was that she was a good six inches taller than me, and about thirty pounds heavier. I would roll and pin her clothes so they would fit. I can't explain why we shared clothes all the time. It's just a thing high school girls do. We would plan what we were wearing over the phone and come to school matching.

One day, in tenth grade, I decided I wanted to wear this new mustard-colored sweater I had bought with babysitting money. I called Sorah because she had this patchwork skirt that would match fabulously with my sweater. I asked her to bring it to school, which was pretty normal for us. She told me that she had accidentally washed it in the washing machine and that it had shrunk. I was ecstatic! It meant I wouldn't have to roll it and pin it! "Put it in your backpack and don't forget to bring it," I told her.

I called her right before she left the house to catch the bus. She confirmed that she had put it in her backpack. So I got dressed, partially. I put on my mustard sweater. Period. No skirt. I had my tights and my socks and my shoes and my puffy, ankle-length winter coat. I was covered head to toe, but I was skirtless. I figured that it was totally safe because the skirt was for sure in her backpack, and my coat covered everything. My high school was literally down the block from my house. I had so many sefarim (Jewish textbooks) that it was too heavy to schlep all of them down the long block to school. I would take one of the many baby carriages that were always floating around the house, and I would put my books in the stroller and trudge through the snow with my baby carriage filled to the brim with books and schoolwork. I was quite a sight.

So, this fine day, I did my usual trek through the snowy street, stroller in tow, with a mustard-colored sweater and a coat. Nothing else. I got to school, not even remotely nervous. I mean, what could go wrong? She had put the skirt in her backpack, right? I walked into school and headed straight for the bathroom. Sorah was already there, waiting nervously for me to appear. She was always nervous, as I tended to come up with crazy ideas and make her come along for the ride. "Do you have the skirt?" I asked. She lifted the skirt out of her backpack. Oh yes, she had brought it. And she had mentioned to me that it had shrunk in the wash. What she had failed to mention was that it was the size of a thimble. It hadn't just shrunk, it had fucking disappeared. It would have barely fit a Barbie doll, and no matter how vertically challenged I was, that skirt wouldn't fit over a finger, let alone my body. I was completely fucked! There was a strict rule in school that you couldn't wear a coat in class. I knew that the second I walked into the classroom, the teacher would tell me to take off my coat. And yet, how could I? I had no skirt on—I was skirtless!

I couldn't walk back home, because the only exit was right by the principal's office, and there was zero chance that someone wouldn't see me. And what would I say? That I left my house without a skirt? I would be immediately suspended! I would never get married! No family would want me! Oh, Julia, she's the girl who came to school without a skirt on. My family would never be able to live down the shame. These are the thoughts that whirled in my mind. I was scared shitless. This was before cell phones, so I would have to go to the school payphone, which was conveniently located in the side stairwell, away from the office, and I would have to make up some story to my mom and beg her to bring me a skirt. With great trepidation, and making sure no teacher saw me, I slipped into the stairwell and made a collect call to my mother. "Can you please bring a skirt to school right this second?" I whispered. She couldn't hear me. "What?" I repeated my crazy request.

A little louder this time. "Can you please bring a skirt to school right this second?" I said. Still, she just couldn't hear me. Finally, with time against me, and frustrated, I yelled, "I'm not wearing a skirt! Please, please bring a skirt to school right now!"

And then I heard a sound and looked up. There she was, in all her frightening glory. Rebitzen Solevetchik, the principal of Bais Yaakov. And she was laughing! This woman who terrorized people on a daily basis, and who had yelled at my friend Mindy Mayer because she thought Mindy's laugh was not tznius, was roaring with laughter. We stood there. I was totally frozen, afraid to say anything and break the spell. She just laughed and laughed, tears streaming down her face. Then she looked at me, wiped the tears, and turned around and just walked out of the stairwell. We hadn't exchanged a single word! I thanked God profusely for this miracle and waited for my mother to arrive with my skirt.

My mother was a math teacher at Bais Yaakov at the time, so it was perfectly normal for her to come into the school, and no one questioned her. She came, bag in hand, and I scurried to the bathroom to put on my skirt. I chastised myself. This had all happened because I cared too much about fashion. I could have lost everything. I would end up being a spinster, just because I wanted to look pretty in my new sweater. That was where vanity and my obsession with clothing had almost led me. I strived to do better and gave myself a stern talking to, and wrote in my book of sins for that day the sin of vanity.

I do need to tell you about the incredible force of nature that was Rebitzen Solevetchik. She came from a long line of illustrious ancestors. She once told me her whole story. I will try to get all the facts right. Her parents had sent her from somewhere in Eastern Europe, all alone, to di goldene medina (the golden land—the United States of America) when she was just fourteen, to work for her cousin and send money home to her impoverished family. They sent her just six months before World War II erupted.

She worked day and night and tried to find out news about her family. When she was nineteen and the war had ended, she found out that only one member of her family had survived. Her parents had hidden their youngest daughter in a convent, and they and the rest of the family had perished in Bergen-Belsen. She set out to Europe, alone and nineteen, while Europe was still emerging from the embers of war, to find her sister. All she knew was that she had been sent to a convent and was being raised by nuns. She went from convent to convent. At that time, many convents didn't want to give up the Jewish children in their care. (After all, in their minds, by chris-tening them, they were saving their souls and protecting them from the hatred that Jewish people always engender.) The nuns refused access to the girls, and she couldn't find her sister. Undeterred, she went from convent to convent, singing a song that her parents had sung to each of them when they were little. She would walk around the convent walls singing as loudly as she possibly could, until the day that a voice on the other side of the wall answered her! She had found her sister. She raised holy hell. She camped outside the con-vent and pestered the nuns day in and day out until they finally let her have her sister. They traveled back through war-torn Europe, back to the goldene medina. That is Rebitzen Solevetchik.

When I met her, she was such a towering presence, even though she was exactly my height—a woman greatly feared by parents and students alike. One negative word from her and your daughter would never get a good shidduch (match). Everyone always called the high school before accepting a shidduch. If you got Rebitzen Solevetchik's OK, the match went ahead. All she had to say was that the girl wasn't aidel (refined), or she wasn't full of chesed (kind deeds), or she wasn't tznius enough, and no one would touch that girl with a ten-foot pole, no matter how much money she had. She wielded an insane amount of influence. You couldn't buy her off. You couldn't beg or cajole. If she didn't like you, for whatever reason, you were toast. No one would date you, because Rebitzen Solevetchik said not to. The stakes were high, as without a husband and chil-dren, what were you? You didn't matter. You didn't exist.

There was a girl in the class whose mother was hated by the re-bitzen because she thought she was too fashionable. Her name was Bayla Rosenberg, and she came from a super-wealthy family that was well respected in my community. She called Bayla's mother in to the school and told her that from now on, she was not allowed to pur-chase any clothing without having a teacher from the school accom-pany her and approve her choices. She told this to a wealthy matron, a scion of the community whose husband supported the school. She didn't care. This poor woman, for the four years that her daughter was in high school, was not allowed to choose her own clothes but had to go shopping with a teacher. It sounds insane, but that's the amount of power that Rebitzen Solevetchik wielded. And she used it tirelessly and fearlessly "in the service of God." I loved and feared her in equal measure.

There is a line in Tehillim (Psalms) that says, "ve gilu bir'ada." It means "rejoice with trembling." Fear and love inexorably intertwined. That's how I felt about Rebitzen Solevetchik. She was such a brilliant woman. She spoke seven languages. She had an almost photographic memory, and I thought she was wonderful. She liked me too, and it hadn't gone unnoticed in my class. Since she barely liked anyone, I was often sent as the emissary to plead for one cause or another. One time, when I came in, she was clearly in a contemplative mood. She just looked at me for a long time, sitting there, her eyes boring holes into my brain, and then, out of the blue, she said, "You remind me of my younger self." It felt like the greatest compliment I had received in my life. And she kept talking, almost as if to herself—ruminating about how she was as spirited and vivacious as I when she was younger, and also that her breasts weren't so low down as they were now. It was a moment of humanity. She didn't use the word "breasts." She just pointed to hers, which were hanging somewhere mid abdomen, and then to my sixteen-year-old breasts, which were quite sizable, and made a rueful remark about remembering the days when hers had looked like mine. It was such a personal thing. So private, somehow. This from a woman who we all almost deified. That genuine, human remark drew me to her all the more. She was human, after all. I floated home on a cloud of happiness that day.

A big drama in tenth grade, however, was the day Rebitzen Solevetchik found out that Tova had a TV in her home. The rebitzen came into our classroom with fury in her eyes, and we sat there trembling in our seats, wondering who was going to bear the brunt of this wrath—each praying that it wasn't us. She started roaring, "I smell TUMAH!"—impurity—"I smell TUMAH!" and walking around the classroom as if trying to find the source of this terrible smell. She stopped at Tova's desk. Staring at her, the rebitzen said,

"There is a person here whose house is polluted with sin and the devil. The stink of this evil fills my nostrils, and I can smell the devil's presence in this room." She pointed accusingly at Tova. "You are stinking up the whole school. You have spread evil to all your classmates." Tova was completely bewildered. She couldn't fathom what she could possibly have done.

"You have a television in your house," the rebitzen continued. "Your parents have betrayed you and your sisters and brothers and this school! Your parents have brought the devil into this room, into your soul! Tonight, you will go home, and you will take an axe, and you will chop, chop, chop your television," she screamed. And while she was screaming, she mimicked taking an axe and smashing the television. It sounds absurd now. You may even be laughing as you see the scene in your head. But believe me, it was anything but laughable. It was terrifying. Of course, the TV was thrown out that evening, and Tova's parents had a very difficult time making peace with the rebitzen after that. That day made a huge impression on me, and it was years and years before I found the courage to turn on a TV.

Every Shabbos (Saturday) afternoon, I would get together with Tova and Sorah and Ruchoma (the girl who called when she had leukemia twenty years later to ask my forgiveness), and we would study a text called *Mesilas Yesharim*. The title means "the path of the straight ones" (the righteous people). Basically, it is a guide on how to live a holy, pure life. We never made it past chapter 10 because that chapter said, "One who has attained this trait has already reached a very high spiritual level," and none of us could honestly say we had, so we would start at the beginning again, hoping that this time, we would be more successful and manage to attain the level of purity that the book promised if one followed its guidelines.

Always the search for goodness, for perfection, which leads to constant guilt, as it is truly impossible to never have one bad thought, to never say or do anything remotely wrong. It was an impossible task we set out for ourselves, an impossible task that our world required from us. Complete selflessness, complete self-abnegation. Say thank you for pain and suffering. Appreciate humiliation. Heady, complicated tasks for sixteen-year-olds.

There's a joke that's told in the world I came from. There was a yeshiva that was known for the study of mussar (ethics). Students there were taught complete self-abnegation. They would purposefully do things to invite derision, in the hope that it would cleanse their spirit from even a minute portion of pride. One day, a student walks into the yeshiva and sees all the students murmuring to themselves, "I am nothing. I am less than nothing. The earthworm was created before me. I am dust and ashes." The new student sits down and begins to murmur the same thing. "I am nothing," he begins. A student overhears him and says to his study partner, "He's been here for five minutes and he already thinks he's nothing. Ha!"

You get the gist. It's very telling, and totally true. This search for humility, for righteousness, engenders its own kind of pride: the pride of being better, more righteous, than anyone else. It's such a high. There is no greater feeling, nothing that makes you feel more whole, more complete, and more powerful. It's pretty ironic. The very thing that's supposed to bring you away from pride and toward humility and self-depreciation makes you feel better than anyone else.

I felt so righteous in tenth grade, my most religious year up till then, and I was on a continuous high, experiencing a mixture of constant shame and guilt that I wasn't yet perfect and the feeling that at least I was better than everyone else. It was an impossible level of spirituality to maintain. I am too innately stubborn, too vain, too conscious of others' attention to be able to maintain this level of righteousness for long. It weighed so heavily on me. I had to battle daily against my desire to look pretty, against my desire to read interesting books—abasing myself on the altar of God, when all I wanted to do was read Jane Austen.

My home life became even more complicated. After Chana and Yitzchok, my sister Naomi was born, closely followed by my brother Yoni, and when I was in tenth grade, my sister Chaviva was born. We were now at six kids. Me and five children under the age of six. My parents finally hired a live-in cleaning lady, because I could no longer manage all the housework, the babysitting, and my homework as well.

My sister Naomi's birth was something of a miracle. My mother always had extremely difficult pregnancies, and Naomi was the most difficult one by far. First my mother developed double pneumonia and was hospitalized. (Pneumonia runs in the family. I myself have had it eleven times.) Then my mom got placenta previa. They told her that they would in all probability have to abort the baby, as the pneumonia could kill her if it continued untreated, and the drugs needed to treat it at that stage would damage the baby. In Orthodox Judaism, the only time you can abort a baby is when the mother's life is in danger. My father was left to make the choice, as by that time my mother was too out of it to think rationally. Like all good Jews, it didn't occur to him to make the decision alone.

At the time, there was a very famous rebbe living in Monsey. A rebbe is a leader of a Chasidic community and wields enormous power. Chasidim don't make business deals, buy houses, or make any decisions without first receiving their rebbe's blessing. There can be many rabbis, but each Chasidic sect has only one rebbe. That's why Chasidim have so much political clout: because the rebbe can promise that all his tens of thousands of Chasidim will vote for whichever candidate he commands them to. There aren't too many constituencies that can deliver 100 percent of their constituents. They are also supposed to have a closer lifeline to God, and their prayers more efficacy. My father called the Vizhnitzer rebbe. The Vizhnitzer rebbe ran a sect called, you guessed it, "Vizhnitz." The Satmar rebbe ran the Chasidic sect of Satmar, and so forth and so on. Each of these names comes from the place in Europe where that particular sect began. So Vizhnitz is actually Vyzhnytsia. Satmar are from the town of Satu Mare in Romania.

The Vizhnitzer rebbe was already in his eighties at the time and very ill. My father had donated considerable amounts of money to the rebbe and was hoping that the rebbe would tell him what to do.

He begged to speak to the rebbe, and that took quite some doing, as hundreds of people lined up outside his home to have just five minutes with him, and so impromptu phone calls didn't really happen. My father promised a huge sum of money if he could just speak to the rebbe for a few short minutes. Finally, the rebbe took the phone. My father explained the whole situation to him and asked him what to do. The rebbe listened carefully and then told my father, "Don't do anything. Your wife doesn't have pneumonia or placenta previa." My father tried unsuccessfully to explain to the rebbe that my mom was in the hospital with both. I was sitting beside him, and he was crying, tears streaming, as he begged the rebbe to help him. The rebbe just kept repeating, "Your wife doesn't have pneumonia or placenta previa." Finally, my father, feeling totally despondent, said thank you and hung up. He looked at me with total despair in his eyes and told me that probably the rebbe was too old and ill to understand his English. Rebbes speak almost exclusively in Yiddish, and my father's Yiddish was basically nonexistent. All my brothers, however, speak Yiddish fluently.

My father drove to the hospital utterly unsure of what to do. When he arrived, it was to find a gaggle of nurses and doctors around my mother. A miracle. In the few hours since my father had left the hospital, my mother's pneumonia had cleared significantly, and her placenta had lifted. Just as the rebbe had said, she no longer had double pneumonia or placenta previa. That is the story of my sister Naomi's birth.

Naomi was a special child from day one. She was incredibly smart and was naturally studious. When she was three, she was diagnosed with a lazy eye, and to correct it, she had to wear these massive, thick glasses. I still have pictures of her. Three years old and so serious looking with her giant owl lenses. My mother also had a lazy eye, but since it was never corrected when she was a child, she had severe issues with eyesight her entire life. You couldn't really see that she had a lazy eye, especially behind the very thick glasses she always wore, but because of it, she had impaired depth perception, and driving in a car with her was always an adventure. There was a prayer book in our car, as we were so afraid every time she drove us anywhere that we'd spend the entire time praying that we would get to our destination alive. To this day, I do not understand how she ever managed to pass her driver's test.

Now, you may read this story of my sister's birth and say, Oh wow, then it's all true, and extreme ultra-Judaism must be the right path since there is no logical way for Naomi's birth to have occurred. That's certainly how I saw it then: further proof of the correctness and truth of our way of life. It is only now, after traveling the world and hearing of miracles that happened to my Catholic friends, my Muslim friends, my Hindu friends, that I've come to my own personal conclusion. I do not pretend to have the answers; it's just what I think and nothing more. I do believe in some higher power, whatever name you care to give it, and I think that people who spend their lives caring for others and being selfless and truly righteous, be they Muslims or Jews or Christians or Buddhists or any other religion, or just good people, have a closer connection to that source of higher power and sometimes can perform miracles. It's not about the religion at all. Or about what you wear and where you pray. Because if that were the case, it would be impossible for miracles to happen within every religion or without religion at all. It's just that selflessness and kindness and a life filled with putting others' needs before your own brings with it some kind of connection to a greater power. Anyway, that's how I see it.

In case you're wondering if my father pressured my mother to have babies every year, believe me, it was not him. My mother would have had ten more if it were possible. My youngest brother is six months younger than my oldest daughter; he's an uncle who is younger than his niece. My mother had me when she was twenty-one, and she had my youngest brother when she was forty-six. She continued to have kids over a span of three decades. She still uses this fact to prove how much she loves children—and to convince my sisters and my sisters-in-law to keep having babies every year. My brother Yitzchok, who is in his midthirties, has eight children. My sister Naomi, who is in her early thirties, has eight children as well. My youngest brother, Shlomo, already has two kids and he's not even twenty-five.

The real irony is that my mother doesn't like babies and children. She never took care of her own. That was left to me. I mothered them so much that when my sisters and brothers found out I was getting married and moving out of the house, they all packed their stuff and wanted to know where "we" were moving to. When I say they called me Mommy, it's not hyperbole.

Although my mother *wanted* to have many children, in general, there is tremendous pressure put on young girls to pop out a child every year. If a woman feels like she needs a break, it means she's not righteous, and people will pity her. No one wants to feel that way. The pressure is intense. And it's not just a fight against your husband or your mother-in-law; it's a fight against nature as God intended it.

That summer, the summer of 1987, I was sixteen, and my parents decided they wanted to go on vacation—by themselves. Since they weren't going to be home, they saw no reason to pay the cleaning lady to stay, so she left as well. So my parents left me, at sixteen, with $200 and five children under the age of six and flew to Israel to vacation. Chana was six, Yitz was five, Naomi was three, Yoni was two, and Chaviva had just been born. She was a few months old. Sorah came over and tried to spend as much time as she could with me, but after a few days, her family left for vacation, and so I remained, all alone. Yechiel would drop in unannounced with groceries, or just a kind word and a smile that said, Your life sucks worse than mine.

I cannot begin to describe the bedlam. The day after my parents left, Yoni came down with some kind of stomach virus and proceeded to give it to all of the kids. I had five vomiting, crying, fevered children. I spent the next two days cleaning up projectile vomit and trying to calm down five sick kids who wanted their actual parents. I called my mother, crying and overwhelmed, and her reply was "You're perfectly capable. Just take care of them and leave me alone. I deserve a vacation." That was it. No kind words. No "Oh, honey, I'm so sorry, you're so amazing for letting us get some vacation time."

I don't even know why I bothered. I think I was scared because Chaviva was just a newborn, and I was afraid she would die. Those nights I was too afraid to even try to sleep—afraid she would choke on her vomit and die, and that I would be responsible for her death.

It was two days of pure, unadulterated torture in the middle of one of the hottest summers that New York had had in years. All humid and sticky . . . wet heat that clung to your skin like slimy tentacles. Finally, everyone stopped vomiting, and I thought that perhaps things would go back to quasinormal. No such luck. All of a sudden, the whole house was blanketed in darkness and the air conditioning stopped humming.

The kids started crying because they were frightened, hot, and miserable. I had no candles and just one flashlight, so I went downstairs and reset the circuit breaker. We had a few minutes of blessed respite before the electricity went off again. Back down I went, only to have it turn off again five minutes later. Leaning against the basement wall in frustration and desperation, I noticed something odd. The wall was burning hot. It felt like I was touching a cooktop.

I called our neighbor, and he came over, and I corralled all the pajamaed kids to his house. He called in a friend who was an electrician to check the circuit breaker. What the electrician told me terrified me. He said that had I turned on the switch just one more time, I would have, in all probability, blown up the house. There were some loose wires in the wall that had severely overheated, and it would have triggered an electrical fire. Had I not leaned against that wall and felt the heat, we would all be dead. For the next few days, we sat in the sweltering heat and darkness until the wiring was fixed. I was shaken for a long time. My responsibility for all these little lives weighed heavily on me.

The kids were tired, scared, distraught, and just generally unhappy, and they let me know it. Even thinking about it now, thirty years later, I'm still filled with that sense of dread . . . that impossibly heavy weight. When I heard the sound of my parents' voices as they returned, I felt this huge wave of relief. They were home, and I hadn't killed anyone. I had managed to keep all my siblings alive.

That year, my gentle little brother Yitzchok, who now won't look at me or hug me, turned five. He and Chana were my favorites, because they were the oldest after me, and at least, at that age, they could talk and communicate, not just poop and pee. He was always such a gentle soul. Every Shabbos, he would walk with me to shul and hold the siddur (prayer book) lovingly in his hands. Other kids ran about and played. He sat solemnly in his little Shabbos three-piece suit and carefully tried to read along. Both he and Naomi taught themselves how to read.

A few days before Yom Kippur that year, after I had done my usual task of putting the kids to sleep, I heard crying coming from Yitzchok's room. I found him sitting up in bed, tears streaming down his face. When I asked him what was wrong, he was so distraught he could hardly speak. Finally, after I held him for a while, I managed to get to the bottom of what was troubling him. He looked at me, tears spilling from his eyes, and in the softest, sweetest voice, told me that he was afraid that he hadn't been good enough all year and that Yom Kippur was coming in a few days and he was sure God was going to punish him. I remember holding him and feeling such love for him. I didn't think to myself: What an awful religion to make a five-year-old afraid of punishment. I was way too indoctrinated for that. What I felt instead was deep shame that my five-year-old brother was better at remorse and repentance than I was. That night, I cried myself to sleep as well and prayed that God would forgive me for not being righteous enough.

That summer of 1987 was two years after perestroika had launched in Russia. My father quit his job at IBM and decided, like so many Russians with this new economic freedom, to start a company that would do business in the Soviet Union. His office was in the laundry room, but when he flew to Russia for work, he had an armored Range Rover and two bodyguards accompanying him. Fake it till you make it, right?

He convinced and cajoled his way into purchasing huge quantities of oil and managed, with a group of other Russians, to build pipelines to bring oil from Russia to Switzerland. I'm honestly not sure exactly where, as any questions I asked were always met with silence.

One time, my father received a call from the president of Azerbaijan in his New York office—aka our laundry room. If I was home when his "office" phone rang, I was supposed to pick up and pretend to be his secretary. After passing my dad the phone, I busied myself with laundry while listening to the phone call. The president told him that he would grant access to the oil in his country if my father would bring him something from the States. My father, of course, said, "Sure, whatever you need," but he later confided that he was totally petrified. What if the president asked for a private jet? Or a million in cash? Or something else totally unattainable for a guy who was faking being an international businessman and working from his laundry room? He waited with bated breath to learn the request.

Underwear. That's what the president wanted. Tighty-whities. He wanted boxes of white Calvin Klein underwear and two pairs of Levi's jeans. After my father hung up the phone, we both cried with laughter. Of course, my father complied, and off his business went.

He would travel monthly back and forth from Monsey to places in Eastern Europe I'd only seen on a Risk board. One time he came home from one of these trips with a jewel-encrusted dagger. My mother was furious. How could he bring such a violent thing into a house filled with children? His response: "Lina, be happy they gave it to me and didn't put it in me!"

I learned many things that year, but they weren't ideas found in a textbook. The most important lesson (which was to stand me in good stead throughout my journey into the outside world) was the power of confidence. Do something or say something with enough confidence, and no one will question you. The most important lesson I learned was to be brazen enough to win, and it's a philosophy I maintain until this very day.

I have a story that illustrates this. When I was in tenth grade, my parents got me a ratty 1970s Buick, as my mother's driving deteriorated and they really needed me to do errands and carpooling. I cannot begin to explain the noise my beloved Buick and I made. You could hear me turning on the car all the way in the classroom. People in school would hear that sound, and say, "Julia is coming." It was such a wreck that we couldn't manage to find a single buyer when we tried selling it. But I didn't care. It was painted a putrid rust color and wheezed and coughed and complained every time I turned the engine on, but it was a taste of freedom, and I fucking loved it.

There was this bagel spot in Monsey called Bagels and More, where I would sometimes drive to get my favorite lunch: a hot bagel, fresh out of the oven, with scallion cream cheese and coleslaw on the side. This was, of course, against school rules. If I was attending school that day, I'd take Tova and Sorah, and we'd have to go so quickly no one would notice we were gone.

We got away with it for around six months, and then one day, as I was pulling back into the Bais Yaakov parking lot, the rebitzen was driving in the other direction. Tova and Sorah ducked down to avoid being spotted, but I was driving, so there was no way for me to duck. She could have reached into my car she was so close to me. There was nothing I could do. So I sat up straight, gave her my widest, most confident smile, and waved. She looked bemused for a second, but I was so calm and confident that she just assumed I must have been out for a legitimate reason. She smiled and waved back. That's the meaning of brazen.

By eleventh grade, we still had very little money, as every cent was being funneled back into my father's business, but we did have some new additions to our family. Now that perestroika was under way, for the first time since the advent of Communism, people could travel to other countries. My grandparents from my mother's side came and stayed with us for nine months. My parents had just con-verted part of the garage into a bedroom for me, as the live-in maid had taken my bedroom. I had gotten to live in my own room for all of three weeks when my grandparents came. Now there was no place for me to go. My parents moved a makeshift cot into the laundry room, and that's where I stayed that entire year. It was so lovely having my grandparents there, though. They helped with the kids a bit, even though neither was well enough to pick up the kids or play with them for any long amount of time, but any help was welcome. And they really loved each other. I could see that my grandmother must have been very beautiful in her youth, and my grandfather treated her like a goddess. It was so wonderful for me to see that.

My grandmother was quite the grande dame and assumed everything would be done for her, as she was accustomed to, but she was the only one who could get under my mother's skin, and this filled me with a very guilty sense of pleasure. Someone getting under my mother's skin for a change? Priceless. Of course, I would spend hours in prayer, begging God to forgive me for my bad thoughts.

Eleventh grade brought other changes as well. I couldn't maintain the intense level of religiosity that I had managed in tenth grade. I started reading secular books again, albeit surreptitiously and very, very carefully. I almost got caught once, during American history class, where I had snuck one of my books in, stuffed into our class reading, so while everyone was reading about some battle during the Revolutionary War, I was reading one of my Regency England romance novels, whose main characters were named Desmond and Desiree. It was during one of our few secular classes.

Our school only taught the bare minimum of classes required by state law to be considered a legal high school, and they only paid the bare minimum to their teachers. What we got generally were religious women with no training whatsoever in their assigned subjects who basically read the workbooks and handed out the prepared questions. They knew exactly as much about the subjects as we did. But every once in a while, if no religious teacher was available, we would get an irreligious teacher for a secular subject. They were usually public-school rejects, who were so bad that even the worst public schools wouldn't hire them. One of them was teaching us U.S. history in eleventh grade. I can't remember his name, but I would recognize him if I saw him again, because he had this one long hair that he would use as a comb-over, and he had this extremely pronounced squint that made him look a bit like a tipsy pirate. I had already read the history book, and other books pertaining to the period, so I was crazy bored in class and was reading about Desmond and Desiree. He caught me. He read the page out loud, except instead of reading it as "Desmond and Desiree," the names of the two protagonists, he read it as "Desmond and Desire." If he brought the book to the rebitzen, I would immediately be suspended and probably never get married. Those were the stakes back then. He saw the paralyzed fear on my face and, luckily for me, took pity on me and didn't throw me out of class.

In eleventh grade, New York State required that all students take the PSAT. I didn't even know what a PSAT was; we weren't told about it, because the school believed it wouldn't affect us, as we would go on to get married or attend seminary and then get married. We were told on a Monday that the next day we would be taking a test required by the state, and that was that. I didn't study for it, and I got such a high score that I received a nice chunk of money from the government to be used for college. But that money would go toward my teachers seminary in Israel, which was nothing like college.

Yechiel and I had now been "together" (I use this term loosely, as we had still never touched) for three years now, and I was still crazy about him. I thought we'd go on like this until we got married, but then one Sunday we drove to Bear Mountain State Park to go hiking. I told my mother that I was studying with Sorah. It was the longest time we had ever spent together alone, and he had brought along a picnic basket. We sat down to rest, and while I was munching on an apple, he sat next to me and laid his head on my lap. I froze. I had no idea what to do. He smelled so good, and it felt so nice to have him this close, with his hair begging to be touched and his head resting so sweetly on my lap. My hand moved of its own volition, and I combed my fingers through his soft, wavy hair. He didn't try anything else, and I didn't move him off my lap.

I was so confused that night. It had felt so right, so natural, to have his head resting on me, and yet I knew it was terrible and wrong.

I determined never to let him touch me again until we were married. I was seventeen already, and in just two years we would be husband and wife, and then we could touch each other to our hearts' content.

It had been my dream for so long, to finally leave my parents' home and have my leader and commander be Yechiel. That was as far as my dream got back then.

It was a normal Tuesday when all my dreams were shattered. A Bais Yaakov twelfth-grader who was known for being "troubled," which just meant that she had normal needs and desires but in our world that made you "troubled," reached out to me. She just walked over and asked for my number. This predated cell phones, and I had used my babysitting money to pay for my own telephone line in the house; it was my only bit of privacy. I was living in the laundry room, as there was nowhere else for me to sleep. It was me and the washer and dryer.

To enter our house from the driveway, which everyone did, you had to walk through the laundry room. So I could never be undressed, as people would walk in whenever. I slept on a folding cot. My desk was the washing machine. So I bought myself a phone line. I would sit in the bathroom and talk on the phone in private. She called me that evening and told me something so earth shattering, so mind blowing, that I almost passed out. Literally. Felt dizzy and weak and sank to the floor. She told me that she and Yechiel had been dating, and that they had kissed, and he had touched her breasts, and she had touched his penis with her hands. We didn't know the term "blow job," but she described it in full detail and told me that I should let him go, because after what they had done, he had to marry her. A religious girl doing that to a guy—I mean, I knew she was messed up, but this was just unthinkable.

I was torn. On one hand, she could easily be lying, as he was a good catch and maybe she'd decided she wanted him for herself. On the other, her words felt true to me. I determined to find out for myself. That week, Yechiel and I met at our usual spot, and I looked him in the eyes and asked him point-blank. He hadn't been expecting it. For a second, his face betrayed him. That second was enough.

The funny thing is, I understood it. I had refused to allow him to touch me. The closest we had ever come was him putting his head on my lap. He was twenty years old and horny, and I wasn't letting him do anything. But none of that mattered. He had betrayed me, plain and simple. I didn't feel anger or hurt. I was just shattered. All my plans, the future I had seen for myself, was now dust and ashes. It was the destruction of the plan that hurt me the most. That was the only thing that had kept me going during high school—the dream of escape, the thought that one day I would be Mrs. Yechiel Horowitz. The hurt over his betrayal and the anger would come later. Now all I could think of was the destruction of my plan. I didn't cry, of course. Never let them see you cry. I walked away from Yechiel, and from our future together, with my head held high.

Those were terrible, sleepless nights. I was at a total loss. For as long as I could remember, since I was fourteen, I knew what my future would look like. We had even chosen the furniture, and now I felt totally untethered, confused, and so alone. He had always been there for me. My knight in the shining green Camry.

He did not take it well. At all. He kept on telling me that it didn't mean anything, and that it was just because he couldn't touch me. He would hide behind the bushes and wait until late at night and come knock on the laundry room door. I ignored it all. Every time I thought about him touching her, I felt totally sick to my stomach. I wasn't angry. I was disgusted.

Life at home became even more unbearable. My father's business was really starting to take off, which meant that he was away more frequently. That meant that even more responsibility fell on my shoulders.

One night, my father needed the laundry room for some late-evening meetings, and my grandparents were staying with us, so there was literally nowhere for me to go. My parents called one of our neighbors, the Goldmans, who had an in-law suite, and asked if I could stay there. It was maybe all of 150 square feet, but it was my own space for the night. It felt like heaven.

Even staying at the Goldmans' in-law suite, Yechiel found me and came knocking at the door. And that night, for some reason, I forgave him. In my defense, I was so unhappy and so alone, and he had been a massive part of my life. He begged me to meet him in the backyard the following night, and I acquiesced.

When I got there that evening, he had a blanket laid out for a full picnic. Food and drinks and beautiful china: he had thought of everything. It was like something out of one of my romance novels. He had lit a lantern, which gave off this soft, romantic glow.

He looked so good, and his eyes were so sad and apologetic. I had heard he had been so depressed that he had stopped eating, and I could see the evidence in his thin frame. We laughed and we talked, and I didn't want the night to end. But eventually I had to pee badly. But if I left to go to the bathroom, that would mean the end of this magical night. Finally, I couldn't take anymore. My bladder didn't care about the moonlight. I started to stand up, too embarrassed to admit how badly I had to pee. He stood up too, and grabbed me, and kissed me. It was my first kiss. And it was awful. His breath smelled like the stuffed grape leaves we had just eaten, and I was hit by a flood of his saliva. I drowned in it, and not in a sexy, romantic way.

So I just ran away—mostly because of my bladder situation, but still, I ran like crazy. I quickly realized I had left my keys in the backyard, but there was no way I was going back to Yechiel. My bladder would no longer be denied, so I peed in the neighbors' bushes. There it is: a shameful end to a very disappointing night.

All I could think was, This was it? This was what kissing felt like? How awful. I dumped him for good because of that kiss. There was no way I was going to subject myself to that for the rest of my life. That kiss was the first and last time I touched a man in any way, even a handshake, until after my marriage.

CHAPTER THREE

In Bais Yaakov, every year, we had something called Concert. It was the Broadway show of our community. In the outside world, school plays are things you're forced to attend if you're related to someone in the play and you can't get out of it. In my community, it was pretty much the only source of entertainment. It got so big that we had to rent out the RCC (Rockland Community College) theater, which seats 2,500 people, and we did the same performance for three days in a row. It was sold out every night, and there were also standing-room-only tickets.

Of course, it was for women only. No men allowed. It was a play, a choir performance, and four dances, all put together into a four-hour show. The plays were always the same—always about women living either in poverty and deprivation or in captivity, sacrificing all so their husbands or sons could learn Torah. Every play, every concert, every book, every story revolved around that same concept. It was told in a thousand different ways until it became the warp and weft of our thoughts and lives. No one came for the play. They came for the choir and the dances.

When I was in high school, ours was the most famous of the high schools in Monsey in my sect, and our show was the most highly attended. Twelfth-graders were chosen to lead the different parts of Concert. I was asked to be head of dance. And trust me, being head of dance in Bais Yaakov Monsey was serious stuff. I was responsible for conducting tryouts and choosing who would make the cut.

I come by dancing genetically—from my grandmother, the Bolshoi ballerina, and from my father, who was also an excellent dancer. I could move. No joke. With no further training than the ballet classes I had taken in Austin, Texas, my body just did its thing. It made me extremely popular, and the star of the Bais Yaakov concert. It was a dangerous gift, though. My dancing was sexy and sensual, and what I couldn't express in real life I expressed when I moved. All that need, that hunger for freedom, for experience, came out in my dancing. So I was always getting into trouble. We had no dance teachers, and we weren't allowed to take normal dance classes, so our dances were, until I came along, more like synchronized calisthenics. I threw in some moves I had learned in Austin. I also found old dance DVDs in the library, watched them in the library's DVD player, and memorized the moves. We weren't allowed to use non-Jewish music, so I worked with what I had. I looked so different from the other girls when I danced that it became a kind of school activity. The girls would sit around me, and I would just dance.

I got called in to the office of the teacher in charge of the concert, who told me that she was concerned about my dancing abilities. Look at what had happened to Barbra Streisand. She had been a Bais Yaakov girl in her youth too, and her singing talent had caused her to leave the community and lose her place in heaven. She was pointed out to me as an example of the evil power of talent. I was so offended. I would never be like Barbra Streisand, I promised. Nothing was more important than my faith, and there was no way ever that I would consider disappointing God and making Him punish me for dancing in front of men.

There was also the issue of the moves themselves. We had rules: No moving your hips. No shaking your shoulders. Those rules were nothing compared with the rules we had when I was head of dance in seminary. There, we weren't even allowed to lift our leg above a forty-five-degree angle. It was so limited and regulated as to barely be considered dancing. My year, I vowed, would be different—we would dance. I had four dance concepts that I was very excited about. One of them was the "doctor dance." I went around to all the religious docs in the community and convinced them to lend me their doctor's coats. The idea was that mitzvahs can cure your illnesses. The second was the "morning dance." The staging started with us waking up on cots, and then it was all about how, from the moment you wake up, your life has to be in the service of God. The third was the fight between good and evil. Half the girls were good angels, and the other half represented the yetzer hara (the evil inclination). The idea was for half the girls to have whips and the other half to fight them with the light of goodness. Now, I had zero clue where to get whips. This was pre-Google. The search engine back then was called the yellow pages. I tried costume shops. I tried prop shops. I finally found a store in Greenwich Village that said they sold whips. I had no clue whatsoever what kind of shop this was. I had never heard of S&M. I thought it was a costume shop. I took the Jewish-owned Monsey Trails bus line—where women and men sit on separate sides of the bus, and there is a mechitza (curtain) between them so that, God forbid, no man will be forced to gaze at a woman—to Manhattan and walked to the Village. I walked past all the titty twisters and other toys and went straight to the front desk, where I asked very seriously to purchase nine whips. I didn't understand the shocked look the guy gave me at all. He looked me up and down, my dowdy shoes, and long, flared skirt, and my shirt buttoned up to the collar, and just shook his head in bemusement. He came out a few minutes later with nine whips, and I was so ecstatic that my mission had been a success. I didn't understand the comment he made about my being seriously twisted. I just looked at him, totally confused, and shrugged to myself. Goyim (non-Jews), they're just weird, what do I know? It wasn't until years and years later that the lightbulb went off and I realized exactly what sort of place I had wandered into, and what this guy must have thought. A Bais Yaakov girl in an S&M shop. Only me. My year was the last year that girls got to perform in pantaloons. The poor girls that came after had to perform in long skirts that precluded the audience from seeing any movement whatsoever. I'm sure it had nothing to do with my dances.

When I was in twelfth grade, Bais Yaakov got a uniform. It was super-itchy, pleated, polyester navy skirts paired with button-down shirts. I detested the uniform. The school also started a new measuring policy, so when we got to class our teacher would make us sit down, and she would measure our skirts to ensure they were four inches below our knees, even when sitting. Our shirts had to be buttoned to the top, and our sleeves always had to cover our elbows. We even had surprise spot measurements. It was humiliating and absurd, but I never got in trouble because I was super tznius and was very careful.

One student rebelled—anonymously—in a clever way. There was an ad in a magazine for elbow macaroni with the slogan: "We dare to bare our elbows." This girl cut it out, made photocopies, and stuck them all over the school. I was both shocked at the audacity and secretly very pleased. That line, "dare to bare," has stuck with me till this day, and now I still think of every low-cut top and every miniskirt as freedom. I get to choose what I do with my body and what I cover and don't cover. I also reject the idea that I am responsible for a man's thoughts, sins, desires. It's not my problem, guys. It's no woman's problem.

I had stopped seeing Yechiel and had also stopped reading secular literature. I was back, stronger than ever, committed to my way of life. It was also in twelfth grade that I decided to change my name. I wanted a good shidduch, and who would marry a Julia if they could have a Rochel or a Leah instead. I was the only person I knew who was called by their English name: Julia. Almost everyone else I knew had a Hebrew name. I wanted a nice Jewish name too, so I decided to name myself. I still don't know where I came up with the name Talia. It certainly wasn't a common religious name, but that's what I chose. And once I decided to have a Jewish name, I stuck to it. It's a testament to my intense stubbornness that the next year, not one person continued to call me Julia. Everyone called me Talia. I made sure of it.

Girls who graduate high school in the ultrafundamentalist community have two choices: stay home and start the process of getting married, or go to seminary, in another country (Israel), all by yourself for a full year. Guess which option most girls choose? It's the closest to freedom we ever get. Without that year, all girls would go straight from being under their parents' dominion to being under their husbands'.

Unfortunately, seminary is nothing like college, which has minimal supervision. Seminary is almost as strict as your parents' house. You have to be back in the dorm by 10:00 P.M. The streets that have boys' yeshivas are forbidden to even walk on. God forbid a young yeshiva bochur (an unmarried student) will be pulled away from his Torah studies by the siren call of a pretty girl. There are whole neighborhoods of Jerusalem that are forbidden because they are considered hangouts where girls and guys can mingle. Cell phones are not allowed. (Obviously, in my day we didn't have cell phones, but the same schools exist today, with the same strict rules, and they ensure that you have no contact with the outside world, as they only allow what are termed "kosher" cell phones, which feature only dialing and texting, no Internet.) You live, for a full year, completely cut off from the world, surrounded by only your teachers and classmates. No news. No clue about what is going on in the world around you. Still, it's as close to freedom as a religious girl is going to get, so every girl tries to make sure she gets into a seminary.

Just like in the outside world, in the religious world you have the "Ivy League" of seminaries. The crème de la crème of the seminaries is a school called Beth Jacob Jerusalem, or BJJ. It's as difficult for a religious girl to get in there as it is for someone to get into Stanford. In the secular world, you want to go to an Ivy League school because that will give you entrée to the best jobs. In the religious world, where you go to seminary will play an immense role in the type of shidduch you are offered. So the stakes are extremely high. Getting into the right seminary will determine, in large part, what kind of man you're going to spend your life with. I decided I would do whatever it took to get accepted to BJJ. I started coming to class. I became editor of the yearbook. I even volunteered for Chesed, a program where they send high school students to impoverished homes with lots of kids to cook and clean for overwhelmed moms.

March, when the final interviews for the seminaries would be done, was fast approaching, with acceptances coming at the end of April. My interview with the woman from BJJ went off smoothly. I knew every sentence from the Torah that she quoted, and I could even tell her what each famous commentary said about every line. I nailed it, but that didn't mean that I had an automatic in. I still came from a ba'al teshuva family. My lineage was garbage. I was also, as much as I tried to pretend otherwise, very different. I waited, with bated breath, for weeks. Ours was the most famous of all the girls' high schools in the religious world, due to the rebitzen being our principal, and generally, Bais Yaakov Monsey had more girls accepted than any other school. But a rumor went around that my year there were many more applicants, and BJJ could still only take ninety girls. So they had set the limit to three girls from any one school.

The day the letter came, I tried to figure out if it was a yes or no by the weight of it, just like anyone holding a college acceptance letter. Finally, with trepidation, I opened it. I'd made it. Me, Tova, and a rabbi's daughter named Rena Schwartz were the only three to get in.

Now that I was accepted to BJJ, I had one more hurdle to overcome in high school: the class photo. The class photo was a drama in and of itself. Since there was no communication between boys and girls, and dating was done through a matchmaker, the picture generally shown to the prospective guy was the girl's yearbook photo. Do you remember your high school yearbook photo? Can you imagine if that was the picture shown to prospective husbands? Horrible. I decided I was going to wear makeup to the picture shoot, which was obviously forbidden in school. Makeup meant you were trying to attract someone, and you shouldn't be attracting anyone, so why wear it? It also meant that you focused too much on the external, instead of working hard on yourself internally.

I came to school with the makeup hidden in my backpack. The

plan was to put it on right before my turn and take it off before any-one saw me. It was a good plan, albeit risky. I applied makeup in the bathroom and tried to walk quickly to where the pictures were being taken. Just as it was my turn, a teacher walked over and saw my mas-caraed lashes, and she had a fit. She got some alcohol and proceeded to rub everything off my face.

A few years ago, I read a book called *Reading Lolita in Tehran* by Azar Nafisi, who describes how when she was a teacher, after the Ayatollah came into power, nail polish was banned. She once forgot to take hers off before she got to school, and she was chased down the hall and made to remove it. Reading that made me think about how fundamentalism sucks in any form—be it Islam, Christianity, or Judaism. It made me feel connected to women all over the world and is one of the three books I credit with truly freeing me from the bonds that imprisoned me.

So, in my yearbook pic, I'm au naturel, without even an eyelash curled. But it got even worse. For the photo, we could wear our own clothes, and I chose something totally covered, of course. But when I sat down, I must have sat oddly, because in the shot, you could see my knees. They only realized this once all the pictures had been de-livered, so I had to sit for hours with a thick black magic marker and black out my knees in everyone's yearbooks.

Of the ninety girls who made up the incoming class at BJJ, Tova and I were the only ones with fathers who were not rabbis. The other eighty-eight girls came from old rabbinic dynasties. I was so ner-vous. I was a bit like the kid from the wrong side of the tracks getting into an Ivy League. I knew everyone around me would be religious royalty. You know, there are those people in the secular world, people who come from old money who have this air of complete, inherent self-confidence. They have nothing to prove. They don't give a flying fuck what others think of them, only because *they* never think about it. It's this insouciance, this innate feeling of belonging, of mattering, that gives them a relaxed, confident air. It's so attractive! It's something I've always longed for, always strived to attain, that feeling of belonging, of innate self-assurance.

Growing up, I watched people like that. I was so attracted to them, longing so to be able to cultivate that air myself. In BJJ, either they were very wealthy or they belonged to Jewish nobility. They had lineage and heritage. They were Jewish blue bloods. Each of these girls knew they would be offered the best of the best in terms of potential husbands. Each of these girls knew they were the crème de la crème of the religious society. And then there was me. Never quite fitting in. No family lineage. A ba'alas teshuva. A father who worked instead of being a rabbi. Even though, at this point, our family finances were starting to turn around, and my father was beginning to make some serious money, we still weren't at the level of wealth where my lack of lineage could be conveniently forgotten and forgiven. I was nisht ahin, nisht aher (Yiddish for "neither here nor there"). That feeling of not belonging has been part of me for so long now that I have accepted it. I'm one of those people who will never fit in, will always be nisht ahin, nisht aher. I obviously don't fit into the religious world anymore, but I don't fully fit into the secular one either. My history, my background, separates me. I'm always the odd woman out. I've made peace with it.

At eighteen, the need to fit in was not only a very emotional one, it was a very practical one. I was petrified that I wouldn't be offered the right type of match and that I would be stuck with a husband who was a dud. I needed to make sure that all these girls, whose fathers all ran yeshivas where the boys who would be husband material studied, would love me and remember me. I not only wanted to become part of that crowd, my future depended on it. That's a lot of pressure to put on yourself. I gave myself a stern talking to the day before I left for seminary. Be friendly. Be positive. Be warm and kind to everyone and work hard and don't make any trouble. I had a much easier time fulfilling the former part of that sentence.

We were three girls to a room that was around half the size of your average college dorm room, with three beds squished in and no space for even a chest of drawers. We had plastic containers for everything. There was a mini closet, which is really stretching the term "closet," and the pièce de résistance was the bathroom. Ah, the bathroom. The toilet was a regular toilet, nothing exceptional, but the shower—now, that was some creative invention! The shower had no ledge or anything with which to hold in the water. It was just a shower head with water coming out and floating all over the room, running hither and yon. Soapy, sudsy water would come oozing out of every corner. If there were clothes or shoes on the floor in the room, watch out!

We cleaned the floors with something called a sponja. Basically, in the center of the dorm room, as opposed to the center of the shower, was a drain. You would pour water on the floor and kind of smush it around with some liquid soap and take a squeegee mop, a sponja, and smush it all around and maneuver all that mess into the drain in the center of the room. It was a disaster. I think nine times out of ten I left shoes, socks, the occasional skirt lying on the floor, and it became a sponja casualty. It never actually cleaned anything either; it was just pushing the dirt from one place to the other.

We were given the names of our roommates a few weeks before seminary started. I was told that one of my roommates was a girl called Basya Fentuch. You cannot imagine how many times I was told, by literally *everyone*, how fortunate I was to have her as a roommate! Her father was the rosh yeshiva (dean) of a very prestigious yeshiva, and a renowned Talmudic genius, and she was supposed to be practically perfect in every way. Forget Mary Poppins. Meet Basya Fentuch. There were all these stories about her. She never got kicked out of class. She never got under a ninety-five in anything in her life. She was pure, pious, perfect, prayed three times a day with extreme concentration, etc., etc. People went on and on and on. I remember thinking to myself, What am I? Chopped liver?

Basya's personality didn't make it easier to like her. She really was "perfect." She followed every rule easily. She went to sleep at nine every night and was awake at six-thirty every morning. She did her homework the second we came back from school. She never looked at boys. She got every answer right. All the teachers adored her, and all the girls admired her. She also never cracked a smile or laughed at a joke or stayed up till 2:00 A.M. whispering secret thoughts. She was definitely brilliant, and had she not been part of the religious world, I'm sure she would be the CEO of some major Fortune 500 company by now.

Writing all these things now, I feel guilty, because I met her many years later during a PTA meeting. They say it's a small world. Well, the ultrareligious Jewish world is even smaller, so eventually your paths are bound to cross, one way or another. It turned out that her son and my son were in the same class. She recognized me. I would have never, under any circumstance, recognized her. Gone were the sharp eyes that saw everything and took careful note. Gone was that confident stride that said, My life is going to be a smooth road to heaven, and it will be wonderful. She looked destroyed. Worn down. Exhausted. Deflated, somehow. My faith suffered a crack that day.

My memory of her, of her indomitable will and determination, her consistently doing the right thing and making it look easy, made her a bit superhuman to me as well. I may not have liked her in seminary, but I respected her tremendously. A huge part of me wanted to be her. I was in awe of her. I had so much difficulty doing the right thing. I was always fighting with my inner "evil inclination," which pulled me to attract boys' attention, to wear things I shouldn't, to question the Torah in my mind (too afraid to ever verbalize my queries), to daydream during prayer. Being good (the way it was defined in the frum world), for me, was an extraordinarily onerous daily struggle. Be obedient. Don't ask questions. Don't want. Don't be seen or heard. Pray, pray, pray. Direct your thoughts to God. She made it look easy. I don't think she ever had an inappropriate thought in her life.

Let me digress for a moment on that word: inappropriate. I am sick to death of being told what is and is not appropriate. Let me make this clear: I don't care. I will not respect a religion that doesn't respect me back and that thinks it can control what I put on my body. I will wear what I want, when I want, and let someone dare try and stop me. Tradition and religion are excuses for some of the worst behavior imaginable. Women's feet were bound in China because of tradition. Women are arrested and imprisoned in Saudi Arabia for being inappropriately dressed, but that's OK, because it's their religion. Women in Russia cannot report their spouses for spousal abuse if it doesn't leave permanent damage on their bodies, because it's the tradition of the Russian Orthodox Church to allow men to beat their wives. I am heartily sick, whether for religious reasons, or traditional ones, or for any reason, frankly, of being told to be "appropriate." Let's exhort and force men to be appropriate for a while and see how they like it.

While my first roommate was the epitome of appropriateness, my other roommate was her diametric opposite. She had a face like Garfield. I remember the first time I saw a Garfield cartoon and immediately thought to myself, Oh my God, it's Tzirel. Tzirel was from Toronto, so an out-of-towner; in the religious world, anyone living outside of either New York or Israel is considered to be living out of town. Out-of-towners were generally a bit more chill than their New York counterparts. They didn't have as many strict chumros and were more connected to the outside world. She got into BJJ on the waiting list, which made it less prestigious, and people gave her grief the whole year because of it. "Oh, she only got in on the waiting list? Hmmm. That means she's not really BJJ quality." That was the attitude. Whereas Basya took everything seriously, Tzirel took nothing seriously. She went to sleep at 4:00 A.M. every night and woke up literally nine minutes before we were supposed to get to class. I was horrified by Tzirel's lackadaisical attitude. They almost threw her out midyear because she so seldom came to class, and she had to beg and entreat them to give her another chance. She started coming to class more regularly, but I don't think she heard a word, and I know she failed every single class she took.

The school itself was a good ten-minute walk from the dorms, all uphill, and you were lugging five pounds of sefarim (religious schoolbooks). It was also directly downwind from the Jerusalem Zoo, so we would sit and study, skirts down to the floor, buttons buttoned to our collarbones, stockings, and no air conditioning, in extreme heat, with the smell of animal excrement forcing its way up our nostrils, trying to concentrate on our subjects. The day began at 8:30 A.M. and ended at 6:30 P.M., with a forty-five-minute break for lunch. There were no secular subjects whatsoever. It was ten hours of straight indoctrination. Of course, then, I didn't see it that way.

I found out later, from a friend of mine who was a friend of Basya's, that Basya didn't like me, because I was "too smiley." It makes me laugh every time I think about it. All that wasted effort! Note to self: Don't give a shit what others think. Be confrontational when necessary. Stand up for yourself. My God. I really wish I could go back in time and yell at my obedient young self. I wanted to be good so badly. It was such a struggle. Arghhhhhhhhhh. Wanting to be loved by my fellow students. Wanting to be loved by my teachers. All that desire to be "appropriate," with varying degrees of success.

You'd think, with two such diametrically different roommates, I would be the friend and intermediary of both, as I was somewhere in between, but no such luck. Basya thought I was too smiley, and Tzirel thought I was too serious. And that was that.

BJJ was run by an incredibly brilliant woman named Rebitzen David. The very first day she came into school she told us, "They say in BJJ we brainwash our girls. Well, whose brain doesn't need a little washing?" I thought it was exactly correct. We were all such imperfect beings. Whose brain *didn't* need a little washing?

I worshipped her. She was so learned, so knowledgeable. In Bais Yaakov high school, it was all do this or don't do that. Wear stockings, not socks, modesty, modesty, modesty. In BJJ, it was the first time we started learning the *why* of things. It was extremely intellectually stimulating and fascinating. I was learning how to learn! Not to just accept things for what they were but to delve into the sources of these laws and try to understand the root reasons for all the rules that dominated my life. Even though I wasn't allowed to, I started using those tools to learn Talmud myself. Studying Talmud (which is all the guys learned in yeshiva, from sunrise to sunset, and where all the laws governing our lives primarily exist) was forbidden to women. The excuse given was that true Talmudic learning required so much time and effort, and a woman's role was to have children and raise children, not to become a Talmudic scholar. As the Babylonian Talmud, Tractate Ketubot 59b, states, "a woman is good for beauty; a woman is only good for children." Plus, we were told, women were too emotional, too touchy-feely to be able to study something so complex and intellectual. You want to know what it says in the Talmud? Go ask your husband, your father, your rabbi. Don't you dare try to understand it yourself.

When I once, at one of her home dinners, very gently broached the topic of why women aren't allowed to learn Talmud to Rebitzen David, she looked at me very intently and seriously and said, "When you finish learning all of Torah and all the many things you *are* allowed to learn, then come back to me and I'll tell you why." Of course, looking back, that was not an answer at all, but at the time it seemed very legit. Why worry about what I'm not allowed to learn when I don't know all that I am allowed to learn? I set about trying to learn everything that I was allowed to, but I still, unbeknownst to anyone, continued my study of Gemara (the Talmud). We learned so much Aramaic in class (the Babylonian Talmud was written predominantly in this ancient language) that I was able to translate the Talmud and its commentaries. It was very slow and hard work, but Rebitzen David had taught me the importance of going back to the source, so I did. I needed it. I really wanted to understand. To learn. To become pious and righteous and stop all these horrible thoughts going on in my mind—this constant pull of the outside world.

Anyone religious who reads what I have written here will stop and say, "Aha, this is where she went wrong" and use me as the perfect example of why women shouldn't learn Talmud. You see? I learned Talmud and I left Judaism. Questioning things is dangerous. Women with too much knowledge are dangerous. Look at Julia Haart, who went off the derech (righteous path)! What a shanda (shame)! Her path to the dark side all began when she tried to learn Talmud. We were told that the few women who had tried it had gone mad and committed suicide. It was only safe for men, with their superior minds. We were taught the story of Bruria, who was so brilliant that she decided to ignore the law stating that women aren't allowed to study Talmud. She ended up committing suicide. The lesson was clear: babies or no babies, a woman's mind was incapable of studying Talmud.

Learning and knowledge for women were for the sole purpose of being righteous wives and mothers. Be it religious learning or secular learning, anything that didn't add to those roles was prohibited. Rebitzen David told us that, having gone to college herself, she had firsthand proof of how evil and dangerous it was, and that going to college would destroy our lives, and we would never be able to regain the spirituality we had lost from being in constant contact with the outside world.

The longer I was at BJJ, and the more acquainted I became with the women there, the more my dreams began to solidify. I became more and more fundamentalist in my views. Gone was the girl who longed to see the world. I tried to dedicate my life to God, and all I prayed for was a good match with a God-fearing man who would dedicate himself to the study of Torah and become a great leader of the Jewish people. I wanted to be the crème de la crème in heaven, which meant suffering on this earth and making up for being born an irreligious Russian.

Girls my age in the outside world may have been aspiring to feminist greatness, having been taught things like "Be the CEO your mother wanted you to marry," but I was, like every other girl at BJJ, aspiring to attain greatness by proxy. I was supposed to dream of being the one behind the scenes, ensuring that everyone else was happy. I was to be careworn so my husband could be carefree. It sounds very righteous and pure when I write it now, but in practice it sucks, believe me. All you end up teaching your children is that women don't matter. Your sons see you in your constantly overworked and miserable state and think that it's OK for their wives to be like that. My mother did it; why can't you? Your daughters see you and think, Oh, this is what being a good woman looks like, and accept suffering and pain as their lot in life. Being a martyr doesn't do anyone any good.

After my year in Israel, I remember landing at JFK Airport and having culture shock. It was not only that I was coming from a different country with a different language. I was also returning to the outside world. I had forgotten what it looked like, what it sounded like. Giant billboards with scantily clad women in cut-off shorts and tank tops. The bare-chested guys in the Abercrombie ads. They all assaulted my senses. I had spent twelve months totally immersed in a place where there were no irreligious Jews, where no cars passed by on Shabbos. Every day, every hour, was spent with those whose entire lives revolved around the yeshiva and the shul. I had not seen a television, nor read a single piece of illicit literature. I hadn't read a newspaper or heard the news or even spent one second contemplating what was going on in the world around me. As remote and separate as Monsey was from the rest of the world, there was still the library, cars with non-Jews in them, billboards and ads trumpeting the messages of the forbidden.

Brainwashing in seminary was so perfectly orchestrated that I never even realized how much I'd changed. If I had been a goody-goody before, I was twenty steps beyond that now. I couldn't manage to stop loving clothes, but I did stop focusing on the physical and the earthly. I had one focus, one single-minded goal: to find and marry a righteous tzaddik (a holy man) who would be a great luminary in the Torah world and to help him and take care of him and raise a family together. That was all I thought about and all I wanted. If I had ever wondered if the life of a rebitzen was for me, those doubts disappeared completely. I was willing to suffer physical and financial deprivation for the sake of heaven. By being the cleaning lady, the sexual vessel to my husband, and the babysitter to my children, I would attain my place in heaven.

CHAPTER FOUR

The summer that I returned to Monsey, all I could think about was how to get a really good, righteous husband and, in the meanwhile, a respectable job. After seminary, there was only one job I was allowed or even remotely qualified to do: teaching. That's what all girls who wanted boys who would learn full time and become rabbis did. It kept you in the community, working with children (a woman's only purpose in life), and it brought in money so your husband wouldn't have to worry about paying the bills.

In this regard, my community has expanded somewhat to consider other professions as appropriate for girls to do (always within the community, obviously). There were only so many teachers that the schools could take, and as people started having more and more kids, and more girls came out of seminary, there just weren't enough teaching jobs for all of them. So, in the last ten years, they've added some additional permissible occupations. They still involve dealing with kids, and to prevent people from having to leave the community to learn these skills, they created "colleges," like the New Seminary, which is a university in name only. I have no idea who they bribed to get some sort of accreditation, but they operate fully within the community, with all-female classes taught by religious women.

Now it is permissible for a woman to be a speech therapist (working for a religious institution), a physical therapist (working for a religious, all-women institution), or an occupational therapist (again, working only in religious institutions). Girls can also be secretaries (working for religious companies only) or receptionists (same rule applies). The community needed to enlarge the career opportunities, as women are expected not only to have babies every year but also to work within the community and bring home the gefilte fish (bacon is too unkosher to use in this sentence, so I've substituted a more proper Jewish food).

The husband should never have to worry about anything whatsoever other than learning Torah. His mind should be clear from stress or responsibility. All the running of the household, the taking care of the babies once you've had them, making money to feed and clothe all these children, falls to the woman. And she should be grateful and do it all with a smile, because this is her only path to heaven. She must take it all on her shoulders so her husband has nothing but learning on his.

In my day, however, none of these jobs existed. You were either lucky enough to get a teaching position or forced to work as a secretary for your uncle's cousin Moshie, who had a dry-cleaning business. Having graduated from BJJ put me at an advantage, although my Russian heritage still made it challenging. I got very lucky and was offered a job at Yeshiva of Spring Valley, my alma mater, teaching fourth grade.

The minute I arrived home from Israel, I was also considered "on the market" for a husband. Basically, I was for sale. Nowadays, people date for years and live together before getting married. I had a few hours to decide who I would live with for the rest of my life—at nineteen years of age, right after coming out of an intense year of brainwashing.

The way marriages are made in the fundamentalist world is vastly different from how it happens in the world you live in, where boy meets girl, or girl meets boy, and they fall in love, and then each brings the other home to Momma. It is a business transaction, and instead of a banker or a lawyer working on your behalf (or, honestly, on your parents' behalf), a shadchan (matchmaker) acts as the intermediary between families, and between the girl and guy themselves.

The shadchan is like a mix between a car salesman and a talent agent. Their stock in trade is exaggeration, and their product is people. They make their money when the match is successful and the boy and girl get engaged. The wealthier and more illustrious the participants, the higher the paycheck. They can make anywhere between $10,000 and $300,000 per match. Just like there are some salespeople who sell Rolls-Royces and some who sell Hyundais, some shadchanim deal with the crème de la crème of frum society and others settle for selling Hyundais—that is, people with no particular lineage or wealth, like me.

Though I had many marks against me, my sisters and brothers had a much easier time of it. They were all born once my parents were religious, and most in Monsey, so they didn't have the stigma of not being frum from birth. Also, by the time my sister Chana (next in line after me and ten years younger) started dating, my family was extremely wealthy. When I was dating, my father was making money—what, to the rest of the world, would be considered living the American dream—but in the Jewish world, where multimillions are needed, it still wasn't enough. Despite all this, I was determined to be among the first girls in my class to get engaged. There was no way I would become a nebbuch—a pathetic, unmarried girl over the age of twenty-one. People talked about you if you weren't married by then.

Guys in the community, however, didn't even start dating until they were around twenty-one, and most started as late as twenty-three or twenty-four. They also had a much longer shelf life. If a guy made it to twenty-seven and was not married, he was a bit questionable, but that still gave guys six years to choose a wife instead of the two years that girls had. This creates a serious logistical problem, because every year girls come out of seminary at nineteen, and they are vying for the same guys as the nineteen-year-olds that came out the year before, who are now twenty. So, with each passing year, your chances of finding a good match as a woman dwindle, and if you aren't married by twenty-two, you're basically left with the rejects, weirdos, divorcés, and widows. The pool of wonderful girls is vastly greater than the pool of eligible guys, and the whole system functions in the guys' favor and gives the families of boys greater power and the ability to be extremely picky when choosing a prospective bride.

You cannot imagine some of the questions I had to answer before I was allowed to date some of these guys. One example: "What kind of bananas do you buy?" If you said, "Ready to eat and ripe bananas," then you were a person who liked spontaneous gratification. No good. If you said, "Green bananas," then you were planning too far ahead and didn't have faith in God that he would provide you bananas when you wanted them. No good. The correct answer was "Slightly overripe bananas." That showed that you weren't spoiled, and that you were careful with money, as they're usually on sale and much cheaper. I kid you not. You never knew what mind games these mothers were playing with you.

Another question I remember was "What kind of tablecloth do you use on Shabbos when you set the table?" If it was a plastic tablecloth, which made it much easier to clear the thousand dishes at the end of the Shabbos meal, that meant you were lazy. If it was a tablecloth made of fabric, they would ask what color it was. If it was a white tablecloth, that meant you were a good traditional family. If, however, you wanted to spruce up your Shabbos table and make it more colorful, you were too wild and too focused on material things.

I remember the shadchan when asking my mother for a picture of herself. Why, you ask? Because the prospective mother-in-law wanted to know the likelihood of her future daughter-in-law becoming fat. If her mother was skinny, it was considered more likely that she too would remain skinny after numerous childbirths. I was asked to measure my hips by one prospective family, as wider hips meant that I would have an easier time at childbirth and be able to pop out more babies. I was even asked if I ever dreamt about my teeth falling out, which apparently foretold that you would die at an early age.

The first shidduch that was proposed for me, that I found out about, was with a guy whose last name I no longer remember. (I was only told about the guys who my parents approved of; most got rejected for one reason or another, and I never even heard about them—with some exceptions.) He was suggested by a rabbi who my parents were very close to. Rabbi Stern was a brilliant and kind man who I very much admired and respected. After a long and arduous process, I finally made it to an actual first date. I still remember what I wore, of course: a black skirt, very slim but not fitted, and a beautiful blouse with a high collar and beautiful sleeves with ruching at the wrists. I looked fabulous, if I do say so myself.

I had never seen a picture of my date, Shlomo, and Rabbi Stern, in typical guy fashion, had told me that he was "average." Gee, thanks. That was helpful. He was to arrive at 7:00 P.M. I was supposed to hide in my room until my mother came and got me. He had to get past my parents first. The kids knew something was up, as they had been told in no uncertain terms to play quietly in the downstairs playroom, and under no circumstances were they allowed to come up.

My parents had prepared the obligatory repast, replete with shining white tablecloth (usually we had plastic tablecloths, but no one needed to know that), and we all sat—my parents upstairs, dressed in their Shabbos finery even though it was a Tuesday, and me made up, dressed up, and nervous as could be, praying to get a peek of him as he walked up the stairs to the front door. From my vantage point on the bottom floor, all I would see of him from my window was his legs.

Seven o'clock came and seven o'clock went. Fifteen minutes turned into thirty, which slowly inched to forty-five. At first I worried that he or his family had had second thoughts, and that the shadchan would call soon and make some excuse as to why his side had changed their mind. Then, when 7:45 came and went, I became genuinely annoyed and was deciding if I had the courage to refuse to go out with him altogether. Finally, at eight, a full hour later, I saw a giant Cadillac pull up to our house.

I had to wait another thirty minutes while he chatted with my parents before I heard my mother's shoes click down the stairs. It was interminable. I knew my first impression of him would be based on my mother's expression, which was a mixture of bemused and amused. "What's he like?" I demanded, grasping at her arm. She released her arm from my grip, smiled calmly, and told me not to keep him waiting, as he was "wonderful and such a genius." "What does he look like?" I asked. At that, the amused look came back to her face. She didn't reply and just pushed me out of the room toward my possible destiny.

He looked like a Teletubby. He was short and chubby, a round little man. Now, who am I to complain about someone who is vertically challenged? I'm minuscule. But that's exactly the point. We always want in a spouse what we lack. And to be attracted, I needed a man with height; I had to give my kids a fighting chance, after all. I thought about how I would have to kiss him, to sleep with him, and I felt seriously nauseous, but I chided myself that I was being shallow and to give him a chance. I know you probably think I'm a proper bitch right now, but I'm telling it like it is. Please don't pretend that you wouldn't prefer marrying a handsome stranger to a short, chubby one.

He was very apologetic about being so late and rambled on about getting lost on his way. I thought it was just an excuse, but after the rest of the evening, where we got lost constantly, I understood that this was a way of life. He was truly an absentminded professor. It drove me completely mad. It took us nearly an hour to get to the Sheraton in Mahwah, even though it's twenty minutes from Monsey, what with getting lost and driving at the speed of a ninety-year-old bubbe. He drove the exact speed limit. If it said thirty miles per hour, he didn't drive thirty-one or twenty-nine; he drove thirty. Who doesn't even drive five miles above the speed limit?

When we finally arrived at the Sheraton—a typical first-date scenario, as hotel lobbies are filled with people and there's no concern about yichud—we only had another hour left, according to the rules, in which to talk. Yichud means "separate" or "alone." Women and men are not allowed to be alone until they're married, and even then they can only be alone with one another. For example, if there is a cleaning lady and a man at home without the wife and he doesn't know when his wife will be back, or she's away for the night, the cleaning lady cannot stay. Forget about kissing or touching, which are governed by the laws of negiah; the laws of yichud forbade even a modicum of privacy to allow the prospective partners to really know one another.

We only had a few hours, always surrounded by people, in which to make this life-altering choice. So we sat there at the Sheraton, trying to peer into our future. He offered me a drink, and I chose a Diet Coke. We sat there as people came and went, dressed in our Shabbos finery, and tried awkwardly to start a conversation.

I'm an excellent listener and am genuinely interested in what someone has to say. I started asking questions about his pulpit and his college students, and soon I had him talking nonstop. I don't think I said a single word myself, other than asking questions in response to his monologue. He was, however, genuinely interesting. I could see why people thought he was brilliant. Once he began speaking about a subject he was passionate about, he was quite entertaining.

The hour sped by in a flash, and it was time for us to go back. I had truly enjoyed the hour in his company. I learned later from Rabbi Stern that he had found me a "fascinating conversationalist," which I thought was hilarious, because I had barely spoken. It's something I've seen time and time again. People love the sound of their own voices. Someone can tell the same joke over and over without getting bored, as long as there are new people who will listen. However, no one on earth likes to hear the same story twice. It's an excellent lesson to learn, the art of listening. "It is amazing what one sees when one looks," my teacher used to say. I would add it is amazing what one hears when one listens.

I came home that night thoroughly confused. On the one hand, he was theoretically everything I wanted in a husband: erudite, rabbinic, successful. On the other hand, he looked like Jewish Santa, complete with beard and belly.

I wanted to like him, I really did, but the thought of having him touch me was repugnant. My parents were both waiting for me when I got home, and I explained my dilemma. They recommended that I go out with him again (if the shadchan called and said he wanted to date me again, obviously). "Perhaps his looks will grow on you once you get to know him," my mother opined, and I agreed. Of course, in my world, getting to know him meant going out a few more times, but to me, that seemed perfectly normal. Plus, it was way better than the Chasidic way of practically not meeting before the wedding at all.

We all waited on tenterhooks to receive the call from the shadchan. It's an awful feeling, not knowing if he likes you, not knowing if the shidduch will continue—not unlike waiting for a guy to text you; just the uber-religious version. Luckily, the shadchan called the next evening (a clear sign that Shlomo had really liked me). We immediately responded in the affirmative, and our next date was set up.

Our second date was at South Street Seaport in Manhattan, which still fulfilled the rule of our not being alone but was infinitely more fun than sitting on an itchy Sheraton couch. I tried to imagine, with all my might, the two of us touching each other, yet my mind refused to cooperate. We wandered around South Street Seaport, and even the fishy smell didn't detract from the adventure. It was as foreign and exotic to me as Fiji. South Street Seaport was a world filled with people who dressed so differently from me, who led lives I couldn't even fathom, Martians in shorts and tank tops, laughing easily on the arms of their tanned boyfriends as they strolled, seemingly without a care in the world. I wandered, long-skirted, long-sleeved, and thick-stockinged, with a total stranger whom I found extremely unattractive. Covered and condemned, convincing myself that I could be happy with the man expounding upon heavy Torah topics beside me, as I prayed that the sweat running in rivulets down my legs wasn't obvious.

We went out one more time after that, and of course, on date three, he officially proposed. He painted such a vivid and detailed picture of our life together, and I tried to insert myself there. Me having his children and setting his table. I just couldn't do it. I refused as politely as possible and came back to tell my disappointed parents.

The second guy Rabbi Stern matched me with came from a family I knew well. I was set up with their oldest son, but I was disappointed, because their youngest son was very handsome. I really wanted to go out with him, but the oldest son had to be married first. Also, Rabbi Stern told me that the younger son wasn't very clever. Their family was significantly more modern than mine, and his mother taught secular studies as opposed to Judaics. What concerned me most was that I heard Chaim, the oldest son, went to baseball games. I found that completely shocking. Truly yeshivishe people didn't waste time on such frivolity.

I still had serious misgivings, but my parents said I had to go, and so I went. He wasn't a fan of sitting in a hotel lobby, so for our first date we went to a kosher Chinese restaurant in Queens. He was intelligent and polite enough to ask me questions about myself. The conversation with him wasn't one sided, and I enjoyed myself. We were in the middle of dinner and I was telling a funny story when, mouth full of rice, intently listening, he burst out laughing. I don't know who was more surprised, he or I, when rice came spewing out of his mouth like a projectile, landing squarely on my face. There we were, me sitting with rice dripping off my face, and him looking so mortified, his face puce with embarrassment.

I tried to contain my laughter, but it was impossible. I laughed till tears streamed down my face. I laughed till he started laughing too, and there we sat, crying and shaking with laughter as I wiped wet, partially chewed rice off my face. We accidentally went past the requisite three hours, and my parents threw a fit, but it wasn't because we had any intention of being naughty. Rather, he had absolutely the most abysmal sense of direction, and we kept having to stop at gas stations to ask for help.

I had really enjoyed myself. He was fun and very respectful of my opinions, and I felt like being married to him wouldn't be such a bad thing. We went out two more times, and once again, on date three, a proposal was made. I didn't know what to do! I really liked him and enjoyed the time I had spent in his company, but honestly, I couldn't respect him. He was too modern, not serious enough for my tastes, and he had zero interest in becoming a rabbi. My dream of being a great rabbi's wife would die if I chose to marry this man. I was in a serious quandary. Thanks to a little luck and some emergency surgery, I managed to postpone my decision.

During this time I was working full time teaching fourth-graders, and to make some extra money, I taught Jewish dance classes in the evenings.

A frum person's life is filled with continuous simchos (joyous events). The family size in my community is generally no less than six children, and more often, at least eight, like my family. Their children all need to be bar and bat mitzvahed, and they all marry at a young age. Basically, from the time you're eighteen until the day you die, you are constantly attending simchos. A frum wedding averages around four hundred people, all smushed together, hands held, running round in a never-ending, sweaty circle that is mistaken for a dance. It's onerous, repetitive, and mind-numbingly boring. Men and women are completely separate, so there's no mixed dancing.

Some brilliant woman came up with the idea of making up line dances for women so they could enjoy the endless stream of simchos a little more. Of course, it was an all-women dance class within the community, and it was to the same interminable Jewish music that would be played at the wedding, but that didn't detract from the excitement. It was an instantaneous hit.

I loved the classes. They were a kosher way to satisfy my love of dance, and they brought with them a unique opportunity. I started taking extra classes so that I could teach the dances myself, and since I was already known as an excellent (albeit slightly too sensual) dancer, people flocked to my class—to relieve the monotony in their everyday lives, to make spending five hours at a wedding a little less dreadful.

I spent my days trying to excite a bunch of fourth-grade girls and my nights trying to teach women, many unaccustomed to exercise, how to move to the rhythm and dance to the beat. It required a lot of patience and very strong vocal cords. All day long, I spoke above little girls and all night long, I spoke above the blasting sounds of Mordechai Ben David from my boom box. It was too much of a strain, the constant talking, and within two months of teaching both, I developed two polyps on my vocal cords. By that point, I could barely talk.

Apparently, whispering is even worse for your vocal cords than speaking, and so the doctor abjured me not to speak for two weeks in the hope that, with rest, they would heal themselves and the polyps would shrink of their own volition. It was, on one hand, unmitigated torture staying silent, being unable to express myself. I did find an inner calm, though. It was so quiet inside my head. I could think to my heart's content and my parents couldn't question me. I couldn't babysit the kids, because I couldn't speak. It was an odd respite of sorts. The only person who understood me without my saying a word was my little brother Yitzchok. It pains me greatly that he doesn't speak to me today, as once, before I became a heretic, he was my voice, and he understood me without my having to utter a syllable.

For two weeks, my dating was put on hold, and all questions pertaining to whom I would marry were left dormant as I focused inward and remained silent, locked in my own dilemma.

It gave me ample time to think, and still the thought of being Chaim's wife seemed impossible.

I always imagined the Shabbos table, with my husband expounding on some complicated tractate in the Talmud, and me glowing with pride at his erudition. It didn't occur to me that I could be erudite myself, or lead the Shabbos table myself—just as it never occurred to me to try and get through a day without taking a breath. Both, at that time, seemed impossible and ludicrous.

After two weeks of being locked in my own mind, my vocal cords were again tested, but to my dismay, all that silence had not done the trick. The polyps were just too large; they had to be operated on and removed. Another week of respite before I made the decision. At the time, I was genuinely happy that I was having surgery. It seemed preferable to having to make a decision that would forever alter the course of my life.

After the surgery was over and two days went by, which was the time allotted to me by my parents, the moment came when I had to make a decision. I called him myself, because I thought he had been so kind to be patient with me, letting me take my time in deciding, and I didn't want the refusal to sound cruel and cold. It had been a heart-wrenching decision, but Rebitzen David had done her job too well. I was too extreme, too indoctrinated to appreciate his leniency. I wanted someone committed to the Torah above all else, as I was. I wanted a man worthy of my worship, of my sacrifice. Please don't judge me when you read these words. I was all of nineteen years old, forced to make an impossible choice in an insanely small amount of time, and fully brainwashed by my parents and teachers. I was a sponge, soaking up their words of suffering for God, of self-abasement in the name of raising children who were righteous, and of allowing a man to reach the highest heights of Torah learning by suffering silently and removing all stress, responsibility, and worry from his mind. It was my duty as a Jewish woman and my only path to heaven.

My parents weren't pleased by my refusal, but when I told them about the baseball games, they understood immediately. They basically told me that unless the next guy was an axe murderer, I would have to choose him. We decided to try a more extremist match-maker, renowned for setting up rabbis' sons with wealthy in-laws who could support the family and allow the man to learn Torah in peace. She was in high demand. I don't know why she agreed to find me a shidduch. Perhaps it was an interesting challenge to her; and though my family was not yet wealthy, they weren't impoverished either. They could pay for the privilege of a shidduch made by her.

I was in awe of her when I met her. She was beautiful, and even though she had nine children, she was thin and incredibly well dressed, sort of like a proper princess. She questioned me, but with such a warm and lovely smile on her face that she instantaneously put me at ease. She told me she had the perfect match for me. His name was Yosef Hendler, and he too came from a ba'al teshuva family, which I found quite disappointing; but she went on and on about how his rabbis saw a bright future for him and that he was brilliant and a true Torah scholar who would one day lead the Jewish world. She described him in such glowing terms that by the time she was done, my parents were convinced and gave their permission for the shidduch.

She said he went to school in Philadelphia, and we assumed that meant the Talmudical Yeshiva of Philadelphia, which was considered the Harvard of the Orthodox Jewish world. I immediately called my friend Basya from seminary, as her father was the rosh yeshiva of Philadelphia Yeshiva, and asked her if she could get the scoop on him. She called me back perplexed because her father had said he had no student by his name. My parents were extremely perturbed and called the shadchan demanding an explanation. "Ah, well," she explained, clearing her throat nervously, "I didn't say he went to Philadelphia Yeshiva, I said he went to school in Philly. I actually meant that he went to the Wharton School of Business. I did mention that he is a ba'al teshuva," she continued. "Well, that's where he became religious, at Wharton, and now he's a very erudite scholar at Yeshiva Chaim Berlin in Brooklyn. Ask his rabbis, and don't hold his past against him," she cajoled.

Luckily for me, I had also gone to seminary with the daughter of the rosh yeshiva of Chaim Berlin, a girl named Simi, and so I called her in search of information. She called me back the following day, and there was clear hesitation in her voice. "My father says that he's one of his best students. He says Yosef is a very holy man with a bright future as a great rabbi and that you would be lucky to have him," she concluded. I heard something in her voice, though, that told me she disagreed with her father but was too proper to say so. I begged her to tell me what she was thinking. We were friends, and I guess she felt a certain responsibility. And so, with clear concern in her voice, she said, "I'm not sure he's the boy for you. He's very straight, and he's very quiet and very serious. I can't imagine you, with all your vibrancy and life, being with someone like that." I thanked her, but inwardly I was fuming. Did she think I was some flighty flibbertigibbet? Who the hell did she think she was, telling me that a serious, straight genius Torah learner was not for me? I so badly wanted to be pious, to be serious, to be less attracted to beautiful clothes, to secular books. Her words made me even more excited to go out with him.

He came to the house in a raspberry-red Toyota Camry hatchback with a license plate that said "REGI" (his mother's name, and his mother's car). I was not impressed. The black hat he wore had such a wide brim that it looked like a flying saucer. I promised myself that if I ended up marrying this guy, the first thing to go would be his hat. A black hat was beautiful and necessary—we were Black Hatters, after all—but that brim was just too much.

It was the middle of the Jewish holiday of Succos, which is bookended by days on which you can't drive or use electricity, but during the middle days of Succos, electricity is allowed. You are not, however, allowed to eat anything more than a fruit or a vegetable outside of a succah (a temporary dwelling that all frum Jews put up and live in for the seven days of Succos), to remind us that God is our shelter, and that everything is temporary.

Yosef, hearing that I was an unusual girl, decided to be creative about our date. He brought a picnic basket and drove me to Bear Mountain State Park, the same place I had gone with Yechiel a few years before. Since we weren't allowed to eat outside of a succah, the whole picnic consisted of apple slices and some honey to dip them in. I sat there on the ground in my Shabbos finery (that's how you always dress for a date), amid the pine cones and leaves—completely frozen, since it was October in upstate New York. I was tired, hungry, freezing, and cranky by the time our date was up.

When we got home, he walked me to our front door, as was customary, but it was locked, and no one was home. I found out later that my brother Yitzchok had injured his eye and had to be rushed to the emergency room. Since this was before cell phones, there was no way for them to reach me and tell me. I assumed he would be a gentleman and stay with me and use this extra time for us to get to know one another better, but he just said, "Oh well, you can always go to your neighbors," and left me standing there, alone and shocked out of my mind at his abrupt and rude departure. I was so cold and so hungry, and I was in desperate need of a toilet, and he had just left me there! Dumped me unceremoniously at my front step and told me to fend for myself! Unfortunately for me, my across-the-street neighbors weren't home either, and I felt like a beggar girl, going from door to door, desperate to use the bathroom. Finally, by the third house (the Gershmans), I was in luck. I relieved myself, reliving every single, solitary embarrassing moment, and my fury and disgust over his behavior grew. There was no way in hell that I was marrying this man.

Finally, with my parents back home, and Yitzchok safe and sound with a patch over his eye but luckily no permanent damage, they turned their attention to me. I told them about the date and the cold and the apple and then, as the pièce de résistance, told them how he had unceremoniously dumped me at the door. My parents told me that I was being ridiculous and that it was probably because he was a very pious young man, and since the permissible three hours had passed, he felt it was wrong to stay.

For days I fought with them, refusing to go out again with a guy who cared so little about my welfare. The shadchan called and begged me to reconsider. Finally, she delivered a handwritten letter from Yosef which "explained" his behavior. He wrote that he was terribly sorry that he had offended me and left me, but that he was starving and desperate to go to the bathroom and was faint with hunger. He also knew the allotted time we were allowed to spend together had passed and therefore felt it was unacceptable to stay any longer. My parents were very pleased with both his humility and his explanation. But didn't he think that if he was starving and desperate for the bathroom, I was hungry and in need of the facilities too?

For two weeks, we argued back and forth—me refusing to yield, them refusing to take my no for an answer. They called everyone they could think of who could influence me. My mother was very persuasive.

"You are very unforgiving, Talia," she accused me. "Do you really want Hashem to respond in kind? Haven't you ever done something you've later regretted? Who do you think you are to judge someone and not accept such a humble and heartfelt apology?"

We had just finished the Rosh Hashanah and Yom Kippur holidays, which precede Succos, and I had spent thirty days in prayer, begging to be forgiven for my multitudinous sins. How could I expect forgiveness if I refused another the same thing? They made me feel so guilty and childish and cruel. And I gave in. I fucking gave in. From time to time in the twenty years of misery that followed, I would go back to that day in my mind, begging my younger self to stay strong.

"Do not give in!" I would beg my nineteen-year-old self in my daydreams. "Stand strong, girl!"

I broke down and finally agreed to go out with him again, and I prayed that I would find something seriously damning, so that I could refuse him. This time, he took me to a kosher restaurant. We started the meal off rather uncomfortably, the memory of his abandonment still fresh in my mind, but he was so earnest and so kind and solicitous, asking me what I wanted to order instead of choosing for me (which was quite unusual). I started to think I had judged him too harshly. He was incredibly intelligent, and I found his shyness charming. We argued about philosophical concepts, and he seemed to really enjoy my opinions. At one point during the meal, he was speaking so passionately about the Torah that he covered my hand with his own to make a point. He immediately realized his faux pas and blushed, apologizing profusely, but I had loved it. No man had touched me (besides that one kiss with Yechiel) since I was a little girl. His hand covering mine felt so nice, so safe. It hadn't repulsed me at all. In fact, it had made me like him all the more.

When we came home, my parents were waiting anxiously. "He's very nice," I said, embarrassed at my previous opinion. "You see!" my mother exclaimed. "I am always right! I know he is the boy for you!"

My "proposal" occurred in a parking lot where we pulled over for him to say the evening prayer. I was sitting in the car, and when he came back in, he said, "Will you be my aishes chayil?" which means "woman of valor."

There is a prayer said every Friday night before the Shabbos meal: "Aishes chayil mee yimtzah" (who will find a wife of valor). It goes on to describe what a wife of valor is: "She brings her food from afar. She rises when it is still night and prepares food for her household. She seeks out wool and flax and works willingly with her hands. Charm is deceptive and beauty is naught, a God-fearing woman is the one to be praised. Her husband is well known at the gates, as he sits with the elders of the land." That is what he asked me, not whether I would be his wife, or his lover, but Will you be my helpmate?

I wanted exactly that. To toil and suffer for the Torah. To be great by proxy, the shadow behind the man. It is all I had been taught to aspire to, and the voice in my head that proclaimed it wasn't enough was thoroughly silenced. I denounced that voice! I swore to myself that I would fight the evil inclination that lived inside of me, whispering forbidden thoughts and dreams in my mind.

There was no turning back now, because breaking an engagement in the frum world is as serious as a divorce. Break your engagement and you can expect that from that moment on, your lot in life will be to marry someone twice your age who no one wanted, or a divorcé or a widower. The shidduch system is very strict and unforgiving, and you break an engagement at your peril. To prevent people from having second thoughts once they're engaged, you're only allowed to speak on the phone three times before you're married, and you're not allowed to see one another anymore.

The day of our vort (engagement party), which took place in our house, was dark and gloomy, foreboding clouds puncturing the skies in ominous disapproval. It was as if the sky itself was warning me that I was making a serious mistake.

I used some of the money I had saved to buy myself a beautiful Dior dress. It was the most expensive piece of clothing I had ever purchased. It had a full skirt, à la Dior circa the 1950s, made of black taffeta and Bordeaux-colored flowers. I loved the crisp feel of the taffeta against my skin, and how the cinched skirt made my waist look infinitesimal. I whirled round and round in my bedroom, loving how the skirt sashayed and swayed with each twirl. I felt beautiful.

We had "tzniafied" the dress by using some extra material to make long sleeves and raise the neckline above my collarbone. We had also lined the top of the dress, so that not an iota of skin could peek out amongst the tulle and flowers. Luckily, since I'm so tiny, we had had extra material from the bottom of the dress with which to work, so it didn't look as mismatched as tzniafying things usually does.

I was so grateful to be engaged at nineteen. I knew full well that my chances of meeting anyone half decent at twenty, with my ba'alas teshuva status and my unimpressive lineage, were practically nil, so I felt enormous relief. I was a kallah—a bride!

The vort was as segregated as the wedding would be. Men and women went to different rooms, the men upstairs and the women downstairs. Yosef and I saw one another briefly before (for photos) and briefly after. I did see the gigantic brim of his hat move from place to place as I peeked upstairs.

Finally, at the end of the vort, we managed to speak. He looked at me in my whirling, twirling, taffeta Dior and at my smiling face, and all he managed to say was "That is a nice dress."

"What about the woman inside the dress?" I longed to ask him.

"What do you actually think about me?" I wanted to know. We were getting married and he had never once told me I was beautiful. He had never once complimented me, and though I knew and understood it was because he had been taught it was immodest, the woman inside me cringed.

"Do you find me attractive? Will you one day love me?" I longed to ask. It destroyed my evening. It hit me how little we knew of one another. How crazy is it to marry and spend your life with someone you can't even manage to compliment?

I knew that I shouldn't have these thoughts, but my very feminine nature rebelled. I wanted to feel admired and appreciated. I needed to see at least a gleam in his eyes, a subtle look of appreciation, unspoken as it may be, to show that he found me attractive. I searched his eyes for a clue, scanned his face for something, anything. I walked away deflated and depressed.

It only got worse after the vort. The three phone calls allotted to us were a disaster. I got this very strong feeling that he had no clue what he was getting himself into, as, no matter how much I tried to suppress my innate nature, I was neither shy nor demure or quiet. I was outspoken and confident and outgoing, and I could tell he expected a proper meek and mild Bais Yaakov "aidel maidel" (refined young woman).

It worried me so much that I decided to break the engagement. I might as well have decided to travel to space. I was told by my parents in no uncertain terms that, since I was a ba'alas teshuva, the stigma of a broken engagement would make it impossible for me to even get a date. They laid my choices out for me clearly: marry Yosef or remain alone and childless and living with your parents for the rest of your life. Those were my options.

The thought of spending the rest of my life subservient to my parents seemed like death. Living alone clearly wasn't an option. Frum girls do not live alone. You live in your parents' house, under your father's rule, until you transfer to your husband's house and live under his rule. Women are too simple and stupid to live alone. They need a man guiding them and managing them. It wouldn't even have occurred to me that living on my own, going to college, and getting a profession and supporting myself was an option. To understand it, you have to imagine a woman in sixteenth-century France having those thoughts. Absurd. Completely unimaginable.

"Who knows?" I tried to convince myself. "Perhaps it is cold feet and you're imagining things." It is one thing I battle with to this day: believing in myself enough to listen to the voice in my head and not letting others talk me out of what it tells me. I get better and better each day. It's practice, like anything else, and success breeds success. I can count on one hand how many times my inner voice has been wrong. Every time I have squelched the voice in my head, I have lived to regret it. I didn't know that back then, and I made a decision. I would marry Yosef and be humble and meek and attentive and work hard to earn his pleasure.

CHAPTER FIVE

In the religious world, just as in the past, there is a dowry given with the bride. The parents of the bride agree to give the couple a certain amount of money and support them fully for a set number of years. The bride's, or kallah's, side also must pay for a silver menorah, which the groom will use to light the candles during Chanukah; the silver tray used in the Passover ceremony; a new pair of tefillin (square boxes containing handwritten verses from the Torah, which men wear on their arms and head during morning prayer); and the marriage tallit (ceremonial shawl) that he is obliged to wear during morning prayer as a married man. They also have to gift him a gold watch during the wedding.

The groom's, or choson's, family must provide the diamond ring given at the vort, a pearl necklace given at the wedding, the cost of two sheitels (wigs), and the candlesticks the bride will use to usher in each Shabbos. The bride's side has to pay for the entire wedding, while the groom's side has to pay for the flowers at the wedding and sometimes, if the family is a bit more lenient and there is to be alcohol, the wine as well.

My parents promised to support us for as many years as Yosef stayed in yeshiva full time. His parents bought me a two-carat diamond ring in a yellow gold setting, which I absolutely detested, but of course, no one bothered to ask me what I wanted. They also gifted me, instead of the antique silver candlesticks that I had dreamt of, a twisted, modern candelabra monstrosity. It looked like a pair of ram's horns.

I had wanted something that looked like the traditional candlesticks I saw in all my friends' homes, gleaming and polished, handed down for generations. I had imbued these candlesticks with meaning, as I wanted to start my own family traditions—to one day hand my candlesticks down to my daughter, who would pass them to her daughter. We would build generations of women who would bless their family each week, eyes closed in concentration, as they said the ancient words of prayer and protection.

Yosef's mother also purchased me one human hair wig and one synthetic hair wig. I was very grateful for the human hair wig. I only wore the synthetic one on the days that my good wig was being washed, and I never went out of the house in it. It was so bushy and looked enormous above my tiny face and body.

Once a girl and boy are engaged, there are generally three months between engagement and wedding, as too much idle time makes for dangerous ideas. During that time, both the groom and the bride attend marriage classes. The girl takes kallah classes from a very holy rebitzen, and the guy takes choson classes from a holy rabbi. Most girls who get married have literally zero clue as to how babies are born and know absolutely nothing about sex. Forget about having a clitoris and what an orgasm is; they don't even know where a penis goes. The kallah classes are supposed to educate girls in the ways of marriage and the marriage bed, and the guys, who are much more knowledgeable, as the Talmud talks about sex in detail, are taught what is and isn't appropriate in bed, and what one should expect from a wife, and what one's duties as a husband are.

My kallah teacher was from a very wealthy, renowned family, and her father had, many years prior, purchased enough land for all of his eight children to build homes on. They all lived in the same neighborhood. All the children and grandchildren ran around playing with all their cousins in a street that was wholly holy. I was in awe of this arrangement, and I longed for just such a holy, pious life on a street where the outside world had no place and was not welcome, and where my children could play in happy abandon with my sisters' and brothers' holy children.

The first time I walked into my kallah teacher's magnificent home, with its sweeping marble staircase and its polished floors, I had my notebook gripped tightly in my nervous, sweating hands. She greeted me warmly, her beautiful wig clearly coming from the most exclusive sheitel macher (maker) in Brooklyn. A human hair wig, usually made from the hair of some woman in India who has sold her beautiful locks for just such a purpose, costs around $5,000. A synthetic wig, however, which mats as you go about your day, costs $300 to $400.

My elegant teacher's name was Rebitzen Golda. She had eleven children, but her family was wealthy enough to afford several nannies. She taught kallah classes as a way of giving back to the community, and to raise her family's standing. It meant her daughters would be a hot commodity, since they had been raised by a woman so pious as to teach other young girls about the proper behavior of a bride.

She was supposed to teach me about sex and the laws of family purity. Suffice it to say that she taught me nothing about sex or pleasure and everything about what I was supposed to do, according to what she claimed was Torah law, to keep my family and my children pure. The one thing she drummed into me during the classes, which took place twice a week every week leading up to the wedding, was that while my husband was "doing his duty," I was not to think of my body, but I was to recite psalms. I was to think of God as his seed spilled into me, as that was the only way to ensure that my children would come out holy. If I enjoyed the physical act too much and allowed myself to lose my concentration and focus, my children would be doomed for life, and it would be my fault, my sin. I had nightmares about this for several years after my marriage and did my utmost to recite psalms in my mind while my husband spilled his seed into me. I was so afraid to ruin my children before they were even born.

I once asked my rabbi how it was fair to punish newborns for the sins and failings of their parents. Why should they suffer just because I am imperfect and didn't think the proper thoughts during sex? The rabbi replied that it wasn't about fairness, it was reality. He used the example of drugs. We were always being told how dangerous the outside world was—a place filled with drugs and drug addicts, who killed and stole and sold their bodies for their next hit. This was the future of anyone who left the community. Their children, and they themselves, would fall into despair and ruin, lost, without purpose and meaning, floundering in an empty existence.

This seemed proven out by the many stories I heard about "off the derech" (off the righteous path) kids who became drug addicts. The truth is that we were so unprepared for the outside world that the shift was too much to handle. It was time travel. It is a devastating fact that many who go off the derech do indeed become lost, and many turn to drugs. It is not the fault of society or their own sins but of the community that forced them to be unprepared for modernity. It is the fault of the rabbis who gave them no choice, no ability to survive in the outside world.

When I asked my religious question, the rabbi responded with a medical example demonstrating the principle. We were always taught that whatever exists in the physical world is mirrored in the spiritual world. Just as a mother taking drugs during pregnancy will affect the mind and body of the fetus, so too, in the spiritual world, if a mother is impure, the soul of her baby will be stricken with that impurity. Fact and reality. Fairness didn't come into it. His answer seemed logical and reasonable, as the spiritual world was as real to me as the sofa in my living room.

My kallah teacher also taught me about the laws of "family purity," the mikvah (ritual bath). When a woman has her period, she is considered to be a niddah (menstruating and thus impure). Her husband is not only not allowed to sleep with her, he's not allowed to touch her *at all*. He cannot sit on the same sofa cushion or pass her the salt or take the baby from her arms. Total and complete separation. The laws of family purity are sacrosanct. Nothing is more important in the Torah than being born kadosh (holy) because your

mother went to the mikvah. How do you go about purifying yourself once you've stopped menstruating? you may be wondering. Surprise surprise, it is extremely complex and, of course, all the laws fall
to the woman. You first have to count seven clean days: days during
which there is no blood. You have to stick a small white cloth into
your vagina two times a day for seven days, and if there's blood on
the cloth or panties, you have to start from day one until you've had
seven clean consecutive days. This is very complicated, because
women secrete things from their vaginal tracts other than blood.
What if it's just discharge? What if it's a yellowy color, or dark orange? What then? Is it blood or not? Does she have to start the count
from scratch? These questions loom large in an Orthodox Jewish
marriage for obvious reasons. It's a constant drama, and there is
much moaning when an uncertain color shows up on that cloth or
your underwear (which happens pretty much all the time). What to
do? You have to bring your underwear or the cloth you've just shoved
up your vagina to a rabbi, who will then look carefully at the stain to
determine whether it's blood (the count must be restarted) or just
some other kind of secretion.

Once you have seven clean days, you then need to go to the mikvah. A mikvah is a ritual bath made up predominantly of rainwater
collected in a sort of deep square in which a woman has to dunk her
naked body three times while the mikvah attendant stands above,
watching her, reciting the words "kosher" after each dunk. If a hair
escapes being completely immersed, she will say "not kosher" and
you have to dunk again. The preparation for going to a mikvah is
also very intense. A single solitary extraneous sliver of anything on
your body will render your mikvah invalid and if you conceive after
that, your child is considered "ruined." You are not allowed to have
anything that is not naturally or wholly attached to your body before
you dunk. This means no nail polish (I was always so afraid that a
minute sliver of clear polish that I somehow missed would make my
newborn spiritually defective), not a single strand of loose hair, no
fake lashes, no scabs that have started peeling off, no dry skin, no
snot in your nose. Not a single extraneous anything. It would take

me at least two hours to prepare my body for the mikvah. Once you get to the mikvah, you need to do another deep clean of your whole body, in case some object attached itself to you on the ride there. Then, when you are done, you press a button and the mikvah lady comes into your room. You have to stand there, stark naked, while she goes over every inch of your body with her gloved hands. If she thinks your nails are too long, she makes you cut them in front of her. If she thinks your heel has any loose dead skin, she cuts it away herself. I would open my vagina to ensure that no discharge had come in the time between my cleaning myself and her examination. It was invasive, uncomfortable, and frankly awful for me. I dreaded going to the mikvah.

It was always supposed to be a major secret when you went to the mikvah, as it was considered untznius for other people in the community to know, because of a law that requires a husband and wife to have sex the night of the mikvah. Imagine how much fun sex is when it's the law that you have to have sex, whether you want to or not. Most mikvahs would keep women apart in different waiting rooms, in case you accidentally bumped into your next-door neighbor, which would have been considered hugely embarrassing. Some mikvahs would make appointments and usher you out through a private door so no one would bump into each other accidentally. That's what I spent most of my time with my kallah teacher doing: going through the intricate and complicated laws of family purity. It was so frightening to me. The stakes were so high. If I didn't do exactly everything perfectly, my child would be damaged goods for life. If I made a mistake, my child would be born tainted. End of story. No one wants to sully their family purity with a child born with a spiritual defect.

As ill-prepared as I was for this marriage, Yosef fared even worse. His choson teacher was one of the strictest, most pious rabbis at Yosef's yeshiva. His name was Rav Reuven, and I will never forgive him, because he made the first years of my marriage so miserable. He told Yosef that it was sinful for him to kiss me too much, to speak to me too much, that having warm feelings about me would take away Yosef's concentration from his studies and be his downfall.

He also taught Yosef a saying from the Torah: "Al tarbeh sicha im ha easha," which literally means "Don't talk to a woman a lot." This saying, believe it or not, exhorts a husband to refrain from speaking too frequently to his own wife! This idea being, if you're not allowed to speak to her often, how much more does this apply to women who are not your wife? Rav Reuven taught Yosef that he shouldn't spend too much time in my company, and that kissing and caressing me before the actual act was not only unnecessary but sinful and harmful to his desire of being a great rabbi. Sex was an act that was a mitzvah, or a positive commandment between a married man and woman, only if it was done with the holiest and purest of intentions and not born from pleasure or desire. Like my kallah teacher said to me, Rav Reuven told Yosef over and over that he should be thinking solely of God when he touched me and had intercourse with me, and that he should be reciting psalms in his mind as he came.

The Torah says, relating to what to look for in a spouse, that he or she should be your ezer k'negdo, which translated literally means "your help against you." This means that your spouse is supposed to challenge you and make you into a better person. But that begs the question: How does your spouse make you into a better person against your own will? How do they force you to choose the path of righteousness? I thought of Yosef and told myself I was lucky. He would definitely be my ezer k'negdo, and he would make me better, more holy, more worthy of building a holy house among the Jewish people.

During the months preceding our wedding, after I would daven shacharis (say the morning prayer) each morning, I would sit and enumerate the few things I knew about him and think how wonderful his middos (character traits) were. I decided not to ever think about him in the bathroom, because the bathroom was the least holy room of the house, and you weren't allowed to think of God in the bathroom, nor were you allowed to make any blessings. Since he was to be my husband, and God's emissary on this earth for me, it would be inappropriate to think of Yosef in the bathroom. Can you even imagine? It sounds hilarious when I write it, but I was so completely ignorant, so ridiculously, absurdly naïve and idealistic. So very brainwashed.

In my mind, I started painting a very lovely picture of how wonderful our life would be. Yosef knee-deep in the Talmud, his eyes shining with holiness as he pored over the ancient tomes, and me knee-deep in children, teaching them the pathways to God, and being pure in thought and deed. I decided I was in love with him (although I had no clue what that word meant), and that I would make him the happiest husband, and be the best wife I could possibly be.

We were engaged in October and married in January, which is the standard amount of time in our world. In the outside world, I later learned, people generally took a year between engagement and marriage, and planned bachelorette parties and honeymoons and bridesmaid dresses. In my world, none of that existed. I had absolutely zero choice in any matter related to my wedding. No one even bothered to ask for my opinion, as it was totally extraneous. I was the star of the show only in theory. In reality I was just a piece on a chessboard to be moved about and placed where needed. Chess pieces don't get asked if they want to move or stay.

Being that I was very interested in clothing, no matter how hard I tried to combat it, I was excited about getting to choose my wedding dress. I couldn't wait to go to the bridal store in our community, which sold only "kosher bridal dresses" that covered you head to toe. I waited eagerly to go. I remember the day so clearly! I couldn't sleep the night before, because the bridal store was in the Chasidic neighborhood of Borough Park, Brooklyn, which meant that I'd get to go to the city in the morning and walk down Thirteenth Avenue in Borough Park with all the religious ladies in their pillbox hats and sheitels, pushing their baby carriages and keeping a loose eye on the other children that spilled, helter-skelter, from the narrow row houses that populated the area.

Borough Park was my Paris! It was so cosmopolitan and exciting compared to Monsey. Everyone said that the best kosher pizza was Amnon's on Thirteenth Avenue. There was the Donut Man of Boro Park, the kosher doughnuts shop, with its enticing smells and sugar-coated delights. On Chanukah, Mr. Donut would sell these dough-nuts that were filled with caramel instead of the usual oozing strawberry preserves. I always longed to taste them, but my family had no business in Borough Park, no second cousins to visit or un-cles and aunts who lived on Eighteenth Avenue, like many of my friends. Yet here I was, nineteen years old, walking down Thirteenth Avenue to the door of a narrow brownstone—the side entrance, of course—where a woman named Chanale sold tznius wedding dresses out of her basement.

There were two approved wedding-dress scenarios. You could rent a dress for the night and then return it after the wedding, or you could have a dress custom made. My mother had been too busy to be bothered with my dress, so my only option was renting one, and she didn't understand why I was disappointed. "What's the big deal?" she wanted to know. "You're only going to wear it for a few hours and never again, so it seems like a waste to make a new one for just one night." It was a moot point anyway, as the only wedding dress maker we knew of was looking at me askance, daring me to question her assertion that no one would make a wedding dress in that time frame.

It was clear to me that I had no choice. I would have to pick a dress from one of those racks in that basement. My mother didn't have time to go and find other dressmakers, and had zero patience. She was very clear with her instructions. "There are plenty of dresses there. Pick one—quickly, please, because we have so many other er-rands to do, and I don't want to have to come back to Brooklyn again. It's such a schlep." It took the whole day, back and forth on the Mon-sey Trails bus. My people didn't travel on regular transportation. Sit with the goyim? Where they sit all mixed together, women and men? Impossible. Our bus only made certain stops, in the kosher parts of the city. Forty-seventh Street in Manhattan for the Chasidic guys in the diamond business, and Borough Park and Flatbush for all the ladies.

I stood there feeling very sad in that dank and smelly basement, looking through racks of dresses worn by other kallahs, on other wedding days. They were all so huge. Most girls are not my size. I'm tiny, heightwise, and I also weighed around ninety pounds soaking wet. So there I was, skinnier and scrawnier than most girls my age, trying to find in these sad, groaning racks a dress I would wear on the day that would determine the path of my whole life. I tried so hard to be cheerful, to yell at myself that it was just a dress, and that my mother was right—I would be wearing it for only a matter of hours. "It doesn't matter," I kept telling myself. I just wasn't doing a good enough job of convincing myself. I so badly wanted to cry, but I hadn't cried in public since that night in the kitchen, and I certainly wasn't going to start now.

Dress after dress was just too large, and since these were rental dresses, no alterations could be done to them. The only allowance was for the length of the gown, as that could be pinned up for the duration of the wedding and then taken down again. But I must have taken too long, as my mother's patience had reached its limit. She grabbed one out of the pile, this hideous monstrosity with puffy sleeves and a thick, full skirt made of some shiny material masquerading as silk satin, with pasted-on flowers and rhinestones in the middle. She pushed it into my arms and said, "Try this one." It had a tiny waist. That was what had drawn her attention to it. It looked like it was my size. I tried to protest, but she was having none of it. I scampered off, head lowered, to the dressing room, praying that it would be too big, too wide, too anything. It fit perfectly. The only dress in that entire basement of dresses. Whoever it was who had originally worn this ugly tablecloth had been as petite and thin as me.

I looked at myself in the mirror. The puffy sleeves were enormous on my tiny frame, and the full skirt swallowed my little body whole. It was the ugliest dress I had ever seen. I hated it. It was tacky and fluffy. I looked like one of those dolls I had seen perched on top of wedding cakes: round and silly, stuffed with fluff. I walked out of that dressing room (it was really a utility closet with boxes and brooms and a mirror stuffed haphazardly against the wall), and I felt like the ugliest, most pathetic creature. My mother said, "It's perfect." And that was that.

The next place on our list was a kosher lingerie store that sold kallah lingerie for that special night and other pieces for the following days. Religious people don't sleep naked. The walls of your house aren't even supposed to see your uncovered hair if you wanted to have righteous children. Just as my wedding dress had swallowed me whole, so did my wedding nightgown. It was meant to be white (easier to spot the blood that way)—and then, for the seven impure days after my period, I had to wear white nightgowns as well, until I reached the mikvah, the bath I would have to dip into again to achieve purity. This made it easier for a rabbi to pronounce you kosher. And then, for the next few weeks until your following period, you were supposed to wear only colored underwear and colored nightgowns, and even your sheets were supposed to be colored, so that some small discharge wouldn't invalidate your "clean days" and shorten the time that you and your husband were allowed to pass one another a saltshaker or sit on the same couch.

Therefore, I needed at least one white and one colored nightgown. The nightgowns I ended up with were A-line and made from scratchy, shiny polyester, and with elastic bands around the wrists and shoulders. I don't think anyone even during Regency England would have worn such monstrosities. Between you and me, I never once wore them.

Oddly enough, by this point, I wasn't afraid of the wedding night. I was excited. All those Barbara Cartland romance novels had done the trick, and I was much more informed than your average religious girl. Barbara didn't talk about orgasms or clitoral stimulation. It was, basically, fall in love and fall into bed and then the rest is magical and mystical. That was my understanding, and I was looking forward to it. I was also dying for my first real kiss. I didn't count what happened with Yechiel, because it had been more a saliva deluge than a kiss. This was going to be it. This man—who I had now convinced myself was a supertzaddik (super righteous), and with whom I was supposed to be one—was going to kiss me, and it was going to be magical, and we would live happily ever after.

I am, by nature, a very physical being, and I love being held and hugged and kissed. I love affection, and this seemed like the most extreme version of affection. It was Yosef's job to love me and to make me feel loved. After all, I had been taught that the Gemara states that for a man to be blessed with a son, the husband must "please his wife first." It means she must come before he does. Of course, neither Yosef nor I knew what an orgasm meant. But I can tell you from personal experience now that that is incorrect, as I had my very first orgasm when I was in my thirties, and it was with a Rabbit vibrator and had nothing to do with my husband.

The day of the wedding arrived amid the outbreak of the Gulf War, with Scud missiles exploding all over Israel. People brought transistor radios to our wedding, because most had relatives in Israel, and they were worried for their loved ones.

Just as I had had no choice in dress or wedding hall or flowers or anything else, no one bothered to ask me who I would want to have doing the makeup at my wedding. I have extremely sensitive skin. Even to this day, a new cream can turn my entire face into a blotchy mess. I don't just sunburn; I immediately get sun poisoning if I don't reapply sunscreen every two hours, on the dot. My mother picked the woman who was supposed to do my hair and makeup for the wedding. There was no practice run, no discussion of what kind of look I wanted. And the beginning of the evening would be the last time in my life that I would be allowed to uncover my hair. I would start the wedding with my own hair, but after the chuppah, the wedding canopy where the actual marriage ceremony would be performed, and the yichud room, where Yosef and I were supposed to go for a few minutes after the ceremony and touch one another for the first time to show we were truly married, I would have to put on my wig. Those two hours before the chuppah would be the last hours ever that my hair would feel the wind or get kissed by the sun.

The woman who did my makeup would have done well as a makeup artist on a set of one of the Star Wars movies. She painted two bright streaks of hot neon pink across my perfectly lovely nineteen-year-old skin, and my eyes were covered in so much green eyeshadow that it was difficult to blink. When she was done, I looked at myself in the mirror. I might not have had much exposure to fashion magazines or movies, but it didn't take a genius to know I looked ridiculous. Between the puffy-sleeved, petticoated gown and the bizarre face paint, I looked like a mad Wes Craven version of a child bride. I couldn't contain my dismay.

I went to my mother and the makeup lady and asked if she could remove some of the makeup. They both assured me that I didn't know what I was talking about, and it was necessary for pictures.

"You don't realize, honey," the makeup artist said, "but I've been doing this for twenty years, and in photos, if you don't put on this much makeup, you will look pale and unhappy. Do you want to look pale and unhappy?"

I wasn't totally convinced, and I snuck off to the bathroom to try and remove some of the makeup, which was also extremely itchy and uncomfortable on my face. I shouldn't have bothered. My mother saw me and promptly made me sit back in the chair and have my makeup reapplied, although I did manage to remove most of the horrible green eyeshadow. I told her that my face was really itchy, and I thought that I was having a bad reaction to the makeup, but I was told that I was being ridiculous and that she had enough on her hands to deal with without having to worry about me, and that was that.

An ultra-Orthodox Jewish wedding is unlike anything you've ever been to, believe me. It begins with two receptions, one for the men and one for the women. The women's reception is called a badeken. The kallah sits on a "throne" (a massive chair covered in fabric), with her mother and her female relatives on one side and her soon-to-be mother-in-law and her fiancé's female relatives on the other side. While they pass out hors d'oeuvres, which can range anywhere from baby lamb ribs and duck confit to herring and crackers, depending on the financial situation of the kallah's family, women go up to the kallah in her grand chair and tell her and the mothers mazal tov and ask for a bracha (blessing), as a kallah is supposed to have a special connection to God on the day of her wedding, and her prayers are supposed to be more readily answered. Women who have been unable to get pregnant, or those poor lost souls who are still unmarried, come to a wedding for the express purpose of getting a bracha.

I was, meanwhile, supposed to be assiduously reciting Tehillim. The day of your wedding is like a mini–Yom Kippur. You fast the whole day (not a single morsel of food nor even a sip of water) until you reach the yichud room, where you are alone for the very first time. This usually takes place around nine at night. On top of everything, I was "unclean" (on my period), which meant that I would still be off-limits to Yosef, and therefore we couldn't actually be alone for the first time in the yichud room. I was going to be a married woman who was still forbidden to even be in a room alone with my husband, let alone shake his hand. But it wasn't proper for everyone in the wedding to know that, so we had to pretend to have a yichud room, where my sister and brother were waiting for me, because someone had to be with us at all times.

I was told that whatever I want out of my future, I should ask for it on the day of my wedding, as it was the most propitious day of my entire life. So I sat there, looking and feeling so ugly, with my face itching and tears running down my cheeks, as I begged God to forgive me for all my thousands upon thousands of sins. (After all, even that special day, I had gone against my mother's wishes and tried taking off my makeup. I was just a horrible sinner and a shallow person, and I begged God to give me more time.)

On the groom's side, men sit around tables and toast and drink schnapps and whisky and vodka in honor of the choson (the groom), who sits surrounded by both fathers, and by all the male relatives of both families. Then the mothers-in-law come in and break a plate together, which is supposed to bring mazal (luck) to the new home, and then the actual badeken occurs. A badeken is when the starving choson is walked by all the hundreds of men who are attending the wedding to the kallah's reception room. By then, the kallah is covered in a veil that is supposed to be completely solid, so you can't see her face and she can't see any of the men descending on the room, and then, once the choson, flanked by a sea of men, is standing close to the kallah, her father lifts her veil to show the choson that there is no chicanery afoot, and the kallah is truly the one promised to him, and then he is walked back to the choson's room amid much singing and dancing (by only the men, of course). Women stand on the edges of the room, smiling and clapping and watching the men escort the choson back to the men's room. This is done because, if you remember the story of Rachel and Leah, their father, Lavan, switched the brides at the last minute, and Isaac was tricked into marrying Leah instead of Rachel. In order to prevent such shenanigans, the choson is allowed to see under her veil right before the chuppah, and to publicly proclaim that she is indeed the right woman.

As I sat trembling and praying under my veil, hearing the tide of male voices coming toward me, I have to tell you, I have never been so afraid in my life. When they lifted my veil and I saw the weak, pale, starving face of my soon-to-be husband, I was filled with immeasurable dread. It hit me then, knocked me in the gut and made it difficult to breathe: the realization that I was putting my life, my future, my everything, in the hands of a total and complete stranger. I knew nothing about him! Nothing! And this was it. Too late to change. Too late to reconsider. He was my future, and I would end up following his command and his rule for the rest of my life.

I was also dying of thirst and faint from hunger, and there was still the chuppah to get through, where I would walk around him seven times, with my mother and his mother, to symbolize the seven blessings that would be said, and the creation of the world, which was done in seven days. Our chuppah was as simple and plain as the rest of my wedding: white tablecloths pinned together to form a tent. White roses (to this day it is the only flower I detest) scattered hither and yon for the walk to the chuppah.

It's not like walking down the aisle in the outside world. There are no bridesmaids or best men. It's just relatives (grandparents and parents and siblings).

He was standing there, also wearing white, praying and shaking with concentration, as I walked solemnly and slowly around him. We still hadn't looked at one another. I was being led by both our mothers, which pretty much symbolized my life, around a man who would take over the role of leader and commander. There was always some yeshiva bochur (student) who would sing you down the aisle. It's haunting, solemn, beautiful music that aptly conveys the feeling of the day. The concept of "ve gilu bir'ada" which means "rejoice with trembling," is very big in my world. Even when you are happy, don't get complacent. You break the glass under the chuppah to remind everyone of the destruction of the Holy Temple. Even at the happiest moments, remember that God is all-powerful and a jealous God, and He punishes sins and sinners.

Yosef was supposed to pass me the wineglass to drink from as the rabbis recited the seven blessings, and he was also supposed to put the ring on my finger, but he couldn't do either of those things, as I was unclean. We kind of fudged it under the chuppah, with the rabbi passing me the wine to drink and Yosef pretending to put the ring on my finger while actually slipping it into his pocket. Because there were so many people standing under the chuppah with us, rabbis and parents, it was very difficult to see from the audience (which is always seated separately, men on the right of the aisle and women on the left) what was actually happening under the chuppah, and so no one noticed. A glass goblet was placed under Yosef's foot, and he was supposed to stamp on it, break the glass, and everyone would scream mazal tov, and we would be escorted to the yichud room by the same throng of dancing men.

Once Yosef stamped hard enough to break the glass, there was a roar of approval from the crowd and that was that. Mr. and Mrs. Hendler were officially (if still only partially) married.

Soon, we entered the yichud room, where my sister and brother, who were nine and eight, were waiting for us, as we still couldn't be alone, although I was now technically Talia Hendler. There was some food in the room, as our fast was finally over, and we both dug in, ravenous with hunger. It was a way to mask the awkwardness of the moment—and a helpful distraction from the reality of the situation. We were supposed to remain in the room for thirty minutes and then go out to take pictures, standing a good four feet away from one another. As we walked out of that yichud room, the pretense, which would last for the next twenty years of my life, began. I knew people expected to see a happy face, and even though the absolute last thing I felt was happiness, I didn't want to disappoint my audience. The show must go on.

We were swept away to our disparate rooms—Yosef to the men's room, where the men danced round and round, red-faced and sweaty, and me to the women's side, where the ladies showed off simcha dances that they had been taught by me. I smiled for my teachers, smiled for my friends, smiled till my mouth ached and my shoulders sagged from the weight of it. I danced and laughed and pretended that it was indeed the happiest day of my life.

It wasn't until later, after midnight, that Yosef and I were able to see one another again. We spent our wedding night in my neighbors the Gershmans' in-law suite. In order to keep private that we still weren't allowed to consummate the marriage, we still had to sleep in the same house, although not in the same room. I slept in a room with Chana and Yitzchok, and Yosef slept in a separate room by himself. There I was, sleeping with my siblings, in my new tichel, which was attached to my head with metal clips that dug into my scalp and caused horrible headaches, a married nineteen-year-old child who was still forbidden from being alone with her new master and husband.

The next morning, I woke up and walked to the bathroom, stepping gingerly over my sleeping siblings, to be met with a face I didn't recognize. As I feared, my face had reacted to the cheap, heavily applied makeup. I wish I had a photo from that day. It was swollen to ten times its regular size. My eyes were tiny slits in the swollen, red mass that masqueraded as my face. Brushing my teeth was absolute agony, and the thought that I would have to attend Sheva Berachos that evening and sit through hours of rabbis' speeches seemed pretty abysmal, to say the least. The seven days after the wedding are called Sheva Berachos, which means "the seven blessings." You have seven of these dinners/events for the six days following the wedding, as the wedding itself is considered the first day.

Each day represents a different blessing. You are supposed to come to meals hosted by relatives and friends, where rabbis expound on the purpose of marriage and exhort the kallahs to be properly obedient to their husbands.

We walked into that Sheva Berachos, and my parents actually grabbed me, took me aside, and asked, "You look terrible, what's wrong with you?" I longed to scream, "I told you the makeup was bothering me." But what would have been the point? My mother was no longer the arbiter of my destiny. That was Yosef's job now. I just shrugged my shoulders and said that I had had a bad reaction to the wedding makeup.

Somewhere in the middle of the fifth speech of the evening, I realized I was hot to the touch. I was burning up with a fever. I excused myself and got a taxi to take me back to the Gershmans' house. Yosef followed an hour or so later, and we repeated the same sleeping arrangement as the night before. I had still not exchanged more than five words with my new husband.

It wasn't until the last night of Sheva Berachos, that last, seventh day, which was being hosted in Brooklyn by his rebbe and his yeshiva friend, that I was able to go to the mikvah and we were finally allowed to be alone together. Yosef and I had spent our first week of marriage pretending to others and being unable to even get to know one another better.

I got back to the Gershmans' house, all clean and holy from dunking myself in the mikvah, and then we were supposed to quickly dress and depart to Brooklyn for the Sheva Berachos. After that, as it was my mikvah night, it would be a mitzvah for us to have sex. That order got completely reversed, because the minute I walked into the Gershmans' house and saw my newly permissible-to-touch husband, I jumped him. Literally. I came back from the mikvah so eager to be a real wife, so curious about sex, and so desirous of being an adult and starting this new chapter of my life that I did what I always do: jumped right in, assuming I would figure it out as I went along.

You should have seen his face. He didn't expect that. Brides were supposed to be shy and scared. I was neither. I was hungry and not hiding it. I wanted to know what the fuss was all about. In the Regency romances I had read, girls changed into women after they had that "special moment." I badly wanted to be a woman. I was trying to kiss him as he was trying to get me off him. But I won. He was still a man, after all, and rabbis or not, here was his wife kissing him, and I could feel him get hard. We got naked lickety-split, and I was so impatient to see him naked too. I'd never seen a penis before, and I was so very curious to see what it would look like. I wanted to know how it would feel, what it would be like to touch it, to hold it in my hand. I was fascinated by how Yosef's grew large and hard when he saw my naked body, and I felt very beautiful at that moment, seeing his obvious desire for me. We fell back on the bed at the Gershmans' house. We tried to figure out how to get his dick into my vagina, but were having no luck. We just had no clue how it worked, and he was too afraid to hurt me. Already an hour had passed and we were no further along than when we started, so we gave up. By the time we got to the Sheva Berachos, the hosts were justifiably annoyed that we arrived three hours late. We couldn't exactly explain that I had had to go to the mikvah and that I had then jumped my husband, so we used traffic as our excuse. They were not pleased, and as this dinner was made by the wives who were part of the new community that I would be joining (Yosef would be continuing his learning at Chaim Berlin), they never let me forget it. They made me pay for it during the two years Yosef was part of the kollel. The kollel was still part of Chaim Berlin, but it was only for married men, and paid a stipend to their students to keep them learning Torah as long as possible.

With the last Sheva Berachos over, we were finally going to spend the night at our new apartment in Flatbush, just the two of us. No siblings, no parents, just us, starting our new life together. The day before, I had taken the bus to the apartment (which I hadn't chosen), and I'd brought streamers and candles and flowers to decorate. I wanted to surprise Yosef with a romantic, beautiful home.

I need to take a moment to describe the apartment. It was on the first floor of a condominium apartment building. We brought down the median age in the building by like fifty years. Our apartment was so small that the kitchen didn't have any counters. It had a fridge and an oven/cooktop. That was it. We ended up buying a countertop at Lowe's that someone had ordered and never picked up and mounting it on the wall with hinges. When the countertop was down, it blocked the bathroom. So I could either cook or use the bathroom, but I couldn't do both. It was a kitchen/living room/dining room all in one, and then one bathroom and one bedroom. I think it was about three hundred square feet. The main living area was painted a nuclear yellow, and our bedroom, Gatorade orange. Atomic orange. I spent the first month we lived there painting. I also taught myself how to lay tiles, and I retiled the floor with excess tiles that, again, had been ordered and never picked up by some customer at Lowe's. I had had enough of sticky linoleum to last me a lifetime. My kitchen was going to have fucking tiles, even if they were tiles I hadn't chosen and that someone else had rejected. It was also on the first floor, with a window that opened to the courtyard, which, in Flatbush, was a very dangerous proposition, as the building was on Avenue I between Seventeenth and Eighteenth streets—a neighborhood famous for thefts.

I would have never chosen it, not in a million years, if anyone had bothered to ask me, but of course by this time I was totally accustomed to not being asked for my opinion, so I looked at that tiny apartment and promised myself I would make it the happiest, loveliest apartment ever!

That night, our first night in our new home, we went inside, where streamers and flowers hung, and my friend Simi (who had warned me against marrying Yosef) had gone ahead and lit all the candles. It was small and ugly, but it looked cheerful and happy and romantic. I walked in, excited to surprise him, but he didn't even glance at the decorations. He ran desperately to the bathroom and spent the next four hours vomiting his guts out. I became genuinely afraid that I would become a widow before I could officially become a wife and called 911. He was rushed to the hospital with severe food poisoning, as the cold cuts he had eaten were completely spoiled. Everyone at the Sheva Berachos who had eaten the cold cuts ended up having food poisoning. Of course, they blamed me and the fact that we had arrived so late.

It wasn't a very propitious start—me swollen and sick the first few nights, and then him hospitalized the day of the mikvah. It was two days before he was released from the hospital, and we were getting into dangerous territory, because you're not technically married until you've consummated the marriage. He and I were both healed, it was finally time to have sex, and I was still beyond enthusiastic. We had two twin beds, but we technically only had to sleep separately when I was a niddah (impure). His choson teacher, however, had told him we should always sleep separately no matter what, and that once we finished having sex he should go back to his separate bed. He had also told Yosef that it was inappropriate to spend too much time making love to me, or on foreplay, although neither of us had the vocabulary to speak about foreplay.

It was finally time to try and have sex again. I wanted to be kissed and explored, and I wanted to do my own exploring. Yosef was well proportioned and slim. I wanted to touch every part of his completely unfamiliar body. But he was horrified. He just didn't expect it, I suppose. He assumed I would by shy and quiet, and that I would lie still and let him do his thing. It wasn't like that at all, and instead of praising his lucky stars that he had such an uninhibited wife, he chastised me and looked so uncomfortable and disgusted with my blatantly untznius-like behavior that I stopped what I was doing and lay still so that he could enter me. But it didn't work.

The night was ruined. Even when he entered me, he didn't manage to break my hymen. It remained totally intact, and all I felt as he moved back and forth inside of me was discomfort. The walls of my vagina were very dry, and the friction felt awful. Of course, at the time, I didn't know about vaginal walls and friction. All I knew was that this was not what I had been led to believe making love would be like. It felt like someone was brushing my teeth really hard and making my gums hurt. Not sexy or even remotely appealing.

We tried again that night and the next night, but now I was no longer looking forward to it. It hurt like hell. I wasn't even remotely wet or lubricated, and there was no kissing or cuddling or anything pre-sex, and every time he entered me, or tried to, I became more and more sore. Finally, I started bleeding, but unfortunately, the rabbi said we needed to go to a doctor, as this didn't look like the right type of blood. My hymen was still intact! The doctor I was sent to told me the blood was from the walls of my vagina, which were bleeding from the constant, dry abrasion that I was suffering every time he entered me. The doctor told us about K-Y jelly, which she said would make it less painful when Yosef entered me. I, of course, had an extreme allergic reaction to it, and became more swollen and sensitive every time he entered me. It didn't occur to me to complain or ask that he stop. It was both our duties, and we had to keep going until he managed to break my hymen.

Let me be very, very clear here: none of this was Yosef's fault. The reality is, we were both just doing what our teachers had told us. He had no intention to hurt me or cause me pain, and in all the years of our marriage he was never physically abusive in any way. We both thought we had a duty, and that to do it in any other way was to harm our children's souls and their very lives. We were so clueless and so sincere and so very wrong. He was as much a victim of the system as I was. What happened to me and Yosef happens to men and women all over the world, in any fundamentalist culture where there is only one way to goodness, and where all other roads lead to hell. Imagine being told that being tender to your wife or spending time embracing her will harm your children. Is it any surprise that Yosef treated me as he did, or that for the first few years I accepted it as my lot in life?

It took several years, and the birth of my second child, Shlomo, when we moved back to my old house in Monsey and changed rabbis, for me to finally feel comfortable enough with our rabbi to ask him what the actual laws pertaining to having sex were. We were both flabbergasted and furious with Yosef's rebbe and my kallah teacher for having taught us chumros (stringencies) and telling us that these were laws. This new rabbi, who was the rosh yeshiva in Monsey that Yosef switched to, was also a black-hat fundamentalist, but at least he was honest in his teachings and didn't add things to the law. He told us that we are absolutely allowed to have foreplay, and though Yosef was not allowed to ever look at my vagina directly, nor to touch it with his mouth, he was allowed to stimulate me with his fingers, and he was allowed to kiss me and caress me, and to touch me and try and please me. It was massively different from everything we had been taught before. We were clearly both victims, trying to do what we had been taught was right.

CHAPTER SIX

On the morning of Sunday, January 20, 1990, I could walk around outside without my hair being covered, just like anyone else, but by the evening, I was no longer allowed to uncover my hair—at all. It was an enormous adjustment, and hard enough trying to remember to put on my sheitel when I went out of the house. The wig was so heavy and itchy, with metal combs that dug into my scalp, which gave me massive headaches. I tried to make do with one clip, but this didn't do as good a job of keeping the sheitel on my head properly. Often, I would pass by a mirror and realize that my "hair" was lopsided and I looked so chaotic, with my wig careening sideways.

It was so hard for me, wearing this mop on my head. I missed my hair. I missed how it moved and how I was able to run my fingers through it. This had been a habit of mine since I was a small child, but now there was no running my fingers through my hair. By the middle of the day, the part that was touching my neck would be all matted and twisted and clumpy, and I would have to go to some bathroom and try and comb out the rat's nest that my hair had become. I had also refused to cut my hair short, which was not "legally required" but preferable. Luckily for me, Yosef detested short hair and was very pleased with my decision. This presented its own set of problems, as I had to somehow stuff all my hair under my wig so that not a single strand of real hair would show. I would roll it up in a bun, squish it under the wig and pin it all together, and clip it into my scalp. I absolutely detested wearing a wig. The other option I had was to cover my hair with a tichel (kerchief). Sometimes I see these ads with glamorous women, hair covered elegantly with a scarf or kerchief, and they make it look chic and fabulous. My face, however, is one of those that needs hair framing it. Put me in a kerchief and I don't look like Grace Kelly; I look more like a matryoshka doll.

In the Talmud it says that if you want to have righteous children, you need to be stringent, and that "the walls of your house should never see your nakedness" (including your hair). My husband decided we would follow this stringency, and he made me wear the tichel even to bed. Since not one strand of real hair is allowed to be shown, it has to sit on your forehead and over your ears. How do you keep it from sliding around and revealing a strand? You guessed it! Metal pins. I had to sleep with shards of metal around my head.

I just couldn't do it. I've suffered from insomnia most of my life, so trying to sleep with metal attacking my scalp was impossible. I tried; I really did. I even apologized to the walls of my house, having forced them to see my nakedness. I first tried to reason with Yosef and explain to him why sleeping with a tichel was impossible for me.

"Why don't you try it, Yosef?" I asked him. "How would you like to sleep with metal pins?

That didn't go over too well. Like one of those records you see in old movies, where it gets stuck in a perpetual circle of repetition, he recited the mantra "The walls of your house should not see a hair of your head in order to have righteous children" over and over.

"All the women I know do it," he would chastise me. "None of them complain that it hurts them. I asked my friends and my rabbis, and they all said their wives sleep with their hair covered. If they do it, you can do it too."

The whole guilting thing usually worked very well, but in this particular instance, I knew that it wasn't the law, and I just wasn't prepared or holy enough to take this particular stringency upon myself.

All through the first few weeks of marriage the tichel debate hung over us like blackout shades, making everything darker and more miserable than it already was. After three weeks of cajoling and debating, I finally had had enough. I knew full well that I would never be able to get a full night of sleep if I had to wear this thing. And so, Tuesday morning, I walked out of our bedroom and told Yosef that if my hair was so objectionable to him and to the walls of our sainted apartment, then my face was going to be objectionable as well. I was going on strike. Either I could uncover my hair when we were alone in our house or I would cover everything, face and all, and he would be speaking to a faceless person whose kerchief not only covered her hair but went down past her chin. He laughed. He said, "Yeah, yeah. Let's see how long that lasts." He clearly didn't know me. He actually *didn't* know me, but that was neither here nor there. I looked at him laughing and proceeded to pull my tichel down over my entire face. There weren't even slits where my eyes were. It was basically like wearing a black sock.

I walked around like that for eight solid days, full face and hair covered. He would talk to me, and I would speak back through my tichel. He had friends over, and since there was nowhere to hide me, he had no choice but to have his friends see me, sans head. I would have kept going, however long it took, but after eight days, and seeing that I was prepared to remain on strike as long as necessary, he relented.

I had won! A small victory for sure, but for me, it felt like a massive one. Of course, it didn't occur to me at the time that a religion that required so much suffering from its women must be inherently wrong. It wasn't the law that wanted me covered. The law of God was sacrosanct and not to be questioned, but this was not a law—it was a stringency.

It never occurred to me to question the stringency, and I assumed that my inability to keep it made me a lesser being, less righteous than his friends' wives who suffered in silence and never said a word of complaint. I believed all that, that it was my inadequacy that made wearing the tichel so unbearable. It is really true that the walls inside our minds, the limits we put on ourselves, are the most damaging ones. Had I not believed everything I was taught, had I not policed myself, had I questioned more and accepted less, I would have left much earlier. I wouldn't have lost twenty years of my life living in a prison. I fought anything I thought was unjust. Unfortunately, I didn't think that my religion was unjust. I could defend myself against all, but I was silly putty in the face of my own convictions.

With the Tichel Rebellion won, I settled in and determined to love Yosef and to make this marriage a happy one. As a married religious woman living in my community, I had basically one creative outlet: the meal. Cooking. It was the only thing in my life that I could get really creative with, and so I embraced it full on. Not being allowed to go to culinary school, of course (a place filled with non-Jews and unkosher food that I could neither cook nor try), I decided to educate myself and to learn how to cook things that were outside the traditional Jewish menu.

However, my first Shabbos meal was a fiasco. Yosef invited friends for Shabbos without telling me until late Thursday night. That gave me practically zero time to buy the ingredients, let alone make the food. Winter Shabbosos begin very early, around 4:30, or at sunset. Once the sun sets, you are no longer allowed to cook or turn on the cooktop or the oven. I was teaching in school, which meant that I had just a few hours to go grocery shopping, get home, do the mise en place, and cook two enormous meals.

I managed to make chicken soup and some salads and some chicken (which I threw, willy-nilly, into the oven), but there was no way I was going have time to cut and peel the potatoes and onions, soak the beans, soak the barley, and brown the meat for the cholent. Our guests were coming to us for Shabbos lunch, and to Yosef it was unimaginable that after a freezing walk from shul to our apartment, he and his guests wouldn't be met with the hot, warming scent of cholent.

Cholent (a stew slow-cooked in advance to allow a hot meal on Shabbos) is the only food that even men make in the frum world. It's kind of like barbecue in the outside world. Many guys are cholent aficionados and pride themselves on their cholent-making abilities.

Yosef offered to make the cholent. To this day, I still have no clue what he put in it, but it was blue. Blue. I promise you. Not the golden-brown that cholent usually is. How that mix turned blue I literally have zero clue, but blue it was, and it smelled like swamp. My guess is that the kishke that he bought was tied with a blue string, and he didn't think to untie it and threw the whole thing into the cholent pot. I felt such a deep shame. It sounds silly now, but at the time, it felt like I had failed as a wife and homemaker, and even though I was angry with Yosef for setting me up to fail, I was angrier with myself. My first Shabbos and I hadn't managed to make it work.

My behavior was also found wanting. Yosef had assumed that I would remain silent at the meal as all his rabbis' wives and all his friends' wives had done when he was an unmarried yeshiva student. I, however, totally unaware of Yosef's expectations, merrily and happily regaled his friends with the comic turn of events that had led to blue cholent and had everyone laughing. I was so happy that even if I couldn't feed them properly, and they would walk away with empty stomachs, at least I could entertain them and make them feel welcome. But Yosef found me too friendly, too talkative, and too at ease with his friends.

"They're all going to be laughing at me behind my back in yeshiva now that I married such an immodest and outgoing woman," he said. Outgoing is a massive insult in our world. "Yatzanis" (she who goes out) is a word from the Torah relating to a woman named Dinah who was raped by a prince in the city of Shchem. Her brothers had to go and kill all the inhabitants of the town of Shchem as a reprisal for her rape. She had been friendly to a prince of the city, and untold disaster followed. It was a lesson to women everywhere. Stay in your tents. Talk to no man. Be rarely seen and never heard. Otherwise death and destruction follow.

I tried reasoning with Yosef.

"How would you feel if you had cooked and cleaned and served and then had to sit through an entire meal without being allowed to participate in the conversation?" I asked him. "I'm not a woman," he replied. "That's not what God wants from me."

He had tradition and the Torah on his side. I had only my feelings on mine. It was not a fair fight at all. So I sat there and took it, and I questioned myself. I promised that I would try and do better. Try to be more like the wife he expected. Try to be more tznius in my actions. I let him rant on and on—sitting there, taking it—because somewhere deep inside, I felt he was right and I was wrong. That it was indeed my flaw, my sin. I simply hung my head while he berated me. It was an awful first Shabbos, but I was stubborn and determined. I would make Yosef proud. I would become the woman he wanted me to be.

I also had my teaching. Just as with everything else in my life, I determined to do things differently. I was going to be responsible for creating thousands of tzaddekeses (righteous women) through teaching, thereby assuring my place in heaven. I didn't want to be a boring teacher who just taught kids to memorize by rote and didn't capture their minds and their imaginations. Teaching allowed me to use my abilities in the service of God. It also gave me a massive degree of freedom, as no one cared what I taught as long as it led to love of God and to happy parents. Girls didn't need to actually know anything just to have babies, so no one asked me what my lesson plans were or if they were learning anything. I had found the only job open to women in the frum world (in my time) where I could have a modicum of autonomy and freedom and use my love of an audience and a story.

I made everything into a story. The stories from the Torah and the Prophets are very exciting if you tell them in story form. I would teach my students about the kings of Israel and the prophets, the wars and tests and adventures, the loves and histories, and I made them come alive. I would come dressed in a costume and assume different voices, and always time it so I left them on some cliffhanger till my next class. I was also supposed to teach them language (Hebrew), so instead of making them memorize conjugations, I made up plays where they each had a part, and they memorized their lines, which contained all the rules I was supposed to be teaching them. They loved it.

In Monsey, for the five months from the start of the school year until I got married, I had taught fourth and seventh grades—Hebrew subjects to my fourth-graders and English literature and American history to my seventh-graders, although I wasn't even remotely qualified to teach either subject, as I had no degree or expertise whatsoever.

When we moved to Flatbush, two different schools wanted to hire me: a Sephardic school, called Sha'arei Torah, and an Ashkenazi one. The Ashkenazi school was a very prestigious ultrareligious high school called Bnos Leah Prospect Park Yeshiva High School, which wanted me due to the massive influx of Jewish Russians, as I was probably the only ultrareligious, Russian BJJ graduate in all the frum world at that time. What had once been a source of constant embarrassment now put me at an advantage.

I wanted to figure out a way to teach in both schools, as that would be double the income. Women, of course, were only paid a third of what men were paid to teach the same subjects. I once asked the principal why male teachers were paid so much more than their female counterparts, and I was told, "Talia, they are working to support their families!" Well, what did this guy think I was teaching for? It was wrong, and I knew it even then, but who was I to argue?

Yosef was earning about forty dollars a week from the kollel, which couldn't even cover our meager rent, let alone utilities and food, so my teaching in two schools really came in handy. I was now teaching from eight in the morning until six-thirty in the evening, five days a week. For anyone who has ever taught anything, you can imagine what a massively grueling schedule that was. It was a ten-and-a-half-hour workday, during which I had to be on and exciting and interesting the entire time. I had forty clever, vivacious, rambunctious, and easily bored seventeen- and eighteen-year-olds, and I was all of nineteen years old. It took massive amounts of energy and creativity and physical and mental strength to keep it up day after day. There were also no workbooks or textbooks, so I had to prepare everything myself. I spent an average three hours a night preparing for the next day's classes, but I loved every single second of it.

This should tell you everything you need to know about the educational system in my community. That I, as a nineteen-year-old high school graduate, with no advanced degree (other than my certificate from my one year at BJJ), with no expertise whatsoever, was teaching girls literally six months younger than I. To say the educational system is abysmal is a massive understatement. It's quite a brilliant system if you think about it. They put in enough classes so they can get government funding, even if the teachers teaching these subjects (like me) were highly unqualified. By not educating people so that they can function in the twenty-first century, you make it nigh impossible for anyone to get out of the community, because we're not educated in the ways of the outside world. Of all the egregious parts of fundamentalism, that to me is by far the worst. There is nothing more powerful and important than knowledge and education, and both were stolen from us, preventing us from relating to the secular, modern world. Do not equate having physical schools with having a real education. So I did the best I could for my students and educated myself as I went along, as I couldn't bear to teach them the way I'd been taught.

I also did all the shopping, cooking, cleaning, and serving at home. I was up at 5:00 A.M., and in bed at 2:00 A.M., and the whole cycle would begin again the following day. I was too tired to think. Too tired to complain. Too tired to hate. Every ounce of energy I possessed went into teaching those girls and cooking creatively. I loved doing both and refused to do either by rote.

At the second school where I taught, Sha'arei Torah, the first day I walked in, the girls looked up at me, noticed that I wasn't wearing anything particularly fabulous or expensive, and decided I wasn't worth their time or attention. I started by introducing myself, but literally no one was paying attention. I needed another approach, so I decided to be mean. I would stare them down with the coldest expression until none of them dared to challenge me. It became my modus operandi to be cold and frightening to every new class I had. I would throw out half the class for the tiniest infraction. I found that once they're afraid of you, and you establish your authority, you can then relax and have fun. The lesson I learned all those years ago, as a nineteen-year-old teaching eighteen-year-old Sephardic girls, has stood me in good stead ever since. People want to be popular, and they want people to like them. As a leader, however—and this applies to any leadership position, be it as a teacher or a parent or a boss—popularity is irrelevant. Most people wander around feeling lost, with no clue as to what they want or how to get it. It has been proven that children do better with a clear and defined set of rules. Kids may constantly try to test those boundaries, but subconsciously they want their parents to be regimented and consistent. It makes them feel that there is order and calm in a very disorderly world.

What I don't think people realize is that as adults, most people still want and need those exact same things. That is one of the most appealing things to many people about religion or any other dogmatic system. People want someone else to tell them what's right and wrong, what to do and what not to do. To decide these questions for yourself is frightening and dangerous and makes you feel vulnerable and alone. Most people want to feel that their leader is smarter and more knowledgeable and knows what's best for them.

That's why people follow charismatic personalities who seem very sure of themselves, no matter how bizarre or irrational their ideology. People want someone else to find them. To structure them. To tell them what the plan is and how to accomplish it. Being weak and trying to get people to like you, when you are in a leadership position, is a recipe for disaster. I promise you the love will come, but first they must look up to you and fear you. Your word must have weight, and going against you must have consequences. You do no one any favors by trying too hard to be popular. To be a leader, you must always be self-assured (no matter what's going on inside your head), and you can never show doubt or nervousness.

You want people to work hard for you? Be sure that they get the message that going against you is unwise, and they will start focusing on the task at hand rather than plotting how to get rid of you and not getting anything done. I've noticed that any company without strong leadership is constantly mired in fights and dramas, as people test their limits and behave badly. And since there are no repercussions, they get caught up in office drama, and very little actual work gets done. This applies to all ages and all people. I am very fortunate that I learned that lesson all those years ago, as a nineteen-year-old teaching girls one year younger than me.

That first day, I threw out the ten girls who were speaking the loudest and seemed to be the ringleaders. And then I got into it. I started off by asking a question they didn't expect. That's the next step in leadership: after you show them you're boss and have their attention, you need to fascinate and educate them. Fear alone does not make a good leader. Once you have their attention, you need to excite their minds.

I asked them why in the world I should be here teaching them a thousands-of-years-old text that didn't remotely apply to their daily lives.

"Most of you are engaged to be married already, and why should it matter to you how Jacob dealt with Esau or how Moshe split the Red Sea? Why should any of this matter to you?" I asked.

That caught their attention. No authority figure had ever asked the question, which to them, in their circumstances, was perfectly logical and understandable. In the Sephardic culture, where they married even younger than in my world, why should they study? What was the point when all they wanted to discuss were the things that were applicable to their lives: how to be the best wife or mother, how to get the best husband, how to have a happy marriage and be respected in your community.

They looked at me with new interest. I seemed to understand their feelings, and I was asking the question that they had all been thinking. That was the hook, but I still had to reel them in. I told them that the Torah was a love song between God and his people. That it is a marriage, and a partnership filled with love and trust.

I asked them, "Do you want to live a happy life? Do you want your husband to love and respect you? The secrets to all happy relationships, the secrets to the meaning and purpose of life, are all within these pages."

I had them all then, pens ready, hearts wide open, eager to listen to the words of wisdom that would flow from my mouth. Now, this only worked because I believed every word I was saying. People can tell when you are faking it. You cannot lead unless you truly believe in the direction that you're taking and the words that you say. To be successful, what you share with others must be real and authentic to yourself. What made me successful was that it was clear that I deeply believed in the path that I was teaching. I made sure to teach them all the parts in the Torah that I thought would interest them and that I could make stories out of. I filled their minds with stories of love and devotion, of sacrifice and purpose, and they loved every word. They cried when their heroines died, and begged me to stay longer in class, as every day, I left them on a cliffhanger, not knowing what would happen to their now beloved prophet or beautiful heroine. In all the years that I was a full-time teacher, I only had one student ever glance at her watch, and it is something I still remember to this day, because my goal every single day of those many years was to capture my audience and bring them into my world. I watched them very, very carefully for the least signs of boredom, which meant I needed to change up my method and do something else to fascinate their minds. I don't know if you get the general idea that I am hopeless at doing things halfway. If I was going to be a teacher, I was going to be the best fucking teacher that any of them had ever had.

I became extremely close to all my girls, and they made my house a cheerful place, filled with their laughter and confidences. The first time I had them over, though, it was a bit of a fiasco. The Sephardic community is extremely insular (as are most sects in the ultrareligious world), and their parents weren't sure how they felt about their daughters coming and spending time in a non-Sephardic home. To assuage their concerns, I decided to invite the entire class and their parents to my home for a yom tov (holiday) meal. The yom tov that

was around the corner was Shavuos, which celebrates the Jews receiving the Torah in the desert, on Mount Sinai, after their miraculous escape from Egypt. I invited them for the second lunch meal, as
all Jewish holidays begin the night before, and so Shavuos was two
evening meals and two afternoon meals. The first evening meal is
always very short on Shavuos, as on this particular holiday, in addition to the usual eating and praying, Jews celebrate the gift of the
Torah by . . . guess what? Studying Torah.

It is a Litvishe minhag (custom) to have a quick meal the first
night, and then return to the synagogue or yeshiva and learn Torah
all night long and not come home until nine the next morning (men
only, of course), and then pray the morning prayers. Because of this,
the first-day meal is served extremely late, as men usually collapse
into bed at 9:00 A.M. and sleep a good five or six hours, until two or
three in the afternoon, and that's when the yom tov meal is served.
It's usually simpler and quicker than other meals, as everyone has to
go back to synagogue in the evening. The second-night meal is also
very late, as Shavuos prayers take forever, and it generally doesn't
begin till ten at night. Therefore, the best meal at which to have a lot
of guests is the second-day meal, after everyone is rested and has
slept and you can begin at 1:00 P.M. and not rush the meal. I invited
over sixty people—my twenty-two twelfth-grade students and their
parents—for a meal. Luckily for me, around thirty people accepted
my invitation.

Now, where was I going to seat all these people, you ask? Just like
Jerusalem was said to expand to accommodate one and all when all
the world came to visit its holy sites, I figured I too would be able to
accommodate everyone, and I had faith in God. I cooked mountains
of food, and there was no way my tiny little fridge could accommodate food enough for thirty people. So I knocked on one of my religious neighbors' doors, a widower, and asked him if I could store
some of the things in his fridge and freezer. The first night, since I
was feeling very connected to God and very holy, I decided that just
as tzaddekeses of old also spent the whole first night of Shavuos up
and studying Torah, I would do the same. Of course, I could go nei-

ther to shul nor yeshiva, as women weren't welcome or allowed, but I could do it in the tznius way: stay up by myself and learn alone in the privacy of my house. That's what I did. I was awake still when Yosef came home, and I had a little kiddush ready for him—wine so he could make the blessing, and some homemade cinnamon buns because I figured he'd be hungry. Once I had served and fed him, we both fell into a deep sleep.

Several hours later, I heard pounding at my door. I was groggy and dressed in my tichel and a really nasty-looking robe. I peered, eyes still crunkly with sleep, teeth not brushed, to see what idiot was disturbing my slumber. Well, with all this foreshadowing, you've probably guessed it. A bunch of eager-faced girls and their parents stood outside my door. It was clear from the shocked look on my face, which I was too groggy to hide quickly, that there had been some misunderstanding. They looked at me and I looked at them, and then a girl named Tamar said, "Oh dear, have we come on the wrong day?"

Trying not to sound as panicked as I felt, I laughed and said (there was zero point in lying, as my unkempt appearance and sleepy demeanor were pretty easy to read), "Well, yes, I had expected you tomorrow for lunch, but no worries at all, come on in and we will have a great time!" I apologized profusely and told them that they would have to wait a bit for the meal, as I clearly wasn't ready.

There were two major issues. One was that, while you are allowed to cook on yom tov, as opposed to on Shabbos, it has to be on an already-lit flame, as the prohibition against lighting a fire holds for yom tov as well as Shabbos. I had one tiny flame on, and an oven that could barely fit one roast, let alone an entire meal at once. You remember Creepy Crawlers and those little ovens that you baked them in as a kid? That was basically the size of my oven, to give you an idea. It would take hours to defrost the challos and the roasts, and hours more to heat and reheat everything.

To compound the problem, most of my food was in my neighbor's fridge and freezer, and no matter how loudly we all pounded on his door, my poor, dear religious neighbor, who was in his midsixties and had also stayed up all night learning Torah, was ensconced in a world of deep slumber from which no amount of shouting or banging could rise him. Forget about being able to defrost or heat my food; I couldn't even get to it!

Here I was, with more guests pouring in every minute and literally no food. There was just no way I was going to be able to serve the food I had intended to serve, and I realized I had to make peace with that fact. I looked at what I had in my apartment, and basically the only things I had in enough quantity to feed thirty people were potatoes and eggs. By this point, we had figured out how the days had gotten mixed up. Apparently, the girls had had a bit of a disagreement as to which afternoon I had invited them for, and instead of just calling and asking me, they had decided to listen to the most popular girl in the class, who insisted it was day-one lunch and not day-two lunch. And that was that. The call went around to all the girls and their families, and since Sephardim generally don't stay up the first night like their Ashkenazi counterparts, no one questioned it. And now ... here we were.

Everyone pitched in. Some people peeled potatoes, others cut onions, some cracked eggs. In my kitchen, which could barely fit one, we had at least ten people trying to help and everyone else squished into my dining/living room laughing and talking. We made it fun. It is still, to this day, the simplest yom tov meal I have ever made, and one of my happiest memories. We ate eggs and hash browns together happily, our sense of camaraderie and good humor saving the day. In the end, everyone thought it was a wonderful success, and they all left still chuckling (and probably pretty hungry; let's be honest) but feeling like we were a team and a family.

Those first few months were pretty crazy, and although I was unhappy at home and feeling less and less connected to Yosef every single day, I didn't have enough time to face how miserable I was. I was just too busy teaching, preparing, cooking, and grading. Yosef and I barely saw one another, as he spent all day in yeshiva and I spent all day teaching and then cooking, and we rarely had a meal alone together, as his yeshiva friends or my students joined us for pretty much every meal—although never at the same time, of course, as it would have been unacceptable to have single girls and guys at our home simultaneously. That was strictly verboten. The rare moments we had alone were uncomfortable, to say the least. We were two strangers, forced together by custom and law into strictly defined roles that neither of us could truly conform to. We realized if we were to have any chance at a happy marriage, we needed to find a way to get to know each other.

Since we didn't get to go on a honeymoon, as that wasn't a thing, in the frum, yeshivishe world, we decided that we would take a month in the summer, as I had a month off from teaching and he had time off from kollel, and we would go on a road trip and try to really get to know each other. We planned on driving through forty states. It was a very adventurous plan, as I had never been anywhere, and I wanted to see everything. We would see the Grand Canyon, Yellowstone Park, Muir Woods, and Bryce Canyon. We were going to go cross-country and then up and down the West Coast from Vancouver to San Diego. That was the plan. Remember, this is 1990, before navigation of any kind. You used maps. You asked for directions. You got lost. That was all part of daily life. We used something called a TripTik. You would send AAA your trip itinerary, and they would send a packet with directions. We had jam-packed every moment and timed our entire trip down to the hour, as it was imperative that we be in a religious community for every Shabbos on which we would be traveling.

For frum Jews, travel is very complicated. We knew there wouldn't be kosher food in many of the places we stopped, so we had to bring enough food to last four weeks. We also had to be sure to end up every Friday evening by a synagogue, so that we could have a proper Shabbos and Yosef could pray with a minyan, a group of at least ten religious men. Our rouge-colored Toyota Camry wasn't going to have an inch of room left once we packed sheitels, hat boxes, Shabbos clothes, and kosher food. We also decided to take a shofar—

a ram's horn that you blow every morning in the month leading up to Rosh Hashana, to remind Jews of the impending judgment day. We planned to be back before the month began, but Yosef decided to take it just in case.

This was going to be the most exciting trip of my life! I had never been on vacation, as my parents always left me with the kids when they traveled. This was going to be my first real adventure. We only had a little cash, which I'd managed to save from working two jobs, so we planned to camp out as often as possible.

We decided to leave the day after Tisha B'Av. Tisha B'Av is the strictest of the Jewish fast days, excluding Yom Kippur. The nine days leading up to Tisha B'Av are also heavily restricted, and it's supposed to be a very unpropitious time for the Jewish people, so you're not allowed to listen to music, or swim (as you might drown), or fly on planes, or do business deals, and you're not allowed to eat meat or chicken. You are also not allowed to do laundry or dry-clean or even wash your towels.

Of course, the nine days are usually smack-dab in the middle of July, so it makes life very annoying, as your kids are stuck at home and can't swim or go anywhere. Those nine days feel interminable. We decided to leave the day after Tisha B'Av, because you can only start doing laundry on the afternoon of the following day. We needed to be in Toledo, Ohio, that first night to ensure that we would be in a city with an Orthodox community on Friday night and have a place to spend Shabbos in Detroit.

It is a nine-hour drive to Toledo. We planned to leave at two in the afternoon and arrive at eleven at night, sleep at a Motel 6, and then continue onward the next morning. Unfortunately, by the time we finished doing the copious amounts of laundry, which we weren't allowed to start till noon, and then packed (or rather stuffed haphazardly) it into the car, we were four hours late. We left at 6:00 P.M. We knew that we would have to drive through the night to reach Toledo the following day, or otherwise we wouldn't make it in time to Detroit, which had a real shul and a minyan, both very critical things for Shabbos.

We were both so exhausted when we left. Between fasting and laundry and packing an entire month's worth of everything, by the time we got on the road, we were both ready for bed. Yosef drove on and on, getting ever more tired. If you've never done the drive between Brooklyn and Toledo, please don't. There's literally nothing to see. It's the most boring drive imaginable. Monotonous and flat. Cornfields followed by cornfields followed by cornfields. Yosef had been driving for a good five hours, so it was now past eleven and we still had four hours to go. I was dozing off and on, and apparently so was he, as he started to weave between the lanes. We were both jarred by the sound of a police siren! The policeman who stopped us was very kind and grandfatherly. He looked at us, very wholesome and covered, and realized we certainly weren't drunk or drugged, but were obviously exhausted. Instead of giving us a ticket, he told us, "Look, you're clearly very tired. Why don't you stop off at the motel down the road, and sleep and then restart your trip in the morning?" Very sound, practical advice. Did we follow it? Of course not. We had to be in Toledo that night! There was no two ways about it; our Shabbos was in danger!

Yosef looked so exhausted, however, that I had a genius idea: I would drive. Of course, I was bone weary as well, but at least I had been a passenger the last five hours. Now it was his turn to rest and my turn to drive. I decided that I would drive around seventy miles an hour, as there was no one in sight and it was a straight highway. I put on a cassette of the Miami Boys Choir (an Orthodox boys-only choir that sings Jewish songs) and blasted it, threw some gum in my mouth, and opened the window so the wind would blow in my face and keep me awake. We didn't listen to goyish (non-Jewish) music, as it could debase our souls. It was now 2:00 A.M., and I was so incredibly tired that I didn't have the energy left to press the gas pedal. Yosef was snoring happily beside me, fast asleep, and I just didn't have the heart to wake him. Then I had another genius idea! I would put the car on cruise control. That way I wouldn't have to expend the energy to press the gas pedal. There was only an hour or so to go till we got to Toledo, and I figured this way I could finish the drive. I put the car on cruise control going seventy miles an hour and then, having nothing to do, promptly fell asleep.

Had I not put the car on cruise control just minutes before, the car would have slowed down, as my foot would no longer be pressing on the gas. However, that car, set to seventy, didn't slow down an iota, and it carried two blissfully sleeping passengers as it barreled down the highway at breakneck speed. The highway ran through all these cornfields, with just some metal barriers every couple hundred feet and large swaths of road and cornfield divided by absolutely nothing. A minute or so after I fell asleep, the car veered off the highway in between two guardrails, and we went flying at seventy miles an hour through someone's cornfield.

I woke up, disoriented and discombobulated, to wide, flat things flying in my face. I had no idea where I was! The slick stalks of corn were like a sheet of ice, and they were flying at us at seventy miles an hour, the windshield covered in giant yellow stalks. I did what any sane person would do in that situation: I slammed on the brakes.

"B'Siyata D'Shmaya" was playing on the stereo. I will never forget it. Those words mean "with God's help," and the sweet sound of those kids' singing filled my ears as the car went flying. The stalks were so slick and slippery that slamming the brakes at seventy miles per hour caused the car to skid into one of the guardrails at a massive speed and intensity, and this is when finally Yosef woke up. We went spinning round and round in the air until we finally landed, tires down, car right side up, in a ditch in the field. When we came to a stop, there was no longer any engine or front tires. The front part of the car had been completely sliced off when it crashed into the rail. Outside the windshield was literally nothing.

We both got out of the car, shaking and completely in shock but totally unharmed. There wasn't a scratch on either of us. Half the car was missing. Only the cabin and the trunk were left; the rest of the car was somewhere behind us. The car had literally been cut in half. And we were totally fine!

My first words were "Does this mean we can't go on our vacation?" That's all I could think of: my first adventure killed in the very first evening. It was impossible! The fact that I was alive and that Yosef and I weren't hurt didn't even register; I was just worrying about how we could continue our vacation without our car. And all of our stuff! Luckily, the trunk and the interior of the car hadn't been touched, so everything was still where we had left it, but how were we going to do the rest of the trip with half a car?

It was almost 3:00 A.M., and an era before cell phones, so we stood there trying to figure out what to do. He decided to copy a move from the Torah. When Abraham was stranded and the king of Egypt was coming out to meet him, he made Sarah hide in a large chest for her protection so that the king wouldn't get any naughty ideas. Yosef decided to do the same, to protect me, and told me to hide in the cornfield while he tried to flag down a trucker (the only drivers on the road at that time of night).

Yosef always says that the guy who stopped must have been Elijah the prophet disguised as a trucker, because after he pulled over and called the police for us on his walkie-talkie, he disappeared without a trace before Yosef could thank him. The policeman who came eventually was flabbergasted. He followed our mad path through the cornfields in his police car. He was a clearly a religious midwesterner, as the first words out of his mouth when he got out of the car were "God must loooove you." He drew out the word "love" until it was at least four syllables.

He had seen our trajectory, he had seen the wreckage, and here we were, standing in front of him in all our religious glory, with nary a scratch on either of us. My nineteen-year-old self, however, felt massively unlucky. My first vacation! My first time out of New York other than a short weekend in Cleveland, and it was *over*? A few hours of driving, to meet an ignominious end in a cornfield in Fremont, Ohio? That's where we were, we found out: a few minutes' drive from Fremont. They towed our car to a garage, and we were taken by the tow truck driver to a nearby motel. We slept like the dead for six straight hours, too tired to make sense of what had just happened and too worn out to figure out what to do next.

When we woke, we realized we had left all our food and belongings in the car. We took a taxi to the body shop. That body shop was the most pristine auto shop I'd ever seen. It was the size of an airport hangar and so clean that I would have felt comfortable eating off the floor. Clearly, in Fremont, they took their cars very seriously.

We expected them to tell us that our car was unsalvageable, and that it would cost more money to repair it than the car was worth. Imagine how surprised we were to hear that they thought they could piece our tiny Toyota Camry back together again. This was wonderful news! Now we just needed to convince the insurance company to pay for the repairs, and also to give us a rental car while ours was being fixed.

I decided it would be best if I called the insurance company. That call was a thing of beauty. By the time I had finished telling my sob story about our ruined "honeymoon," we had gotten a promise that the company would issue us a credit toward a rental.

The local Chabad rabbi offered to pick up our car when it was finished and to host us for a hot, homemade meal. It's one of the things I love most about my world, that Jews will help each other without question and allow a stranger into their home.

Yosef and I learned a lot about one another on that trip. I was still trying to be physically loving, only to be constantly rebuffed. Everywhere we went, I would find some nook and try to kiss him, but he would disentangle himself from my arms and tell me how inappropriate it was. By the end of that trip, I had given up. I clearly wasn't going to get the physical contact that I so desperately craved. He thought it was shocking and awful that I wanted him to touch me for no reason other than physical closeness. It was not how a true bas Yisroel (daughter of Israel) should behave, and he looked at me like I was the devil incarnate for even trying to touch him. I was so hurt and so saddened, but again, that voice that told me that I was a bad person and that my needs were wicked and wrong—and that God couldn't love me because I was such a horrible sinner as to want to have some kind of physical closeness with my husband—would play in my head, and I believed it.

There were also some really funny moments. Don't forget that most of the time, I wore a tichel and a long skirt and was covered head to toe in the scorching heat. The only uncovered parts of my body were my hands and my face. We looked very odd, to say the least, and we stood out among the people all around us in short sleeves, shorty shorts, and bathing-suit tops. Wear a long, flared skirt? Stockings with socks? Tichel on your head? Yup, you're an Orthodox Jew, but in the places we were driving through, most of the people had never seen a frum Jew. We were somewhere near Idaho, where we'd stopped at a rest stop to fill up on gas and get some sodas, when I was asked an awesome question by a total stranger. I was super tan, really dark from all the sunshine and traveling (my face only, obviously, as the rest of me was totally covered, legs, elbows, and all).

"Hi, I'm Pueblo," this lovely woman said. "What tribe are you from?" I smiled and told her, "I'm from the Tribe of Israel," and we both stood there and laughed, as she had assumed that I was Native American.

The most frightening part of the trip was driving through Coeur D'Alene, Idaho, which is home to the country's largest population of skinheads. Both Yosef and I were worried that somehow, someone would realize we were Jews and try to hurt us. That was how we saw the rest of the world anyway, and Coeur D'Alene seemed to be a very large, looming reminder of how hated Jews were in the outside world. As we approached, there was some kind of fire in the distance, and we nervously chuckled and said, "I guess they already know we're coming."

When we made it to the Grand Canyon, we had to blow the shofar. Because of our car accident, we had to extend our trip by a week, as the car still wasn't ready to be picked up in Toledo. We were very grateful that we had thought to bring a shofar, just in case, and were very excited to blow the shofar at the Grand Canyon. It made it even more meaningful and special somehow.

Jews everywhere were blowing the shofar to confuse Satan because it was getting close to Rosh Hashanah and Yom Kippur, a time when all Jews are focused on good deeds. The shofar served as our wake-up call. We found an edge right off the Grand Canyon, and Yosef put on his tallis and tefillin, and we both started davening shacharis (saying the morning prayers), right there on a ledge of the Grand Canyon. It was a very special and mystical moment, praying to God as we watched the sunrise, smiling at each other—in harmony with ourselves and the world around us. The beauty of the Grand Canyon filled my heart with gratitude to God for creating such a glorious world for us to live in. We were so deeply immersed in prayer, rocking back and forth as we said the ancient words, that we failed to notice that we had an audience.

A family was on the ledge above us, snapping photos of us, and when we finally noticed them, they were all gawking at the strange sight of a man wrapped in a white blanket (the tallis), holding a ram's horn and saying foreign-sounding words. It was clear that none of them had ever seen a religious Jew before. Yosef told me in Hebrew to just ignore them and not to speak English so that they would go away. Then he picked up the shofar to blow it, and the grandfather of the family called down to Yosef, "Miiiighty big peace pipe you got there." He thought we were Native Americans doing a prayer ritual and greeting the sunrise! I feared he would fall off the ledge when Yosef blew the "peace pipe" and they heard the haunting sounds of that shofar fill the air around the Grand Canyon.

I am sure that somewhere on their mantel is a picture of us that they have shown to all their friends as they described the Native Americans they saw performing a sunrise ritual. I always imagined that one day someone would visit them from New York or Miami and break the news that those people weren't Native Americans but ultra-Orthodox Jews. I would love to be a fly on the wall the day that happens.

Although Yosef and I had wonderful moments during the trip, our differences came out in stark relief. In Los Angeles, we spent Shabbos with a friend of his who was an outreach rabbi—someone who goes to less religious neighborhoods and tries to get people to learn Torah. His wife had six children, ranging in age from seven years old to a few months old, and barely any help. I could tell that some time ago, she had been really pretty. There were still tiny vestiges of that beauty—her full lips, her hazel eyes. But her mouth was turned down at the corners, and she looked perpetually annoyed. She wasn't very welcoming or friendly when we arrived, but I understood quickly enough that she had no energy left over to be kind or entertaining; it took every ounce of strength she had to be kind to her own family. She had none left over for mine. She had had her first child exactly nine months after her marriage at nineteen, and she had been having babies every single year since. She was still in her late twenties, and she looked fifty. Her sheitel was bedraggled, and she was clearly overwhelmed and miserable. I looked at her and was afraid that I was looking at my future self. Was this what I wanted? Was this the path I had chosen?

Her husband was that type of man I dislike most: amiable and jocular to everyone else, and a miserable shit to his family. He didn't smile at his wife or kids once the entire time we were there. In the two days we were at his home, he never once said thank you to his wife.

Of course, at Shabbos, I got in trouble with Yosef for being my usual outspoken self. I was an embarrassment, and the other men were talking behind his back about me. I spent the night crying. Was he right? Was I really an embarrassment? My heart told me that I hadn't meant any harm, that I hadn't been flirting, that I'd just enjoyed good conversation with people who treated me as an equal. My mind told me I was a monster, and that I should be ashamed, and that I needed to subdue my nature and stop being the center of attention.

During Shabbos lunch I stayed silent to try and please him. My meek behavior helped, and by Sunday, he had forgiven me my lapse.

I remember the outfit I wore that Shabbos. It was a yellow Teri Jon suit that I thought was the height of fashion. And I was definitely the only woman there wearing sunshine yellow. Even in those days, when I looked askance at anyone who talked about secular topics at the Shabbos table, read no secular literature, and didn't even have a radio or newspaper in my home, I still couldn't resist sneaking color into my wardrobe. "Where does it say you have to dress in black and dark blue and brown?" I would always ask. "Show me where in the Torah or the Talmud it says that Hashem doesn't approve of colors. Aren't flowers colorful? Didn't Hashem create those?"

That first trip solidified the dynamic in our relationship that would continue for the next two decades. He would rebuke me, we would argue, then he would sulk for days and punish me for my brazen behavior. I would be penitent and try harder until the next time, when it would begin all over again.

Many girls got pregnant within the first three months of getting married. We had now been married over nine months and I still wasn't pregnant. Yosef was starting to get worried, and he would go to the rabbis to get blessings. This had been the first nine months since I was ten years old that I wasn't changing diapers every day, and cleaning babies and feeding babies and putting little kids to sleep. I had been a mother to six kids, my siblings, for the last nine years of my life, and I was only nineteen. I didn't want a baby. I was sick of changing diapers. But I also felt like a huge sinner. What kind of woman was I? All women must want children. Children are the very purpose of our existence.

It was the only reason Hashem created women in the first place. We were supposed to either be pregnant or be nursing until we were too old, and then we were supposed to help with grandchildren. What kind of monster was I? What was wrong with me?

My prayers to Hashem would go something like this: "Thank you, Hashem, for understanding that I'm not ready to have a baby yet. Oh, Hashem, I'm so, so, so sorry that I'm such an imperfect and horrible girl that I don't want to have a baby yet. Please, Hashem, make me a better person so that I will be grateful to have a dozen babies." Confusing, right? Well, that's what my head was like for more years than I'd like to count.

It became a huge issue, my not being pregnant. We were married on January 20, 1990. I became pregnant in April of 1992. Two years! Two years that I didn't have to change diapers. For me, it had been a huge godsend. For Yosef, it was a nightmare and a punishment for the fact that I was such an outgoing and untznius woman. He had been praying for me to have a baby, and I had been secretly thanking Hashem for not giving me one.

I knew immediately that it was a girl. I could feel her personality. I knew from firsthand experience how useful an eldest daughter was, as I was one. But I promised myself that I would never do to her what my mother had done to me. She would have a real childhood. I couldn't wait for her to be born. She would be someone to love who would love me back. I was desperate to feel loved and to love. I was so miserably unhappy with Yosef, but I knew my baby would give me a reason to live, and I was determined to be the best mother possible.

Meanwhile, I had to survive the pregnancy. The poor kid had nowhere to go in my tiny body, and midway through, she kicked me in the ribs and cracked my rib cage. Every time I breathed or moved, deep spasms of pain would cascade through my body. I wasn't allowed to take any pain medication, so I had to suffer as she grew inside me. I also had sciatica and anemia and was constantly fainting. I gained over forty pounds, which was a little under half of my regular body weight. People would pass me on the street and not recognize me.

From all my pregnancies, there exists only one photo of me pregnant. I wouldn't allow anyone to photograph me, as I was hugely embarrassed by my massive size. My nose expanded and covered half my face. The front and back of me had different zip codes. I wasn't a house; I was an apartment complex. I felt so unwieldy and uncomfortable and just plain miserable. I was still teaching in two schools throughout my entire pregnancy, on top of doing all the shopping and cleaning and cooking. I was constantly tired, miserable, and in so much pain. My poor students really got a fright when I fainted in the middle of teaching one day.

Yosef got really lucky, though, because I'm not moody at all when I'm pregnant. I didn't cry all the time or want pickles and ice cream. Nothing like that. I didn't have the luxury of being irrational, and I hate crying. There was only one thing I wanted. My nesting instincts were at an all-time high, and all I longed for was furniture. Funnily enough, this happened with each single pregnancy. Some people want turkey sandwiches or hot dogs. I longed for couches and tables. And I couldn't even fathom living in our minuscule apartment with a baby.

Luckily, we ended up moving to a beautiful place. It was truly a find. My friend's parents had bought the house next to theirs in Flatbush, Brooklyn, for their daughter and their soon-to-be new son-in-law when she got engaged. Their daughter's apartment was the top floor of the house, and they had done it up beautifully: new kitchen, with marble countertops and marble floors. It was 1,200 square feet, which felt palatial to me. Then their daughter's engagement fell through, and so she didn't need the apartment after all. Because I was her friend and didn't yet have a dozen children, they decided Yosef and I would be the perfect tenants until their daughter got engaged again. They only let us take a one-year lease, in the hopes that within that year their daughter would manage to find her bashert (chosen one) and would move into it once again. They gave it to us at an incredible price, and because I was working two jobs, we were able to afford it.

Yosef was still learning full time in kollel and bringing in just five hundred bucks a month now, but I was making over $65,000 a year by teaching in both schools, and so we would easily be able to make the rent. I even convinced Yosef to let me have a cleaning lady twice a week, since I was massively pregnant and had broken ribs. Of course, technically, it was my money, as I was the one bringing in the income, but it didn't occur to me that this gave me any rights as to how we spent it. It was Yosef's money, and I had to beg and plead to get that cleaning lady.

Our house was so close to our neighbors that we could pass one another sugar or flour from our respective kitchens without even having to stretch out our arms. Our new neighbors had sixteen children! I would watch in awe from my window at how they made Shabbos. I thought the woman of the house, Mrs. Katz, was a miracle worker and prayed that one day I would have such a beautiful family. The entire year that I lived in that apartment, I never once saw her lift a finger in the kitchen. There were always at least four kids cooking and cleaning. Even her sons cooked and cleaned, which I found fascinating. I'd never even seen a man do anything in a kitchen except eat. Yosef didn't even know where anything was and had to ask me where we kept a knife if he ever needed one. I would stand in my kitchen, cooking and cutting, making Shabbos or dinner, and watch in awe at the concert of cooking right across from me. One son would cut veggies while another made soup, and a daughter made chicken and another son busied himself with cholent. We would wave to one another, and literally pass condiments through the window. I loved that apartment so much and couldn't wait to make friends in my new neighborhood.

In the frum community, the way you make friends is in synagogue. We moved in right before Shavuos, which was at the end of May, and I thought that would be the perfect time to meet my new neighbors. I decided to go to shul in the morning, figuring I would get to meet the women who had come in the morning to pray. I remember exactly what I was wearing: a beautiful white Tahari suit with mother-of-pearl buttons that I thought were the height of elegance at the time, and a new real-hair sheitel. Even though I was covered head to toe, I felt very good about how I looked and was excited to introduce myself to the new neighborhood. I went to sit in one of the front rows, as that was one of the only seats still open in the women's section. In a frum shul, men and women don't sit together, and there is a mechitza (a thick curtain or wooden wall) between them, so that women and men can't see one another.

Of course, the rav and the Torah are on the men's side, and the tefillos (prayers) are all read aloud by the chazon on that side, so the women's section is pretty cut off from the action. If you want to see the Torah scroll or watch the chazon davening with kavana (deep concentration, rocking back and forth as he prays the ancient words), you have to sneak a peek between slats in the wooden wall or a crack in one of the curtains. I didn't even bother. I was concentrating deeply on my own tefillos, and I didn't need to see the Torah to feel Hashem's presence beside me.

Toward the end of the service, I noticed that everyone was staring at me. I attributed this to the fact that no one here knew me at all. I was so happy that I had worn something nice, because all eyes were focused on me. Then a very kind elderly woman tapped me lightly on the shoulder and, in a very pronounced Brooklyn accent, said, "Dahling, I think you should go to the restroom. You have a brown stain right in the middle of your skirt."

I twisted my skirt around and sure enough, there was a giant brown blotch smack-dab in the middle, right by my ass. It looked like I had shat myself. I looked down at my chair and understood why that seat had been empty. Some guy, the night before, while he was learning Torah, had spilled coffee on the chair and never bothered to clean it up.

I wanted the earth to swallow me whole. It was hard enough coming into a new neighborhood and trying to make friends; now I had this humiliation. The davening was finally over, and I slunk against the wall and inched my way out of the shul, managing to get outside without anyone else seeing my backside.

I waited there for Yosef to come out—praying, praying for him to hurry up so that he could walk behind me and shield me from everyone's gaze. He walked out with a few men from our neighborhood, and they collected their wives and he brought them over so that the wives could say hello. The women had seen my stained skirt and looked at me with pity in their eyes. A few were clearly trying very hard to hold back laughter. While I stood there, and I cannot make this up, a bird flew above us and pooped on my sheitel. There I stood, pregnant, with brown gloop covering my behind and bird poop dripping down my new sheitel. I don't remember how I managed to get home without crying. I was so totally mortified.

I laughed at it later, because it was so absurd, but for the entire year we lived there, I never once went back to shul, and not a single woman from my neighborhood ever came over to say hello or welcome me. Not one person.

That might have been the final straw, but I was already realizing how hard it would be to have a baby in Brooklyn. My community, as opposed to Chasidim, doesn't believe that you can have an eiruv on Shabbos in a busy place like Brooklyn. An eiruv is a string that goes from telephone pole to telephone pole to enclose the space within. You are technically not allowed to carry anything outside of your home on Shabbos—ever—but an eiruv extends the area considered your "home" and thereby allows you to carry things within the confines of the religious community. In Monsey there is the Monsey eiruv. In Brooklyn, because there are millions of people, the rabbis of our community decided that it was too busy to utilize the leniency of an eiruv. That meant that all women with small children were forced to spend Shabbos inside their homes every single week, because you weren't allowed to use a baby carriage or carry your child, or diapers, or wipes, or snacks, or anything. Shabbos lasts from sunset Friday night until an hour after sunset Saturday night, every single week of your life. You aren't allowed to use electricity, and if you can't even socialize or take your kids to the park, you are truly screwed. I couldn't imagine living like that.

At least Chasidim use an eiruv in the city. My community didn't. I told Yosef that there was no way I would manage to stay cooped inside for the next twenty years of my life, alone in the house, while he went and hung out with his yeshiva friends and learned Torah and socialized. I had had enough and was sick of Brooklyn. No one had been kind or friendly to me, and I didn't have anyone to talk to.

I wanted to go home to Monsey, where I had friends and family and somewhere to go with my baby.

It was an easy decision to make because the lease on the house was up anyway. Of course, that meant Yosef would have to leave his yeshiva and find a yeshiva in Monsey, but that wasn't too difficult, as the rabbi who had helped him learn Torah when he first became religious lived in Monsey as well.

We couldn't afford a house, and at the time there were only two apartment complexes in the community. One was called Blueberry Hill, and the other was called Victoria Gardens. They were both ancient and decrepit and filled with young frum families with many babies. But if you're a young couple and you don't have in-laws who will buy you a house, that's where you go. We ended up at Blueberry Hill, which was the nicer of the two. Despite this, the walls of our apartment were a color I would generously call "rat-droppings brown," the fridge was mustard-yellow, and the kitchen walls and countertops were a color called "opaque couché," which is a very chic way of describing a mixture of muddy grass and projectile vomit. But this was going to be our home, like it or not.

Batsheva arrived two weeks early. My water broke in the middle of teaching a class (I was still teaching in Brooklyn), and they rushed me to the hospital, where I was given Pitocin to supercharge my contractions. If anyone reading this has ever had to take Pitocin, you know exactly how excruciating that is, as it causes contractions that are twenty times the strength of natural ones. It cannot be done without an epidural, but of course I had wanted a natural birth, and so by the time I gave in and agreed to an epidural, I was already screaming the roof down.

I was in labor for sixteen hours, even with Pitocin, and I barely had the energy to push Batsheva into this world when she was finally ready to arrive. I gave birth to her at Good Samaritan Hospital, where most of my siblings had been born, and my mother and I used the same ob-gyn. Did I mention that my mother and I were pregnant at the same time? She got pregnant during my sixth month. We used the same doctor, who was religious and therefore was not even remotely surprised that my mother and I were pregnant simultaneously. By the time I gave birth, she couldn't help at all, because she was going through a horribly difficult pregnancy of her own, at forty-six years old. It was her eighth baby.

My daughter was born on Shabbos, so luckily no one from my family was there during the birth; but the second Shabbos was over, both our families descended. My mother-in-law's first comment, after mazal tov, was "You look different without any makeup." I ignored her, until the next comment came out of her mouth: "Oh my, you're still so fat. It doesn't look like you lost a pound with this birth. You still look completely pregnant."

At that point, I will admit, I began to cry. I had just gone through sixteen hours of labor, I was twenty-one years old, and my self-control wasn't at its finest. I screamed at Yosef to get her out of my room. They left, and I had a few moments of respite. But it didn't last long. They came back in with my parents to argue about whose house I would go to, and they stood over me, voices raised and angry, arguing about my baby as if I didn't exist. I looked to Yosef for help and realized that none would be forthcoming. I pressed the button for the nurse, and when she came in, I was hyperventilating. She shooed everyone out of my room and promised me she wouldn't let them back in. I was finally alone with my baby, for the first time since I had given birth.

My love for this little bundle of humanity hit me with the force of a UPS truck. My life finally had meaning and purpose. I was going to do everything in my power to give her the best life imaginable. I looked at her tiny, scrunched-up old-man face and swore to her that she would have a happy childhood, and she would grow up feeling like she belonged, and confident in her own self-worth. I couldn't bear for them to take her away from me. I had been told that to give her a bottle would seriously damage her for life, and so I never once gave her a bottle; I nursed her until she was two years old. We looked at each other those first moments, and I breathed in that delicious baby scent, and my heart felt like it would explode with love.

Yosef and I decided to name her Batsheva, as she was born on

Shabbos, and Batsheva means the "daughter of seven." Batsheva was also the name of King David's wife, who bore him the most famous king of Israel: King Solomon. The nurse asked us if we also wanted to put an English name on the birth certificate, and I looked at her like she was mad. My daughter was a bas Yisroel who would spend her life in holy pursuits and become a famous rebitzen. God forbid that she should have a goyish English name.

The first month was hell on earth. All babies breathe through their noses when they are born, and not through their mouths. For Batsheva that was dangerous, as she hadn't managed to sneeze out all the amniotic fluid, and her nostrils just weren't wide enough yet, so we constantly had to aspirate her. An aspirator looks like something you'd baste a turkey with. It has a long nozzle that you stick into the baby's nose, and then you slowly release the bulb so it sucks out the liquid to open the airway. She screamed bloody murder every time we did it, and I'm sure I would have done the same.

We had to aspirate her every thirty minutes for the first week, or she could literally stop breathing and choke to death. It was horrible. We couldn't sleep at all, as someone had to be on constant watch to be sure that she wasn't choking on the amniotic fluid. The more times we put the aspirator in her nose, the more inflamed her poor nostrils became, and she would flail and scream and twist her body in every direction—which made aspirating her all the more difficult. I think I slept maybe fifteen minutes the entire week. Add that to the fact that I was nursing and not using the bottle at all, and I was a total wreck.

Winter turned to spring, and spring into summer, and I spent my days cooking and cleaning and watching and nursing Batsheva. I don't remember doing anything else. I was the perfect little home-maker. And then fall was upon us, and I had to go back to work, or we wouldn't be able to afford the apartment. My parents weren't giving us the money they had promised, so I found two schools to teach at in Monsey, as the commute to Brooklyn would be impossible with a seven-month-old who had to be nursed.

As in Brooklyn, I managed to negotiate a little over $65,000 between the two schools. It was an insane schedule, as I was also nursing Batsheva and refused to give her a bottle at all, so in between classes, every three hours, I would run home, nurse, and then run back to school. I was teaching at ASHAR (Adolph Schreiber Hebrew Academy of Rockland), which was the most modern school in Monsey and, if you recall, was the first school that I had gone to when I arrived in Monsey as an eleven-year-old. By the time I taught there, it no longer had mixed-gender classes. There was a new principal and a new, more fundamentalist mandate. I taught girls-only English, history, and writing classes. That was my afternoon job. Of course, I learned as I went on, as I had no degree in any of these subjects and was a twenty-one-year-old mom. (Again, that should tell you everything you need to know about the level of education in our schools.) My morning job was at Bais Rochel, a Chasidishe school for girls. They were as disparate as my Sephardic and Ashkenazi schools had been. ASHAR was leaning closer to the Modern Orthodox world, and Bais Rochel was totally Chasidic. In that school, forget about girls not even being allowed to learn Talmud or any of the other tomes that boys and men studied. In Bais Rochel, girls weren't even allowed to learn Torah—not even the stories in the Bible! They weren't allowed to read about Rochel and Yaakov (Rachel and Jacob). The five books of the Torah, the history of the Jewish people, were considered inappropriate to them. They studied from *Tz'enah Ur'enah*, the dumbed-down retelling of a story that some man had written. At that school they believed any sheitel over chin length would attract male attention, and so I had to cut mine to be able to teach there. They hired me even though I was Charedi, which is another name for the black-hat or yeshivishe community, and not Chasidic. Among the influx of Russian immigrants who had arrived in the United States during perestroika were many who had become Chasidic, and now their daughters needed to be taught the ways of the Torah and Chasidus. They understood that as a Russian ultra-Orthodox woman, I would be able to connect with them on a level that no one else could. My Russian birth again helped me.

Plus, I had gone to Bais Yaakov and BJJ. I was a rare bird and in high demand.

I was still also doing all the household chores and food shopping and cleaning and cooking, of course. I had hired a nanny to care for Batsheva while I taught. One day, one of my classes was canceled, so I ran home to check on the baby. I walked in the door and I heard a *radio*. I could not believe my nanny had brought a radio to my house and was listening to non-Jewish music. I went ballistic. "You've poisoned my daughter's neshama (soul)," I screamed. "You've sullied our house and my precious child!" I let her have it, tears streaming down my face, panicked and horrified that she had let such impurity into our holy home. That night I cried for hours, scared shitless that I had ruined my daughter for life by allowing such an insidious influence into our home. When Yosef came home and found out what happened, he was equally horrified. The nanny was totally religious, of course, but she was clearly not as holy as I thought. That's how utterly brainwashed I was. We had absolute, complete isolation from the outside world, and that was how I wanted it.

It was hard to admit, but the real problem was that I was miserably unhappy with Yosef. I didn't enjoy his company, and I didn't want to be his wife. We didn't fight so much as just coexist. I felt like I was always being judged and found wanting. I was never tznius enough, never appropriate enough. I talked back. I had opinions. I wasn't what he expected in a wife, and he kept trying to change me to fit the mold of the aishes chayil, the woman of valor he had wanted to marry.

I was so unhappy, and feeling so alone and miserable, that I called my parents and told them that I wanted to divorce Yosef. They came over thirty minutes later, both of them, and, sitting at my tiny kitchen table, painted a very dismal picture of what my life would look like if I left Yosef. "You will be a divorced woman with a baby who's also a ba'alas teshuva, and your family is Russian. Do you know what that means, Talia? It means you will be alone for the rest of your life."

My father was gentle yet stern. "Do you really want to spend the rest of your life alone? A nebbuch [pathetic person] who has to live with her parents?" In my world, women didn't live alone. For those who claim that the world I lived in was not that disparate from the modern world, I always ask, "How many women in our community live alone? How many women own their own homes? How many women are career women and not just working to support a family that they were forced to start as teenagers?" The answers are tragic. Women in my world do not live alone unless forced to do so by being widowed or divorced and old enough to have too many children to move back home with, or by becoming an agunah. An agunah is one of the worst fates a woman can suffer in my world. An agunah is a woman whose husband refuses to grant a "get." A "get" is a Jewish divorce. The secular divorce provided by the U.S. courts is completely irrelevant in my world. Unless you receive a get, you are still married and you cannot remarry. The law works as follows: A man can divorce a woman for any reason whatsoever. There are actually examples in the Talmud of what are perfectly legitimate reasons for a man to divorce his wife. If he doesn't like her perfume, a man can divorce his wife. If she burns the cholent or annoys her husband with the tiniest infraction, those are all deemed utterly acceptable as reasons for divorce. A man doesn't really need any reason. If he wants a "get," he goes and gets one. A woman, however, is not allowed to divorce her husband *under any circumstances* without his approval. He can beat her daily, humiliate her, demean her, torture her, he can abuse their children, do literally anything he wants . . . it makes zero difference. She still needs his permission to get divorced. How many abusive men do you know who would willingly divorce a woman they've been tormenting for years?

What makes it even worse is that, because in my world a woman cannot be alone in the same room with a man she's not married to, let alone have a relationship, she is forced to live alone for the rest of her life. Add to that the fact that the whole community and religious observance is structured around the man, so without a husband, she is a zero. Men do all the forward-facing daily religious observances. They're the ones in shul. They're the ones leading the Shabbos and yom tov table. They're the ones talking to your son's rebbeim (teachers in school). Many schools won't even take a kid if the mom is alone. I have many friends who have to beg some man, a rabbi they're close to, or their father, to call on their behalf, as the school doesn't want a family that doesn't have a man leading it. A family led solely by a woman? There must be something inherently wrong with her that she left her husband. "We don't want her kind in our school" is the basic attitude. In my world women who are forced to live alone disappear. They are nebbuchs. A woman needed a man's guidance, his oversight, or she was bound to do something terrible. Twenty-year-old divorcées moved back home with their parents, whether they wanted to or not. What other choice did they have?

My mother said, "You need to figure out a way to be happy with Yosef. He is such a tzaddik! What does he do to you, exactly, that makes you so unhappy? Does he hurt you? Hit you? Harm you in any way?"

"No." I tried to explain. "He doesn't hurt me physically in any way at all, and he's not mean or horrible. He just wants me to be someone I'm not. He wants me to be quiet and meek and obedient, and I can't do it." I went on, trying to make them understand, trying to make them see that I felt like I was disappearing.

My mother looked at me and said, "He is your ezer k'negdo [husband who helps you by berating you], and he is doing his job, which is to make you into a better woman. Poor man, he's stuck with a woman who's too untznius! You should be thanking Hashem for giving you such a wonderful husband. Love? Love is something made up by goyim that only exists to draw you away from Hashem."

She continued with a point that she had drummed into me my entire life: "Where does it say in the Torah that we are supposed to be happy? You are spoiled and selfish! Who says you need to be happy? Who says that's what you deserve in life? Life is about serving Hashem.

"The question you should be asking yourself, Talia, is whether he improves your service of Hashem, and from everything you've been saying, he is doing his absolute best to mold you into a proper bas Yisroel. You should be on your hands and knees in gratitude and thank Hashem for giving you such a righteous husband, who you clearly don't deserve. Stop being so selfish and thinking about happiness," she rebuked me. "You don't need to be happy. You shouldn't concern yourself with your own happiness. That is the road to gehenim (hell). Stop thinking about yourself and what you want. Only think about Hashem and what He wants, and you will find happiness."

My father had painted a bleak picture of what my life would look like, and my mother filled me with shame and remorse for wanting more. I was done and defeated. I never again, until the day I left, shared my unhappiness with another single solitary soul. I learned my lesson that day: if I wanted to change my life, I would have to do it on my own—and I would have to do it in secret.

CHAPTER SEVEN

I knew it was crazy and impossible, but part of me kept whispering that I should figure out a way to save money—just in case, just in case, just in case. Of course, my mind wouldn't let me think about what that "just in case" really meant, but it seemed like a way to have a little freedom, a little insurance if I couldn't make it as Yosef's wife. It didn't occur to me back then that I would use it as my "escape my world" fund. Back then, the only thing I wanted to escape was Yosef.

Teaching wasn't going to make me enough money—and certainly not money that I could have for myself, in my own account. The problem was, I didn't know how to do anything else. I had no skills, no degree, and I didn't know anyone in the outside world.

I needed to do something outside of my community, so no one would know. I still had my job teaching in two schools, so I worked on reducing my class load. I also had no college degree. All I had was my teacher's certificate from BJJ, which wasn't worth the paper it was printed on in the outside world. I believe, to be a successful teacher, you have to be both an actress and a salesperson, so the first thing I thought about was sales. As a teacher, you need to "sell" whatever it is you teach, so that your students "buy" the lessons you teach them. I would also often act out scenes from history and the Torah to make it come alive for them. I figured I had had plenty of practice in capturing minds and exciting people.

We only had religious newspapers in the house, so the next day, I drove to 7-Eleven and bought myself a newspaper. That first day, I scoured the want ads to get an idea of what kinds of sales jobs were available. I couldn't work in a store, as those jobs required working on either Saturday or Friday, which would be impossible for me. It was also too public and too dangerous.

It took me several weeks of stopping at 7-Eleven and buying papers until I came across an ad that made me sit up and take notice. MetLife said they would train you to be an insurance salesperson, and no experience and no college degree were required. The ad also said you could make hundreds of thousands of dollars in your first year there. It sounded too good to be true, but I was desperate.

It took me a few days to summon up the courage to dial the number listed, but eventually I did. I was told that all I had to do was to go and get my Series 6 and 63, and that both tests cost only seventy dollars. Those were the tests needed to get an insurance license. If I passed, I would come to one of MetLife's training seminars and they would decide if I was salesman material.

I studied for the tests all over the place—in my car, driving to do food shopping or from one school to another, while I was home alone and nursing Batsheva. I often studied in the bathroom. I stole moments wherever I could to learn about mutual funds and annuities, and term and whole and universal life-insurance policies, and the differences between them. I passed on my first try. Now all I had to do was convince someone at MetLife that I could sell.

I went into those training seminars completely covered and tznius, with a sheitel on my head, and my thick stockings, and my clothing that covered everything except for my face and hands. Not one person realized! I just looked like a very proper librarian, or some senator's modestly attired wife. My conservative and concealing clothes made me seem serious and reliable, which I realized helped me significantly.

The woman who ran the Rockland County MetLife office was named Sandy Weiss. I was so excited—a fellow Yid! A Jewish woman would decide whether I got the job. Even if she wasn't re-motely religious, she was still one of the clan, and that boded well for me, I thought. At the time, I still didn't know a single non-Jew. And on my first day of training at MetLife, I found myself sitting in a class filled with them. I spoke to no one and no one spoke to me, but at least the head honcho was a Jewish woman, and that gave me hope that I could pull this off.

When Sandy interviewed me, I told her nothing about my life or that I was religious. I'm sure what she saw in front of her was a very determined and dowdy-looking twentysomething. About halfway through, she asked me the one question that I had dreaded: "So, Talia, do you have a group of people that you can sell life insurance to? To be a good agent, you need a good Rolodex. You need to grow your contacts so that word will spread, and one person will tell an-other about what an excellent agent you are, and that's how you can grow your business."

I lied by omission. I said, "Well, Sandy, I have a lot of very influ-ential Jewish friends who are extremely wealthy, so I do indeed have an excellent Rolodex." All of that was very true. I did indeed know a lot of very wealthy and influential Jews. I just left out the fact that they were all extreme, fundamentalist, ultra-Orthodox Jews, and that none of them would ever know I was selling life insurance. I simply looked at her with such confidence she believed me. And I got the job.

For the first time in my life, I was going into an office with goyim. You would think that I would have made friends or become more a part of the outside world or come to understand the inherent flaws in my world. None of that occurred. It was us and them. They were the "others": not to be trusted or befriended. I couldn't go to lunch with them, or to a bar (totally forbidden), and so I never got to know a single person in that office. I kept myself to myself and stayed out of everyone's way. I was taught that the most dangerous goyim were the ones who seemed nice. Germans had seemed nice too, and had allowed Jews into their schools and businesses, and then, overnight, your goyish neighbor stuck you in concentration camps and turned you into dust and ashes. Never trust those smiling goyim, I was taught, and it was a lesson I believed wholeheartedly.

I always think of MetLife as the beginning of everything. I learned so much at MetLife that stood me in excellent stead when I left my community behind eighteen years later. I owe a huge debt of gratitude to MetLife. Many of the business techniques I learned there I utilized when I started my own business. The place was very cleverly run. The first thing they did with the new hires was to invite them to the home of the boss, in this case Sandy Weiss's brand-spanking-new McMansion. The message was: if you work hard and are successful, one day you can have a McMansion of your very own.

Being shown Sandy's house taught me an excellent lesson. When hiring new people for any job, show them the endgame, the goal they're striving for. Make them see the big picture and help them envision a better future for themselves and they will work twice as hard to achieve it. You can talk about success, or you can show what success looks like. Showing is more compelling than telling.

I also learned that Sandy Weiss wasn't even Jewish. Her last name was Weiss because she had married a Jewish man; I was in complete shock. An intermarriage was the biggest sin in our world and meant the destruction of the Jewish race, as a child born to a non-Jewish mother isn't considered Jewish. I looked at her like she was a rare and endangered species after that, but I was also confused. I had always thought of those who intermarried as monsters, but here was this kind and lovely woman who had given me a chance. I decided to put it out of my head. Maybe she was the exception to the rule.

The second step in the training process was to go with experienced agents to their sales meetings to see how it was done and how to deal with different types of people. I was fascinated. I watched my instructors avidly and stored all the lessons in my mind. When I think about those days spent running from one school to another and selling insurance on the side, then running home to nurse Batsheva, I don't really know how I managed. Add housework and

Shabbos and cooking for and feeding not just my family but the many yeshiva bochurim who still came to our house, and you can get a sense of how overworked I was. Looking back now, it was fantastic training for the future. I work twenty-hour days now, and I love it. I learned to juggle a thousand balls in the air, and I've been juggling ever since.

My preparation was finally over, and it was time to begin. The first test we had was cold calling. This was prior to the do-not-call laws that mean telemarketers can't harass you anymore. We would be given a list of random phone numbers to try. Whoever was able to get the most appointments booked would win a four-hundred-dollar bonus at the end of the week. For the entire time that I worked at MetLife, I won every single time.

I learned some excellent techniques there too. Never ask, "Would you like to meet me so that I can talk to you about your future and your needs?" That gives the person the opening to say, "No thank you." Instead, always say, "What day works best for you? Monday or Wednesday? Shall I come to your house, or would you like to meet in the office?" Give them choices that assume that they've already agreed to meet and have them pick a date and a place and you're in. Couch what you want as a given and people will give it to you—a good lesson for life.

I started selling at a high volume, but I quickly realized that wasn't enough. I needed a group of people who were really tied to one another, who would talk about me and spread the word about this amazing new life-insurance salesperson. In the end, I decided on policemen. I figured they would all want extra insurance, and they all talked to one another. It worked like a charm.

The only other memory I have from that time was Purim. As usual, we had a bunch of bochurim over for Purim, and it's a mitzvah for men to get drunk on Purim. (Of course, that mitzvah is *only* for men; who's going to clean up after them or serve the food or wash up the vomit if not for women? Typical.)

I dreaded Purim for that very reason. This year, I decided, I was going to exact some tasty revenge. After a huge Purim meal that I had cooked and served, I brought out dessert: caramel apples. I made the apples super chewy and sticky. I watched gleefully as each guy took a deep bite into his apple. I wish you could have seen it. They all sat there trying in vain to separate the caramel apple from their teeth, completely stuck and unable to speak, consternation growing, as they were too drunk to have real motor skills. I sat there and laughed and laughed and laughed. My little revenge for torturing me every year. A solitary moment of comeuppance in a life where I had little say and no way to make my pain felt.

When Batsheva was six months old, my mother gave birth to her final child, my youngest brother, named Shlomo Betzalel after my mother's father. My mother had a condition that rendered her unable to produce milk, and it was one of the things that really bothered her—that none of her children had been able to get the benefits of being nursed. I was still nursing Batsheva and could have given a group of cows a run for their money. My mother asked me to express my milk so that she could feed it to her child, and so that's what I did. I nursed my own brother, in addition to my daughter.

To complicate things even more, I got pregnant again around this time. I was sure that I couldn't get pregnant while still nursing, but that is an old wives' tale, because I was nursing two babies and still became pregnant. I tried so hard to pretend to be excited, but no matter how often I told myself that I was happy, I knew it was a lie. I quit my job at MetLife and decided to try again to be a proper bas Yisroel. I was only going to work in religious institutions and try to be a true rebitzen. No more foolish dreams. I was going to have child after child, every year. There would be no escape. I would just have to figure out a way to be OK with it.

It was midsummer, and we spent the Succos holidays with my parents, as I was pregnant and still nursing while also teaching. Preparing for Succos, an eight-day holiday with its three-course meals, in addition to Shabbos was just too much to handle. My mother, by this time, had a massive amount of professional help, so when she invited us, we agreed.

The second day of the holiday, I started having horrible pains in my side, excruciating jabs that would twist me in two and render me immobile. On the holiday you can't use cars or electricity or phones unless your life is at risk, and I didn't want to break yom tov by complaining. But by midday I could no longer hold back. The pain had gotten so bad that I told Yosef I needed to go to the hospital.

My family decided I had appendicitis, and they broke yom tov to call a cab to take me to the emergency room. No one could go with me, as it was only my life that was possibly in danger, and so I was the only one allowed to break the yom tov. I so rarely got to be alone that, even in pain and worried about my appendix rupturing and dying, I was glad for the solitude.

It wasn't my appendix. I miscarried. Of course, since we weren't allowed to communicate or use the phone, my entire family had to spend the whole holiday worrying about me and not knowing what had happened, or even if I was dead or alive.

They had to perform a dilation and curettage procedure, which was a terrible experience. But after that, I had an entire day to myself to recover. I was probably the most cheerful woman they'd ever met after a miscarriage. I still hadn't recovered from my first pregnancy, and I just wasn't ready. I was twenty-two years old, and I already felt like I was fifty. My fears had come true. I looked in the mirror and the face staring back at me reminded me of that poor woman in L.A.

The year Batsheva turned one, my parents really made it financially, and so they decided to move out of the Smolley Drive home where I had grown up and build a McMansion of their own in a very affluent neighborhood of Monsey. We were all happy, as this meant better shidduchim for my siblings and, one day, for my own children. Another plus was that my parents offered to let us live in the Smolley Drive house rent-free.

We were barely scraping by financially, even with me working in two schools and Yosef's kollel stipend. Kosher food is much more expensive than regular food, not to mention that there would be private schools to pay for; and there were also the Shabbos meals, which were like Thanksgiving meals every week of the year. It's expensive to be a fundamentalist Jew.

We both wanted Yosef to be a Torah scholar, but we were also sick of having no money, and he did have an incredible degree from Wharton School of Business. Reality and ideology weren't gelling. That was among my earliest realizations of the vast difference between what I had been taught to believe was a beautiful way of life and the struggle of living in that reality. What I had thought of as an embarrassment, that Yosef was a ba'al teshuva and had gone to a goyish college, was now going to serve us in good stead.

Yosef finally agreed to leave the kollel and started searching for a job as a trader. But it was really difficult, because he hadn't ever used his degree. The first question everyone asked was "What have you done since you graduated?" and the answer—"became a Torah scholar"—didn't make a very positive impression in the world of finance.

It took six months of trying before someone gave him a chance. His first job, as a trading assistant for Lehman Brothers in Connecticut, only paid $30,000 a year. He would leave the house around 5:30 A.M. so that he could be there at eight sharp, and he often got home after 10:00 P.M., so the only time he would get to see Batsheva was on Shabbos and Sunday. I was proud of him for working so hard and would have Batsheva kiss his picture good night before she went to bed.

Batsheva was the joy of my life. She was very quick and intelligent and started walking at ten months. She also had an uncanny ability to sniff out chocolate. I was a chocolate fiend at the time (although in my late thirties, I developed a chocolate allergy and now have a really bad reaction to eating anything that has cocoa in it), and Batsheva would find all my hiding spots, no matter how high up they were or how out of the way. She would climb out of bed in the middle of the night, and I would wake up in the morning to her entire face covered in chocolate, a guilty remnant of her nighttime escapades. She was like a truffle-hunting piglet!

She was also incredibly neat. When she ate, there would always be a pile of at least twenty napkins beside her, as she would want to wipe her hands and her face after each bite, and each wipe required a new napkin. We called her a mini mefunak, which means someone who's very conscientious and particular. It was really funny watching her eat.

Despite the chocolate, she kept her clothes immaculate even from an early age and would never be untucked, even when she was just one year old. Other than not wanting to sleep, she was a good child, very cheerful and not prone to kvetching. I hated kvetching more than anything and would ignore tantrums and crying fits until she got the message that it was not the right way to communicate with me.

I became pregnant again, and with school out for the summer, I took a job in a religious day camp called Camp Regesh as the head counselor so that I could bring in some extra money. I did this despite the fact I had sciatica and anemia again, not to mention a one-year-old to contend with. It was one of the hottest summers in Rockland County history, with temperatures regularly reaching over ninety-five degrees, and there were over three hundred campers to organize, as well as counselors and parents. I would probably have enjoyed it had I not been pregnant, but with an additional forty pounds on my frame, in the excruciating heat, it was torture.

A bit insanely, I also took on a second job as the principal of a young-adult-education school called JEP, or Jewish Educational Program. It helped educate kids who didn't go to religious school to learn about their Jewish heritage. It was a lot of hard work, but it brought in extra money, and I loved it because it was challenging. I was in charge, and I was really good at it.

By August, I was so out of steam that I managed to come down with an illness that is common in children but very rare in adults: croup. It was the best thing that could have happened to me, though, because I was forced to lie in bed and stay inside, away from the heat. I got a ten-day respite from my jobs, which I desperately needed.

◆   ◆   ◆

The first week I was back, I decided to go swimming with a group of girls from Camp Regesh. I was less than thrilled with that decision when the nurse came to tell me that that bunk had lice. Shit. As the bunk was all girls, I had taken off my sheitel to go swimming with them and hadn't even worn a tichel—very naughty of me—and now God was definitely punishing me. I asked the nurse to check my hair for lice, with sheer panic in my eyes, because the thought of having lice while being pregnant and wearing a sheitel was just too much for me to bear. Luckily, the nurse gave me a clean bill of health.

It was really strange, though, because suddenly my hair really started to feel itchy, and I was constantly scratching my sheitel, as my hair underneath it was very uncomfortable. I again asked the nurse to check my hair and again was told I was fine.

A few weeks went by, and now my head was so uncomfortable that I decided to go to my ob-gyn to try and understand what was happening. The nurse at the doctor's office also checked my hair and couldn't find a single louse or egg. The doctor told me that some pregnant women get a very dry scalp, because the baby sucks nutrients away from the body. He told me that that was what I was experiencing. He prescribed a protein-rich shampoo. I would soak my hair for ten minutes with the shampoo and let the protein really soak in every day, in the hopes that the itching would stop.

Summer had ended, and I was back to teaching in two schools, Judaics in the morning and secular subjects in the afternoon, but my itching hadn't abated. It was mid-October, I was in my sixth month, and I was washing dishes when a bug fell into the sink, followed by a few more. Lice, colonies of them. We called a nurse to come to my house, and this time she had no problem in spotting the lice. My head was an entire city, with apartment complexes and entertainment centers filled with lice. Lice need protein—that's how they grow and multiply—and I had been soaking my head in protein-enriched shampoo for nearly three months. I didn't just have a lice infestation; I had a lice nation.

It was impossible to get them out of my head. My head was shaved, as nothing else seemed to work. Batsheva had them too, of course, as did Yosef, and their heads ended up being shaved as well. I always think that Batsheva's hair came out thicker and better after that, so you're welcome, Bat. It was a nightmare of unmitigated proportions. They had been living in our home since August, and it was October. Our entire house had to be fumigated. Every T-shirt, jacket, piece of linen, everything, had to be dry-cleaned. It cost thousands of dollars that we couldn't afford. We took apart our entire home trying to rid ourselves of this curse. Was it all because I had swum in that pool without my tichel? Hashem was really punishing me with this plague, and my poor family all had to suffer because of my aveirah (sin).

And the sheitels? The sheitels were filled with lice too, but those I couldn't shave or throw out, because I would have to buy new ones, and that would have cost thousands of dollars as well. I was told to soak them in a lice-killing shampoo and then to cover them in mayonnaise to drown anything that was left, and then to put them in the freezer for a month just to be sure. That meant that for a month, I would have to teach in a tichel (one of those ugly head coverings that I hated so much), and that I had to attend any event in that month in a tichel as well. Horrible.

Though fashion felt so far from my life, I was always looking at the shop windows and scouring fashion magazines surreptitiously. I even found a store that specialized in selling hard-to-find European fashion magazines like *L'Officiel*. I would use some of my carefully earned money to buy copies and use them as inspiration to draw my own renderings, which I would then stuff in random spots throughout the house. It was the only activity outside of caring for Batsheva that gave me any joy. By November, in my seventh month, I was so enormous that even walking was difficult, but I would still drive to Manhattan occasionally to shop at Saks or just walk down Fifth Avenue.

One day I was walking along, slow and ungraceful, when a fire truck pulled up beside me. The guy driving had real concern on his

face and asked me if I needed help or if he should call an ambulance
to get me to the hospital. The guy had thought I was ready to pop,
and I still had months to go! I wanted to cry, but instead, I just smiled
shyly and told him that I was only in my seventh month. He looked
at me incredulously, trying to imagine how that was even possible,
and told me to stay safe and take good care of myself.

It turned out he was closer to the truth. A few days later, Yosef
and I were having dinner at Glatt Wok, a kosher Chinese restaurant, and when I got up to get some extra napkins, my water broke—
then and there, two months early. We rushed to the hospital and
waited for contractions to start, but no such luck. So they put me on
Pitocin to try to induce labor. This time, I asked for an epidural as
soon as possible.

I don't know if I still hold the record today, but at the time, I
ended up with the dubious honor of the longest recorded induced
labor in the hospital's history. We came to the hospital on Thursday
night, and when Saturday morning arrived, I still hadn't delivered.
Twenty-nine hours of induced labor and nothing was happening. I
had been without food for over a day, pumped full of drugs, and I
was totally delirious. I don't remember any of this, but Yosef tells me
that I was hallucinating and talking to my students and to Batsheva,
who obviously weren't there. By Saturday morning they decided it
was dangerous to wait any longer and they were going to have to do
a C-section.

Usually, they don't put you under when they perform a C-section;
they just use local anesthesia. I was so far gone, though, that when
they tried explaining to me that I was going to have surgery, I started
screaming and fighting the hospital staff and refused to lie still. So
they had no choice but to totally knock me out to deliver this baby.

Shlomo Nochum Hendler was born on November 11, 1995, a Saturday morning. I woke up several hours later—ravenous, groggy, and
nauseous—to be told that I had a son. Shlomo was four pounds,
eleven ounces when he was born, and if that wasn't worrying enough,
he was born with a condition that still hasn't been diagnosed till this
day. He came out with red hands and red feet. I don't mean red hands

like when your hands get cold and they turn a reddish pink. I mean red hands like you took a bright red lipstick and covered your hands with it. No one in the hospital had ever seen anything like it. He was put in isolation in the ICU, and dozens of pediatric surgeons and doctors from all over New York came to see the baby who had been born with red hands and feet. They had no idea what was wrong with him, where it came from, or if it would ever go away.

On top of being horribly worried about Shlomo, the day after I gave birth, while the nurse was helping me walk to the bathroom, a bug fell out of my hair. Somehow, somewhere, some small egg had stayed in one of my tichels and I had lice all over again. I had no choice but to tell the nurse, as I didn't want anyone else to get it, and for the next two days, whenever someone came into my room, they wore hazmat suits. I saw how they looked at me, this religious woman in her tichel with dirty lice. This time, I shaved my hair myself, down to the nub, totally bald. Anything, *anything* to get rid of the lice.

We eventually had to go home without Shlomo, as they needed to keep him under observation because of his small size and the red hands and feet. I remember the ride home being excruciating without having my baby with me. Every day I would drive back and forth to the hospital so I could nurse him in the ICU and hold him and tell him that I loved him. Batsheva also didn't understand why her baby brother wasn't home yet, and I didn't know how to explain it to her.

After two weeks, the red hands and feet crusted over, and the crust fell away, leaving normal-looking appendages in their place. It was the strangest thing. When he finally came home, he was only four pounds, three ounces, as he had lost some weight in the hospital. For you to get an idea of what the next three months looked like for me, all I can tell you is that on his three-month checkup a mere nine weeks later, he weighed twelve pounds. Because his stomach was so tiny, he ate practically nonstop: every forty-five minutes, twenty-four hours a day. It didn't occur to me not to nurse him, and so it never occurred to me to give up and give him a bottle or ask for help. I was up twenty-four hours a day, every single day of every week, for nine straight weeks. I was so exhausted that I couldn't function, and there was no respite at all. I watched him grow stronger and chubbier, and it gave me great happiness, but I also felt my life draining out of me.

The other difficulty was the boredom. Try nursing every forty-five minutes, twenty-four hours a day, without being able to watch anything. I would spend the days and nights literally staring at the walls as I nursed him, too tired and drained to read. By week five, I couldn't take it anymore. We had recently switched rabbis, and I was totally thrilled with our new one. He was much more lenient than the one from Chaim Berlin and didn't mix chumros (stringencies) with actual halachos (laws). He seemed more normal and rational than any of the previous rabbis we had asked our shailahs (religious or moral questions) to, and I was very grateful for his guidance. In my world, you didn't make a major decision, even ones unrelated to Torah and the mitzvos, without first seeking the bracha (blessing) and advice of your rav.

After five weeks, I mustered up the courage to ask the rav if I could have a television in our home. Not cable, I promised, not anything inappropriate, just the basic channels, so that I had something to watch while I nursed my baby twenty-four hours a day. I broke down crying from severe exhaustion and misery when I spoke to him, and the wonderful man took pity on me. I was allowed to have a TV in my house! Of course, we weren't allowed to tell anyone about it lest people got the wrong idea about us, and I wasn't going to have cable or anything. With those guidelines in mind, we bought ourselves a TV/VCR combination, and for the first time, I brought a tiny sliver of the outside world into our lives.

I was very, very careful with what I watched. I didn't want an impure child, after all, but I had certainly become less strict than when I had had Batsheva. With her, the sound of a radio bleating for a few minutes in our house had caused me alarm, and now here I was bringing the outside world, albeit a world that didn't really exist anymore, into our home.

Before the seventies, women and men on TV slept in different beds, and there was only a little bit of kissing allowed. Men were the bosses and women were homemakers on television, so it was a world more similar to mine than the current modern world I actually lived in.

I watched every episode of *I Love Lucy* over and over on the VCR. Lucy was always portrayed as inferior to her husband, less intelligent, and had to ask his permission to do anything. She was always getting into trouble when she wanted to go out of the house and work, so it was a world that seemed a lot like my own.

I watched *Leave It to Beaver* (a very wholesome show that ran from the midfifties to the early sixties) and *The Three Stooges* and *Father Knows Best*. They subscribed, in large part, to the same male/female philosophy, so it felt proper and less wrong to watch them. I watched *The Addams Family* and *Gilligan's Island*, which was a bit naughty because it had a very scantily clad Ginger in it, and Yosef would always be very disapproving when it was on. Among my favorites was *Get Smart*, because it had a female spy, who, though still subservient to her male counterpart, was clearly his superior. I was obsessed with her. I also loved *Bewitched*, as the main character was a proper stay-at-home wife and mother but had superpowers and was strong and in control, even if she had to hide it from the world and from her husband. I also loved *I Dream of Jeannie*, as Jeannie was also a good and proper housewife who did what Captain Nelson told her to do. She was supposed to fulfill his wishes, but very often she got her own way. She too had powers, and that made me happy—to dream about women that could, in some small way, make their own destinies. Yosef didn't approve of that show either, because she was inappropriately clad, but he didn't make much of a fuss, because my life really was quite miserable, and I was up all night every night. The seventies were totally off limits, although I badly wanted to watch *Wonder Woman* and *Charlie's Angels*. I would sneak into the Blockbuster on Route 59 and take out all the classic movies. I watched *Arsenic and Old Lace* with Cary Grant. All the movies that I watched ended happily ever after, with the female protagonist properly wed and happily listening to her husband.

I loved all the Cary Grant movies. *The Bishop's Wife* and *His Girl Friday* and *Bringing Up Baby*. That was one of my favorites, as it introduced me to the inimitable Katharine Hepburn, who didn't look like any of the other prim and proper women of her time, and who dressed more like a man and always wore pants. I thought she was so marvelous and brave, and I loved her style. I think I must have watched *Adam's Rib* with her and Spencer Tracy a dozen times. A female lawyer! Who argued with her husband! *Wow!*

I also fell in love with Audrey Hepburn. I saw the movie *Charade*, and I had never seen a more elegant or beautiful woman in my life. It would be many, many years later that I would get to see *Breakfast at Tiffany's*, because even though it was a sixties movie, it was about a young woman who lived by herself and slept around. There was no way I was bringing that kind of nonsense into my home. I stuck to the movies where everyone was either married or trying to get married. Independent women were too far out of my reality and too inappropriate and wrong, and besides, Yosef would never have allowed it. I remember that he once came in during *Leave It to Beaver*, which was as prim and proper as you could get, and it just happened that at that moment, the husband and wife kissed, and he was horrified that I was watching such a promiscuous show. But I swore to him that it had just been bad timing and that it was very wholesome, and he believed me and allowed me to keep watching it. Phew!

It didn't occur to me at the time that it was patently absurd for a twenty-four-year-old mother of two to have to ask permission from her husband to watch *Leave It to Beaver*. I was too busy feeling grateful for being allowed to watch it at all. Technically, I was supposed to get rid of the TV once Shlomo started sleeping more normally, which happened when he was around three months old. He was so chubby and normal and large by then that he started sleeping for a good six hours straight, and it felt like absolute paradise.

I thought about it. A lot. Should I get rid of it? The rabbi had only given me permission for a very specific amount of time. It was now time to throw it away, or at least store it in the attic until the next baby. I just couldn't bring myself to do it. I told Yosef that I would only watch while I was nursing, and that he could approve every show, and it wouldn't be every time I nursed but only at night when I was too tired to read a proper Jewish book about some tzad-dekes or other. He agreed, and the TV stayed, and I got to watch *North by Northwest* and *To Catch a Thief*, and Audrey and Katharine became my companions on those quiet, magical nights.

When Shlomo was eight months old, Yosef asked how I would feel about leaving Monsey. He was considering a job at a company called Southern Energy, and it was in precisely the field he was interested in. He was earning so little, and the job would pay much more, but the catch was, it was based in Atlanta, Georgia.

Anywhere in the United States that wasn't either Monsey, Borough Park, Flatbush, Williamsburg, or Lakewood, New Jersey, was considered "out of town." Out of town meant that there was a large ultra-Orthodox Jewish community, and that there would be separate girls-only and boys-only elementary schools, and also a yeshiva or a kollel and generally a yeshivishe, black-hat high school as well. It just wouldn't be the size of the New York or New Jersey communities, as those were the largest in the country. Of course, the out-of-town communities would be just as religious, just as separatist, but in a more relaxed, out-of-the-way, smaller version.

I was both frightened and excited by the idea. I was still very close to my mother and father, and we were under their constant scrutiny—not to mention Yosef's parents' scrutiny. The idea of being far away from both sounded absolutely fantastic. It also sounded like a wonderful adventure. Since I was barely a child, I hadn't lived anywhere other than New York City, and to move to a different state, where people didn't know me and my parents wouldn't be watching my every move, sounded fucking fantastic.

I asked for two things. I wanted a large enough community to have a kosher supermarket and at least one kosher restaurant, even if it was only a kosher pizza store, in addition to the schools and the shul and the kollel and yeshiva, because I needed to have someplace to go once in a while when I didn't feel like cooking. I still remembered the ultra-Orthodox community of Texas where even milk had to be flown in frozen from Brooklyn, and you could never go out to eat, as there were no kosher restaurants. The community we lived in had to have all the necessities of our lives. I knew Yosef would never move us to a place without a kollel or a shul or a proper separate school for our children, but I didn't think he would care about the food, as he never cooked anyway, so it would make very little difference to him either way. He promised to look for exactly that, and we got very excited about moving far away from our families.

Two months later, he got an invitation to come to Atlanta and interview for a trading job with Southern Energy, which at the time was one of the largest energy companies in America. He was being offered a salary of $150,000, a princely sum to us. Plus, the cost of living in Atlanta, Georgia, was much lower than in Monsey, New York. The city also had all the prerequisites that I had asked for: one kosher restaurant, one kosher food store, and of course, a kollel, and a yeshiva, and a shul with a very famous rav. The school met the highest standard of Torah observance, and the teachers were all wives of the kollel members. There were even religious doctors and lawyers and bakers and teachers, so the community was very proper and totally separate from the rest of the world, just like the one in Monsey.

If that weren't wonderful enough, there was also a Modern Orthodox Jewish high school where they would probably love to have a qualified, proper, and pious Monsey teacher (the epitome of top-class in the frum world) instructing their students—so it would be easy for me to get a job too. We decided to fly down to check it out. Yosef would interview with Southern Energy, and I would meet with Rabbi Cohen, the principal of Yeshiva Atlanta, which has since become Atlanta Jewish Academy.

Despite having all the necessities, when compared to Monsey, the Atlanta frum community was minuscule. Monsey has hundreds of shuls and over thirty elementary yeshivas, not to mention separate high schools for boys and girls. There are over twenty kosher restau-

rants in Monsey proper, in addition to restaurants and kosher grocery stores nearby in Teaneck, New Jersey, and the dozens of kosher
restaurants in Manhattan and Brooklyn. Where we lived, there were
over a hundred kosher options, and we were going to a place that
had two—a pizza store and a milchig (dairy) restaurant, something
like a small café, that served pasta salads and iced coffee. It was called
Broadway Café although it was far, far away from Broadway.

The frum community in Atlanta is in a neighborhood called Toco
Hills, which is a stone's throw away from Emory University, and
right next to Druid Hills as well, and yes, it is quite hilly. The story
goes that the city bought all of Toco Hills from a single landowner,
and part of the deal was that he would be able to name many of the
streets. Being a good Christian, he went with Merry, Christmas,
Jody, Bramble (his wife's name). Many of the most rabbinic and religious people in all of Atlanta lived on Christmas Lane.

Rabbi Cohen and I hit it off right away. He was very different
from any rav I had ever met, and much more open-minded. He
smiled and looked me straight in the eye when he spoke to me, and
it was clear that I was going to get the job. I came from the Harvard
of seminaries, and I was teaching high school at Bais Rochel in Monsey. There could be no better qualifications for a Judaics teacher.

Even with two babies in the house, I would be teaching a multitude of Judaic subjects to ninth- through twelfth-graders. I would
be at school from 8:30 A.M. for davening (morning prayers, which I
had to attend and oversee) until 5:00 P.M. I taught Historia (Jewish
history), Navi (the prophets), Chamesh Meglilos (the five books of
scrolls, which include the Book of Esther and Ecclesiastes), Yahadus
(a catch-all for life in general, including the role of women in our
world), Jewish holidays, and Mussar (words of rebuke to help you
live a holier life). I also taught Chumash (Bible study), and Parsha
(the weekly Torah reading).

Though we had a nanny, it was a massive load—especially since,
as in Monsey, there were no government-provided textbooks or cur-
ricula, and I had to write everything myself. I did already have years'
worth of notes, so it was slightly easier than before, though I had to

tailor the classes, because in Atlanta, they would all be taught at a slightly lower level than I was used to. What I found out later was that most of these girls weren't religious at all, but their parents sent them to a Jewish school because they wanted their kids to have a Jewish identity. And this school did have an excellent secular department taught by actual teachers who had graduated college. I was offered a great salary, commensurate with my experience and the fact that I was from the heilige Monsey (holy Monsey). It would be the first time in my life that I would be teaching all my classes in English.

Yosef's interview was a success as well, and we both knew we had made the decision before we even said the words out loud to one another. We decided we would live there for no more than three years, because we were concerned that an out-of-town school, no matter how holy the rav, wouldn't provide the level of piety we wanted for our children.

We chose to rent a house rather than buy one, in case we really hated it, and within two days, we picked one out on Bramble Road, a lovely 2,500-square-foot home. Yosef would be an energy trader for Southern Energy and finally make more money than I did, and I would still be a mother and a teacher, and a homemaker and a wife. We broke the news to our parents, and when Shlomo was ten months old, we moved.

I was so excited, the happiest I'd been since the day (before) I got married. I couldn't wait to make new friends and to meet different people, and somewhere deep inside of me, in a place I tried not to visit often, was the thought that living in Atlanta meant I would be a little more connected to the outside world, a little more "with-it"—an odd expression used in my world for people who knew what was going on outside our community.

Our first stop when we landed was Broadway Café to inaugurate our new life in Atlanta. They made beignets, a southern version of a doughnut, and they were the most delicious thing I had ever tasted. We also ordered their four-cheese pizza, which I thought was the height of culinary sophistication, and we surveyed the other religious people there. This was the South, and as such, our frum compatriots were very friendly. I think every single person in the restaurant came over to say hello and to welcome us to the neighborhood. In such an insular community, a young family with two kids was big news. Everyone wanted to know who we were and where we were from. But the minute I said my name, everyone knew exactly who I was, because they had all heard of the new teacher who was coming from holy Monsey. I wasn't used to such warmth and friendliness. The frum community in Brooklyn, and even the one in Monsey, was snobby and standoffish. The entire year I had lived in our second apartment in Flatbush, not a single person had so much as said hello, and here I was surrounded by a dozen new faces, all eager to welcome us.

I felt instantly at home and happy with our choice. The other thing I noticed was that these women weren't fancy. There were no Chanel dresses and Dior suits. I was by far the poshest-looking person in the café. I always loved clothes and getting dressed up and trying to look as chic as possible within the confines of Jewish law, but I never judged people based on their attire. I was an anti-snob, and that was a thing about the New York frum world that I had always hated. People would look you up and down and try and calculate how much your clothes cost, and if you bought them from the outlet store a season late or if they were au courant and straight off Madison Avenue. The ladies in Atlanta were bargain shoppers, most of them dressed in long-sleeved Gap T-shirts and flared denim skirts.

I could also see that a lot of them were ba'alos teshuva. It's difficult to explain how frum people can tell whether you've been frum all your life or not. Sometimes the sheitels are a dead giveaway, because newbies don't really know how to care for them or style them, and they can look like hairy doormats perched on one's head. Other times it's the attire. When a woman looks truly out of the 1900s, or like a prairie woman, it's a dead giveaway. Generally, when you see a longtime frum woman from my community walking down the street, you'd never know she was religious or that she was wearing a sheitel. She dresses kind of like a president's wife: elegantly, in a fitted Dior or Chanel suit if she can afford it. It wouldn't occur to you that it wasn't her hair on her head; her wig is that good. When I show people pictures of me from Atlanta, I always get comments on how "normal" and "regular" I look. I learned how to dress elegantly and even slightly sexy while still staying totally within the confines of the law. Of course, there was no décolleté, and there were no elbows or knees or even collarbones showing, not to mention, God forbid, pants, but if you didn't know to look for that, you wouldn't think twice. I just looked fancier than most people do during the day, as it's much easier to dress that way if you dress in business attire as opposed to casually. Think of what you wear to look casual: jeans and tees and shorts and tanks. All those were forbidden to me. T-shirts, the kosher kind, were impossible to find. They not only had to be thick enough to not be even remotely see-through, they also needed long sleeves, and such tight crew necks that your collarbone wouldn't show at all. Forget boat necks or regular crew necks. What most women did was wear two shirts. One was what we called a Kiki Riki, which was the "shell." It was an undershirt that was skintight and covered you from the neck, above your collarbone, all the way down to the wrist. Then frum women would put the fun or cool T-shirt they bought in a regular store on top of that. Think layering—not because we wanted to, but because it was the only way we could wear casual clothing.

Ba'alos teshuva hadn't learned all the tricks yet, and I could generally spot a novice a mile away. Even though I was a ba'alas teshuva, no one here knew that, and to them I was simply a very frum woman from a holy city.

Life in Atlanta was so different from the one I had known in Monsey. We moved into Bramble Road and were inundated by Shabbos invitations from all our neighbors. The entire street was yeshivishe, and we had one of the head rabbanim from the Atlanta Scholars Kollel (ASK) living on our block. I found out that the entire kollel in Atlanta was made up of Ner Yisroel transplants. All the rabbanim that were learning at ASK had gotten their smicha (rabbinic ordination) from Ner Yisroel.

Stubborn since birth. Any wonder
my nickname was Blintzy?

Dancing in the Bais Yaakov concert.

Always cooking and exhausted.

Graduation photos day. I tried to sneak on mascara, but I got caught and they removed it.

Going on a hike with my classmates from Beth Jacob Jerusalem (BJJ).

My vort (engagement party). As usual, the men are singing and dancing on the main floor while the women and I are downstairs in the basement.

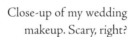

Close-up of my wedding makeup. Scary, right?

This is just part of my family on my wedding day: Naomi, Chaviva, Chana, my mom, my dad, Yitzchok, and Yoni. Not pictured here are Yehuda and Shlomo Betzalel, who were both born after I was married.

Our cross-country trip. Always covered, always the odd person out, never free.

Pregnant, nursing, miserable, and exhausted. I thought my whole life would be this. I have four children, but I was pregnant ten times and had six miscarriages.

Camp Ema adventures in Atlanta.

Shlomo and Batsheva.

Batsheva's wedding: me, Batsheva,
and Yosef sitting; Aron on the floor;
and Shlomo behind Yosef.

How I work: lots and
lots of pictures.

My first Cannes experience.

The drawing of a new design. I convinced Swarovski to create crystals that won't attack your ankles or poke holes in your hosiery when you cross your legs.

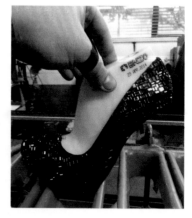

Design in process.

The finished product with flat crystals.

Julia Haart shoes at Galeries Lafayette.

Platform shoe with thinly
sliced stone encasing the heel.

Shoes inspired by Las Setas in Seville, Spain.

Drawings to design.

Inspiration everywhere, from sculptures to flowers.

Modeling the Swarovski crystal shoes, a favorite pair.

In our world, Ner Yisroel is somewhat of an anomaly. They are totally black-hat yeshivishe, but since they were out-of-town, they had some unique features. They had a deal with Johns Hopkins University, so that the courses that yeshiva guys took in Ner Yisroel would be transferrable, and you could get a Talmudic degree from Johns Hopkins without ever having to step foot in the college. It was the only yeshiva at the time (other than Yeshiva University and Touro, both of which were just independent Modern Orthodox Jewish colleges) that had any program that connected it to a purely non-Jewish and secular university.

The other unique thing about it was that, again because it was out-of-town, it had a strong proselytizing arm and would conduct outreach to irreligious Jews to bring them back to the fold. There wasn't a single other "mainstream" yeshiva that did outreach to irreligious Jews. As opposed to frum communities in New York City, out-of-town communities need to do a lot of outreach and bring Jews back to the fold, not just for the mitzvah, but for a very practical reason: they needed the community's support to survive and get paid salaries. Whereas in places like Monsey or Brooklyn, no one would even dream of questioning why a bunch of grown men sit around studying ancient tomes all day and don't bring in enough money to feed or clothe their constantly growing families, in out-of-town cities, where the predominant makeup of the community was either very modern or wholly irreligious, you needed to learn how to interact with these people, as they were your support and lifeline. If an out-of-town kollel can't make people religious or at least excited about religion, it's game over.

This kollel in Atlanta was a Ner Yisroel outpost. The wives of the rabbanim were as super frum as the women I had grown up with. They dressed very tznius and not stylishly at all. They had no TVs or VCRs in their homes. The difference was that they were vastly less judgmental and more open-minded than their Monsey counterparts. They had to be, as they were an outreach kollel, and they had to be OK with having all sorts of irreligious people wandering through their homes. They had to learn how to deal with the outside world to some degree, even though they, like I, viewed the outside world with utter contempt and distrust. They were willing to brave the tempestuous temptations of the secular for a very worthy, holy cause: to bring lost souls back to Judaism.

Like the Lubavitch who had brought my parents to this world, they went from town to town, in and around Atlanta, and helped Jews find their religious roots, hoping to make them into ultra-Orthodox Jews. They were extremely successful. It didn't hurt that literally every guy in the kollel was hot. They were all bearded and black hatted, but they were all very handsome. Like the handsome priests who ensured high attendance at church, these guys were great at getting college kids and families alike to come to Torah classes and Shabbosos, etc.

Everyone there still had six-plus kids, and the women were always pregnant, exactly like I was used to, but they allowed irreligious college kids to come to their houses for Shabbos and learn what a real Shabbos experience was like. I loved this. It reminded me of all the outreach my family had done when perestroika brought tens of thousands of Russian Jews to New York. And it allowed me to get really creative with my cooking and feed dozens of people, from all walks of life, every week.

Life in Atlanta was so different from the one I had known in Monsey. My favorite part of the week was Shabbos, because every single Shabbos, the major part of the community would come together for a kiddush in shul (synagogue) after the davening (prayer) was finished. "Kiddush" literally means the prayer that is said over wine during the Shabbos meals. "A kiddush," however, means the equivalent of a cocktail party. You usually make kiddushes for special occasions like a bar mitzvah or an engagement, or if your son has finished a mesechta (tractate) in the Gemara and you want to celebrate his accomplishment with your neighbors. Here in Atlanta, they made a kiddush for no reason at all, other than for people to socialize! And it was mixed! Men and women walking around the same room, eating from the same kugel tray and standing in the same line for different types of herring! The height of excitement, you're probably thinking to yourself. But where I came from, this was basically the equivalent of a wild, raucous party! Of course there was nothing even remotely wild or raucous about it, and it was filled with mothers, surrounded by the same dozen children and baby carriages and diaper bags, and men and women weren't partying together, but at least we were in the same room, and we weren't being stuffed behind a smelly, dank curtain with some sad pieces of food that the men didn't like, which happened all the time in Monsey.

And it also meant that I was able to meet many of the women in my community in one place. It was awesome. I'd never been with a group of such friendly, open, accepting people in my entire life!

Of course, its being a frum community, even a small one, meant that there was more than one shul. There's a frum joke that's told in my world:

A guy gets stranded on a desert island and is there for many years, all alone. One day, a ship comes to his island. He's finally going to be rescued! Before he leaves, he shows one of his saviors his island. There are two rather large wooden buildings, one only a hundred feet from the other.

"What's this building?" his savior asks.

"It's my shul," the man replies.

"And this other building here?" queries the man.

"Ah, that's the other shul," says our stranded friend.

"What? But I don't understand," the perplexed sailor says. "I thought you were the only person on the island."

"Oh yes," the man replies. "That's the shul I *don't* go to!"

It's a very telling joke. Get a bunch of yeshivishe frum Jews together and they will want ten different shuls. The differences would seem insignificant to an outsider, but to the men who daven there three times a day, the little things make all the difference. For example, will the shul have a "Naytz" minyan (which means a quorum of ten men that daven really early, sunrise to be precise), which is great for men who work in the "outside world"? Another issue might be how long the chazon takes to go through the entire tefilah. This is actually a really important one, especially for the lonely women waiting at home for their husbands to come from shul so they can feed their hungry families Shabbos dinner or lunch. If the chazon really gets into it, and draws out every note, davening can take from 8:00 A.M. until 12:30 or 1:00 P.M. every single Shabbos, which is very difficult and onerous for the little children hungrily awaiting Abba (father), as lunch can't be served until Abba comes home from shul and makes kiddush. You are not allowed to eat food on Shabbos without having first recited kiddush.

It becomes even more critical during the yomim tovim (the Jewish holidays like Pesach and Shavuot and Succos), because the davening is two to three times as long as regular Shabbos davening, and if the chazon is slow, the men don't get home until two or three in the afternoon!

In Atlanta, when I lived there, there was our shul, the Sephardi shul, the Modern Orthodox shul, and a Persian shul. A couple hundred or so of ultrareligious Jews and they had five shuls within a five-block radius! I really loved Atlanta. It was the first time in my life that I was an insider and someone that others aspired to be like.

I felt the constraints of my life loosen ever so slightly as well. I was away from the severe fundamentalism of Monsey and my mother's ever-watchful eye. Life took on its own rhythm, and I loved teaching at Yeshiva Atlanta. My time there can be summed up with a few short stories. My classes were very popular. I made everything into a story. I spoke with passion and excitement, and it was readily apparent that I believed and loved what I was teaching. I would get complaints from the parents that their kids were spending more time on their Judaic studies than on their secular ones. Since these were predominantly irreligious families, they wanted their kids to focus on the AP courses and be sure they had good GPAs so they could get into the best schools, and here I was, getting them all excited over ancient texts and esoteric principles. Suddenly their kids were talking about Esther and Chana and Yonatan instead of about logarithms and the Revolutionary War. They called the principal, concerned. I took it all as a huge compliment and patted myself on the back. My place in heaven was secure, since I would be instrumental in bringing so many lost Jewish souls back to Judaism.

After my first few months of teaching there, the school staff became perplexed over a very curious situation. Students were disappearing from their classrooms, and they weren't congregating in the bathrooms or the halls or in the woods behind the school. No one could find them. They would just disappear, dozens of them, for forty-five-minute intervals. So the administration asked the teachers to start taking roll call twice during class, to figure out exactly when kids were disappearing.

I never took attendance. I found it an utter waste of time. I figured that these were young adults, and it was their responsibility to show up to my class, and if they didn't, and didn't make up the work, they would fail and that would be on them. But now I had no choice, as the principal was asking for the rolls.

I started taking attendance and found that every single person who was supposed to be there was. But then I noticed something. There were a good twenty more people in my classroom who were not on any attendance sheet. It turns out that kids had been sneaking out of their other classes to take my class. I had just assumed that the class assigned to me was over fifty kids, and although I thought it was a large size for a class, I went with it. Imagine my surprise when I realized that all the missing kids weren't playing hooky or smoking in the bathrooms but were sitting quietly in my classroom, taking copious notes for a subject that they weren't going to get tested on.

I went home that night and cried tears of gratitude. I loved teaching, and I felt I was sharing the secrets of the universe with these kids and helping them live purposeful, meaningful lives. It gave me strength to continue, and to ignore the misery that was still brewing at home.

Once, however, we had a heated conversation about why it was wrong to go to movie theaters. I couldn't tell them not to watch TV, as I was watching TV myself, albeit still only shows from the fifties and sixties. I did, however, argue vehemently against going to movie theaters and sitting amongst the goyim. Laughing with the goyim, that shared camaraderie—it was dangerous. Why were the Jews almost destroyed in Egypt? Because they started going to the Egyptians' "teatrot" (theaters). We were taught that they were all enslaved as God's punishment for mixing with the non-Jews. If we don't separate ourselves, I warned my students, God brings anti-Semitism and the goyim kill us. Better to self-segregate than to have God do it for us through anti-Semitism.

In my world, we were all taught that it was no coincidence that World War II and the Holocaust started in Germany. That was the birthplace of the Haskalah (Jewish Enlightenment) movement (that inspired Reform Judaism). The German Jews were completely integrated into German culture. They intermarried at alarming rates, and unlike in the rest of Europe, where Jews lived in shtetls and wore payos and were immediately identifiable and religious, their German brothers and sisters had given up their Judaism and assimilated into the German culture. "They think that Berlin is Jerusalem . . . from there will come the storm winds that will uproot them," wrote Rabbi Meir Simcha of Dvinsk, years before Hitler came to power. The birthplace of the Reform Jews was the birthplace of the genocide that almost succeeded in consuming the Jewish people. An accident? Not according to my world. It was God punishing the Jews for assimilation.

The lesson was clear and very frightening. Separate yourself, or God will send anti-Semites to do it for you. Getting too comfortable in the outside world? Watch out; your next-door neighbor will turn on you and send you to the gas chamber. I believed every word I told them. It's what I had been taught and indoctrinated with my entire life. I genuinely believed that going to a movie theater was equivalent to rebelling against God Himself! It was dangerous and possibly deadly and in direct defiance of God. With all my elegant clothes and my slightly larger exposure to the outside world, I was as brainwashed as ever, and I proceeded to try and brainwash others.

At this point, though we had not been married all that long, Yosef and I no longer slept in the same bedroom. He snored loudly, and for an insomniac like me, it was a nightmare. Finally, he agreed to move out of the master bedroom and sleep downstairs, in a guest bedroom. I would have happily been the one to move out of the master bedroom, but I had little kids who still woke up at night, and I had to be on call for their cries.

For the first time in my life, even if it was just for sleeping, I had an actual bedroom (as opposed to a laundry room) all to myself. We'd still have sex in there, and Yosef would come in every morning and get his stuff and use the master bathroom, so it wasn't my very own; but it was damn close, and I loved it.

In addition to continuing to make my drawings of dresses and outfits, I found a religious woman who was a very sought-after seamstress and paid her to teach me how to sew on a real sewing machine. She, like the woman I had met all those years ago before my wedding, would design and sew beautiful, tznius gowns for the holidays and for weddings and bar mitzvahs and the like. My sewing and pattern-making skills grew exponentially, and I loved my sewing machine more than any other physical thing I owned. I would spend every available second drawing designs, making patterns, and sewing clothes. Of course, they all had to be super long and super tznius, and I chafed at all the myriad restrictions, but it still gave me great joy.

My days and nights took on a steady rhythm. Before I went to bed every night, I would write in my diary, recording my sins and mitzvahs of the day. And then, sometimes, when I was feeling particularly miserable or Yosef had gotten angry at me for being "too friendly," I would write alternate lives for myself. Yosef always died of natural causes in the beginning of the stories, and then some knight in shining armor, generally an Australian, as that seemed to be as far away from my world as I could imagine, would come and rescue me.

It never occurred to me then that I could rescue myself. I couldn't imagine a world where women lived alone and supported themselves and were their own bosses. I was sure I needed a man to rescue me. I was sure that somewhere out there, there would be some wonderful guy who would sweep me off my feet and take care of me and get me out of this misery. I was still religious in these stories. I loved the Torah and God and I didn't want to rebel against Him or His commandments. I just didn't want to be married to Yosef. He was trying so hard to force me to be someone I just wasn't. Remember that it wasn't his fault. He was just as brainwashed as I was. He was taught that he had to rebuke his wife and enforce the laws of tznius, or his children, his community, and his very soul would suffer the consequences. He believed that, and he took his responsibilities very seriously. He did nothing wrong, and I have zero anger in my heart toward him. He was following the laws that dictated his behavior as much as I was, and he genuinely believed he was doing the right thing.

Many years before I left, I stopped dreaming of a knight in shining armor coming to save me. I decided to save myself. I no longer yearned for someone wealthy, handsome, and loving to come for me. I longed for freedom, for wealth I had earned, for silence and solitude. I never again would allow myself to rely on another person—especially not a man. I would rather starve than ever ask permission. I wanted to earn my keep and to make a difference and to do something wonderful and useful every day of my life. I would never again be made to feel less than, or that I needed someone else to survive

With Yosef, I couldn't seem to do anything right, and often our fights would come back around to my clothes. I was by far the best-dressed person in our community in Atlanta, and although I was technically always tznius, I managed to look as good as possible under those constraints. I couldn't show cleavage, obviously, but I could wear a tight shirt that showed every curve. I pushed the envelope as far as I could without ever going against the law.

In fact, the only time every single one of my students got a question on one of my tests right was when I asked, as a joke, what outfit I wore the first day that I taught them. My clothes were such a topic of conversation that there wasn't a single girl in the class who got the question wrong. I used their admiration as an argument for my right to wear the clothes, as it made them trust and like me more, which boded well for my ability to shape their minds and win their hearts.

Not everyone agreed, including Yosef. But I argued that I was teaching girls that you can be both tznius and fashionable within the confines of Judaism. They thought that to be religious, you had to turn into a major nerd and stop taking care of yourself, but I was showing them that you could look good, be fashionable, and still be totally tznius. It was a good argument, and the principal of the school heartily agreed with me.

One night, a famous rav flew all the way from Israel to give chizuck (religious strength and fervor) to our community. Of course, he wouldn't address ladies directly, but he deigned to speak to us through his shamash (a personal secretary who took care of the rebbe's every need), his eyes cast downward so as not to gaze upon a woman. When we had questions for the great saint, we had to write them down on a piece of paper and then his shamash would read them out loud, so the rav wouldn't have to hear female voices.

One of the questions came from a rebitzen whose husband was part of the kollel. Her question read, "Is it proper and appropriate for a teacher who teaches impressionable young bas Yisroels to dress fashionably? Doesn't it send the wrong message?" Every single person in the room knew exactly who she was referring to—yours truly—and the entire room looked at me. I was sure I was in for it now.

But his answer caught everyone off guard. He said, "This is a stupid question! You are in this city to bring lost souls back to the Torah. That is your purpose here. And if you dress somewhat fashionably—of course, within the confines of the laws of tznius—and cover everything that should be covered, you are OK. This will make it easier to relate to you, as you won't look totally different from them, and your words will find a place in their hearts with greater ease." I was ecstatic. I now had free rein to be unabashedly fashionable, and no one could say a word, because the rav had OK'd it. I've often found that the women in my world, the rebitzens, who ran the schools and taught the classes and were supposed to be our guides as to what a bas Yisroel should be, were often more stringent and militant with girls and young women than the rabbis were. It used to bother me so much, and I struggled to understand why. The only rationale I can come up with is that forcing other young women along the same path they were forced to follow themselves is the only thing that makes life tolerable. It makes sense of your misery, that all your suffering was for a just cause and that your path is the correct one.

Can you imagine the mental anguish of finding out at forty-five, or at sixty-three, that all that suffering, all that shrinking yourself down until you disappear altogether, was for nothing? That it was all a lie? I can think of nothing more painful than that. So, the women uphold the system and are sometimes even more extreme than the men.

It was a huge triumph for me, and I went home and shared the rav's comment with Yosef, but he didn't like it. "He is a holy rav and he's probably never seen anyone who dresses like you, so he has no idea what he just said yes to," he said. Nonetheless, I felt vindicated and righteous. In this city, at this particular time, it was a mitzvah to dress as I did: tznius but fashionable. I was doing it in the service of Hashem, clearly. The little voice inside my head that told me I was doing it because I was obsessed with fashion and clothes and design and color, that voice, as usual, was silenced.

CHAPTER EIGHT

Two summers after we moved to Atlanta, my family came to spend Succos with us. I was ecstatic, because I missed my siblings so much. I had raised them during their younger years, and I was very close to them. My mother would no longer allow any of them to visit me without her, because she felt that I wasn't religious enough. Though I had cried copious tears years ago when the nanny had turned on the radio in our home for two minutes, now I did indeed own a TV, albeit one with only four channels and a VCR. My mother thought I had gone soft and was now too modern.

Succos was a favorite holiday of mine. You had to make a succah—a hut-like structure—to remind yourself that all your material possessions are really in the hands of Hashem, and that at any moment you may have to leave the comfort of your home. Everyone made their own succah, and it had to be big, as you weren't allowed to eat any food (nothing with wheat or grain) outside of the succah. The men were even supposed to sleep in there. It was your makeshift home for the seven days of the holiday.

I would feed an average of thirty people at every single meal, as my house became more and more known as a place to go for a good kosher meal. We had guests every Shabbos and every holiday. The cooking was an enormous task, especially with the nine members of my family arriving, but I did it with joy and pride. It was my only creative outlet, after all, and I love feeding people. Of course, my mother spent the entire holiday displeased. There were too many irreligious Jews around. There were too many men. Why wasn't I more reticent? More appropriate? Quieter? And the knees! My skirts were too short. They covered my knees when I was standing or walking, but when I sat down, they would ride up, and you might get a glimpse of half of my knee. Are you fainting with desire yet? It's about as sexy as it sounds. In my opinion, knees, like elbows, are far from sexy. Why seeing a part of my elbow was supposed to cause paroxysms of desire in some random guy I have no clue, but there it was. And so she admonished me to make sure that my skirts were at least four inches below my knees, so that no matter the position that I sat in, not a millimeter of my knee would show. I also didn't sit properly. Crossing your legs is untznius, as it focuses the eye to the vagina and is therefore improper. I was always crossing my legs—it was my go-to comfortable seated position—and that too was an issue.

I took all her advice and nodded and smiled and ignored her completely. She wasn't my boss anymore, and I had enough with Yosef constantly telling me how to dress and always checking my skirts for me when I sat down. Several times a day, he would tell me that I was somehow being untznius.

That fucking word haunted my dreams. It was constantly there. The bane of my existence. It summed up all my inadequacies. My entire being, my personality, the very fiber of my essence just wasn't tznius. Try as I might, as religious and covered as I was, I couldn't manage to not stand out. I stood out everywhere I went. It was inevitable. My nonconformist nature was in constant battle with my regimented and conformist lifestyle. I so badly wanted to be good. I taught Torah all day, and then I came home and took care of my husband and my children. I prayed three times per day and spent at least thirty minutes a day reciting psalms before I went to bed. I had guests (a great and powerful mitzvah) almost every day of the week. I was involved in helping irreligious Jews come back to the Torah. Still, it wasn't enough.

Every single solitary day was spent in the service of others. The concept of "me time" didn't exist in my world. All I did, all day every day, was in the service of Hashem. That was what I had dedicated my life to, and I was all in. And yet, with all that, I was always found lacking. If I could have just managed to be less fashionable, less concerned with my appearance, I would have been a respected rebitzen. It was all that was missing—the one thing that I just couldn't quite fix in my personality. I just wasn't tznius enough for anyone's liking. My outgoing personality was a giant problem. "Outgoing" and "tznius" cannot coexist. I chastised myself as much as they chastised me, and yet I was drawn to clothing, to fashion, to art. I couldn't help myself. I found my mouth opening to question some man, to impart knowledge when it wasn't my place to do so, to argue about tractates I wasn't allowed to be learning in the first place. My nature was the problem, and although I swore to subdue my nature, to change into the quiet, demure woman everyone wanted me to be, I couldn't manage it. My entire life may have been in the service of Hashem, but my attire ruined it all. And lest you think I was truly inappropriate, I ask you to turn to the page with the photos of me from Atlanta. In them, I'm always covered head to toe, wig on, all things covered. You'll look at me and see a very modestly dressed young woman, twenty-five or twenty-six years of age. To you, I will seem the height of tznius, but in my world, my clothes were too colorful, too fancy, too tight. Too everything. Did you notice Talia? Well, there you have it: the problem in a nutshell. Talia was noticeable. And that was, at its very core, the opposite of tznius.

There are two different kinds of days during Succos. There are the yom tov days, when you can't use electricity, and you have a long holiday davening in shul that lasts till after twelve, and then there's the meal and a few hours break and then it's back to shul for the next davening and the next meal. There are also a few days that are called chol hamoed. They're still part of Succos, and they're still festive, so you're supposed to be dressed in your Shabbos finery, but you can drive and use electricity. You're still not allowed to work, or eat outside of a succah unless it's just snack food, but you can do other things.

My father convinced my mother that it would be a great idea to take the kids to Disney World on one of these days. None of us had ever gone, of course, since my parents didn't take us on vacation when I was living at home, but they were wealthier now. They felt it was safe to go to Disney World, since the boys were still very young, because once they got older it wouldn't be tznius for them to go to an amusement park with half-dressed ladies in bikinis. Yitzchok, my oldest brother, was around twelve years old, so it was now or never. There was even a kosher restaurant in Orlando, and a Chabad house where they could daven with a minyan. The Chabad house had built a giant succah for all the religious Jews who were coming to Orlando during chol hamoed Succos.

The kids were ecstatic, except for Batsheva, who hadn't been invited to go and keenly felt the slight. My mother didn't want my daughter around my siblings because she talked about *I Love Lucy* and the seventies version of *Scooby-Doo*, which were the only things I would let her watch, and so she felt Batsheva was too "modern" and didn't want her to influence my siblings.

They were gone for a few days and were supposed to be driving back to Atlanta for the last days of yom tov. The night before they were to return, I woke up because a dream had shaken me. It was so disturbing that I went downstairs and woke up Yosef. In my dream, someone had died, and I awoke with an impending feeling of doom. About thirty minutes later our phone rang. It was my father, and I couldn't understand a word he was saying, because he was crying so hard. A feeling of dread settled in my body, and it would be many years before it began to dislodge itself.

It was pouring rain, and my parents had rented a twelve-passenger van for the drive from Atlanta to Orlando. There were nine of them, after all, and they wouldn't fit into a normal car. The roads were slick with rain, and my poor father lost control of the vehicle as it skidded over a sheet of water. The car spun round and round, totally out of control, the wheels slipping and sliding over the wet road. Somehow, the back seat of the car had not been properly attached, and all of it, with my brother Yehuda strapped to it by a seatbelt, broke off and went flying out of the car. He was five years old. My brother Yoni, who was ten, tried to catch onto the loose seat and hold onto it as he saw Yehuda being dragged and thrown with the seat. Yoni's entire arm was nearly torn off, the skin and muscle of it ripped and shredded. Yehuda was killed instantaneously. I write these words now very matter-of-factly, but my heart is breaking all over again as I relive that night.

I remember sinking to the floor, my grief so enormous there was no containing it. I couldn't speak or breathe. I couldn't even tell Yosef what had happened. I sat on the kitchen floor, curled into as tiny a ball as I could manage, and rocked back and forth, trying to wrap my mind around the enormity of what had happened.

I had seen him just a few days ago. He was my darling, cherubic, sweet little brother who played so beautifully with Batsheva, who was two years younger than him. He was such a sweet and likable child, like all my brothers. Never an unkind word, always a smile. He was blond haired and hazel eyed, and his entire face lit up when he smiled, and I adored and loved him as if he were my own child. They all felt more like my children than my siblings, and my father was telling me that Yehuda was gone. It was too unthinkable. Impossible.

Yosef couldn't get a word out of me. I don't know how long I sat there rocking back and forth, trying to compress my body into the smallest imaginable space so that I could disappear completely. That seemed vastly preferable to feeling this much searing, unbearable pain.

In our world, a body must be buried immediately, so that the soul can find peace in the World to Come. Because it was yom tov and no one is allowed to drive or to be buried during a holiday, we had to wait for two days before the funeral. My parents and siblings remained in Florida with my brother Yoni, who was hospitalized, as half of his arm had nearly been ripped off when he tried to save Yehuda. After yom tov, he was flown back to a New York City hospital so that my family could go home and bury little Yehuda.

I flew home the moment yom tov was finished, to sit shiva with my family and to just be together. Yosef stayed back in Atlanta with the kids, as I didn't think it would be healthy for them to see so much grief and suffering at such an early age. To lose a child is something none of us wants to contemplate. I will never forget the sounds that came out of my mother. It wasn't crying or keening or wailing. It was a sound of such incomprehensible anguish that it is forever imprinted on my mind. She was inconsolable, engulfed in her unimaginable grief. I wanted to hold her, to help her, to try and alleviate some of the pain, but I knew that nothing I could say or do would make it better. I couldn't bring Yehuda back. She would sit on a stool, as during shiva you sit on either the floor or a tiny stool or a pillow. You're not allowed to shower or even change your clothes for seven days.

She would just sit on the little stool, eyes glazed in disbelief, and make this grieving sound, rocking back and forth, her body unable to contain the pain.

And my poor father. He was driving the car. It wasn't his fault at all, of course. The police determined that the van was faulty and that the rental company hadn't attached the back seat properly. Intellectually, he knew he had done nothing wrong. Yehuda had been wearing his seatbelt. And yet it had been his hand on the steering wheel, his foot on the gas pedal. It haunted him, but he couldn't focus on his grief. He focused on his wife, because we were all afraid that she was suicidal. She would sit and scream, a sound that got inside your bones, that would fill the rooms and halls of their beautiful home until it seemed as if the walls themselves were wailing.

It is in times of travail that our community really shines. Give them a crisis and everyone is there, pitching in and helping in a thousand little ways. The entire community gathered around my family. There were always people there during shiva, sitting with my mother, just holding her hand. There were people who cooked and others who made sure the house was clean. I remember being so touched when I saw Yankel, the CEO of a very successful company, with mop in hand, washing my parents' floors. It is one of the most beautiful aspects of the world that I come from, their compassion and caring for one another. Being compassionate, selfless, and caring are all traits that are drummed into us, instilled in us from the moment of our comprehension, and it colors the way you view the world. I am grateful that I was taught this way. I think it has made me a more compassionate person, and I know my children feel the same.

In the end, I didn't spend too much time in the house, because Yoni needed so much care, and he was just ten years old. He had watched his brother die and been unable to save him and had half his arm ripped off to prove it. He had to have multiple skin-grafting surgeries, and he couldn't stay in the hospital all alone. My parents clearly weren't up for taking care of anyone, so it fell to me. I sat shiva in the hospital, in Yoni's room, by myself.

Through it all, Yoni was incredible. He never once complained. He was in so much pain, and his arm was unrecognizable: mangled, and skinless; and yet he would just lie in that bed as doctors came to poke and prod him, and he would ask thousands of questions. We ended up spending almost a month there, and we grew incredibly close. The only time he cried was when he thought about Yehuda; and then I would sit on his hospital bed beside him, and we would hold each other.

I think Yehuda's passing was the death knell to any sense of religious balance for my mother. The only way that she could manage to live through the unthinkable was to believe that there was a meaning and a purpose behind Yehuda's death. Some of our neighbors told her that a child, when taken so young, is often an old soul who had to come back down to earth to make up for some horrendous sin in a previous lifetime, and that when the soul had been cleansed on this earth, they died and their soul went back up to heaven, purified. The rav told her that it was only very strong and special people who merit being the parents of these recycled souls. And that it was because Hashem knew my mother was so holy and pure that he gave her Yehuda for a few short years until his task on this earth was completed.

These kinds of thoughts were what prevented my mother from spiraling completely into despair. They gave her strength and answered the question that couldn't be ignored: Why Yehuda? Why this beautiful innocent child? The idea that those questions had no answer was unthinkable. There had to be a reason and a purpose. It couldn't just be a random act. It needed to have meaning. Otherwise, what was all this suffering for? What was life for?

And so my parents became even more fundamentalist than they had been before. In my mind, there is BY and AY: before Yehuda's death and after Yehuda's death. You may think to yourselves, Wait. Weren't her parents already totally fundamentalist? And you would be justified in asking that. But there are myriad nuances that make up the Orthodox world. After Yehuda's death, they broke their final connections to the outside world.

There are thousands of examples, but what impacted my family the most was how my mother changed her parenting style. Yoni felt the brunt of this. In the hospital, he had become fascinated with doctors and medicine and made me buy him books on anatomy and biology to read. He would pepper every doctor who came to visit him with questions and would ask for the details of what they were doing and why. His doctors were generally lovely and answered his questions with great patience. He became quite a favorite in the hospital, as he was so clearly fascinated by their work.

We were sitting there one evening, and he looked at me and said, "I want to be a doctor and help other people like these doctors helped me." I could tell this wasn't some childish whim. He meant it. In the years that followed, he snuck medical books into the house and would read them in the bathroom. Imagine a world where wanting to be a doctor could get you into trouble. That was my world. My mother hated the idea. From now on, she had determined that there would be no working men in our family. All her sons were going to be great rabbis. She didn't care what they wanted or needed. She was going to mold them into Torah scholars if it killed her—or them, for that matter. She wouldn't leave poor Yoni alone. She spent countless hours talking to him, convincing him, proving to him that to be a doctor, to be anything other than a rebbe, was to waste one's life. It was a purposeless existence. There was no point to anything but the Torah. The Torah was all that mattered.

Within a few years, her relentless campaign had worked. Yoni felt ashamed that he had ever wanted to be a doctor. I reminded him of it years later, a few days before his wedding, and he looked at me, his eyes filled with sorrow, and told me, "I don't know what you're talking about. I never wanted to be a doctor." My heart broke for him all over again that day.

Today, Yoni is a rebbe to fourth-grade boys. My brilliant brother, who so badly wanted to save lives, teaches little kids about what not to do, and makes a minimal salary. To me, that's tragic. He was so talented and so hungry and fascinated by medicine, and now he's just like hundreds of thousands of young men in my world, whose only choice is to become rebbeim in elementary school or high school, or if they're very lucky, in an adult yeshiva, where other young men will come to learn to be rebbeim in elementary schools and high schools, and the cycle continues forever. It pains me to think about it and makes me mourn for the loss of my brothers, who had so much potential, so much intellect and uniqueness, and never really got the chance to choose.

Of course, if you ask them now, they will all tell you how happy they are, how content they are with their lives and how much they love learning and teaching Torah. It's because they're such genuinely good and honorable people who believe everything they were taught and live that way for the best reasons imaginable, because they truly believe it is the path of righteousness and goodness, and that it is what they were born on this earth to do. You can't miss what you don't know. And they know nothing of the outside world. Yes, they know of its existence, and they talk endlessly of its problems and issues and are not shocked by the constant acts of anti-Semitism that have again become the accepted norm. They "know" about the outside world like a person can "know" about chocolate without ever having tasted it. Their knowledge of the world is even less than mine was at their age. It's all esoteric and theoretical. They cannot fathom its beauty or opportunity or that there are other ways, equally vibrant and viable, to live your life. They are the Chosen Ones. They are the fortunate few to whom God has given His answers and His Guidelines. That is the brilliance of religion: it makes you believe that the freedoms you have given up were sacrificed for a good cause, the best cause. It makes you police yourself. You feel as if it is your choice, and you don't realize that you haven't really been given a single choice since you were born. The heavily indoctrinated rarely recognize their own indoctrination, and they defend their indoctrinators with all the power at their disposal.

My parents also started practicing all sorts of crazy chumros (stringencies). A simple example would be that on Passover, or Pesach, you're not allowed to eat anything with gluten: no cookies, crackers, cakes, etc. (Matzoh is unleavened, hence it's eaten on Passover.) Another chumrah is to not buy anything in *any* store over the holiday, even if the food is labeled kosher for Pesach, and a rabbi has certified it as such, in case some tiny leavened crumb from some worker in some factory accidentally got into the kosher-for-Pesach mayonnaise. That's a chumrah. Of course, somehow all the chumros add work for women, not men. Men make them up, and women's lives get harder. Who suffers when you can't even buy mayonnaise or ketchup and must make it from scratch? The women.

My mother adopted every single chumrah she could find. Literally. My family stopped eating berries of any kind, lest there be some tiny, unkosher bug hiding within the center. That is a chumrah. In Judaism, you can't eat bugs, but if the bug is invisible to the eye and is hiding in the confines of your celery stick, you can eat the celery stick without being afraid that you're eating an unkosher bug. If the eye can't see it, you don't need to worry about it. Those who follow the chumros, however, have decided that any bug, even those invisible to the eye, renders fruits and veggies unkosher. Rather than accidentally eating a bug, better not to eat the fruit or vegetable at all. Fresh strawberries, raspberries, blackberries, broccoli, spinach, etc., all became verboten in my household. Any food that was prone to attract bugs became unkosher to my family. Artichoke? No way. Too buggy. You know all those brain foods that are supposed to be so good for you? My family stopped eating them lest some microbial bug find its way into their body.

Other chumros followed. Clothes became even dowdier and

frumpier looking. High-heeled shoes were totally forbidden. Anything above a two-inch heel and you might as well be a prostitute. My parents still had some old books down in the basement from their early days: Rex Stout and Agatha Christie and Dorothy Sayers—books that we weren't supposed to know about. Now they were all unceremoniously dumped in the trash. Whatever vestiges of the outside world remained were eradicated wholly and completely. After Yehudah's death, I had to go back to Atlanta. Soon after, I got pregnant once again, but miscarried twice. I knew I was supposed to be sad, but the idea of having another baby was too much for me. I was so grateful to Hashem for understanding that and giving me miscarriages. But my respite didn't last for long, and I soon got pregnant again with my beloved Miriam.

Miriam was born in 2000, when Shlomo was five years old and Batsheva was seven. It was the first time I had any exposure to a non-Jewish doctor, as the community in Atlanta only had a few religious doctors, and there was no religious ob-gyn. Yosef found me a Catholic doctor, because he reasoned that a Catholic doctor would have similar beliefs to an ultra-Orthodox Jewish one, so there was less risk that he would tell me something inappropriate.

Miriam was by far my largest baby, weighing in at eight pounds, five ounces, and yet she was my easiest birth. In the end, it only took seven hours of actual labor, which for me was a joke, and then she popped right out. I lay in that hospital bed and thought about what the rest of my life would look like. I knew I would have to have more children. It was inevitable. I still had the savings I had earned from MetLife hidden away, but every new baby I had was another chain that tied me to Yosef and made my nascent dreams of escape seem even more impossible.

When the doctor came to check on me—a slim, handsome southern gentleman with peppery gray hair—I couldn't contain my misery, and it all came pouring out of me. "I'm going to be in the hospital giving birth every year until I'm too old," I sobbed. "I'm going to be changing diapers and having babies for the rest of my life." I cried piteously. He looked at me, perplexed.

"Why not take birth control?" he asked me, calm as a cucumber. As though he were suggesting, "Why not have a glass of water?" He told me about IUDs and birth control pills that were 99.9 percent effective.

In the Gemara, it says that technically, for two years after you give birth, you're allowed to take some form of birth control to give your body time to recover. You can also, and again I use the word "technically," use birth control after you've had one son and one daughter, as that is deemed by some as fulfillment of God's commandment to be fruitful and multiply. The reality, however, is completely different. Taking birth control is regarded as going against God and your purpose in life as a woman. No one I knew took birth control.

Between Shlomo and Miriam, I did take the frum version of birth control. It's a pill, but its efficacy is super low. I would call it birth control lite, as it is as likely as not that you can get pregnant on it. The idea is that between the pill and nursing, you'll have enough time to recover before you get pregnant again. I knew women who specifically nursed for two years so that they wouldn't get pregnant, but as I discovered before, nursing as a means of birth control is a myth.

It was the matter-of-fact way that the doctor told me about it that just shattered me. This meant that it wasn't just up to God if I got pregnant. He didn't look at me like I was a monster, or an ungrateful woman. He smiled calmly and spoke without any rancor or disapproval. He gave me permission to choose. I will never forget the debt of gratitude that I owe this man. He changed my life.

I started taking the birth control, of course telling no one, and felt as if a weight had been lifted off my shoulders. I knew that I still had to have more kids; I only had three, and that is not a respectable number in my community. Anything under six and you are considered biologically damaged. If I told you how many lovely, well-meaning women said that they prayed for me all the time, that Hashem would open my womb so I could have more babies, you wouldn't believe it. It was done out of total kindness and love. It occurred to no one that my inability to get pregnant was a chosen one. I knew I would eventually have to have more kids. I would feel too guilty; it was too horrendous to contemplate. But at least I could get a real break, and know with almost certainty that I wouldn't get pregnant.

I would sit there as they looked at me with pity in their eyes, davening to Hashem to open my womb, and I would pray to God not to answer their prayers. It was still not 100 percent effective, this birth control, and I had constant nightmares that Hashem would punish me for taking it by making me pregnant anyway. These nightmares lasted well into my forties when I finally decided, while I was still in the community, already out the door even if my physical body was still there, to get my tubes tied. I would wake up from my nightmare drenched in sweat, heart pounding wildly, afraid that I was somehow pregnant again. I had raised my seven sisters and brothers. In my mind, I'd already had ten children. I'd been changing diapers and wiping noses and doing homework and cleaning up vomit since I was ten years old—thirty years of babies. I had had enough. And pregnancies, for me, were a nightmare. But for now, I had given myself permission to choose, permission to have a hand, however small, in my own future. And it changed something deep inside of me.

I wanted to know what other knowledge there was out there. I wanted to know what else I didn't know. Atlanta gave me the perfect opportunity to do that. I had more freedom from prying eyes here than I ever did in Monsey. I didn't want to read anything dirty or bad, I just wanted to know more about the world outside. That world might have been on another planet for all the connection I had with it, but at least, I thought to myself, I could learn something about the other planet, even if I would never be able to travel there or be part of that world.

I became a Barnes & Noble regular. I devoured everything. I read Voltaire, Descartes, Spinoza. I gorged myself on the classics. And the words—those beautiful, mellifluous words. My old love for words came rushing back. I wanted to know every word, to understand its meaning, its nuance. I was fascinated by the etymology of words. I loved the way a new word would feel on my tongue. I delighted in the sounds, in the experience of constantly learning something new.

I read a lot of British authors, and I did read Russian literature, Dostoyevsky and Tolstoy, but they were too depressing for me. I wanted happy endings. I wanted to lose myself in a world foreign to my own. I wanted the lives of those who existed merely in someone's imagination to be happy and full of joy. It loosened the burden of my existence somehow, imagining others happy and content.

Reading, to me, was a privilege not to be taken lightly, and yet I see that in the outside world, most people have constant access to any book they desire, any knowledge they want to attain, and so many take no advantage of this. Reading was the path to my escape. It was my education. Books saved me, and I am very conscious of the power of words—the way they express who we are, the conduit for thoughts that lie deep in our souls. As Cicero said, "As reason is the glory of man, so the lamp of reason is eloquence." I read every history book I could get my hands on. I learned about India and the World Wars. I read *The History of the Decline and Fall of the Roman Empire* by Edward Gibbon. I loved Winston Churchill and read all his books, and George Orwell really spoke to me in *Nineteen Eighty-Four*. It sounded not far from the world that I was currently living in.

It is only now that I realize that most of the literature I read was about ancient times, or times when the world outside and my world weren't so different. In all the books I read, women's roles were similar to mine. They were married off by their parents, allowed an education, if any, of sewing and piano playing and "comportment." I think I stuck to the past because the current world was too frightening for me to even read about. It was too different, too extreme. Women living by themselves, getting jobs, not getting married. It all sounded like the outside world was wild and dangerous. I wasn't ready to read about modern-day society yet. Even Rex Stout and Agatha Christie wrote during a time when a woman's place was still in her home. I read no contemporary literature at all. The classics and modern literature, yes. Anything current, no way.

I found that I had a huge penchant for mystery writers. I loved trying to figure out who the murderer was before the book told me. I adored Raymond Chandler; I loved fiction the most, as it allowed me to escape my reality and made me feel connected to the world at large. Or at least connected to an outside world, even if it no longer existed. I read Albert Camus and marveled at the fact that some of his lines came straight from Ecclesiastes. I recognized the passages instantly and was shocked and pleased that a non-Jew had ever heard of Ecclesiastes. Once I started, I couldn't stop. I read every spare second I got and would read well into the wee hours of the morning, an insomniac as always, reading in my bed while the rest of my house slumbered in peaceful ignorance.

Atlanta was the slow squeak of a very heavy, unused-for-centuries door—the first step to being less fundamentalist. I quit teaching once Miriam was born, and our lives fell into a steady rhythm. I would walk with her in her carriage for hours, thinking about my life, trying to convince myself that it was enough.

Although I was no longer teaching a heavy load of young students, I started teaching adult education classes and became quite comfortable with public speaking. I taught Judaic studies to irreligious Jewish women, and I would give lectures on subjects like "the Torah and its relationship to food" or "Why did God give us tears?" Of course, I only taught women, because I thought it was inappropriate to stand in front of men and have all that male attention. But I found I really enjoyed public speaking. It was only many years later that I spoke to my first mixed audience—still about the Torah, but I had gotten special dispensation from a rav, just for this once, as the women of the community where I had been teaching wanted their husbands to hear my words of wisdom and had begged for them to be admitted. It was my first time speaking in front of men, and I chose my attire very carefully, lest I accidentally gave a man illicit thoughts. The last thing I wanted, while doing the mitzvah of spreading the word of Torah to lost Jewish souls, was to ruin it by having Hashem angry with me that I caused some man to have improper desires. I was surprised by how comfortable I felt speaking to that mixed crowd. It didn't bother me at all, and after the first few seconds, I stopped thinking about them as men or women and spoke to them as people, as equals.

I became more adventurous with the kids too, and Camp Ema (Camp Mom) was created. Camp Ema was what I called all the adventures we went on together. We did things that in my community were extremely rare, if not just totally unheard of in that time. We went tubing in full skirts and long-sleeved shirts, soaking wet in attire you would associate with a nice dinner in the city. I never took off my wig. That's how we dressed, no matter what activity it was. I learned to play tennis (with only women, of course) in a super-long skirt so that my knees wouldn't show no matter how much I ran or jumped. I fell in love with tennis. It was such a mind game, and you could play it on a quiet court where no guys could see you, which made it, while very unusual, still wholly acceptable in my world.

We hiked, we biked, with kosher food in backpacks and in long sleeves and long skirts, but we still did it. We even went to a county fair, which was really questionable, as there were goyim everywhere, eating giant turkey legs that filled the fair with the most deliciously smoky scent. I looked at the food longingly, wishing I could taste cotton candy or a churro at a fair, like everyone else was doing. And those giant hot pretzels! How I longed to taste one, but of course, no desire was worth incurring God's wrath, and so those desires stayed safely in the theoretical realm. The Torah said it was OK to wish that you could try nonkosher food as long as you didn't act upon it, as controlling your desire is in and of itself a mitzvah.

The first time I got to taste cotton candy at a fair was in Copenhagen, in Tivoli Gardens. I was forty-five years old. I don't think I've been to a fair since, so I still have never tasted one of those turkey legs they walked around with all those years ago, but I'm sure one day, maybe with my grandchildren, I'll enjoy that as well. My first churro was in Venice Beach. The gooey, sticky, cinnamony deliciousness was almost too much for me. I moaned as I ate it, eyes half-closed with concentration, with great pleasure and enjoyment. I remember the kid who sold it to me being amused by my clear obsession and excitement over the churro. He looked at me and laughingly said, "Damn, I've never seen anyone eat a churro like that before. You would think it's the first churro you've ever tasted!" I laughed and didn't reply. Yes, buddy, it *was* the first time I ever had a churro, actually, and it was fantastic.

In between taking care of the house and the kids, I spent an inordinate amount of time in the kitchen. My house had an open-door policy, and people would stop by for a hot meal whenever they were hungry or had nowhere to go. I shopped and cooked and prepared alone. I had no help, but I loved it. I adored meeting new people, and I have an innate need to feed people, so it gave me great pleasure. I made beautiful menus and created different table settings. For Purim, we had over seventy people for the meal, and I told everyone not to bring anything, that I would cook it all. Everyone had to bring a funny story or a song so that we could make the Purim meal lively and entertaining.

Yosef and I even started going to drive-in movie theaters. I remember the first movie we saw together: *Men in Black II*. We loved it, and we didn't feel too guilty, because we were still separate from the goyim. After all, we were in our own car, with our kosher snacks. Our relationship was very difficult at this point, but I was determined to make it work and convinced myself I could be happy with him.

I turned thirty in Atlanta and hinted that I wanted a real party, maybe even a surprise party. But in the end, it was no surprise at all, and I ended up cooking for it and cleaning the house for it and ordering the pizza. My thirtieth birthday was just like all the rest.

I was still too friendly, too outgoing, too open with men for Yosef. My clothes were still too tight. My anger with him grew, although I kept it all bottled up. We never raised our voices in front of our children. I didn't want their childhoods marred by screaming parents. I was going to appear to be happy no matter what.

We knew that we couldn't stay in Atlanta forever. We were both concerned that if our kids stayed in these out-of-town yeshivas, they wouldn't get the right shidduchim (marriage matches). And then, when Southern Energy, the company Yosef was working for, failed, we knew it was a sign that it was time to move back to Monsey.

Back in New York, Yosef started working at an energy company founded by a frum Jew, and this time he got a piece of the company. I was torn between excitement at being back and fear that the days of stringencies would return in full force. We also needed to find a house, and in the end, we chose one that was just a stone's throw away from my parents. I fell in love with the house because it was on the very edge of the community, and there were ten acres of forest right next to it, which offered a modicum of privacy from nosy neighbors. And it was close to Starbucks, which my community now frequented, as the coffee and some of the pastries were kosher. My Starbucks obsession began then and has lasted till this day. It was a symbol of the outside world just on the edge of mine, and it was fucking delicious.

As much as people assume that my awakening was somehow instantaneous, and that one day I just woke up and decided that I was finished, that's not how it happened. It took over twelve years from the day Miriam was born until I left. There were a thousand gradual steps in between while I lived inside the community. I slowly became less and less fundamentalist. I still kept every single law, but I was done with the chumros and the extras. I wanted to live in the frum community, but it was no accident that I chose a home on the edge, as close to the outside world as I could get. I don't think I was aware of this dichotomy at the time, but looking back now, I know it was my unconscious way of starting to connect to the outside world. I was on the cusp.

And how I loved that house! It was over six thousand square feet, and it was totally new construction—not even a year old. The rooms were spacious, and there was a gargantuan jacuzzi in the master bathroom that almost made me swoon the first time I saw it. My very own jacuzzi in my bathroom—how very decadent. And the kitchen. It was only partially completed, so I got to finish it myself, and I chose a soft light wood, stained to look like it was very old. It

lent the kitchen such a delightful air of coziness and warmth. The
kitchen was definitely the center of the house. Since I spent so much
time cooking, everyone would congregate in the kitchen, and the
kids would do their homework or play with their friends and swipe
tastes of whatever it was I was making. Thursdays the smell of bak-
ing challos would permeate the entire house, and you felt that there
was calm and peace here.

We sent our son, Shlomo, to the same fundamentalist school my
brother Shlomo (who was six months younger than my daughter
Batsheva) attended. It made sense to send him to a school where he
would have a friend and protector. The first day, we walked him into
class, which looked so different from the school he had attended in
Atlanta. Here there were no colored shirts, no sneakers. Everyone
was in white shirts and black or dark blue pants and dress shoes.
Learn Torah in sneakers? God forbid. His rebbe, who didn't deign to
say hello to me, smiled at Shlomo and asked him what his Yiddishe
name was. Shlomo replied, "I don't have a Yiddish name, only a Hebrew one, and it's Shlomo," and everyone in the class laughed because here Yiddishe means Jewish, so the question meant "What's
your Jewish name?"

Shlomo had a terrible time of it at school. He is such a kind and
gentle soul. He became the kid who would take in the kids no one
else would play with. Teachers began seating new students next to
him, because they knew that he would be kind to them. But because
we came from "out of town" and had fewer stringencies than his
other classmates, he was teased mercilessly.

In our world, rebbeim smack kids as an acceptable form of punishment. One of his friends lost partial hearing in one ear because
his rebbe pulled him by the ear all the way to the principal's office
and broke his eardrum. Shlomo saw kids getting slammed against
the wall. He hated it. You're probably wondering why I didn't switch
his school. It honestly didn't even occur to me. All yeshivishe yeshivas were like that. It was totally normal in our world and something
that I had accepted, like all the other garbage I accepted as part of
life. I, however, didn't want anyone touching my child, so I went to

the school, and while his rebbe looked at the floor instead of at my face, I told him that if he ever so much as touched my son in any way, shape, or form, I would go to the goyish police (worst threat ever) and I would turn him in for child abuse. Not one single rebbe in that school ever laid a hand on my son, because they knew that they would have to face the wrath of his insane and obnoxious mother.

For half of elementary school, Shlomo wouldn't go to school at all and would just stay at home with me, and I would do his lessons with him. I couldn't bear to see him unhappy, but of course sending him to a more modern school, where rebbeim didn't hit their students, was unthinkable at the time. I still wanted my son to grow up and become a great Torah scholar. Where you went to school, even at such an early age, played a huge role in your shidduch and also your siblings' shidduchim. If one of the child's siblings was in a more modern school, that meant they were a problem child, and therefore no match with the family would happen. The more fundamentalist your school, the better of a shidduch you were likely to get. The kids in Shlomo's class called him Santa Claus (in that world, a massive insult—like saying you're really a non-Jew), because he ate non–cholov Yisroel, that is, not superkosher. I explained cholov Yisroel in the beginning of the book, so I won't bother you with it again. Suffice it to say, he was the only kid in his class who was eating M&M's (which are totally kosher, with a proper kosher symbol and everything), but not cholov Yisroel. It took years for him to make friends, and even then, he still always felt the odd man out.

Secular studies, as in my time, were basically nonexistent. Everyone knew that they only had these classes due to governmental regulations. After all, none of these boys were going to college. They were all going to go to yeshiva in Israel, and from there to yeshiva in Lakewood or Brooklyn, before getting married—the usual plan for a yeshiva bochur. What was the point of bothering with secular studies?

We sent him to a slightly less yeshivishe high school that, if you saw it from the outside, looked exactly the same as the others. The differences were minuscule, but in our world, they were still important. The main one was that all their secular teachers actually had degrees in the subject matters they were teaching. That was the most important distinction as, in the other schools, a rabbi who knew as much about the Revolutionary War as I know about nuclear physics might be teaching American history. The attitude toward secular subjects, though, hadn't changed at all. But even in the slightly more modern high school, he was still the odd man out. It wasn't until college, in a wholly secular world, that Shlomo, for the first time, made really close friends.

The other problem with the schools in Monsey was that there was a strict no-TV policy, and we still had a TV. We hid it in the bedroom, and of course we had no cable, because you would be able to see the cable wires from outside, and that was a sure giveaway. Before they accepted your children into school you had to sign a document that you had no TV, computer, or other such goyish nonsense in your home. I signed the paper. I lied.

Batsheva had a much easier time of it. She's very outgoing and friendly by nature, and besides, they don't care if girls learn anything anyway, as girls are supposed to become wives and mothers. You don't need math or science to do that. They learned halacha (Jewish laws), and stories from the Torah and beyond about righteous women whose self-abnegation was extreme. These stories demonstrated what they should strive for.

A perfect example was a story that always drove me crazy, even if I refused to see why at the time; it is the story of Rabbi Akiva and his wife, Rochel. Rabbi Akiva's wife, Rochel, was a constant source of "inspiration" in every girl's school. She lived in 50 A.D. She came from a wealthy family who owned countless fields, and she lacked for nothing. She saw something in this man, R' Akiva, that told her that one day he would be a great scholar and that he would inspire the Jewish nation. He was penniless and his parents were gerim (someone who converted to Judaism). Although, like ba'alei teshuva, gerim are supposed to be beloved by God and therefore on equal if not greater footing than frum-from-birth Jews, the reality is very different. Marrying a ger is considered demeaning in my world, which I think is horrible, but it's true. Her father wouldn't hear of the match, but she went against her father's wishes and married him anyway. Her father disowned her. Now the couple didn't have a dollar to live on. She told R' Akiva not to worry, that she would manage somehow, and that he should leave their small village and go to the yeshiva to become a great scholar. She bore him children, and then he left her, not to return for over twenty years. He became a very famous and renowned scholar whose students followed him everywhere and hung on to his every word. On one of his journeys, Rabbi Akiva, in a carriage flecked with gold, passed through the town where his wife lived in abject poverty. He was surrounded by throngs of adoring people. When Rochel heard that R' Akiva was in town (notice he didn't come to her first, and she had to hear about his arrival from others), she ran out of her shanty to see him, and when she saw him, she fell to his feet and started to cry tears of joy for the great scholar he had become. His students tried to shoo her away because she looked like a beggar woman. Her clothes were old and torn, her face lined with worry and poverty. She was so thin because she could barely feed her children, let alone herself. R' Akiva told his students to leave the beggar woman alone, that it was all thanks to this woman and her sacrifice that he became the great scholar that he was.

The inherent message of this story is that a woman should let herself go in rags, almost starve, and sacrifice her own happiness and well-being in the service of her husband, so that he can become a great Torah scholar. Not that the woman herself has the capacity to become a great scholar. Not that she can achieve her own greatness. It is only greatness by proxy. You're the doormat that the great man gets to stand on, and the more you can remove any concept of self—the more you can make yourself nothing more than a receptacle—the better a woman you are. That was the role model that girls ingested from the moment they were old enough to understand a story. There were thousands of stories like this that every girl was taught, over and over, throughout their lives. That route was the only route to goodness, to success as a human being for a woman. She could never hope to achieve personal goals or greatness. She could never have the throne. She had to be the one to clean the throne and prepare the throne and be the step stool for her husband. That was what they inculcated their daughters with. A constant barrage of brainwashing. It works incredibly well.

Batsheva tuned most of it out. If something the teacher said bothered her, she would just shrug it off and move on. She was a happy kid and made friends easily, and if she had questions about what she was learning, she either asked me or kept them to herself. She never openly questioned her teachers.

We had been back in New York for a little under a year when my guilt started consuming me. Miriam was about to turn six, and all this time, I had been on birth control. I was messing with God, and it was starting to freak me out. I kept hearing speeches about the purpose of a woman's life and how children were what Hashem wanted from me, and here I was, with a five-year-old daughter, and I was still taking birth control. I would wake up shaking and go daven to Hashem to not kill me that day. The guilt was consuming me.

I had made two new friends in my community, and each had five kids and was still getting pregnant. Another one of my friends had nine, and another, eleven. My guilt grew and grew. I stopped the birth control and immediately became pregnant. Three months later, I had another miscarriage. I was thirty-four when I became pregnant again. I'd had six miscarriages and three full-term pregnancies, and my body was tiny and ill prepared for another one. I knew it was going to be a boy almost immediately, and as with Miriam, I had the same dream night after night. In my dream, an old man came to me and told me I should name my son Aron after the brother of Moses who was the first holy high priest in the Jewish world and who was known for making peace among the people. I dreamt that my son would be a peacemaker, and indeed he is. He is such a warm and loving person. Everyone adores him, and he's always cheerful and happy. Aron is also brilliant and funny. He's got a fantastically acerbic sense of humor and is so confident and an excellent public speaker, and he's only fourteen. He's definitely not shy. I wonder where he gets it

from. He also has a real talent for filmmaking and is an aspiring director. Back then, of course, he was just a little nugget growing in my
belly, but I was already madly in love with him.

My pregnancy with him, however, was a disaster. I developed sciatica again and had to go on bed rest for the last six weeks of pregnancy. My body also became severely calcium deficient. I got a cavity
that turned into a root canal, which caused dry socket. And if being
bedridden, pregnant, and in excruciating pain from my mouth wasn't
enough, the tooth's nerve became infected and shut down half my
face. The left side of my face was horribly swollen and the swelling
reached my left eye, which was unimaginably painful. It then affected
the nerves below my mouth and I lost all feeling in the bottom half
of my face, below my lips. You could have stuck thirty pins there and
I wouldn't have felt a thing. So while half my face was in excruciating
agony, the other half was utterly numb. I was on very little medication,
because Aron was almost due, and it was the first time my kids ever
saw me cry. Since I had made that promise to myself in my youth, I'd
never cried in public, and yet the pain was just too unmanageable.

At night, Miriam and Shlomo and Batsheva would bring their
sleeping bags into my bedroom and sleep on the floor, in case I
needed something in the night. I was so touched, and even through
my pain, I marveled at how fortunate I was to have such incredible
kids. Eventually, they were going to have to operate on my mouth,
because the pain was too intense. I went to the hospital on a warm
day in June, crying the entire way. They were halfway through surgery when I felt something wet trickle down my leg. My water had
broken. I didn't know whether to laugh or cry. I was so delirious with
pain by that point that I don't remember giving birth to Aron at all.
All I remember is waking up screaming for morphine, and the nurse
coming in and asking me. "Oh, hun, is the afterbirth bothering you?"
And I responded "Afterbirth? Who cares about the afterbirth? It's
my *mouth*. My face is on *fire*." After I gave birth, they completed the
oral surgery, wheeling me from one corner of the hospital to another.
It was absurd.

✦　✦　✦

My exodus truly began when Miriam was five and I was thirty-four. Miriam was my little feminist rebel. From such an early age, she was different from any other little kid. First of all, she was a total nudist. I couldn't manage to keep a single outfit on her. She would start the day fully dressed, and by midmorning she had hidden all of her clothes and was walking around the house sans attire. It drove Shlomo crazy. Little girls in my world were supposed to be covered. It was the chumrah and the minhag (custom), although totally not law, that even at three, a girl's knees and elbows and collarbones had to be covered. No one bothered to ask the question as to what kind of sick pedophile mind would find a three-year-old girl's elbows sexy; that was beside the point. Even at three, a woman was a woman, and as such, her body had to be wholly covered up, lest a man come to have sinful thoughts. End of story.

And Miriam? Forget about long socks and stockings; I couldn't manage to keep undies on her. No matter how many times I put her clothes back on, she would shed them just as quickly and off she'd go. I couldn't bring myself to chastise her at all. I fucking loved it! I loved her spirit, and the fact that she didn't give a fuck what anyone thought. Shlomo could yell at her, Yosef could chastise her, all to no avail. She was comfortable without the constraints of clothes, and that was that. "Make fun of me? That's fine, go ahead" was Miriam's constant attitude. She generally didn't even bother noticing what anyone thought about her. It just wasn't part of her equation. She is the most confident, inwardly focused person I've ever met.

Some of Shlomo's friends weren't allowed to come to our house, because the mothers found out that there was a naked girl running around the house, and they didn't want their sons seeing anything that disgraceful.

When she was in second grade, her teacher gave an assignment to the class. The question was: "If you could walk in someone's shoes, whose shoes would you walk in?"

A few days later, all the parents went to the PTA, and hanging there on the wall were the essays that all the little second-grade girls had written. I wandered around looking at the different answers. Most girls said things like "My grandmother. She's a big tzaddekes [righteous woman], who had fourteen children after the war and lived through hunger and poverty." "My mother, because she is a big tzaddekes and she takes care of our family and davens," ad infinitum.

Every single little girl had written about some righteous tzaddekes woman who had dozens of kids and whose husband was a Torah scholar, etc. And then came Miriam's paper, and I stood there, tears streaming down my face, as I read my six-year-old daughter's essay. She wrote, "I don't want to walk in anyone's shoes. My mother's are too high and my father's are too big and I can't play or run or jump in any shoes that aren't my own so I choose to always stay in my own shoes thank you." My little rebel. I understood. I was awed by her courage and her stubbornness. She wanted to forge her own path.

Miriam and Yosef and Shlomo would argue incessantly at the Shabbos table. Miriam wanted to play soccer. And basketball. There were all sorts of boys' yeshivas that had teams (the modern ones obviously), but not a single one of the yeshivishe girls' schools had them. She was told it was untznius for a girl to play sports. The conversations always went something like this:

"Abba, I want to play soccer," she would say.

"Soccer isn't tznius," he would reply.

"But why, Abba? It's only with girls. What's not tznius about playing with only girls?"

"Because what if a man walked by the field that you were playing on, and you were running or kicking the ball, and he got to see your knees or your legs," he answered, "and that man would start thinking about how beautiful you are, or have other inappropriate thoughts about you. That would be your fault. So that's why it's better if girls don't play sports, so they don't accidentally lead some poor man to sin."

"That makes no sense," she would say, face tight with confusion. "Why is it my fault if he thinks bad thoughts? If I think bad thoughts, is it Shlomo's fault, or your fault? Shouldn't everyone be responsible for themselves and their thoughts? I can't do anything or play any sports because some random person might think something? That makes no sense," she would opine.

She loved singing and would look forward to Pesach, when we would be singing beautiful songs while reading the Haggadah. But of course, she wasn't allowed to sing. Girls couldn't sing or dance in front of men for the same reason that they couldn't play sports: not tznius. Too impure. A danger for men. She questioned it all it so logically, so rationally, and she was a just a little kid.

"Exactly!" I wanted to scream. "That makes no sense! Why is it her problem if some guy stares at her? Why is my life so small because it's my responsibility to ensure that no man strays in his mind?" I had been asking myself these questions all my life, but I had always, always assumed that I was somehow flawed, broken. If I really loved Hashem and was a good person, I would be totally OK with subjugating myself and living in the service of men. Of course I should cover myself. I didn't matter. If I were truly holy, I would know and accept that. My world had convinced me that I was evil and flawed, that I was somehow less than for questioning the inequalities and injustices of my existence. And yet, no one, *no* one, could convince me that my little daughter was flawed. She wasn't getting those ideas from me. I kept those burning thoughts and questions squarely in the realm of the unspoken. I was too afraid to say them out loud. I was ashamed that I couldn't stop thinking them. That was bad enough, but now here was this little girl, pure and untainted by sin, and she was asking these self-same questions. Now, there was no way it was because she was evil. She was too young to be evil; it was impossible.

For the first time in my life, I decided to give myself permission to question. Permission to say the things out loud, the words that had always stayed locked within my mind as dangerous thoughts. Why should my life be so small, and why should women be ashamed and cover their bodies and their skin? Why can't I sing or dance? Why can't I, why can't I, why can't I? Now, thanks to Miriam, I was free to acknowledge the inequity of my existence. It was exactly then that the nugget of desire for freedom left the world of imagination and landed squarely in my reality. I began to read books with a purpose— not for entertainment or mere curiosity, but with the implicit intention to learn enough about the workings of the outside world to actually consider being a part of it. I began to read *current* books about the world outside. I began to truly educate myself. No more fiction. I was reading with a serious purpose now. I started reading only nonfiction. I wanted to fill my mind with as much knowledge as possible, as I knew the transition from my eighteenth-century world into the current one would be agonizing. My freedom money was going to be used to escape not just my stifling marriage but my stifling world! It would take eight more years, however, before I would finally summon the courage to walk out the door; before I was finally ready to leave everything and everyone I knew behind.

In the meantime, I became less and less fundamentalist. I moved Camp Ema to Monsey, and that summer we had all sorts of adventures. We went rock scrambling (in skirts of course). And I started really making friends. There was Sandra from my former high school, Bais Yaakov. She was the only woman I knew with an actual career, and without a Yiddishe-sounding name. She had gone the usual route—high school and seminary and then married off and immediately having babies—but somewhere in the middle, she had decided she wanted more. She was an actuary, and she went into Manhattan every day, to a real office. Her husband was a stay-at-home dad. That was a real anomaly in my community and engendered a lot of conversation. She was super tznius and covered herself head to toe and didn't allow the outside world to intrude on her family life at all. Her work acquaintances never became friends; she didn't do anything with anyone from her office. She went to work and came home, just like most men in the community, and left the outside world outside. People gave her a lot of shit for working outside of the community and were always making snide remarks about how her place was in the house, and what a shanda it was that her husband was Mr. Mom. She ignored them all and made sure that her family was as super frum as everyone else, so that her children's shidduchim wouldn't get harmed. She had six children and married each one of them off, exactly as one should, when the girls were in their late teens and the boys came out of the "freezer." The term "freezer" refers to the fact that men are not allowed to date or speak to women until it's time for marriage. So you're "frozen," and no one can date you.

We had a little crew—me and Sandra and her two next-door neighbors—and we were the crazy, adventurous ones. We went bike riding with all our kids on Sundays, again covered head to toe, but still, it was very unusual and rare in my world. They were super religious and totally part of the community, but they were definitely more with-it and lax about activities, and not as fundamentalist.

My mother didn't approve of my new friends. She thought they were too modern. Some of them watched movies and had TVs (although hidden), and some even went to movie theaters. I know it's difficult to understand, but even with all that, they were totally divorced from the outside world. It was still "us and them." In all these families, all the kids got married off at eighteen or nineteen for girls and twentysomething for the guys—whenever they got a good shidduch. Those friends are all grandparents now. Their kids all had babies immediately. They cooked and cleaned and made Shabbos and yom tov and took care of their families. Still, a movie out with the husband was totally acceptable in their eyes, and my parents thought them horrible for it. But such nuances look minute and minuscule to anyone from the outside.

Yes, they had TVs and movies, but they still knew nothing about the outside world. When I try and explain that to people, they look back at me, perplexed.

The best analogy is to imagine that you've never tasted chocolate. Imagine if you read a book describing what chocolate tasted like, and then you went and saw a film that showed you chocolate. Is that equivalent to actually biting into a delectable morsel of chocolate? Can you really understand what chocolate tastes like without ever tasting it? No, you cannot. You can't understand a world or "know" about it until you really live in it, until you experience it. There is no substitute for biting into a chocolate bar. People can describe the sensation and the taste, and you'll still have no clue until you yourself put a tiny, delectable morsel in your mouth.

That was my friends and I and the outside world. It was just no substitute for experiencing life in the twenty-first century. We were still bringing up our daughters to be wives and mothers. We still thought of the outside world as a dangerous place. We all thought that the only true way to live a good life was ours.

I began getting more daring with my television watching. I was watching current TV shows now—not openly, of course, but in the confines of my home. My brother Shlomo stopped coming to my house because he felt it was inappropriate to be in a home with a TV in it. My kids watched TV too—while very heavily monitored, of course, but at least they got to watch something. I always chuckle when Batsheva and Miriam compare their childhood. Batsheva wasn't allowed to watch anything until we lived in Atlanta, and then it was only the original *Scooby-Doo* (as I thought the modern version inappropriate) and Winnie the Pooh movies and the like. By the time Miriam was old enough to watch, I had massively relaxed the restrictions. She got to watch *Hannah Montana* and other Disney shows that I wouldn't have ever let Bat or Shlomo watch.

Every year I was moving a little further away from fundamentalism. I stopped wearing tights all the time and would go bare legged occasionally. And when I say "bare legged," I'm talking about the small part of skin in between my long skirt and my ankles. I was still otherwise covered head to toe. Not a strand of hair escaped my sheitel, and I prided myself on the fact that although I was "too colorful" and my clothes were still too tight for everyone's liking, you couldn't say that I had gone against a single law of the Torah. I just stopped doing the chumros. And I now had a computer and got to use Google for the first time, which was the most miraculous thing I'd ever come across. I was slowly, ever so gradually, bringing us closer to the outside world, without technically dipping a toe in. We were closer to the beach, but none of us were swimming in the water, I told myself.

One year, Yosef decided to take me with him to the Consumer Electronic Show, or CES, a huge trade show in Las Vegas, since his company had a booth there. There were so many frum Jews attending that a generous man had even started a Shabbos meal plan for those who wanted it. There were hundreds of men at the Shabbos table. I think I was one of only three women sitting there. While Yosef went to the show, I walked around with giant eyes and looked at the gondolas in the Venetian (where we were staying). Everything looked so interesting and so foreign.

That's another question people always stop and ask me: Do yeshivishe Jews travel? Yes, they absolutely do. They just make sure that they bring their own food with them, and that there will be a minyan, and that none of the restrictions ease up. You're still looking at the outside world from a far, far distance, even if you're standing in the middle of it. I mean, think about it: Monsey is less than an hour and a half away from Manhattan. Chasidic women shop at Bergdorf and Saks, but they're still totally separate. They don't make friends with the goyim. They can't sit at the restaurant and have a bite. You have no idea how that divides you from the rest of the world. Imagine going to Spain and not being able to taste Spanish cuisine at all, and eating cans of tuna fish that you brought from New York City. You don't understand the culture or truly experience a place if you speak to no one and eat nothing. It's a marvelous lesson in the success of brainwashing. Even when you're away from the fold, you're so sure that Hashem is watching you, so busy policing yourself, that you actually see nothing, and you experience things only tangentially.

But that trip to Las Vegas was a mind-blowing one for me, in more ways than one. One afternoon, I was resting in our hotel room when a rerun of a TV show called *Sex and the City* came on. Now, that sounded too risqué even for me, and I balked at the title, but then this incredibly well-dressed woman came on the screen—Sarah Jessica Parker—and I was fascinated. I watched the whole thing.

These women were living unimaginable lives just a few miles away from my door. I was swept away. I downloaded the rest of the episodes and proceeded to gorge myself on a life I couldn't ever dream of having. A life that seemed so exotic and exciting: living alone, choosing your lovers, supporting yourself. And then came the episode about a mystical device called a "Rabbit." I watched as Samantha pleasured herself repeatedly with this magical thing, a vibrator. I'd never heard of one. Here I was, with four children, in my midthirties, and I'd never once had an orgasm. Not once, not ever. I was determined to go and find myself a vibrator that very day.

I wandered the streets of Las Vegas until I found a sex shop that had vibrators in the window. I sauntered in, outwardly calm, as if visiting sex shops was a normal Tuesday for me. On the inside, however, I was scared shitless. I was wearing my usual uniform of buttoned-up blouse and long skirt and sheitel. I was aware of the incongruity, but my desire to experience an orgasm overcame my discomfort at being in the store. Rabbit vibrator in hand, I walked back to the hotel room feeling exhilarated, daring, and very frightened all at once.

The first few times I tried it, I peed myself. I'd never experienced that level of physical release, and it scared me. I kept coming close to orgasm and then stopping because it was too intense. It took a bunch of tries before I managed not to pee and had my very first real orgasm. I lay there in bed, drenched in sweat, heart pounding, body liquid and lethargic, and felt like I was alive for the very first time. Quickly, I became obsessed.

It wasn't easy hiding the vibrator when we got home, as it was quite large and made lots of noise, but I managed and would only use it during the day, when the kids were at school and Yosef was at work. It was the most pleasurable thing I'd ever experienced, and what I loved about it most of all was that I was pleasuring *myself*. There was no man involved. The idea that I could please myself, that it was in my power to give myself this much joy, felt like a brand-new kind of freedom.

CHAPTER NINE

Back in Monsey, I made a conscious effort to make more friends, which is never easy for me. I had befriended four women named Layla, Nechama, Shira, and Daniella. I genuinely liked them, and I so badly wanted to be like them. They were so happy in their lives, so content. They were kind, lovely women who spent their days taking care of others. I always felt like the odd man out. I was openly reading secular books now, and many of them read secular books as well, but those tiny forays into the outside world seemed enough for them. They were content to continue the cycle of family, marriage, births, grandchildren, and so on. But it wasn't enough for me. I would sit there while they talked around me and pray and dream that I could be like them. Why couldn't I just be happy with my life? My misery was growing by leaps and bounds. Why wasn't it enough to look at the outside world from a faraway lens? What was it I wanted?

Batsheva was in high school now, at my alma mater, Bais Yaakov. I hated that she was going there. Their fundamentalist views had only become more extreme. I wanted to send her to a slightly more modern school, which still was anticollege but at least slightly less fundamentalist, but she adamantly advocated for Bais Yaakov because all her friends were going there.

I remember the interview that I had with the principal before Batsheva was accepted into the school. She told me she wouldn't accept my daughter unless I gained five pounds, because it wasn't tznius to be so thin and fit. I still managed to get her in, which pleased my parents inordinately, as it increased her chances of getting a really good shidduch. Once again I was forced to sign a paper saying there was no hidden TV in my home. Again I lied. Batsheva ended up hating it, and having nightmares for years about her principal, Rebitzen Paretsky.

I remember a few incidents that describe her school experience perfectly. One day Batsheva came home from school, and while we sat down, she told me that the night before, a twelfth-grader had gotten married, and the class and teachers had all been invited. Batsheva said that at the following morning's daily announcement, R' Paretsky had commended the class on their exemplary behavior at the chasunah (wedding).

"I was so pleased to see all of our girls dressed in black and not dancing wildly and being very serious. It almost felt like a funeral. I am so proud of all of you girls," she told them.

She was commending them for being funereal at what was supposed to be a joyous occasion! There was no room for joy in our world. Black and somber. The life and pleasure sucked out of everything, even a wedding.

Batsheva also got in trouble for being too fashionable. Like mother, like daughter. Rebitzen Paretsky called Bat into her office one day and sat her down and told her, "Batsheva, you're a really good girl, and you have very fine middos (character traits). I am concerned, however, by the fact that your clothes, albeit tznius, are too fashionable."

She looked at Batsheva, her eyes intense with zeal and fervor. "In the Torah, it tells us the story of Yosef, who, when faced with the temptation of a woman trying to seduce him, closed his eyes and saw the image of his father, Yaakov. It was the image of his holy father that stopped him from committing adultery."

She continued, "Batsheva, from now on when you shop, have the image of your mother . . ." And then Rebitzen Paretsky paused and shifted uncomfortably in her seat and corrected herself. "Emmm, uhhumm, well, upon further thought, perhaps it's best if you think of me and have my image pop in your mind so that you won't be tempted to sin."

Batsheva came home and told me the story, and we both laughed and laughed. The rebitzen had started saying that Bat should imagine her mother so that she wouldn't be led to sin, and then, thinking about who her mother was (yours truly), a woman who was constantly getting into trouble herself for her fashionable attire, she had to correct herself and tell Batsheva to imagine her instead. Clearly, I had quite the reputation. Mine was not an appropriate image to conjure up to help prevent someone from sinning. I was too much of a sinner myself!

There was something else that occurred while she was in high school that really shook us both. I was getting my nails done in a salon that was frequented by women in my community, who generally did either clear polish or some very proper pale pink. By now I was wearing red nail polish. No more chumros for me, thank you very much. Sitting in the chair next to me was this young woman, barely twenty, swollen with pregnancy, crying hysterically, tears streaming down her face as she sat there. Everyone was looking at her, concerned, but too afraid to ask any questions. I finally couldn't bear it, and asked her, "My dear, is everything OK?" She looked into my eyes and understood that I was not a judgmental woman, and she proceeded to tell me a story that made every hair on my body stand up.

"I was shopping in the kosher supermarket, and I'm in my eighth month, so it's really difficult to walk around. I was getting all the groceries I would need to make Shabbos when this woman walked over to me and began berating me publicly about my attire."

I looked at her, utterly perplexed. I mean, no one could describe her as sexy. She was enormous and swollen with child. She was covered head to toe, just as I was, and was wearing a sheitel, full stockings, etc.

"What did she mean?" I asked.

The young woman continued, tears still streaming down her face, the memory of her public shaming so fresh in her mind. "This lady started yelling at me, in front of the entire supermarket, with everyone watching, that I was destroying my unborn baby's neshama (soul) because my shirt was too tight over my belly and she could see the outline of my stomach."

She could barely continue, she was so distraught. She looked at me with panic in her eyes. It was clear she was a child herself, already married and pregnant and doing Hashem's work, but that just wasn't enough. She was made to feel so much shame because the outline of the top of her stomach was showing.

"Do you think I've destroyed my baby?" she asked me, panic and dread in her eyes. "I wear this shirt because I can't really afford to buy more maternity clothes, and even though it was super loose a few months ago, it's slightly tighter now. Is Hashem really going to punish my baby? What if Hashem kills my baby?" she asked me.

It hadn't occurred to her that the monster who had so publicly shamed her was in the wrong, as we were so accustomed to being constantly rebuked. She was truly afraid for the health and safety of her baby! I was filled with such rage. I got out of my chair, nails wet, and held her as she cried. I promised her that Hashem loved her and wasn't angry with her. That day, I came home feeling so much anguish. Life felt too painful to live. My world felt so unjust.

But the story doesn't end there. That same day, Batsheva came home from school and asked if we could talk. I could see she was perturbed. Batsheva generally didn't let what was taught to her bother her. But I could see that something had shaken her.

"What's wrong, Bat?" I asked her.

"My teacher told us this story, and she was so proud of it, and she told us we should use it as an example and do the same," she said.

I was really curious now. "What was the story she told?" I asked her.

Batsheva proceeded to explain. "Our teacher told us that she was shopping in the kosher supermarket and that she saw this untznius pregnant woman and publicly shamed her to be more tznius in order to save the baby's life! I don't understand, Ema," my beloved Batsheva told me. "How can it be right to shame someone? Is that really what Hashem wants us to do?"

I sat there in shock. It was her teacher who had caused this trauma. Her teacher who had shamed this lovely woman and made her worry that she would lose her baby. I told Batsheva about my experience in the nail salon, and that her teacher was very, very wrong.

"That is certainly not what Hashem wants from us," I told her. My pain and disillusionment with my world could no longer be contained.

For more than two years after high school, Batsheva would wake up, shaking and soaked in sweat, night after night, with nightmares about Rebitzen Paretsky. Like all of us, fear ruled her life wholly and completely.

When Batsheva was in twelfth grade, a little less than two years before I left for good, I convinced her to come to the movie theater with me. By that time, I was openly going to movies and not caring who saw me or what kinds of obnoxious comments I would get. There was no law in the Torah that said that I couldn't watch movies, and as I said before, I was done with all the extras, all the chumros, that made our religion so intolerable.

I desperately wanted Batsheva to go with me, but she was too afraid that someone from her school, or even more likely, someone from the community, would see her and inform on her, and she would get thrown out of school and never get married. I told her that anyone who saw her would only see her because they themselves were there, so it was a mutual-destruction kind of thing. If they told on you, you could inform on them, and you'd both be in hot water, so it was very safe, as it was in everyone's self-interest to keep it quiet.

"What if someone outside or driving by sees me going in?" she asked. She was too afraid. Then she had a genius idea: she would wear a disguise. She took one of my sheitels and put that on her head. She took a pillow from our couch and stuffed it under her shirt. Now she looked like a nice, newly married, newly pregnant, frum woman. No one would recognize my slim, beautiful daughter with a sheitel and a belly. That was how we went to the movies together: she literally had to pretend to be a married, pregnant woman. She was that afraid of getting caught in the evil sin of going to a movie theater.

Miriam had an even harder time of it. We kept moving her to more and more modern schools, but it still wasn't enough. It was still an all-girls school. They were still doing the same plays about Rochel and Rabbi Akiva. They still advocated getting married as a teenager and teaching that every woman's purpose in life was the same. Miriam was such a rebel, and she utterly and unapologetically refused to conform.

When she was in seventh grade, she got an F on an essay she wrote. She came home, smoke coming out of her ears, storming around our dining room table—so angry she could barely speak. I read the essay myself, and it was an excellent essay. The subject had been "Tell the story of the name your parents gave you." Miriam has a great story for how she was named. When I was pregnant with Miriam, I had a nightly recurring dream. In it, an old woman came to me and told me I was going to have a girl, and I should call her Miriam. She came night after night and finally, convinced that this was a sign, I told Yosef my dream, and we decided that we would indeed name her Miriam. Imagine our surprise when my mother broke down crying at the kiddush when we revealed her name. My mother told us that she had recently paid someone to research her lineage and had found a great-great-grandmother named Miriam in her family tree. No one had ever been named after her, and it was considered a great honor to name a child after a deceased relative. Perhaps it was this woman who came to me in my dreams. I was so happy that I had named this bundle of joy Miriam.

It was a special story, and she had been excited to tell it. I couldn't understand why in the world her teacher had given her an F. Could it be that she just didn't believe the story and thought that Miriam had made it up? I looked at Miriam, completely flummoxed, and asked her why she thought she had gotten the F.

"I know why I got the F, Ema! I just think it's wrong and unfair and I don't understand," she said. "The morah [teacher] told me that I got an F because I used an inappropriate word in the story."

I reread the essay and, not finding a single inappropriate word, looked at her, now even more confused than before.

"What's the word?" I asked.

"Pregnant," she answered. *Pregnant.* That was the inappropriate word. The morah told her that you were supposed to say "expecting" when you talked about a woman who's having a baby. Saying the word "pregnant" was absolutely verboten and showed a lack of tznius.

Excuse me? What? So, we women are supposed to get pregnant by eighteen, nineteen years old, that's totally appropriate, and be pregnant every year until we hit menopause, but the word "pregnant," that's bad? She got an F for writing this sentence: "When my mother was pregnant with me, she had a dream." That sentence negated all her hard work and her beautiful story. It was OK to *be* pregnant, just not OK to *say* pregnant.

In February 2012, a mere eight months before I left that world behind forever (although at that point it still felt like an impossible dream), it was time for Miriam's bat mitzvah. I was becoming less apologetic about wanting to be Modern Orthodox. Most Modern Orthodox people observe Shabbos and keep kosher and follow the laws of family purity, but they don't follow the vast array of tznius laws that made all of our lives a living hell. They go to real colleges, and women and men are treated equally. That was all I wanted. No more chumros. No more being made to feel that I was less than because I was a woman. I wasn't buying this bullshit anymore, and I didn't care who knew it.

We made Miriam's bat mitzvah into a fun extravaganza—as far away as possible from my afterthought, pizza-on-the-back-porch, impromptu, oops-we-forgot-about-you bat mitzvah. We had held Shlomo's bar mitzvah in a fancy hall just a few years back, and I was determined that Miriam would feel just as special as Shlomo had.

Shlomo's bar mitzvah had been typical of my world. Fancy meal, lots of crystal, and rabbi after rabbi expounding on the Torah, followed by a speech by Shlomo and then some dancing for the men while the women sat back and watched. By the time Miriam's bat mitzvah came around, I was much more daring. We were, of course, only inviting women (other than family members), and as such, no mechitza was needed and the girls could all dance, as no boys were invited. We decided to do a seventies dance theme, and the girls all learned some fun moves. Miriam had taught herself how to play guitar from YouTube. Her first year having a computer in her life, and she taught herself how to breakdance, and also how to play the guitar. By the end of the next year, she managed to teach herself how to code—purely from watching YouTube!

I started taking piano lessons so that Miriam and I could perform together. Again, because no men were invited, we could sing and perform at her bat mitzvah. Of course, none of this would have been allowed if any guys were present. Once again, I had managed to keep the letter of the law while kind of playing with the spirit of the law. Yes, women could sing when only in the presence of other women, but goyish music? I had made up a song about Miriam to the tune of a Beatles song. "Here comes the sun" became "Here comes Mir-yam," and my sister Chana and her eldest, Aliyah, sang the words I had written about my beloved Miriam while Miriam played the guitar and I played the piano. Not at all a typical bat mitzvah in my world. All bat mitzvahs in my world were extremely serious, with rabbis staring at carpets while abjuring the new young woman entering adulthood to be a good aishes chayil, blessing her with finding a good shidduch and having righteous children. Then kugel and gefilte fish were served, and then you called it a day. People didn't do disco balls and sing goyish songs. Hers was fun and irreverent and unlike any bat mitzvah party of her friends. Instead of the usual rabbi's speeches, Miriam sang some songs with her guitar, giving solo performances, and that was it. I was happy for just a few hours, seeing my daughter as the center of attention, knowing that I was skating on the edge. I hadn't broken any commandments, but I was really pushing the envelope.

When it was over, reality once again set in. I could keep my unhappiness at bay for a day here and there, but my prison walls were closing in on me, and I didn't know how much longer I could stand it. My life seemed like never-ending drudgery. The days blended together. I had no outlet, no right to work in the field I loved—fashion. It was just impossible. The anger I felt, the feeling of being wholly and utterly trapped, the smallness of my world, they were just getting to be too much for me. No matter what I did, I couldn't tamp down the growing anger and frustration. I could hide it no longer; it was oozing out of my every pore. The misery I had been fending off for over twenty years could not be contained, but I was still too afraid to leave. I wasn't equipped to handle the outside world, and I knew it. I decided to kill myself.

Miriam recently found the diary in which I spent months deliberating which was the best way to commit suicide. I knew that if people realized I had committed suicide, then my kids would never get good shidduchim, and their lives would be ruined. I ruled out overdose (where would I get pills, anyway?) or hanging myself or slitting my wrists. What if my kids found me? They would be scarred for life. And then it hit me! I could starve myself to death! I was always thin, so it wouldn't take much. Fifteen, twenty pounds would finish the job. And I thought it was a genius idea because no one would realize it was suicide. They would think I had an eating disorder, which didn't carry the same stigma with it. It wouldn't ruin my children's chances for good shidduchim. So, I began, systematically and purposefully, to starve myself to death.

Everyone was too busy to notice. We had other important matters at hand. Batsheva was now eighteen, and it was time for her to start dating. She didn't want to go to seminary, and her only other option was to get married. We were doing well financially, and so were my parents. It was now well known that she came from a wealthy family, and she was warm and funny and stunning—a good shidduch—so the calls from the matchmakers started rolling in.

I was so happy for her in the beginning. It still hadn't occurred to me that marrying someone off at eighteen or nineteen was wrong. That was the way of the Torah and what Hashem wanted, and that was that. And that first match was a doozy. I thought my mother would literally pass out with joy. He was from one of the wealthiest families in our world and was supposed to be handsome, worldly, and not overly fundamentalist. That boded well for Batsheva. It meant he wasn't the type of guy to force her to sleep with her tichel on. Maybe he would even stay in the same bed with her after they had sex.

She was excited to go out with him. And the night of their date, we waved goodbye and off they went. Dutifully, as per the rules, they came back exactly three hours later, and I could see by the look on Batsheva's face that things had not gone well. We sat down, and I asked her, "So? How was it? What's he like?"

"I don't think I like him. When we got to the car, he didn't come around and open my door, and I thought that was very rude," she replied. She looked at me to see if I would understand. I remembered so clearly standing in front of my mother, praying she would understand why Yosef leaving me stranded made me not want to marry him. My concerns had been ignored. Hers would not be. She didn't care how wealthy he was, or how comfortable her life would be. She didn't like him, and that was that.

There was also the fact that she had met a boy named Binyamin at our friends' Shabbos table. It was obvious they liked each other, and he would come to our house and hang out all day. I thought it was wonderful that Batsheva had met someone she liked, and I didn't want it to end like Yechiel and me. I didn't want her sneaking out to meet him. I wanted her to know that whatever she did, I wouldn't judge her, and I approved of her getting to know someone outside of the shidduch system.

So we told the matchmaker no thank you, and she was completely flabbergasted. No one had ever said no to that family before. He was such a catch, and he really wanted to go out with her again. Was I sure? I explained about Batsheva feeling that he wasn't polite, and her response was, "You are not doing your job as a mother. This is a nonsensical fantasy of a teenage girl. Love, opening doors, what does any of that matter? Good yichus and a wealthy family, that's all that matters. It's your duty as her mother to force her to continue going out with him."

I thanked her kindly for her words and hung up the phone. I was done taking bullshit from anyone, and there was no way that I was going to force my daughter to go out with someone she didn't like. Yes, she was a teenager, but if they deemed her old enough to marry, then she was also old enough to make up her own mind.

My mother, however, was enraged that we had said no to the shidduch. She tried calling Batsheva to change her mind, but I put a stop to that immediately. I told her it wasn't her place, that she wasn't the mother but the grandmother, and that it was none of her business. I told her that if she had any issues with the way I raised my children, she should take it up with me.

My mother couldn't believe my chutzpah. She reminded me that in many houses, the grandparents make the decision about the shidduch, and she was right. In the homes where the grandparents supported all the kids who were busy learning Torah and couldn't support themselves, the grandparents often did make the decision. In our system, you were never really allowed to grow up, because you never learned a trade or profession that could help you be financially independent. To this day, all my siblings except for Chana and Chaviva are supported by my parents. What choice do they have? They weren't afforded an education, and they were taught that if you weren't a rebbe or a rav, then you were useless. So they were forced to continue being supported by my father. When their kids are old enough to be married, it will be my parents who decide who they will marry. He who has the money has the power.

I reminded my mother that that was not the case with me. They were no longer supporting us, and I didn't want a dollar of her money.

It came with too many shackles attached. The reality was—as I was coming to realize—that I was grateful that Batsheva wasn't getting engaged. I didn't want a teenage bride. I wanted her to experience life first a little, to go to college before she settled down. Of course, I meant religious life. I still wasn't thinking in terms of leaving the community. I just wanted her version of Judaism to be a more modern one, where religious women get degrees and can live by themselves before they get married and start having babies. Yes, she would get married, still at a very young age, but at least she would have had a few years to truly form her character, to get to know herself. My thinking was evolving, and I thought maybe she could get married at twenty-two or twenty-three instead of nineteen. That was all I dared hope for.

But it was too late. She and Binyamin were in love, and they were both nineteen and super horny, and there was no way on earth that they would break the laws of negiah, which literally means "touch" and forbids physical contact with a member of the opposite sex outside of wedlock. They came to me month after month, begging me to let them get married. Finally, we made a deal. I told them that I would allow them to get married if they would promise me that they would not have children the first five years of their married life. I painted a very stark picture of what it was like to be pregnant, to have and take care of a baby. Batsheva's childhood experience was so vastly different from mine. She hadn't changed endless diapers or cleaned the house ever.

They knew that taking birth control before you have at least two children, and not just two children but one girl and one boy, was a giant no-no. This wasn't some chumrah; this was a sin. They thought I had lost my mind, and they were too afraid to do anything that was so against the law. Finally, we came up with a solution. I told them that I would write down on a piece of paper, and sign it like a contract, that if, when they died, Hashem asked why they had used birth control, that they could say they had no choice, because they were following the mitzvah of honoring one's father and mother. I swore I would take full responsibility for the birth control in front of

Hashem, and that the sin was on my shoulders and my shoulders alone. They accepted my offer.

Those months before Batsheva's wedding were probably some of the most difficult in my life. I was slowly unraveling, and the stress of making the wedding, in addition to dealing with the unbelievable fact that Batsheva, who was only nineteen, was getting married, was just too much for me. I could contain my misery no longer. And my first child was leaving the nest. My whole life had been in service to my children. I realized that, one after another, they would leave me. And then what? I hated my life so much. I struggled to contain the constant voice in my head that told me that my life wasn't worth living.

On October 17, Batsheva got married, and it was a stunning wedding. By that point I was down to seventy-three pounds. I was still too afraid to leave, too afraid to make the change. My plan to escape through death was moving steadily forward. Making Batsheva's wedding extraordinary took on a special meaning. I wanted to give her as many happy memories of us together as humanly possible. I got her a stunning Carolina Herrera gown, which we tzniafied. We had fun shopping for her sheitels (at that point the idea of not wearing a sheitel was wholly inconceivable to both of us), designer dresses for the Sheva Berachos, and lots of sexy lingerie. We became closer than ever. I wanted to take every possible moment that we still had together. I wanted to make it as memorable as I could. I wanted her to feel loved and unique.

I got a massive band and even hired a dance teacher to teach us the "Jai Ho" dance from *Slumdog Millionaire*. We played pop songs until one of Binyamin's rabbis told us, "Genugt" (enough). The rabbi said if we didn't stop playing goyish music he would shut down the wedding and make sure everyone left. The wedding still had a mechitza (the wall dividing men and women), but for some of my more moderate friends, I had seated husbands and wives together— what a scandal it was! There were steaks and sushi and carving stations and flowers suspended on invisible strings from the ceiling. We invited more than six hundred people, and I think almost every single one of them showed up. We rented out a country club in New Jersey called the Rockleigh, which had the most stunning pastoral views. It was a special night that people spoke about for many months afterward.

The following day, however, was surreal. Batsheva and Binyamin surprised me that afternoon by showing up at the house, both looking very uncomfortable. Batsheva told me that they needed to speak to me, and we all went into what just the night before had been Batsheva's bedroom. They looked at me, clearly unsure as to how to start. I waited, smiling, so curious to hear what they wanted to talk about. I was worried that they were going to renege on their promise to take birth control, but I tried to keep an open mind and waited to see what they wanted.

Finally, Ben, clearing his throat multiple times, and after much hemming and hawing, looked me straight in the eye and said, "Can you help us? We can't figure out how to have sex. We tried it last night and nothing happened." I could not believe that my daughter and brand-new son-in-law felt so comfortable with me that they came to me to ask me this question. My eyes welled with tears of joy. How different my relationship with my children was from the one I'd had with my mother.

But I was also filled with sadness that these two young kids, who didn't even know how to have sex, were forced to marry just to have it. They had never been allowed to experiment, to play. But I pushed those thoughts aside and explained to them what I wished someone had explained to me. Not like my kallah teacher who told me to recite Tehillim while my husband entered me. I was explicit and unabashed. My daughter wasn't going to have a loveless marriage where sex was just another chore to do. I wanted her to enjoy herself, to be able to pleasure herself and to be pleasured. I told them everything I knew.

CHAPTER TEN

A week after the wedding, Hurricane Sandy struck. Outside my home, it was madness. Live wires sparked menacingly on the ground, daring those intrepid drivers mad enough to venture outside to cross their path. Trees torn asunder. It looked like nature's child had had a massive temper tantrum and thrown the world into disarray. Thick branches blocking roads, homes upended. It was impossible to get gas. Anyone unlucky enough to not have backup generators, myself included, was without power for over ten days.

Inside, my house was cold and dark. The nights were freezing, and we had no light and no heat. Batsheva and Ben had left to go to Israel, to start their new life—both nineteen, so incredibly young and clueless. The house felt empty now. Shlomo was in yeshiva, and in less than two years he would be away in Israel, fully immersed and lost to me. As it was, most days he didn't get back home until nine or ten P.M., because the yeshiva he was in had very long days, so that they could learn Gemara constantly and truly immerse themselves in it. Busy boys stay out of "trouble." It seemed so quiet without Batsheva. The wedding had been its own tempest, but now, with Bat gone, I could no longer ignore the pressure building up inside my head. The madness outside was perfectly echoed by the hurricane in my mind. I was just so angry. It burned inside of me, this whirling dervish of intense anger and frustration and misery. I couldn't control it any longer. I couldn't hide my hatred of my life.

I longed to leave this life. I had dreamt of it, yearned for it, for so many years, and yet it still seemed completely unrealistic. Where would I go? Who would I be? Are you still someone if no one knows you? If you have no shared history with the world outside your door? The thought of leaving, of packing up and moving out, seemed insane. And who was to say it would work? I would still have to face God anywhere I went. Suicide still seemed the safest bet.

I was standing in my driveway, surveying the wreckage that remained from the storm, when my friend Layla called. She was sick and tired of being inside. Her house, which was twice as large as mine and even had backup generators, still felt confining. She wanted to go out, and I was more than happy to oblige.

Layla had recently become one of my favorite people. She seemed content with her life. She had grown up Chasidishe, and her head was shaved under her wig, yet she had modernized herself. She read secular literature, and she loved going to Manhattan. Even though she was as modest as any of my siblings, inside, she was infinitely more with-it and curious about the outside world. Of course, this meant curious about the world like people are curious about indigenous Amazonian monkeys. Or curious about Martians. The people in the world outside were a different species. She enjoyed studying them, as did I. But she was content with viewing the world outside from afar. I was not.

Layla and I decided to brave the weather and go to a restaurant in Manhattan. It was still pouring rain outside, which made it seem more like an adventure, and we made plans to go that evening to the one kosher restaurant that seemed as posh as the nonkosher ones we saw in the movies.

A few minutes after I got off the phone with Layla, my friend Elana called from the city in a total state of panic. There was no gas to be found in Manhattan for love or money, and she was stuck. I was going into Manhattan anyway, I told her, and in Rockland County, it was still possible to find gas. I would go, fill up a canister, and bring it to her. Ironically, she was going to the same restaurant as us that evening with her husband and her husband's boss. It would be so easy—and a mitzvah.

I told Yosef that I was going into the city to help Elana, since she was stuck without gas. I thought that would go over better than saying I was crazy enough to brave the weather just to go out to dinner. I was still asking permission, still waiting to be told. But it worked, and Yosef let me go.

Layla didn't fare as well. Her husband kiboshed the idea, telling her it was irresponsible and dangerous to drive to the city in this weather. But I had gas, and a mitzvah to do, so I decided, feeling quite pious and proud of myself, to drive all the way to Manhattan, give Elana the gas canister as promised, and drive straight home. Elana was counting on me, and I had given her my word. I was wearing slippers (with heels of course), a ratty T-shirt, and a skirt I only wore around the house. I decided not to change, as I wasn't even going to get out of the car. So, canister in hand, I started the perilous drive to Manhattan.

I have to admit it was pretty crazy out there. The hurricane had left severe damage, and the Palisades Parkway was shrouded in mist and darkness. You could barely see through the windshield. I veered around trees lying prostrate on the ground, and live wires dancing recklessly. It was pitch black outside, and vast tracts of the Palisades (which at the best of times has terrible visibility) had no lights at all. I was the only person crazy enough to be on the road. It was wonderful! I felt like a fearless adventurer, alone in an upside-down world, with winds whispering wonderful words about the dangerous unknown. I drove smiling, eyes shining at the challenging conditions, determined and alone.

That gas canister was going to change my life forever. I didn't know it then, but I was truly driving into the unknown, toward my future. To say that drive was the most meaningful one of my life is not an exaggeration. A drive toward a future that I would have to grasp alone, without anyone or anything familiar to help me.

I arrived and parked across the street from the restaurant. Elana and her husband, Leibel, were eagerly awaiting me. I didn't want them to know I had made the trip just to bring them gas, so I hadn't told them that my dinner had been canceled. I got out of the car and handed a very grateful Elana the canister.

I got back into the car, and that's when Elana realized that I wasn't coming into the restaurant after all. She couldn't believe I had come all this way just to bring her gas, and she wouldn't hear of it. "You must come with us to dinner," she cajoled. "Leibel's boss is a man named Ephrayim Lerner, and his family is massively wealthy and he's in the shmatta business." ("Shmatta" is a Yiddish term for a garment, literally meaning "rag," so when people in my world say they're in the shmatta business, it means they're in the cheap clothing business. Many frum Jews are in the shmatta business, as it's not technically fashion. Think of places like J Stores or companies like London Fog; those are considered perfectly appropriate businesses for frum men to run.) "He's a brilliant man," Elana continued. "He will be happy to meet you. You have to come with us!" Leibel cheerily seconded this notion.

I tried to refuse. I had no makeup on. I was practically wearing rags, and this was as posh as restaurants got in our world. I was too embarrassed to go in. I wanted to go home and read a book. But Elana wouldn't hear of it.

I walked into the restaurant, feeling extremely underdressed. Ephrayim and his wife, Sima, were already seated at the table, and they politely added another chair. Though Sima looked at me askance, as my attire was clearly not up to par, Ephrayim eyed me with interest.

That evening was one of the most bizarre and memorable evenings of my life. Ephrayim was fascinating—well read, funny, completely unabashed. He looked me straight in the eyes when he spoke to me. He had read nearly as many secular books as I had. The world fell away. We verbally sparred as we debated pantheism, Locke. He knew what pantheism was, and was comparing it to Rambam—how fascinating! He was totally different from anyone I had ever met. Although totally Chasidic on the outside, he was clearly a rebel on the inside. And erudite. And he was taken aback by my knowledge. He was fascinated by it. Intrigued.

At one point, Ephrayim even asked me what I did. What did I do? No man had ever asked me that question before. No one in my community had ever assumed I did *anything*. It was a given that I was a mom. What else would I be doing, exactly? I could only be a teacher, a secretary, or a doctor's assistant. That was pretty much it, and yet I could see that he wasn't thinking along those lines. He assumed that someone with the mass of knowledge I possessed must be doing something. He had never met me before, and because my clothes (although I was technically covered) were tight, he assumed I was Modern Orthodox, which meant that even though I wore a wig, I would probably have a profession.

And for some odd reason, although till this day I don't know what it was—perhaps the heady wine of having a man take me seriously for once—I told him the truth. I had applied to the Sotheby's training program. I knew I wanted to be around art and fashion, and I also knew that I was great at selling, so I thought I would become an auctioneer. It sounded like so much fun, and I was already known as an auctioneer in my community, as I raised money for the many charities I was involved with by doing live auctions. I was in very high demand for the women's events. I could sell anything, and I could make auctioning off a cheesecake interesting. I knew how peanut butter was invented, because I needed some fun facts about peanut butter pie. I could tell you when the first carrot cake was made, and the history behind the Harvey Wallbanger cake.

I had no idea how I would pull it off and keep it a secret from everyone, but the part of me that didn't want to give up, that didn't want to die, was trying to find a different path.

I told this all to Ephrayim. And then, to my utmost surprise, I shared my fantasy. I told him that I was obsessed with designing, and that my true dream was to be a fashion designer. That night was the very first time I said it out loud. I had never even voiced it to myself. Had never dared. My dream solidified that very second. Hearing the words out loud made it real.

In Judaism, when you are doing teshuva (repenting for your sins), you have to say your sin out loud—to take it from the intangible realm to the tangible one, as if by hearing yourself utter the words, you will it into existence. There is great validity in that. I know one psychologist who tells her patients who suffer from insecurity to look at themselves in the mirror every morning and chant a positive mantra. "I am worthy. I am beautiful. I matter. I can accomplish what I set out to do." Say something out loud often enough and you will start to believe it. Say something out loud often enough and it will become a self-fulfilling prophecy. To the converse, if someone is told often enough that they are stupid, worthless, and useless, that is what they believe. Words are power. "Hamaves vehachaim beyad halashon" (Death and life are in the hands of the tongue), the Torah taught me.

It is indeed very true. I always tell people that they should talk to themselves, out loud. There will be so many voices that tell you you're less than, that you are incapable of accomplishing your dreams, that you need to wait your turn and ask permission. Your voice needs to be louder than theirs. Your voice needs to drown out the hate, the self-doubt. Say what you want to yourself out loud every single day, and you can will it into existence.

For me to say those words, to even think them, was equivalent to you waking up one morning and saying, "I think I will be a time traveler." My dream was no less improbable or absurd. And yet, Ephrayim didn't laugh. He didn't look at me oddly or question my ability or my credentials or my education. He just nodded. By this time, our table was the only one left at the restaurant. It was past midnight, and I heard the impatient scraping of chairs against wood. The staff wanted to go home.

It was clear Ephrayim and I had totally monopolized the conversation all evening when I finally looked around me. Elana was bemused, and Sima appeared scandalized. I couldn't blame her. I had been rude and overshadowed everyone and made this an intimate dinner for two. Ephrayim was short and chubby, with a disheveled beard and a stained shirt. His hazel eyes, however, sparkled with intellect and humor. And he had listened. He heard me. It was exhilarating, and I had never experienced anything like it before.

I didn't want the night to end. I wanted to keep talking. But it was time to go. In my world, women don't give men their phone numbers. Your only male friends are husbands of your actual friends. I barely had any male contacts on my phone. So we didn't exchange information that night. I assumed I would never see Ephrayim again, as he lived in Brooklyn, in the Chasidic part of town, and our sects generally didn't interact.

I drove home in a daze and dreamt about being a fashion designer that night, about drawing clothes that people would actually wear. I dreamt of making shoes that would make women feel beautiful. I woke up the next morning more depressed than usual. My question, "What do you want?" had been answered, but what I wanted was impossible.

I was literally sitting on the toilet when my phone buzzed with an unfamiliar number. It was Ephrayim. I couldn't believe it. I found out later that Leibel had taken my number out of Elana's phone when she wasn't looking, and that Ephrayim had gotten it from Leibel. His text was very terse and to the point. "Come meet me in Manhattan, I have a job offer for you." I mean, he owned a shmatta business, after all! Perhaps he wanted to make it more fashionable and wanted me to design some pieces? That sounded super exciting! Hey, designing anything other than the meals I served my family sounded like a dream come true. Whatever it was, I had to find out.

For the second time in twenty-four hours, I took the Palisades to the city. I don't know how I managed to make it there in one piece. I was driving on autopilot, my mind whirling with different shmatta designs. We met in the lobby of a hotel on Madison Avenue. It was an odd choice that I only understood later. When I got there, Ephrayim was clearly excited. He didn't waste any time.

"I'm buying a handbag brand called VBH. I want to expand it to include shoes. How would you like to be the head shoe designer?" he asked. I sat there, totally stupefied. I am never speechless, but at that moment I was completely without words. In my wildest dreams, I'd never thought that I would actually get to design shoes. I never thought it would ever happen.

And yet here was this incredible human being, offering me that very job, even though he'd never seen a single one of my designs. Even though I could have been terrible, for all he knew. He had seen my hunger and determination, and he had felt my frustration. It echoed his own. He was just as trapped in his world as I was in mine. Our sects had different names, but our lives were the same. We were bound by our shared dissatisfaction. We were both caged lions. His cage, as a man, was bigger and more diverse than mine, but it was still a cage.

I tried to hide my shock and excitement. I wanted it to seem as if I received offers of heading a shoe division for a well-known hand-bag company on a daily basis. I mean, Sotheby's had wanted me. Why wouldn't Ephrayim? Once I said yes, he jumped up, knocking over the chips and soda on the table between us, and propelled me out the door and across the street to where, I soon learned, VBH had its store and headquarters.

The space is now an Apple store, but in 2012, it was one of the most beautiful stores I'd ever been inside. Until that day, I'd never even heard of VBH. It was a very chichi and expensive brand. Michelle Obama had carried one of their bags on a trip to Russia, and a picture of her had a place of honor in the store. The building had originally been a bank, and VBH had kept the vault to use as their VIP space for special clients. They took me into the vault itself and offered me champagne, which of course I didn't drink, as I didn't think it was kosher.

The whole day had taken on a surreal quality. Ephrayim introduced me to the staff as the new creative director of the shoe division that they would be opening. They looked at me, and even though I was in full religious regalia—wig and totally covered—they didn't seem to think that was insane. I fully expected them to burst out laughing and tell Ephrayim to not be absurd. How could this clueless, nun-looking, and wholly covered housewife be a designer? I thought that they would see right through me and understand how useless I was. I tried to pretend that walking around the store, being spoken to as someone whose opinion mattered, who knew about skins and leathers and factories in Italy, was perfectly normal. My own skin was on fire. My hands were shaking, and I could barely breathe, and yet I walked around calmly, nodding about Texan croc versus French croc, and even pretended to have a preference, although I literally had no fucking clue what they were talking about. One of the managers asked me where I had trained and where I had worked as a designer before, two questions that I obviously had no good answer for, and I just replied that I was totally self-taught, although in reality, at that point I hadn't a clue as to how a shoe was made.

He was a bit taken aback by my lack of experience, but he knew the company needed funding, and if Ephrayim wanted to hire an inexperienced designer to man the new shoe division, more power to him. I'm sure they figured they would just change everything I made and get rid of me once the deal was done and signed. Honestly, I didn't blame them. When I asked Ephrayim why he was taking a chance on me, as it clearly wasn't based on logic or shoe designs, he told me that I looked so determined and seemed so intelligent that he figured I would succeed at whatever I wanted to do.

All my later investors would tell me the same thing. By that point, I did have shoes to show, but it was my determination and drive that convinced them. They didn't just believe in my shoes, they believed in me.

Since we were both from the religious world, there was no contract to sign, and everything was done with a handshake, which was common practice. This would get me into massive trouble later on, but at the time, I didn't know better. That was just how people did things in my community. Ephrayim offered me $100,000 as a starting salary and a bonus of $30,000 if the shoes sold well. I would have done it for free, but I accepted without any haggling. We shook hands (very daring of us, as that's technically breaking the laws of negiah), and that was it. I was now a shoe designer. To say it was a dream come true was silly. I hadn't even dared to dream that big. My challenges had seemed insurmountable, and now, because of a canister of gas, my dream had literally fallen in my lap.

I knew there would be serious logistical issues to consider. I knew

I needed to leave Yosef and the community. What I had really needed was a plan, a purpose, before I could even contemplate leaving. And now that opportunity had come to me.

I drove home that day with shoe designs dancing in my head. That building I passed looked like a super-cool design for a heel. Why had I never noticed that? Look at that red on that store awning! Wouldn't it be a perfect red for a shoe? I was brimming with ideas.

I stayed up all night thinking about what would make my shoes different from anyone else's. Originally, all I thought of was making shoes that were so unique and beautiful that women would feel confident and special wearing them. Shoes had always been a love of mine. I'm five feet tall and wear a size 4. I've been wearing five-inch heels my entire life, and though it constantly got me into trouble in my community, I had refused to give them up, since they couldn't actually point to a commandment that said I couldn't wear high heels. More people have seen me naked than have seen me sans heels. It made complete and utter sense to begin my design career making shoes.

For the next few days all I did was take care of lunches and dinners for my family and draw. And draw and draw. I had thousands of ideas. I wanted my first collection to be architectural, so I scoured magazines for interesting buildings. A building I saw in a magazine about Seville called Las Setas (which I got to see with my own eyes several years later) became one shoe. The Chrysler Building became the inspiration for a heel. I designed a heel with stacked gold coins (if this sounds familiar it's because several years after my shoes came out, a few designers copied me and made shoes with stacked coins as well). I had drawn over fifty shoes, and I loved them all.

The first collection was only supposed to have thirteen shoes. I don't know why Ephrayim chose this number specifically, but I wasn't asking questions. I was supposed to present the shoe designs to him the following week. I had to perfect and winnow, which to this day is the most difficult thing for me to do. I always have so many designs floating around my head. When the day came,

Ephrayim studied my designs intently. He looked at them again and again. Then he said, "I love them."

Meanwhile, I kept asking Ephrayim when I could start going to an office, when the deal with VBH going to be signed. Ephrayim kept delaying. I waited impatiently. My designs were sitting there staring at me, begging to be made.

Two miserable weeks went by before I heard from Ephrayim again. He simply texted, "Come to the city." I asked for more details. None were forthcoming. When I got there, he didn't mince words. The VBH deal was dead. He no longer felt it was a good investment.

It had been too good to be true. My dream had been given to me and then taken away. I felt faint. But there was more. "I was just thinking." He rose out of his chair and began pacing back and forth, in the same hotel lobby that we had met at the very first time. "Your shoes are incredible. So different and creative. Why do I need to buy a brand? Why don't we just start a shoe brand together?" I will be honest: it hadn't even occurred to me. I was too conditioned to think that women couldn't be *business*women. Women didn't start companies in my world. And they certainly didn't own them, unless they were selling tznius clothes to women or had a store that sold baby carriages and baby clothes or chasuna dresses, all within the community, of course.

He told me he would be a silent partner, as starting a business with a woman would be considered the height of impropriety, and he would be kicked out of his synagogue. So I was sworn to secrecy; and I was fine with that, as I knew my husband would have a heart attack if he knew that Ephrayim Lerner was my business partner.

I was still petrified of my husband back then. The days when a man can scare me are long over. Let someone fucking try. I will hit right back (metaphorically speaking, obviously), and I will make them pay. People mess with me at their own peril. I may be tiny, but I can be deadly.

Start my own brand? My very own? Have my own company? It sounded like a daunting task, and I knew nothing then about business planning, accounts, taxes, and all the various and sundry items that you need to be very familiar with to have a business. I'd literally never even heard of an invoice. But Ephrayim was looking at me expectantly and offering to help me with the business side of things, and it was the only way to keep the dream alive, even though it sounded absurd. I didn't know anyone in the fashion world. I had no idea where to produce a shoe, how to even make a shoe, and yet here I was, starting a shoe brand. It was as mad as it sounds. I didn't care.

I still wasn't ready to leave Yosef or my world, but I had an idea, an excuse to use. I would often go with my friends to kosher restaurants in the city, so I decided that would be the perfect cover. I figured that as long as supper was on the table, and that as far as he knew I wasn't doing anything inappropriate, e.g., spending time with men, he wouldn't care. I'd been such a "good" wife for so long that I figured it wouldn't occur to him that I would actually be doing something so forbidden.

Ephrayim and I got an office on Madison Avenue at WeWork— a tiny cubicle for a one-woman shoe company that cost $1,100 a month. To me, it was paradise. I knew it was an unsustainable arrangement. There were only so many lunches I could pretend to have, but I was still too afraid to leave. I just couldn't fathom it. Leaving everyone and everything I knew behind still seemed like an insurmountable challenge, but I knew that I would end up having to give up this endeavor if I couldn't leave. Death was still looming over me.

The same day that I stepped into my very first office at WeWork, I came home to a crying Miriam. Miriam is like me: she doesn't like to cry. I couldn't remember the last time I had seen her cry, and now she was inconsolable. Her teacher had publicly accused her of cheating. Miriam, who aced everything and had skipped two grades! The kids in her class decided to hit her when she was down. She was such an anomaly. She wore sneakers instead of pretty bowed school shoes.

She did splits and ran and wanted to play soccer and basketball. Girls in my world play jump rope and a game called machanayim (a form of dodge ball). That day, they taunted her, calling her a lesbian. (She didn't even know what that word meant, and I had to explain it to her.) Funnily enough, those girls were almost right. Miriam is openly, proudly bisexual, but then, she had no clue about her sexuality. I don't know which girl in the class even got that word, but one girl had told the others, and they labeled Miriam a lesbian. She was too sporty. Too driven. Not a normal girl. The combination of being accused and then taunted was too much for my beloved, extraordinary, mind-blowingly brilliant daughter. She was so hurt. She felt so different and so alone.

I called her teacher and made her feel so guilty for having publicly and falsely accused my child that she began crying and begging for forgiveness. "It's not my forgiveness you have to ask for—it's Miriam's," I said. "And since you publicly shamed her, your apology has to be public too." The next morning, in front of everyone, the teacher asked for Miriam's forgiveness and then taught a class on the subject of embarrassing others. But the damage had already been done.

That was the moment I realized that killing myself wasn't the solution. It wouldn't save Miriam. She was as unhappy and miserable as I was. I had to be brave for her. I wouldn't allow them to do to her what they had done to me. They wouldn't destroy her uniqueness, her individuality. They wouldn't force her to conform and be silent. I fucking wouldn't let them. This was the last push I needed. I was done. I knew in my bones that it was time to go.

I was also worried about Shlomo. He was getting more and more extreme every day. He no longer looked up as he walked down the street, but rather, stared at his feet to keep his eyes from accidentally landing on an inappropriately dressed woman. He kept bumping into things, because walking without looking up, as you can imagine, is difficult and dangerous. A few more years and he would be gone for good, becoming another mumbling, fundamentalist rabbi, completely divorced from the outside world. That night, speaking to him on the phone, I was consumed by a feeling of deep dread. Was it too late? Miriam was thirteen and Shlomo was soon to be seventeen. Had I left it too long? Could they adjust to the outside world? Did I even dare to try?

We had been planning on going to Florida for the yom tov of Succos. Miami has a massive ultra-Orthodox community, and often, we would rent a house near my sister Chana and spend the holiday with her. This year, my son refused to go. He said there were too many immodest women in Miami, too many tank tops and shorts. I knew I was losing my son. There was no more delaying. It was now or never.

I knew if I left, I wouldn't be able to bring Aron with me. Yosef would never allow his youngest son to be taken. Plus, the law was on his side. In New York, thanks to the power that the Chasidic community wields, there exists a "status quo" rule, which means that if a couple had been raising their child in an ultra-Orthodox setting and one of the parents chose to leave, the child was generally given to the spouse who stayed, in order to maintain the child's "status quo."

It would be torture leaving him at home, but I had a plan to convince Yosef to let me see him every week, and I knew I had no choice. I couldn't wait until Aron was older; I would be dead by then, and Miriam would be destroyed, and Shlomo would be too fundamentalist. It had to be now. I had to create a life for us so that when Aron did become a little older, he could choose to live with me. I would pave the way and then we would all be reunited. I knew I had to do it, but it was the most difficult thing I've ever done.

The next morning was the morning I would go. I spent all night considering how—how would I leave without Yosef trying to stop me? How would I escape in one piece? I decided to pull a King David. When King David was being pursued by King Saul, who wanted him dead, he hid in the least likely place that Saul would look: in the land of Israel's then enemies, the Philistines. The only problem was the king of the Philistines didn't want him either. They eventually found him hiding in a cave. David knew they considered him a threat, but he figured out a way to save himself. He acted like he had gone stark raving mad. He ranted and mumbled and threw things and acted so bonkers that they decided that all that hiding had unhinged his mind. A lunatic ex-king of Israel posed zero threat to them, and so they left him in peace.

So, that day, the day of my personal Exodus, I ranted, I raved, and I actually threw things. I screamed like a woman who had lost her mind, all the while putting clothes into suitcases and stomping around, slamming doors, and acting like I had gone completely berserk. I was frenzied, wild, red in the face, and shaking with years and years of pent-up anger and frustration.

Yosef watched me in stupefied confusion. He didn't try to stop me. At that moment I think he was just afraid. Of course, it didn't occur to him that I was leaving him for good. Why would it? Until then, at age forty-two, I had never once even slept alone, as even though Yosef and I had been sleeping separately for years, it still wasn't my room. All his clothes were there. He would come in whenever the mood struck him, to have sex or use the bathroom. We might have been sleeping separately, but it was his room as much as it was mine. I'd never even spent a night in a hotel by myself. Women don't do that where I come from. I, who had always asked permission (or at least, to his knowledge had always asked permission), stomped out of the house like a fury possessed, and he didn't stop me.

Honestly, I don't remember much about those first days. My mind felt lost, trapped in a sluggish fog of fear and confusion. I knew only one thing: there was no going back. I didn't know who I would be, what I would become, but I could no longer live a lie. Come what may, I would be true to myself.

In the end, Yosef and I made a deal. If I wanted to see the kids, I would have to come upstate and sleep at home as if all was fine and hunky-dory. We would pretend that we weren't separated, that I wasn't leaving. I would be "traveling for work" and would come home every Shabbos and yom tov and many of the days that I was in the country. If I was in New York City, I would sleep upstate at least 50 percent of the time. I did that for the next six years.

I was still totally and wholly religious. I just didn't want to be fundamentalist anymore. I wanted a gentler, kinder, more advanced and open form of Judaism. I wanted to be Modern Orthodox.

Yosef assumed that I'd had a mental breakdown and would soon regain my senses, and the world would right itself. In the eyes of our community, I was still living with my heimishe (it means more than just yeshivishe, a step up in the holiness chain) husband, and my only sin was that I was working outside of the community. In reality, I was straddling two different worlds, two different centuries.

Miriam changed to a Modern Orthodox school where girls played basketball and wore shorts. She now had AP courses. She was around girls who went to movies and wore pants and yet were strictly kosher and didn't drive on Shabbos or use electricity. Her new friends would still marry at nineteen or twenty, but at least they would date the guy. They had choices, options.

I know that to anyone reading this, it sounds completely mad. How could I go back? How could I wander around the same house, sit at the same table, while living a totally different life the rest of the time? How could I willingly condemn myself to go back to prison?

What choice did I have? If I hadn't, if I had forced the issue and left for good, I would have lost Aron and probably Miriam as well. As horrible as it was to make that drive home, back to misery and pain, it was vastly better than the alternative. I couldn't lose my children. The whole point of this madness was to give them a freer, better life. If I had to suffer through years of going back, it would be worth it. Yosef didn't care what I did when I wasn't home. It was the bargain we'd struck. He asked no questions, and I gave no answers.

The days I slept over in the city, I had a totally irrational fear that Yosef would change his mind and forbid me from seeing the kids, so I moved around, using fake names and changing hotels in case anyone came looking. Writing it now, I realize how illogical that sounds.

I was just so afraid that Yosef would make an impromptu visit and see my new "goyish" lifestyle and refuse me access to my kids, so I took every precaution I could think of. He never did.

I had learned long ago that change is more palatable to those around you if it comes gradually, in small increments. I would wait until everyone got accustomed to change number one before revealing the next change. This gradual withdrawal is one of the main reasons that I managed to bring the children—slowly, ever so slowly—with me. Had I done it all in one fell swoop, they would have been so horrified and ashamed of their mother that I would have lost their trust and their respect. When I finally screwed up the courage to let my hair see the light, it was six months before they knew about it. I just kept putting the wig back on every time I saw Shlomo or Aron.

I know it's difficult for anyone who hasn't lived through leaving a cult or a very insular community to understand. I am convinced that it was the right way. My children now have normal lives, with the whole world and all of its opportunities available to them. They are my biggest supporters and my closest friends. And Yosef and I are now really good friends, and respectful to one another. He's become Modern Orthodox himself and is much happier for it. We still do Pesach and Succos together, as it makes the kids happy. Our relationship now only proves what I knew all along, that he was blameless for my misery. He was a victim too. Batsheva's therapist said she had never seen such an amicable separation in her life. Usually, when a parent leaves the community, their children cut them dead. They are too indoctrinated. I evaded that fate by making that trek back to Monsey for six interminable years. Sometimes, on the drive back, my hands would shake and silent tears would run down my face. I did the drive anyway.

Those first months, I was barely functioning. I may have looked sane, but I was not. I was so filled with rage, confusion, and fear. Yet, through the haze of my misery, something stronger emerged. My will to create a life, to build something I could be proud of, saved me. My determination drove me and compelled me to take each frightening step.

CHAPTER ELEVEN

My days became surreal as I journeyed from the eighteenth century to the twenty-first and back again. During the evening, I would do homework with the kids, we would have dinner together, and things proceeded mostly as normal, but during the day, I was slowly acclimating to modern life.

Suddenly, I was building a shoe brand. I still hadn't decided what I would name it. I couldn't decide exactly who I wanted to become. Did I still want to be Talia? I had given myself that Hebrew name when I was eighteen so that I could fit in and get a better shidduch. I certainly didn't want to be Hendler anymore. Hendler was my prison name, a reminder of how powerless I had been, how trapped and alone. But what should I call myself? I had a moment of divine inspiration and chose "Haart." My maiden name is Leibov, and in Hebrew, "lev" means heart. It felt like a tribute to my past but on my own terms: modernized, reborn. I added the second *a* because I thought it was chic.

After a few weeks, I switched my first name back to Julia. Now that I no longer cared about fitting in, it felt right and authentic. I became Julia Haart. Miriam loved it. I loved it.

It's difficult to explain, but my entire life until that moment, I had felt itchy inside my own skin, as if it were foreign and unfamiliar. I had spent so many years trying to be something that was antithetical to my nature. Living in such perpetual dissonance made me feel as if my body was this thing that I had to stuff myself into every day. When I became Julia Haart, I became my true authentic self and suddenly my skin didn't feel stretched and misshapen; my body and my mind were finally in harmony. I felt more whole than I had ever felt before.

I made it official by ordering a sign for my door at WeWork. Thus Julia Haart LLC was born. Ephrayim did the paperwork, and I just signed what I was asked to sign. At the time I trusted him implicitly, still unused to questioning men.

I don't think anyone who hasn't experienced it can comprehend what it feels like stepping into a new world at forty-two years old. When you step into a roomful of new people, or into a new role or position, you have your history, your past, your reputation to protect you. You find mutual friends or experiences. People my age, in the outside world, have been working since their early twenties. They have social circles, people to vouch for them, people who connect them to the global community. They have high school friends and college friends and work friends and neighborhood friends. They exist because people know of their existence. Until the end of my forty-second year, I did not exist. I could point to no one who knew me. I couldn't say, "Look at my reputation. Look what I was able to accomplish at this company, in this position." I had no one to attest to my character. I was a zero. A nonexistent, invisible, time-traveling, clueless woman, unceremoniously hurtling herself far outside her comfort zone into the vast unknown.

It was so easy for people to take advantage of me, to use me as a scapegoat. After all, I had no friends, no one who cared what happened to me, so who would defend me? It is the loneliest, most difficult thing I have ever done. Till this day, I am still having to constantly prove myself. With every success those voices grow quieter and quieter and my reputation continues to grow, but I am still always at a disadvantage. I'm a disrupter by nature, a lightning rod for controversy, because I forge my own path and see the future with as much clarity as others see the present. Being a disrupter is a very lonely place for anyone, as people around you don't understand what you're doing and are so uncomfortable with change and the unfamiliar. Not having a strong past and a large social circle makes it all the more isolating and difficult.

My innovations constantly threaten the establishment, who have seniority and image, experience and connections on their side. I have only will, intellect, determination, and a clear understanding of what the future will bring on mine. As Gertrude Stein's brother Leo once said of the cynical visitors to their famous salon: They come to mock, and they stay to pray. People mock me until my latest innovation succeeds, and then the mockery turns to respect. Perhaps with enough success, the mockery will be replaced by trust, and I will one day come to a place where it will be vastly more difficult for my enemies to hand over my accomplishments to some man and deny my hard work and leadership. Women's accomplishments have been gifted to men since time immemorial. It's time to change that. The only way to change that is to demand recognition, to overcome our natural, innate modesty and loudly declare our victories.

There is also an advantage to being a zero at nearly forty-three. I hadn't had access to computers or social media for so many years. I was a blank slate. There were no pictures of me from high school, no silly stories for people to look at. Until that day, I didn't exist in the outside world. I could create myself totally from scratch. It was exhilarating and wonderful! I could be anyone I wanted to be. It was almost as if I was trying on different skins, deciding who I really was, what I really wanted.

I knew ageism was rampant in fashion, and I already had too many marks against me, so I thought this was something I could control. Do you know that TV show *Younger?* Well, I did that in real life. I pretended to be eight years younger than I really was. I figured 1971 and 1979 were close enough and told people I was thirty-five, and everyone believed it. I didn't want to tell anyone about my past. Plus, I figured being in my forties and just starting in the fashion world was too pathetic. And my skin, except for my face of course, hadn't seen the sunlight since I was ten years old. My body, untouched by sun exposure, was incredibly smooth, so it was an easy lie, especially since it's much easier, with creams and Botox and fillers, to make your face look younger. It's generally the body that's the dead giveaway, and mine was supple and unlined. I had no stretch marks from any of my pregnancies (the one benefit of having children so early in life is that your skin is more elastic and snaps back into shape if you're careful).

Of course, the difficulty was that I had a daughter who was nineteen and a son who was sixteen. That put a kink in my story. So Batsheva became my sister, and Shlomo became thirteen, which made more sense for a thirty-five-year-old mother, and at the time, he was quite short and cherubic looking, so everyone believed it. Bat didn't love it, but she understood that I was trying to build a future for us, and that the more successful I became, the better her life would be, so she grudgingly went along. So now, here I was, a thirty-five-year-old mystery.

The first group of people I met in the outside world were at WeWork. The company next door to mine was owned by a woman named Luisa, and I thought she was wonderful. I was a disastrous judge of character those first years. I was like a newborn. I was absurdly naïve, and I took everyone and everything at face value. She seemed so helpful, introducing me to her friends, teaching me the WeWork ropes. For the first time in my life, I had non-Jewish friends.

I also got asked out on my first date. I had passed this guy, Brian, in the hall and bumped into him in the communal kitchen on several occasions, and finally, he stopped me and, easy as you please, said, "I'd like to get to know you. Can I take you out to dinner?"

My very first date! I'd never gone on a date before with someone I myself had chosen, not for marital purposes, but for my own personal pleasure. I'd never even spent time alone with a man of my own choosing, aside from Yechiel, and even that had been for the purpose of marriage, and all we'd ever done was one sloppy kiss. I'm not sure that counts.

He owned a few liquor stores and was also an accomplished acrobat who had performed in Cirque du Soleil some years back. He was beautiful. A little over six feet tall, with dark, deliciously thick hair and green eyes and freckles smattered hither and yon. His eyes crinkled when he laughed, and he seemed to be always smiling. He was so nice and approachable. And his body! All those delicious muscles. Orthodox men aren't often muscular. Working out is considered to be too focused on the physical, so very few men in my community are fit.

Even though there were legalities to work out, I considered myself divorced from Yosef, and therefore free to do as I chose. It would not be until eight years later that we finally got a legal divorce. When I left, I told him, "I no longer want or accept to be your wife." And that was that.

Brian took me to an outdoor restaurant and had no clue that I was going on my very first date. What woman in the world hasn't been on a date by the time she's thirty-five? I still wouldn't eat unkosher food, but I would eat kosher food in a nonkosher restaurant. I remember that his shirt had two buttons undone, and I could see his sandy-colored chest hairs. We told one another our goals and dreams, and he showed me pictures of his dog, and we laughed and laughed.

He didn't try to kiss me on our first date. I must have looked too nervous. I'd never kissed someone that I'd chosen before (besides Yechiel, and he chose to kiss me without my permission). For the first time in my life, a relationship was going to be on my terms. I was so scared. On our third date we went for a walk, and he asked me if I wanted to see his new apartment. I understood what that meant, and I was shaking with excitement. I was going to have sex—with someone I was wildly attracted to! All the movies I'd watched and all the books I'd read made sex sound incredible. Sex as I knew it was awful, and about as exciting as getting my teeth pulled. I was curious to see what everyone raved about, and I figured a hot young acrobat who sold alcohol for a living would be the perfect candidate.

He had his own tiny flat on the Lower East Side that I thought was magical. I'd never owned anything of my own before. Even though I'd always brought in money, it was not mine to spend. Every purchase required Yosef's permission, and he would get notifications every time I spent a dollar. Even after I left my world behind, I lived in various hotels and never even rented an apartment. My entire life could fit into one suitcase. For now, I was the quintessential wandering Jew.

And here was this marvelous, happy-go-lucky guy, who owned his home, the master of his domain. I'd never been the master of anything! It seemed the ultimate in freedom to be able to live alone in a place that you paid for. We had a drink, and then he leaned over to kiss me, and I just went for it, tearing off his clothes, running my hands down his body. He was a good ten years younger than me, and his body was breathtaking. Whereas in the past, sex was about being dutiful and took a few minutes, with him it was all about pleasure and exploration. We drew out the pleasure for hours. He was endlessly creative and tirelessly energetic. He taught me positions I'd never seen, and I was a very apt student.

We did it right there on his couch, and I felt like a true twenty-first-century woman, except for one thing. I had sex with him with my wig on! I was still too petrified to take it off. Somewhere midway through, he realized something was up with my hair and stared at me, a bit bemused, but I just said, "Leave it alone." And then made sure his attention was directed elsewhere. I was fine with having sex with a non-Jew, but so conditioned about the fate of someone who removes their wig that, although I was stark naked, I still had it on. Brian was a wonderful first lover. He was very attentive, eager to please, and a bit in awe of me.

I learned something else about myself that night: I am a squirter. It was as if my body, now removed from a world in which I had to be constantly fake, decided to ensure I could never fake anything again. It is impossible for me to fake an orgasm, because when I orgasm, there is clear liquid evidence. I don't know who was more surprised when I squirted, me or Brian. I think it made him feel wonderful and accomplished, and I left that night feeling fantastic about life in general.

I'd been there for three hours. It was getting late now, and I was supposed to drive up to Monsey so I could see Aron. I walked into that prison house with someone's cum deep inside of me and felt so surreal. It was disconcerting, coming back there, cooking dinner, doing homework, when all I wanted to do was to go outside and scream "Sex is awesome!" to the whole world.

I couldn't tell any of my friends in the community, obviously, and the rumor was already making its way around town that I had lost my mind and spent time in hotels in Manhattan. I was still dressing properly, always covered head to toe, so no one thought I was "off the derech," meaning that I had left the path of goodness. They just assumed that my marriage was rocky and I had had a nervous breakdown or something. I had no one to confide in. I couldn't risk telling anyone anything. I had no one to share this incredible experience with. I felt elated but very, very alone.

The next time I went out with Brian, he begged me to tell him about my past. So I told him my father was a dangerous Russian mafioso who I had run away from. I said I was living under a fake name, and that I moved from hotel to hotel because my father would send goons to bring me back if he found me. How my father would have laughed to hear himself being called a dangerous criminal. But I am an excellent storyteller, and think I scared Brian. The poor guy was sure my father was going to hunt him down. He bravely said that no matter what, he wanted to keep dating me, and he looked so sincere when he said it that I felt bad. I am sorry, Brian, but at least the sex was good. We slept together one more time, and then I broke up with him. I was already bored and wanted to try sleeping with someone else.

Meanwhile, my fledgling company had hit a wall. I didn't have a production person. I didn't even know anyone in production. I had no idea where to find a shoe factory. I was lost and clueless. In the midst of desperately trying to figure out how to actually produce shoes, Ephrayim invited me to Las Vegas. He had just opened one of his shmatta stores, and he had invited some celebrities to launch it there.

Ephrayim figured it would be a good place for me to network and meet people. Yosef and I had struck our bargain, so I was free to travel. He had basically stopped asking me where I was going in general; he didn't want to know anymore.

I flew first class and ended up sitting next to a nice Jewish guy named Chris. You won't believe what he did for a living—he was in shoe production. He had worked for Nine West for years and had just recently left to start his own consulting firm for small brands. I told him about my brand, and that I wanted to make extremely luxurious shoes that made women feel special, confident, and unique. He told me that he would gladly take on my company's production. Have I mentioned that I was ridiculously trusting back then? At the time, it seemed like a miracle—and it was, in a way, because he would start me off on the right path, no matter how terrible what happened afterward was. This would be the second in a series of serendipitous meetings that would greatly impact my life.

I arrived in Las Vegas feeling like a massive weight had been lifted off my shoulders. I had been really stuck, and now, thanks to an airplane ride, I had someone who would take me to Civitanova Marche, in Italy, where he told me all the high-end shoes were made. I didn't know it at the time, but that was a lie, as most high-end shoes are actually produced in Padova, but back then, Civitanova Marche sounded as exotic as the moon, and I couldn't wait to get started making the shoes I had designed.

There was an event that night, and I wore a skintight Hervé Léger dress, and even though I was still covered head to toe, I looked fucking sexy. I'd bought designer clothes for years, just ones that a president's wife or a school principal would wear, but now I started buying some that were sexier, clothes that were tznius and still in the confines of the law but not in the spirit, some might say. Hervé was a particular favorite of mine at the time.

I walked into the room, trying to spot Ephrayim, as he had promised to introduce me to a famous female celebrity, and a giant behemoth of a man walked up to me. This giant's name was Samuel Solomson, and he looked like a lumberjack in Chasidic clothing. He was six-foot-three and physically enormous, and he had two tiny slits for eyes that were almost wholly swallowed by the vastness of his beard. Coming from my vertically challenged vantage point, he was quite overwhelming and unattractive. He was Ephrayim's best friend, and the CFO of Ephrayim's shmatta business. Ephrayim had managed to keep Samuel totally out of this shoe company, and Samuel had found out about it and was fuming at Ephrayim for hiding a business venture from him. They shared everything, and Samuel wanted to understand why Ephrayim had kept me from him. I would later learn that Samuel is extremely possessive and lives his life vicariously through the people he likes. Ephrayim was his obsession until I came around and that obsession transferred to me.

As he introduced himself, I told him I was an open book and happy to answer any questions he may have. My forthrightness disarmed him. I wasn't what he'd expected. After I'd expounded on some esoteric principle, he realized that I was a massive head rush for Ephrayim. Until he met me, he had thought Ephrayim was having an affair. That evening, he realized it was not an affair of the body but of the mind—a sexy woman who could argue about Locke and Kant.

Samuel was a total nonbeliever, just like Ephrayim, and stayed religious purely for business, as it was directly linked to his standing in his community. He also had to ensure that his daughters got good shidduchim, so he had to behave carefully. He felt as miserable as both me and Ephrayim. He was incredibly intelligent and very well read, but he was the most insecure human being I have ever met. Trapped in a world he hated, with a wife who made him miserable, he was as depressed and down as I had been. The similarity ended there. I learned that he luxuriated in his misery, loved blaming his life on fate, others—anything but himself.

I watched as his beady little eyes turned from distrustful to impressed. I wasn't the bimbo he had been expecting. I was determined, focused, steady. I did my job a bit too well. He became instantaneously fascinated, although he kept it well hidden and was a total gentleman and didn't scan my body with his eyes. He kept his glance squarely on my face, and I was grateful for it. I liked this giant, I decided. He was just like I had been: trapped in a world he didn't choose, living a life in a prison of rules. We understood each other. We bonded over our shared prison cells.

Ephrayim was thrilled that Samuel and I were getting along so well. He had been worried, and I realized that in addition to wanting me to meet the celeb, he had set this up so that I could meet Samuel, in a formal setting where Samuel wouldn't get too much alone time with me but just enough to understand a bit of who I was.

My meeting with the celeb, whom I shall keep nameless, was underwhelming. She was very polite but extremely standoffish. I think she figured that I was of no importance—some religious compatriot of Ephrayim's and therefore not worthy of her attention. She smiled and immediately found an excuse to walk away.

I also met a wonderful Armenian woman named Alin who worked for Ephrayim and was very well versed in all things fashion. She was five-foot-ten and statuesque, and she carried herself with grace and style. She had such kind eyes. We hit it off and left the party. As we wandered around the casino, I peppered her with fashion questions. She offered me a cigarette, and since I'd never had one, I tried it. It was the first and last cigarette I ever tasted.

Unbeknownst to her, she had a massive impact on my journey. Our conversation became deep and philosophical, and we somehow strayed onto the topic of the Holocaust. I made some comment as to how no group of people had ever been hated and persecuted more than the Jews. My whole life, I'd been taught that no other people had been the victim of attempted genocide. The next words she said were to have a massive impact on my connection to my beliefs.

She told me about the attempted genocide of the Armenians by the Turks. She told me to read a book called *The Burning Tigris*. I couldn't believe it. One of the precepts of my community is that we are the *only* ones who have been punished by God to the extent that genocide was attempted to exterminate the Jewish race. We were taught that it was no accident that Berlin was the birthplace of Nazism, as it was also the home of the Haskalah movement (Reform and Conservative Judaism). We were taught that our very suffering was proof of our chosen-ness. God loved us so much that when we didn't follow the laws of Torah, which were meant to keep us separate from the rest of the world, He sent Hitler to remind us, and to do the separating for us. The Holocaust was not just proof of how evil and dangerous the goyim were, it was also evidence of God's love for the Jewish people. Being the only victims of genocide was one of the cornerstones of my belief system. I was so shocked that I could barely breathe. I couldn't believe it! Another lie! Perhaps we were the only ones who the Western world had wanted to annihilate, but here was another group of people, equally innocent and good, who'd met with the exact same fate. Then I found out about Rwanda. I was so furious. Another lie. I devoured the book Alin had suggested, and a giant crack in my connection to religious Judaism was created. It was the second of three books that would help me decontaminate my mind from all of the indoctrination and brainwashing I had been subject to for the last thirty-two years of my life, the first being one I had read when I was still in the community, *Reading Lolita in Tehran*.

The flight back was as eventful as the flight there. This time, I sat next to a man who was tall and extremely handsome. He was also throwing back Bloody Marys like there was no tomorrow. His name was Arjun and he ran a hedge fund in New York. We got to talking, and after I had a few Bloody Marys myself, I shared a bit of my real story. I told him about the world I grew up in, and although I still lied about my age and my children, I told him a bit about my journey. He was fascinated. I told him about my brand, and right then and there, he said he wanted to invest in my company. I was sure it was just one of those things that people say but don't really mean, and besides, he'd had a lot of Bloody Marys. I figured he would forget all about it. Imagine my surprise when he called me the following day and genuinely wanted to invest.

I was relieved. Although I wasn't actively looking for another investor, my and Ephrayim's relationship had taken an uncomfortable turn, and I wanted to find someone else to help fund my brand. In

Las Vegas, he had proclaimed his love for me. He even wrote me a poem.

That night, he went on to tell me that he was planning on leaving his wife once his girls were off and married and in homes of their own, and that when that happened, he would marry me. He didn't even ask. He just assumed that I would be massively grateful to be his wife. Can you imagine? I was so tired of men assuming they owned me, that they could control me.

I said we would never have a physical relationship, and that he should be ashamed of himself. Let's just say it was not a pleasant conversation, and for all I knew, come Monday morning, he was going to stop funding the company. We had no contract after all, just a handshake. He owed me nothing. So meeting Arjun was fortuitous, to say the least. This is why I still believe in a higher power, call him God or fate, whatever name you like: because my entire personal exodus was filled with one miracle after another.

Arjun became my new partner, and Ephrayim agreed to personally withdraw control from the business. He apologized for his behavior and said that he would keep funding it as promised if Samuel could control the money. I had just met Samuel, and he had been such a gentleman. He wasn't Ephrayim, I told myself. He was a mensch. I thought I was set.

That same week, Luisa from WeWork introduced me to a fashion photographer named Tom, who was quintessentially midwestern, with perfect manners, a bit of a drawl, blond hair, and blue eyes. Tom was in his late twenties. He invited me to go to this bar called PDT (short for Please Don't Tell), which is one of the only speakeasies left in Manhattan, accessible only through a phone booth in a hot dog stand. He ordered me exotic drinks with marvelous names, and I tasted hush puppies for the first time that night. By this point in my life outside, I had gained a good eight pounds. I was happy and no longer trying to starve myself.

Tom was so gentle and beautiful. We rubbed our legs against one another's sitting on those bar stools, our bodies touching slightly, ever so slightly. We walked a bit afterward, and we kissed, and his lips were so warm and firm, exploring my mouth. I'd never really spent any time kissing anyone, and it was marvelous, just kissing, with the cool night air caressing my skin. We said good night, and I walked away feeling so light, so full of hope for the future.

I'd still only had sex with one person (besides Yosef), and I was eager to try it again with someone else. Sex would have to wait, though, as I had no time for dating or socializing without the express purpose of helping my brand. Chris, my new shoe production manager, and I met and made a deal (again with just a handshake—no paperwork and no contract; I didn't know any better). I would pay him a salary and a commission on each shoe sold if he introduced me to a factory in Italy and convinced them to make my shoes.

Chris came through, and within three months, I was off on an Italian adventure. It was the first time I'd left the country alone, other than for seminary. Even though Chris was technically traveling with me, we weren't seated together, and I had no responsibility to entertain him. And he worked for me, not vice versa.

My God, how I love to fly. Even today, though I sleep more often on a plane than in my fabulous penthouse, I still love it. The feeling of adventure, of heading toward some exciting unknown, has never gotten old. I love traveling alone, eating alone. My whole life had been spent surrounded by people who I had to obey and serve and take care of. Being alone was a privilege I didn't take for granted. It felt so incredibly extravagant. I so zealously guarded my solitude that it was two years before I would let anyone share my bed with me. Until then, I would have sex with my current boyfriend and then kick him unceremoniously out of my bed.

Before Chris took me to Civitanova Marche, we stayed in Florence, because Sergio, the product manager we'd be working with, lived there. I had to convince Sergio to take me on as a client, so I took them both to a restaurant that Chris had recommended and plied Sergio with wine and compliments. I quickly figured out that it made sense to stay in the finest hotels and take the largest suite, so that no one would think to question the financial stability of either me or my fledgling company. I dressed conservatively but very elegantly. It is a method that has never failed me.

Fake it till you make it is my modus operandi, and it is actually found in the Torah: "Meetoch shelo leshmah bah leshmah," which means "What's not for its own sake will come to be for its own sake." Do something over and over, even for the wrong reason, and eventually it will be real and true.

Sergio was a rabbit of a man: timid, shy, tall, and stooped, as if all the cares of the world weighed heavily on his shoulders. He had a very negative, can't-do attitude, which I quickly found is endemic in the fashion industry, especially in Italy. The first answer is always a no. Luckily for me, I am impervious to the word. I don't hear the word "no." No, to me, is a slow yes.

I told Sergio I wanted to make heels out of stone, and I wanted to make a real Murano-glass slipper. I had so many ideas. The answer to each of my queries was a very glum no. I just smiled and said, "Well, let's see." Sergio and Chris would look at one another, and it was clear they thought I was a crazy, but hey, I was paying, and they were more than happy to take my money. My ideas always sound impossible until they work.

I wasn't even remotely disheartened by his wet-blanket attitude. I was here in the city of Florence, walking the same streets that the Medicis walked, and if that wasn't a miracle, I didn't know what was. I had read all about Cosimo and Lorenzo de' Medici, and how they had championed art and science in the face of the likes of Savonarola, a religious fanatic who sounded frighteningly like some of the rabbis I knew. I felt a connection to this Italian family because they fought for intellect and art over religious zeal—freedom of expression against the pernicious closed-mindedness of fanaticism.

I wandered the city, an adult in mien but not in attitude. I was a little kid, fascinated with the world around me. That first trip was solely to meet Sergio, but I had tacked on two extra days so that I could see the city. I went to the Uffizi Gallery and stared, mesmerized, at Michelangelo's *David* at the Accademia. I walked around the

Palazzos Medici and Pitti. I imagined their lives back then and marveled at the beauty that surrounded me. I took literally nothing for
granted. Everything was so astounding! I must have looked so funny,
wandering the streets in perpetual fascination, dazed and overwhelmed by the grandeur of it all.

My last evening at the Four Seasons, the hotel was filled with the
sounds of laughter and lively music. It was an Italian wedding. I'd
never been to a non-Jewish or even an irreligious Jewish wedding,
and it was incomparable. The bride was dancing with her incredibly
hot Italian groom. They just looked so happy, and everyone there
seemed to be having so much fun. I looked on—a bit wistfully, I
suppose—and before I could get out of there, one of the guests,
clearly a groomsman, walked over and asked me if I'd like to come in
and join them.

It was a small wedding party, probably no more than sixty people,
and to someone like me who was used to giant weddings filled with
four-hundred-plus people at minimum, it looked so much more real
and authentic. The people clearly wanted to be there. This wasn't an
onerous task they had to fulfill a couple of times a month. This was
a true celebration, honoring love.

It didn't even occur to me to say no. I accepted with alacrity and
eagerness. I wanted my life to be like this: normal, with men and
women interacting as if they'd known one another forever. No awkwardness, no stolen glances between thick, dreary curtains. I tried to
imagine what it would be like to be one of them, to have lived like
this from the time I was a child. It seemed so glorious and free and
open. I wanted so badly to be part of it, even if only for a moment.

I will never forget their kindness, though I have long since forgotten their names. They all welcomed me in, the bride and the groom
and everyone. Most of them spoke some rudimentary English. They
all complimented my shoes. I told them about my fledgling brand,
and we drank and danced, and they just took me in, a total stranger,
alone in a hotel. It was one of the most fun nights of my life. It was
also the first time I had a one-night stand! As the party was winding
down, the groomsman who had let me in asked me if I'd like to go

for a walk along the river. We wandered the river and laughed and talked about absolutely nothing. I was feeling too languorous to make up a story about myself, so I just told him not to ask any questions and to tell me all about himself instead. I loved hearing about his life.

He looked exactly as I had imagined an Italian would look from the books I'd read and the 1960s movies I'd seen. He was quite tall—slightly over six feet—and lean, and his arms were muscular and tanned. His Mediterranean skin was beautiful, caramel and unlined. He was thirty-three years old and a lawyer, and he was impeccably dressed. His wavy brown hair looked thick, and I wanted to run my fingers through it, to touch the superfine wool of his suit. I was so curious what his skin would feel like. We probably walked around for an hour and a half, and then, feeling very courageous, I asked him if he wanted to come upstairs. I didn't even bother pretending that it was for a drink. He answered by kissing me deeply, and without saying another word, hands intertwined, we made our way to my room. It was so odd getting undressed in front of a total stranger, watching a man I didn't know at all removing his clothes. It felt wild and daring, and I was so proud of myself for having had the guts to invite him in. There was always the issue with the wig, which was annoying, but I was still too afraid to take it off. He tried removing it, bemused as to why a woman would be wearing a wig while totally naked, but like before, I made sure to divert his attention to other body parts, and he left my head alone.

The sex wasn't great. I felt deflated and yucky. The minute it was over, I wanted him out of the room. Clearly, one-night stands weren't for me. I wanted to be alone, to relive this marvelous day, to savor every delectable detail, and here he was, a large, naked man, intruding on my treasured aloneness. He had promptly fallen asleep after he'd come, and I had quite a difficult time in waking him. He was far from pleased to be unceremoniously kicked out of my room, but he was a gentleman and left without argument.

I flew back to New York, having secured Sergio as my product manager on the ground. I would return the following month, drawings in hand, and begin the process of working with a factory to make my creations a reality.

When I returned to New York, I was surprised to find that the rent at WeWork hadn't been paid. Ephrayim was supposed to be paying it directly, and he hadn't said a word to me. I had yet to spend any real time with Samuel, and I realized I had better fix that, as dealing with Ephrayim was clearly not an option, and he wasn't fulfilling his part of the deal.

Samuel and I met at the rooftop bar of the Library Hotel. I loved the names of the drinks: Tequila Mockingbird and Catcher in the Rye. I'd read both those books, and now here I was, sipping drinks named after them on a rooftop, like a proper Manhattanite. That week, I had tasted shrimp for the very first time and was blown away by how delicious it was. I didn't feel even remotely guilty. I was still modest in dress, with a wig on my head, but eating popcorn shrimp at Nobu.

My plan was to have a real heart-to-heart talk with Samuel, so we could set clear boundaries from the get-go. I may have been naïve, but I am also a fast learner. I make thousands of mistakes, but I try not to make them more than once.

I told him that I would love to be great business partners and good friends, but that was as far as it was ever going to go. I said I would never have a relationship with a business partner, and that if he was truly going to act as my CFO, I needed to hear from his own mouth that he understood this dynamic. He acted offended that I would even think that he had any other intentions. He told me he was married and had children whom he loved very much, and his only plan was to be part of a brand that both he and Ephrayim believed in. As before, he spoke respectfully and intelligently. We can really be friends, I thought to myself, and with his financial expertise and my drive and creativity, we could do something extraordinary.

Samuel seemed eager to please. I told him about the missing rent, and that Ephrayim wasn't fulfilling his part of the deal. He apologized on Ephrayim's behalf and promised to fix it immediately. Sure enough, the next day, the bill was paid.

Within three weeks, Samuel and I were texting every day. We didn't see one another often, as he was also the second-in-command in Ephrayim's shmatta business. I started to rely on him more and more to take care of the nitty-gritty financial aspects of the company. Finally feeling that it was on more steady ground, with a CFO who knew about running a successful business, I was able to go back to Italy.

The first time I went to Civitanova Marche was overwhelming. On one hand, it seemed like a dream come true. I was in a real shoe factory, with people who created actual shoes. They were turning my drawings into physical objects, and I was going to be a shoe designer in more than just name. I envisioned my own Julia Haart store on Madison Avenue, with people lining up to buy the most beautiful shoes ever made.

But the factory itself gave me pause. It was a family-owned factory called Calzatura Scarpe, and the mom and dad who ran it were intelligent but spoke no English, so I had to rely on Sergio's translations. I had a feeling that what he told me and what they told him was vastly different. I may not have known anything about shoes, but I did know quality, and this factory's shoes didn't look high-end to me at all. They assured me that the shoes on display were for a specific client and were extremely cheap, and they were completely capable of making the most exquisite shoes in the world. I had my reservations, but what did I know? As usual, not listening to my inner voice led to disaster. Every time I have ignored that inner voice, I have paid for it dearly.

Their two children—a girl and a boy in their midtwenties—were also involved in the business, and they were the most vapid and unpleasant people I had ever met. Sergio promised that they had very little to do with the business, but I left that first meeting feeling concerned about our new partners.

Sergio took me from there straight to my hotel. He said there was only one decent hotel in the area, and although it had three stars, "decent" was a bit of a stretch. It was clean; that's all that could be said about it. The part I hated the most was that the bathtub was in the middle of the room—not in the bathroom but next to the bed.

Chris had disappeared the minute Sergio took me on, but I was fine with that, because Chris was sort of shady, and I felt more comfortable with the morose and taciturn Sergio. He took me to his favorite restaurant near Civitanova Marche, set high on a mountain, and the view was breathtaking. The restaurant was owned by two sisters, one of whom took care of the service and the other who was the chef. There was no written menu. They had a farm in the valley below, and the menu depended on what they had harvested that morning. One of the sisters would read you that day's menu from a tiny notepad, and you chose from the three or four options. The food was outrageously good. I stuck to fish and pasta, as I still had never had unkosher meat, but I ate crustaceans with wild abandon. I still dream of her macaroni and cheese, although she'd probably be horrified to hear it called that. The pasta was hand rolled and served with five different kinds of cheese, one of which was scamorza, a smoked cheese that was so insanely good that I understood what a foodgasm was for the first time. I adored going there to eat. In addition to the crazy-good food, I loved the sisters, the quaint atmosphere, and the magnificent views.

I was not there to eat, however. I was there to learn. I met with mold makers, who told me how prohibitively expensive it would be to create my own deeper molds. I needed to make my own molds so that I could alter the arch of the shoe, thereby distributing the pressure points evenly across the foot, rather than having the entire weight of your body resting on the toes, causing pain and discomfort. Additionally, by making them deeper, it would allow me to embed an anti-shock, cooling gel insert to make it as comfortable and sneaker-like as possible. A shoe mold is the foundation of the structure of the shoe. Every shoe is made with molds and lasts (a foot-shaped form that determines sizing). I met heel makers, who looked at my complicated drawings and shuddered. But none of this dampened my enthusiasm. I simply couldn't fail. I knew that if I failed at this, I would have to go back to Monsey, and that was un-thinkable. This shoe brand was my road to freedom, to making a name for myself, and I wasn't going to let anything stop me.

We also needed to ensure that my shoes would be both func-tional and wearable. My first collection was predominantly plat-forms, as I found them infinitely more comfortable. I chose my materials . . . beautiful leathers, Swarovski crystals, stone treated with a special chemical and sliced so thinly that it could be wrapped around a heel. Every piece of stone was unique, which would mean every single shoe would be slightly different, like a piece of art. I found whisper-thin metals that enabled me to make a heel out of coins.

It was already summertime, and the factories would be closing in August for their summer holidays, but I wanted to have my first shoe display ready for fashion week, which, for the uninitiated, is actually a misnomer, as it's a series of fashion weeks lasting approxi-mately a month. I entreated, I convinced and cajoled, to try to get everyone working.

When I flew back home eight days later, I was significantly more knowledgeable about shoes and their makers. I'd learned so much in such a short time. I'd asked a thousand questions. I'd dug and dug. It's the way I've gotten anything done in this new world. I like to learn how things *are* so I can make them into what they *should* be. The words "this is how it's done" to me always have one more signifi-cant word attached. "This is how it's done *now*." That doesn't mean it's how it should be done. The whole world was new to me, so I had no pre-existing notions and was ready to tear it all down.

Although being new to everything has made my life extremely difficult, it has also been a tremendous help. My mind is elastic, not mired in the old ways, in tired paths that have long since lost their efficacy. I am a disrupter, because I take nothing as a given and never assume that the old way is the best way. I think that's so important in life. It's not about your age; it's about how open you are to new ideas and new ways of thinking or doing things. "Forward" means untried and untested. It means embracing the unknown. The minute your mind stops growing, evolving, accepting new concepts, you are already dead. Forget about zombies—that, to me, is the true definition of "the walking dead."

I came back home to Yosef and Aron and Miriam, my veins thrumming with excitement. My kids never once complained about my absences. They all knew why I was doing it, and they understood, in their own ways, that their lives would be better for it.

My deal with Yosef was working well. He didn't ask where I'd been, and I offered no information. We managed to live in the same house over Shabbos and weekends, without speaking to each other. We had both accepted that we were no longer husband and wife, even though there was no piece of paper stating that fact. We managed it so well, in fact, that the kids didn't even realize that we barely said a word to one another. I would still cook and serve, and then we would sing songs, and the kids would talk about their week. It was still difficult for me to look Yosef in the face, even though it wasn't his fault in any way, as he still felt like the physical embodiment of my servitude, and it felt like walking back into prison every time I drove up the driveway, but we managed it.

The business, however, was hitting another major problem. Ephrayim's money was coming in trickles; Arjun's investment couldn't cover everything. I had to pay in advance for molds and lasts, materials, and labor, and I was having difficulty paying on time. I texted with Samuel constantly about getting more money from Ephrayim. But he wanted to text about philosophy and books. He told me about his family, his relationships, his problems, and I became his unpaid shrink.

When I got back from Italy, I realized things had gotten serious. The company wouldn't survive without funding. We certainly wouldn't be making money for at least another year. Even if, on my first fashion week, I managed to sell anything, it would be about five pairs of shoes. And then we had to produce them, which takes an average of six months. And then stores have ninety days before they must pay. Without investment, my company would die before it even started to live.

When I told Samuel about my financial problem, he said that he felt confident that we could make real money, and that being in fashion was such fun for him, and so different from the Chasidim he had to deal with daily, that it was worth it to him to ensure its success. I was surprised. I had assumed that Ephrayim had all the money, and that Samuel was just his number two. I was wrong. Samuel was adept at hiding wealth.

I didn't know about his shady dealings back then. He told me that he had made his money investing in real estate, and my regard for his business acumen grew. If he could accomplish that without an education, without daddy's money (Ephrayim's money was inherited), then he must indeed be an excellent businessman. He offered to put $1 million into the company. *One million dollars.* That would certainly see us through until we started making sales. I was so grateful. He wasn't just spouting words of encouragement; he was putting his hard-earned cash into the business. Little did I know how much that money would actually cost me. He swore up and down that it came with no strings attached except that he would be in charge of the finances, and we agreed and shook hands.

Ephrayim transferred his ownership (on a napkin that said, "Samuel can have my shares in JH"), and that was that. We now co-owned the company. I would own 51 percent, and the only person who would get to make decisions about it was me. Samuel held the purse strings, though, so he did have significant control. His financial validation meant a lot to me. I wasn't exactly a safe bet, with my lack of experience, but I was so good at the design part, and at selling my vision, that he chose to invest. Not many people would have, I thought to myself.

But partnering with Samuel had costs. I would try to not get impatient with the thousands of texts he bombarded me with daily. It wasn't easy. His neediness was distracting. All I wanted was to focus on my business and spend time with my children and occasionally have sex with someone. I had neither the time nor the inclination for a best friend. But at least he hadn't ever said anything remotely inappropriate, and his interest in me seemed to be purely in terms of friendship and the money we could make together. He hated his life, his community, his father, his brothers, and his wife. I sympathized with the misery, but I couldn't stomach his passivity. He never did anything about it. In my deepest, darkest misery, when I was slowly starving myself to death, I had never complained, never taken anyone into my confidence. I'd known I had to save myself and that no one would do it for me.

I spent thousands of hours trying to encourage him to make changes in his life. He was also extremely sensitive. If I didn't answer a text immediately, he would call a dozen times until I responded. He was so difficult, greedy, always demanding more and more of my mental concentration and my time. He complained that our friendship was one sided, and that I never confided in him, and that it was always him doing the talking. I told him that all I wanted to talk about was my business, and that I wished he could focus more on that and less on our friendship.

He didn't deposit the $1 million he had promised immediately, or all at once. He kept it coming irregularly, so that I was always worried when the next amount would be deposited and whether I would be able to pay my factories on time. I understand now that it was his way of keeping control, of ensuring that I would have to call him to remind him to put in the next sum, a way of making sure I kept on saying please and thank you.

Each time I went back to Italy, I learned more and more about the shoemaking process, and I was getting concerned that the shoes wouldn't be ready on time. I threatened and cried, because I had no legal recourse if the factory didn't deliver, and no contract to protect myself. Because I was an unknown entity, they had made me put 80 percent up front, so I only had the 20 percent I had yet to pay as my bargaining chip. I just prayed that they would be done on time. I figured if I nudged them enough, they would finish the shoes just to get rid of me.

The big question was where I was going to launch my brand. I googled "fashion week" and saw that there were four cities where the event reigned: New York, London, then Milan, and finally, all of it culminated in Paris. To me, Paris epitomized fashion. I'd read numerous books of the storied ateliers that had made Paris so central to the fashion world. That would be the city where I would launch my brand.

I decided to go to fashion week in New York and Milan to see what fashion week was like, because I knew nothing about this world and this industry, and I had to gain as much information as quickly as I could. I had no idea how to get invited to any fashion event. I had no clue how to get in to see a show. I just thought I'd go and figure it all out. The factory owners had sworn on the lives of their unpleasant offspring that they would deliver the shoes in time for Paris Fashion Week. The downside was the fact that the first time I would see the shoes would be when I arrived in Paris for my presentation.

New York Fashion Week in September of 2013 was my very first. Tom, my photographer "friend," got an invite to the *Vogue* kickoff party, and he told me he wanted me to come as his plus-one so that I could meet some of his "influential" fashion friends. One was an actor who was known for his style and was always being photographed. The other was this guy named Victor, who was a Washington bigwig by day and owned a jewelry brand on the side. I wore a silver Hervé Léger dress. I thought I looked good, and that gave me the giant boost of confidence that I desperately needed.

Victor was Russian, so we had that in common. He had sandy-colored hair, with a square jaw and visible muscles. I couldn't take my eyes off him. I was there to meet fashion people who could help my brand, and I kept myself focused, but it was difficult with Victor standing next to me, whispering that I looked beautiful.

The actor, whose name was Zack something, was too suave, and I was hesitant about him. He did rise in my estimation, however, when he introduced me to a giant named Alexander Skarsgård. I was impressed that Zack seemed to know famous people and imagined the actresses he could introduce me to, who might even wear my shoes.

One positive aspect of entering the twenty-first century at the age of forty-two is that you take nothing for granted, and firsts take on a deeper meaning. Newness is wasted on the young. I treasured each first I had that evening, and I had a bunch of them. At the *Vogue* party, they served warm champagne and sweating hors d'oeuvres, and I thought it was the most glamorous party I had ever been to—never mind that it was the *first* fashion party I had ever been to. I wandered around, taking note of people's clothing and looking down at their feet. The more I saw, the more confident I felt that my shoes would be a success. Everyone's shoes looked the same. Mine would be different.

Tom and his friends were heading to some after-party, and I followed. The after-party was crazy difficult to get into, but Zack managed it. I was so pleased when the bouncer looked me up and down and ushered me inside. We secured a futon, or rather Zack did, and we all sat, shoulders and knees touching, taking vodka shots and laughing and talking. Victor kept brushing against my body with his. I definitely wanted him.

We made prolonged eye contact, and that lead to another first: we ended up having sex in a bathroom. I could barely believe it as it was happening. It felt like a totally delicious out-of-body experience. The fact that this gorgeous younger man wanted me was mystifying to me. The party was filled with stunning women, and yet after we locked eyes, his never left mine.

It had been a magical night, but it still wasn't over. We were starving, and so we trooped, in full evening attire, to McDonald's. I'd never been to McDonald's. I'd never even had a cheeseburger, or eaten unkosher meat, or mixed meat and cheese together, which is a big no-no. That night, feeling wild and totally reckless, I ate my first cheeseburger. It tasted like heaven.

We sat around the Formica table, the men in suits with ties loosened, me still in my skintight silver Léger, and as we munched on burgers, Tom taught us how to do the "cups" song from *Pitch Perfect*. We laughed over nonsense until almost 2:00 A.M. I was too excited to be tired, but I still had to drive home, because I was supposed to spend the night in Monsey.

When I got back to my car, I noticed dozens of missed calls from Samuel. His messages claimed that he was very concerned that someone had harmed me. His last messages were fully panicked. I texted him back saying that I was OK and driving back upstate. Thirty seconds later he called me, and I had to replay the entire evening to him—who I met, who could help the brand, what connections I had made. Of course, I left Victor out of my story, and I managed not to fall asleep as I drove.

The next morning, I made breakfast before I got Aron off to school. I whirled around the kitchen, reliving moments from the night before. Aron and I laughed, and he told me about his favorite teacher, and it was a glorious morning. I even managed to get out of the house before Yosef came home from synagogue. It would have ruined the magic of that moment and my night of incredible firsts.

CHAPTER TWELVE

Then it was off to Milan for fashion week. I wasn't sure exactly what I would do once I got there. Whereas in New York City I had made a few acquaintances, I knew no one in Milan. I knew Sergio couldn't help. He clearly wasn't fashionable, nor did he attend fashion events. Besides, he was such a wet blanket.

I looked at the fashion week schedule and managed to convince a hotel concierge to tell me where one of the shows was being held—Alberta Ferretti—and strode into that show as if I belonged there, and it worked. I was still wearing my wig, but only another religious Jew would ever be able to tell. I was dressed very stylishly, in a Miu Miu dress, and I walked around with such an air of confidence that no one asked me if I belonged. The show itself was a bit of a letdown. There was so much waiting and then just a few minutes of actual clothes. I didn't want it to end. "More clothes, more deafening music, please," I wanted to request. I walked back to my hotel with a spring in my step. My very first show!

I didn't want to lose a single opportunity or new experience. Here I was, in a stately old hotel, in the epicenter of Italian fashion, so, of course, I wanted to explore. I walked down Via della Spiga and Via Sant'Andrea. I stopped in Gucci, Prada, Hermès, marveling at their grandeur, dreaming of having my own designs gracing the street. I ate an anchovy sandwich in Cova, which I had read about being a must-stop destination in Milan. This trip, I didn't frequent museums and historical monuments. It was a fashion adventure through and through.

I walked down Via Montenapoleone where, a mere two years later, my designs would indeed be gracing La Perla's windows, but at that moment, it was enough to just wander the streets alone, watching beautiful, fashionable people who all looked like they had important places to go and powerful people to see. As I was walking, I noticed the woman in front of me. She was at least five-foot-ten and had a perfect body. And she was wearing the most glorious, skintight black leather leggings I had ever seen. I was enchanted.

I followed her for blocks, mesmerized by her pants. I had never in my life worn pants, hadn't even considered it. I had made many changes in my life but hadn't yet crossed that line. Finally, feeling utterly silly but quite determined, I went up to her and asked her where she got her leather leggings. I gushed about how beautiful they were, and though she was clearly a bit baffled, she didn't brush me off and instead told me that she had recently purchased them from Saint Laurent. I knew Saint Laurent was on Montenapoleone, so I went straight there. I wasn't sure what I was going to do, whether or not I would have the courage to buy them, but I just wanted to see them, to try them on in the privacy of a dressing room.

I walked into YSL, and there they were, in all their glamorous glory. The thinnest, tightest, sexiest pair of black leather leggings I had ever seen. I ran my hands along the creamy, supple leather, marveling at its softness. I inhaled the scent, and my hands shook as I asked a store assistant if I could try a pair on. I looked at myself in that dressing room mirror, and I couldn't stop staring. My butt looked so nice and perky, encased in supple leather that felt more natural and right than any long, buttoned-to-the-neck polyester dress from my old life had ever felt. They were perfect. They represented everything I was still too afraid to do. I wanted them. I needed to have them. Those pants belonged with me, their siren call reaching deep into my psyche, stronger than my fear. I paid for them with great trepidation. I'm sure the assistant thought I was nervous because they were so expensive. If she had only been able to read my mind and understand that this was the absolute first pair of pants I had ever purchased, I'm sure she would have been gobsmacked.

I walked directly back to the hotel, looking as furtive and guilty as if I had been carrying cocaine. It *was* contraband in that bag—the devil's handiwork. The fact that God punished those who uncovered their bodies had been so thoroughly drilled into me, I couldn't imagine that it wasn't true. I got to the hotel room, dropped the bag with the leggings on my bed, and ran right out, unable to look at my naughtiness. I don't even remember what I had for dinner, but finally I had no choice. I had to go upstairs and decide what to do with the evidence of my sin.

I laid them out on the bed, and the pants and I stared at one another. The pants, defiant and sensual, daring me to be bold and brave. I was afraid to even touch them. But no matter how hard I tried, I couldn't stop staring at them. "You are as bad as Yosef has always said you are," I told myself. Somehow, in my mind, to put these on, to wear them in public, would be more shameful than the sex I had had in that bathroom. Obviously, that was a giant no-no, but I considered myself no longer married to Yosef, and non-Jews didn't really count in Jewish law the same way Jewish men did. It was somehow easier to stomach having sex than it was to put on those pants. Fear is rarely rational, especially if it comes from years of indoctrination and mental abuse.

I barely slept. I spent the night tossing and turning and dreaming of the ways God would punish me if I wore those pants. It wasn't until two days later, the day I had to go back to New York City, that I decided, Fuck it! If I'm going to die, at least it will be on my own terms, in the most magnificent leather leggings ever made. This was the most momentous first of all.

I put them on. They were long, but I tucked the excess length into my boots. I looked fabulous except for the sweat pouring down my face. My entire body was perspiring, and I was so afraid to go outside that I could barely breathe. It took me a while to get the courage to go out of the hotel room. Before I walked out the door, I called all my kids to say goodbye. I figured that there was a strong chance that God would kill me, so I didn't want to die without say-ing goodbye. Of course, I didn't call and say, "Hi, guys. I think I'm going to be killed by God today, so live good lives." I just told them that no matter what happened, I would always love them and be with them.

And then, I opened the door and walked out of my room. I walked around Milan in a daze, waiting for some assassin to jump out of a store and stab me. I watched the cars carefully, wondering which one would mow me down, punishment for being so improp-erly attired. I didn't walk into a single store. I didn't notice a single store window. I just wandered the streets and, with each passing mo-ment, gathered courage and strength. That walk was the single most difficult, courageous act that I've ever done. In walking around, I was defying years of brainwashing, years of conditioning.

Those pants changed everything for me. I still wouldn't allow my-self to be photographed in pants, as I was afraid that if Yosef saw a photograph of me in pants, he would be so enraged that he would refuse me access to Aron. I didn't wear low-cut tops, that was still going a bit too far, but those pants had broken down the wall of my fear. Freedom had touched my shoulder that day, and I would never be the same.

Finally, it was time to head to Paris and premier my shoes. I knew no one there, so I followed the only strategy I could think of. I would stay in the chicest, most expensive hotel, in a giant suite, which would double as my presentation room. I thought that if people could see the shoes (which even *I* had still not seen in real life) in such a glamorous, expensive setting, they would be impressed, and someone might take a chance and order a pair. I had asked around, and it was clear that the fanciest hotel was the George V. I booked a massive suite that cost thousands of euros a night and waited impa-tiently for the shoes, which were supposed to arrive with Sergio the next day.

You cannot fathom my excitement when he walked through that

door. I tore open the boxes, and, my God, the shoes were beautiful. I lovingly cradled each one in my hands, marveling at the fact that my ideas, once ephemeral and intangible, were now real, solid shoes. I will admit that I cried a little when I saw them. There were some covered in Swarovski crystals, some that had my gold-coin heels (which weighed significantly more than I'd been promised), and sexy cowboy boots that had steel-toe embellishments and scallops on top but were very form-fitting and feminine. I had always loved cowboy boots, as they reminded me of my beloved Austin, but I hated how they were bucket-like in their width. I could fit three of my legs into a traditional cowboy boot. My version was fitted to the leg, and of course, being a JH shoe, was made with a platform and a sky-high heel.

The deal with the factory had been that they would make two sample sets, one in my ridiculously small size, and one in the traditional size 37, which is the sample size. I was going to be the emissary for my company and wear my shoes everywhere. I'd be a living, breathing one-woman PR machine.

The room was beautiful and filled with glamorous marble columns. I placed some of my most precious shoes on top of those, and then used some other surfaces to elegantly display all of them around the room. It was lovely and chic and unexpected.

I only had two problems. The first was that half of the shoes were unwearable. I tried on one of the 34s, and the heel promptly broke. The factory, of course, assured me that it was because these were not for wearing, but just prototypes, and that it was the way things were always done, and you cannot wear prototypes. It seemed highly suspicious to me, but what did I know? And besides, they were all I had. I just hoped that no one would ask to try them on. Thankfully, the cowboy boots were fine, and so I planned on wearing them as much as possible.

The second and more pressing problem was figuring out how I was going to get anyone into the room to look at those shoes. I didn't know any PR or fashion people; I didn't know anyone at all. So I sat in the lobby of the George V, dressed to the nines and wearing my fabulous boots, in the hopes that someone would strike up a conversation with me.

Every morning I would go downstairs and sit in the lobby. So that I didn't look totally pathetic, I would move from the lobby to the bar and back. For three straight days I sat there and tried to look busy and interesting. I was starting to get very disheartened when, on day four, my luck took a turn. I was looking particularly chic that day, and this really well-dressed man sat down next to me and started talking to me.

We had been laughing and talking for some time when he got up and said he had to go to this fashion event being held that night. It was for some company whose name starts with a *B*. Bottega? Berluti? Balmain? I cannot recall. He asked if I wanted to join him. My enthusiastic yes surprised him, I'm sure. Little did he know I had been sitting in that lobby for four days for precisely this purpose.

We hopped in a cab together, and when we finally got to the event I could hardly breathe. I was here. I was not exactly sure where "here" was, but I was here nonetheless, at my first Paris fashion event. I wandered around, looking at all the people who clearly knew one another, and I felt so down. What now? I was so far behind. I had lost so many years, so much time. Could I ever catch up? Could I ever be as confident and carefree as these people here? There were several rooms and two floors, so I wandered around, smiling and trying not to look as forlorn and lost as I felt.

I was upstairs, in a tiny room that was a bit less crowded than the others, when a woman came and stood next to me and struck up a conversation. She was in her late fifties, attired in the kind of style I associate with first ladies and members of the royal family: proper and expensive. Very classic. She looked down at my shoes and asked me whose they were. I almost cried with gratitude and wanted to hug her for noticing my creations. "They're mine!" I replied, the joy and pride of it obvious in my voice.

"I understand you own them," she chuckled, and added, "but whose brand is it?" That was all the incentive that I needed. I launched into the story of my brand and regaled her with details of the different materials I was using, to be truly unique in the market-place. She opened her handbag and took out a card and proceeded to change my life.

"Have your salesperson call me so that I can set up an appointment," she said. And I stood there, mouth open, nodding my consent as I stared at the card in semidarkness. I couldn't read the small lettering, so I didn't know if she was a buyer or a media person, but either way, she seemed to be interested in seeing the shoes, and she had said she would come to my showroom. We did a double-cheek kiss, which I was still getting used to, and she left.

With that connection made, I gave myself permission to leave the party. It wasn't until I was in a taxi back to the hotel that I was able to really look at her card. It read: "Patricia Clark, Shoe Buyer of Harrods." Of all the people, at all the events, God had placed the one person most likely to help me right beside me.

I, of course, didn't have a salesperson, I was a one-woman show, but that wouldn't do, so I cajoled poor Sergio, who was about as good at sales as I am at sailing, to pretend to be my sales manager. The following morning, we created an email for him, and he was now officially christened our new head of sales. He wrote the email to Patricia, and we both waited, constantly checking our phones, for her to reply. She answered within the hour and asked to come that afternoon to see the shoes. I danced around the room and hugged Sergio, who rewarded me with a rare smile.

When Patricia arrived, being a 37 herself, she asked to try one on. I prayed with all my might that the shoe wouldn't break while she was wearing it, but luckily, it wasn't one of the bad ones, and she walked around the room marveling at their beauty. She spent over an hour wandering the room and picking up shoes. She then asked me to send her the line sheet (I learned later that a line sheet listed the shoes and their retail and wholesale prices, with little check boxes for the buyer to indicate the shoes that they wanted to buy), and that her assistant would send over their order in the next few days. This was really happening.

Sergio was gobsmacked, but we decided not to celebrate until the actual order came in. We tried very hard to contain our excitement until we saw the order. Although it felt like forever, the order came through four days later. She wanted 250 pairs. It was unimaginable. My shoes were going to debut in Harrods. She asked for exclusivity, and she was only buying them on consignment, which meant there was no money for us unless they sold, but she was putting them in *Harrods*. And they would advertise my brand and send emails to help launch it.

The next day, I walked around Paris in a daze. I wandered the streets marveling at the magnificent architecture, the numerous cafés that grace the city.

That first trip, I was so focused on having someone see the showroom that I'd barely left the hotel until the very last day. I ended my one day of sightseeing at the Musée d'Orsay and was overwhelmed by the beauty of it all. Though my taste is predominantly for modern art, and some contemporary art as well, my first love was Impressionism. This was probably due to the fact that I loved Gertrude Stein, who championed the movement, and I knew that the Impressionists had been huge disrupters in their time. The Académie des Beaux-Arts in Paris had refused to show them. They had broken the rules of art that existed. I felt such a strong connection to those brilliant disrupters. I wandered Rodin's garden and daydreamed that I had met all these incredible creators and artists. Paris was so overwhelmingly beautiful. I couldn't wait to get back.

I flew home, half-panicked and half-euphoric. Samuel and I celebrated at Aquagrill, where I ordered an entire tower of crustaceans and taught him how to eat oysters and snails. I felt very proud of my newfound skills.

I told the kids about the orders, and they couldn't believe it. Honestly, none of us thought I'd be able to pull it off so quickly. Miriam was ecstatic, and though Aron didn't quite understand what was exciting about a couple hundred pairs of shoes and he'd never heard of Paris, he joined in the merriment.

Batsheva, who was living in Israel, wasn't as excited. She was still upset with me, and rightly so, for not being there for her properly in her first year of marriage. Her entire life, we had spoken every day for hours, and now I was rushing around, opening a business, traveling, and doing God knows what. She was a newly married woman who, although happy with Ben, wanted to talk with her mom. She felt abandoned and hurt, and I felt so bad that I couldn't be there for her the way she wanted and needed me to be.

Back then, I felt more alone than ever. I had never fit into the uber-religious world I left and had always felt like an outsider, wondering what was wrong with me. But I didn't fit into the twenty-first century either. I was living in a no-man's-land—a woman with no one to call friend and no place to call home. It was wig on in Monsey, wig off everywhere else. Yes, I loved trying all these new experiences, and I was obsessed with and fascinated by the world outside, but inside, there was so much turmoil. It's very difficult to explain. On one hand, I was happier than I'd ever been. I felt hope and joy for the first time in a very long time. On the other, I was filled with so much anger and rage at the years that had been stolen from me, at the lies I'd been taught. Those days, it was a very thin line between laughter and tears.

I can't recall the particular moment I decided to go without my wig, though I still kept my wig on in Monsey. One day I was simply ready to let it go. I also wore a long skirt in Monsey, and skintight leggings the rest of the time. I was still between two worlds and not fully in either. It was unbearably lonely in the beginning, but loneliness was far better than despair. Loneliness I could learn to deal with and move on.

Plus, I had two major logistical issues that needed to be addressed. First and foremost, I needed to figure out how to produce these 250 pairs of shoes, and to produce them on time, and to make sure that they were wearable. I didn't trust Tweedledum and Tweedledee at Calzatura Scarpe, the factory in Italy. And I knew I had only one chance with a place like Harrods, and I couldn't mess it up. The second issue I had was how to get people to know about the shoes so that they would go and buy them. Harrods is a behemoth of a store. Patricia had ordered thirteen styles—more than half my collection. But still, thirteen styles sitting alone among thousands of famous brands would be hard to find. I desperately needed PR and marketing, and I didn't have any.

I imagined my shoes, alone and forlorn like me, competing with the hundreds of brands that had been born years and years before— names people recognized and knew and respected; brands that weren't starting from zero. That was me. I was a total zero, an unknown entity. You cannot fathom how daunting and awful that feels. I was a giant question mark. I couldn't bear the thought that my shoes, newly born and as unknown as I was, would be left sitting silently and invisibly on a shelf in Harrods somewhere. I needed to get the word out. I needed to introduce people to my creations, the part of myself I was sharing with the world.

I also had to design the boxes that the shoes would come in. They were beautiful: red, with my heart-shaped logo proudly displayed in the middle.

Luisa, my "friend" at WeWork, offered to make the boxes for me. Her company made merchandising items for brands. She told me that making shoeboxes in Italy was going to be prohibitively expensive, and that I should have my boxes made in India. That seemed to make perfect sense, although I didn't know at the time about shipping and tariffs and taxes and the rest, which made it actually much more cost-effective to make the boxes in the same country where you made the shoes. But at that point it made sense to me, and I trusted her and so met with a guy who had a box factory in India.

Tom, the photographer, then introduced me to a PR person named Alan. Alan also said that he was friends with Ken Downing, the head buyer at Neiman Marcus, and that he could get Ken to see my shoes the following fashion week. Ken was one of the most powerful people in the industry at the time, so it was a critical connection to make.

Alan also suggested we go to Art Basel in Miami that December, as it's a huge networking event with a lot of fashion elite and celebrities attending, and I acquiesced. I could see my sister Chana, who was living in Miami, and I was becoming obsessed with art, so off I went. Samuel was starting to get annoyed at my constant travel, as he was always wanting to meet and talk and talk, and he would literally text me hundreds of times a day with a thousand questions, but so far my methods were working, so he couldn't complain too much.

That first night at Art Basel, I wore a Christopher Kane minidress with a circular ring in the middle, holding the bralette and the skirt together. It was crazy risqué, and I wouldn't let anyone take pictures, because if they somehow got online, I feared Yosef would see them and I would never get to see Aron again. On top of that, the party was on a Friday night, which presented a big problem for me. Even though by that point I had eaten unkosher food and was wearing whatever I wanted, I still hadn't broken Shabbos. I had never turned on a light, used electricity, or gotten into a car on Shabbos. This Friday night would be *the* night, the first night that I broke the laws of Shabbos. I wasn't driving the car, and I wouldn't even open the door, because that would make a light go on, but I did get into the car and have someone drive me. It's a very slow and painful process, this deprogramming of what has been hammered into your brain from early childhood. It's mental detox, and it's frightening.

The next few months passed by in a whirlwind. It was over to Italy for shoes, back to Monsey for Chanukah, back and forth like a yo-yo, half religious Jew, half irreligious fashion designer. Every time I had to put on my wig and go back upstate, it felt like walking back into a jail cell, but I told myself that it was worth it. That one day, all of this would ensure that my children had a chance at a full, unfettered existence. So I did the drive and smiled when I walked through the door and held the emotions that were bubbling inside me at bay every single time.

On Chanukah I made latkes for the kids, and sufganiyot (doughnuts filled with caramel), and we sang songs, and the kids danced around the room with Yosef as I sat watching, and then I handed out presents. I was happy to be singing Chanukah songs with my kids, happy to get to spend some time with Aron.

I spent New Year's Eve with Tom and Victor and a few of their friends, and it ended in my suite at the Standard Hotel. Victor and I had slept together a handful of times, and we made love for the last time that night. I knew I was ready to move on. I told him that I felt myself falling too deeply for him and that, because of my situation, and my children, a real relationship was impossible, but oh, how I wished it was. I was an expert breaker-upper by that point. I was always super kind and careful with the male ego, so we remained friends.

The following week, I flew back to Italy and met with the mold makers, the heel makers, and the last makers. I made myself a total nuisance there, but I didn't care. Those shoes couldn't break when a person wore them. It was thirteen styles and numerous colors, which was hell for the factory, where they were used to making 250 pairs of each style in each color. My order was too small for them to make real money, and so they weren't pleased, but they knew, as did I, that this small order could lead to a bigger order. And so they worked with me, grudgingly, to make the shoes on time.

We had until the end of January to have them delivered to Harrods, and it was already the second week of the month. While I was there, Samuel called me, excited. He had managed to get me a meeting with someone who was a higher-up at Condé Nast and said that if he liked me, he could introduce me to an editor at French *Vogue*. I was ecstatic. The guy, Mark, wanted to meet on Tuesday, and it was Monday, so it meant that I had to hop on a plane that day and go to Paris, and then fly right back to Civitanova Marche the next morning.

Late afternoon, I landed in Paris and was ravenously hungry. I checked into the George V and went downstairs to the lobby. I decided to splurge and order myself some caviar. I had just recently tasted it for the first time, as caviar isn't kosher, and I was obsessed. It was like tiny explosions of flavor in your mouth. And the condiments—I love a condiment! I adored the blinis and the sour cream and the onions. I love complicated food that takes time to eat. I enjoyed the entire process of building my own little caviar delicacies.

I was sitting there, relishing each mouthful, when a woman came and sat in the chair beside me. She was dressed in a suit and shirt, but it wasn't a woman's suit. It was a man's suit, and it looked perfect on her. She was also clearly wearing men's shoes. I liked her unapologetic style and her bright, inquisitive eyes. She had this lovely, warm smile, and since I was sitting alone and knew no one, as usual, I smiled back.

She asked me who I was and what I was there for, and I launched into the whole story of my new brand and what made my shoes so unique, and how I was here in Paris to meet with a guy who would hopefully do a profile on me. She looked me up and down, taking in my expensive clothes, my fabulous shoes, and the fact that I was sitting in the George V, happily munching on $800 caviar, and she made a decision.

I learned her name was Emira, and she was Saudi. She asked me if I had any shoes with me, which of course I did, as I was planning on showing them to the *Vogue* editor. She asked for nothing that first day and offered to help me launch my brand. She said she was incredibly connected in Paris, and I believed her, because as we had been sitting there, at least six people had stopped by our table to say hello.

We went upstairs, and I noticed that she had a very pronounced limp. She had clearly been through some sort of trauma, and that made me like her all the more. She walked into my palatial suite, and I could see that she was impressed. Just like everyone else who met me, she assumed I was fantastically wealthy and super successful. As I said, I was my own one-woman PR show. She wandered around looking at my shoes, and I could see she really liked them, which warmed my heart. Her English was flawless, and she spoke a mile a minute, talking about taking me to shows and to meet designers and that she would make sure they used my shoes on their runways. She spun a golden web of connections and events and stores, and I drank in every word, mesmerized by the magical picture she painted. We hugged and exchanged numbers, and she disappeared into the evening as quickly as she had appeared. She seemed like a fairy godmother who had materialized out of thin air.

The next day, I waited for the editor to call me and tell me what time to meet with him. He kept changing the times and moving our meeting later and later. Finally, right as I was about to give up, he texted me and told me to meet him in his room at 10:30 P.M. I may have been clueless, but I wasn't totally stupid. I refused as politely as I could and said that that was too late for me, and that perhaps we would be able to meet another time. There was no way in hell I was walking into a male stranger's hotel room late at night. I flew back to Italy the next morning with mixed feelings about the trip. I hadn't met the Condé Nast guy, but I had met the marvelous Emira, and I had a strong feeling that I would hear from her again.

The end of January was approaching, and I still didn't have a single shoe to send to Harrods. What if my shoes weren't ready on time? What if I had to call Harrods and tell them I had nothing? It was so stressful, and of course, since this order was a consignment, I was swallowing the whole cost. If no one bought them, if they didn't appear on time or were unwearable, I would have no recourse.

I had paid most of the money to the factory up front, as they refused to work with me otherwise, and to find a new factory with so little time was impossible. Plus, Sergio told me that every factory would ask for the same, since I was an unknown entity. This was actually true, as I found out when I tried to get a new factory the following season. I had no choice but to wait and nudge and pray that the shoes would be ready on time.

I was still in Italy when Emira called. "Come to Milan right now," she said. The haute couture shows were going on, and Dolce & Gabbana was throwing a party, and she had gotten me an invite. She told me that she wanted me to meet Domenico Dolce and Stefano Gabbana. I almost fainted.

She also told me that she would introduce me to her friends who were attending, one of whom was Kara Whyte, a famous socialite from an unbelievably wealthy family with shops all over the world. She said her entire crew of very wealthy women, and a bunch of Russian oligarchs and Middle Eastern sheikhs, were all there, and that she would introduce me to all of them so that, when my shoes got to Harrods, all these ritzy people would buy them and make them popular. I was dizzy with excitement. I thanked her profusely, packed a bag, and took the train to Milan.

I asked Emira if I could pay her, or give her a percentage of royalties, but every time I brought up payment she would cut me off and tell me we would worry about it another time. This is a good lesson for anyone in business. Please always be sure that you get concrete terms in a contract, and don't accept favors from anyone, as the price you pay for favors is vastly greater than that of a straightforward business transaction. I don't take favors anymore. I like things clearly spelled out in a legally binding contract from day one. Then, however, I was bewitched—grateful, and constantly pinching myself because this fascinating and powerful woman had taken a liking to me and was taking me under her wing. I didn't understand why she was doing it; I was just very grateful that she was.

I booked a nice suite at the Armani Hotel in Milan, and she met me there and took me with her to the Dolce & Gabbana store, because I couldn't wear a different designer to the Dolce dinner; it would be too rude. We picked out a gown, and she asked me for a hundred euros, which she then passed to the shop assistant, and begged her to alter it for me before that evening. Luckily, the hem just needed shortening, and with her puppy-dog eyes and her hundred-euro incentive, Emira managed to convince the seamstress to have it ready for us and to have it delivered to the hotel.

I was just floating along in Emira's wake, following her instructions and letting myself be carried by the tide of her personality. As I was getting dressed in my room, she was smoking this funny-smelling cigarette, and I asked if she would smoke outside, as I am particularly sensitive to smells. Yes, it was pot, but I'd never smelled pot before, so how was I to know?

After the dress arrived, we hopped in a car, and I thought we were on our way to the Dolce & Gabbana dinner party, but she told me she wanted to make one stop first and directed the driver where to go in Italian. She turned to me and said, "I need cash. Take out five hundred euros right now and give it to me." She didn't ask me, she told me, and frankly, if this whole evening was going to cost me five hundred euros, it was totally worth it. Taking out cash as a form of payment seemed quirky but not crazy, and so I complied. I didn't want to offend or annoy her—and besides, I figured the fashion business was like the shmatta business, where people did deals with handshakes and paid with bundles of cash.

After I handed her the five hundred euros, I thought we would be on our way, but she told the driver to take us to the train station. I was confused, and asked her why we were going there. Were we picking someone up, perhaps? She told me to never mind, it was just a quick stop, and she was edgy and sharp with me for the first time. She tossed and turned in her seat, urging the driver to hurry, and jumped out of the car the moment we got there and disappeared into the terminal. I sat in the car, perplexed and feeling uncomfortable, very impatient to get to the dinner. It was probably fifteen minutes before she appeared at the car again, smiling beatifically, good mood restored, and told the driver to hurry and get us to the dinner.

No more was said about our odd trip, but I had a very bad feeling that she had bought drugs or some other illicit thing with my money. But all of that was forgotten the second we walked into the dinner. Domenico himself complimented me on how I wore his dress and said it looked fabulous on me. I was at a dinner party, talking to Domenico Dolce. I could not believe it.

Emira was as good as her word. She pushed and pulled me from one person to another, introducing me to everyone, talking about my beautiful shoes. She was very loud and would interrupt people who were speaking to one another, but no one seemed to mind, and they all appeared to be very familiar with her strange ways. Her hair was slicked back in a ponytail, and she didn't have a stitch of makeup on. She barreled through people, her limp and her clothing making her stand out from the elegant crowd, and with my hand secured in hers, I followed.

She was obsequious to some and obnoxious to others. She kept up a steady stream of gossip, whispering people's secrets in my ear. I was fascinated and repulsed at the same time. She told me who was cheating on whom, who had slept with whom, who was pretending to be wealthy but was actually in deep shit, and who was fabulously dangerous and connected to the mafia.

The people she was rude to, I found out later, had slighted her in some way, imagined or otherwise. She was a woman of massive extremes. She either detested someone or was wholly obsessed with them. People were either the most wonderful human on the planet or the most bestial and despicable creature on earth. And when I say that someone had slighted her, I mean that she would say something like, "Three years ago, Julia, when I was sitting at the George V, so-and-so didn't come over to kiss me, and so we don't speak to her ever." She had an incredibly tender ego—worse than any man I had ever met, and that was saying a lot.

But that night, it looked to me like everyone not only tolerated her but enjoyed her company. I was becoming more and more uncomfortable in her presence, as she was very volatile, and if someone said something that she took offense to, she would just start screaming at them. I watched as all these very elegant and civilized people took her in stride, and I told myself that I just wasn't familiar with the ways of this world, and that I should stop being so judgmental.

She indeed introduced me to Kara Whyte, who was blond and beautiful. She had the loveliest smile, which started from her eyes. She seemed kind and warm, and she treated Emira gently, like a lost soul. The way she carried herself—you cannot fake that. I've only seen it on people who have had enormous wealth their entire lives. They don't concern themselves with fitting in. They assume that whatever they are doing will be followed and copied by others, and so are supremely unselfconscious. It has always been something I admire. I had spent too much of my life trying to fit in.

I sat there surrounded by these glittering, fabulous people and marveled at how far I had come. These people were masters of the universe. They owned banks and department stores and yachts and had chalets and villas. They were media moguls and Russian oligarchs and princes of various Middle Eastern countries. They were intelligent, educated, knowledgeable, and worldly. They had been all over the planet a dozen times. I marveled at their ease and insouciance.

It was getting close to 2:00 A.M., and I had had enough. The stress of pretending that I knew what everyone was talking about was taking its toll. I wanted to go to bed. But before I left, Kara invited me for the weekend to her chalet in Courchevel. Emira and Kara's son and her boyfriend, Frederic, all urged me to accept. Chalet? Courchevel? I had certainly never been to a chalet or to the French Alps. These people were all total strangers, but then everyone in the world was a total stranger to me, so what did it matter? I accepted, and we decided to meet the following afternoon to head up to Kara's chalet.

As we were leaving, Emira said, "I told you that I will get you an entrée with the most powerful and elegant people in the world, and here you are, going to Kara's chalet after just one dinner!" She was clearly very pleased with me as well.

That night, I told her the compressed version of my story: that I was raised in a fundamentalist community and hadn't been allowed to travel or work. She never asked a single question or brought it up again. But she was always watching me like a hawk from then on, to make sure that I didn't accidentally commit a faux pas, for which I was very grateful.

Emira wanted to make sure that I had the proper attire for a weekend in Courchevel, and the next morning she showed up at my hotel to take me shopping. And by that I mean that she told me where to go and I paid for everything. She was constantly asking me for a couple hundred here and a few hundred there. I now understood why they knew and loved her at every hotel. Although I had yet to see her spend a dollar of her own, and I don't think she even bothered carrying a wallet, she was constantly gifting people money that had, mere seconds ago, been gifted to her. She tipped waiters and concierges and hotel staff and doormen with reckless abandon. I never questioned her when she told me to give her money. I would just run to the nearest cash machine and withdraw whatever sum she was demanding.

Samuel was justifiably mystified by these constant withdrawals, but Emira had gotten me an invite to Kara Whyte's home, and Samuel and Ephrayim understood what that meant, since they were in the shmatta business. Kara was renowned in their world, as her family's multibrand stores were everywhere, and Samuel was already dreaming of partnering with Kara in some new venture.

That day I bought a warm hat, a fabulous Moncler ski suit, and a bunch of sexy sweaters from Versace, Chanel, and Saint Laurent. I also bought a few cocktail dresses that I could wear with my own shoes. Emira said that every evening would be a party. Kara had a driver pick us up. We were quite the entourage: four cars and two giant vans carrying everyone's luggage.

Emira was very cold on the trip up there, making constant reference to my ignorance in the ways of the world. I was so pathetically clueless, and she seemed to derive great pleasure from making me feel inadequate and ignorant. It was just the two of us in the car, and she tormented me the entire ride up there. I finally asked her what her problem was, to which she replied, clearly miffed, that it had been over two hours since I had thanked her. She actually said, "You should be thanking me every single hour!" And she didn't mean it figuratively. She was completely serious.

Kara was the most perfect hostess, and her house was lovely. She had a few Damien Hirsts scattered about, and a magnificent Andy Warhol. I was in awe. I was fascinated by art, and here was a home that had works that I had just come to learn about, by artists I had only seen in museums. I had never been in a home that embraced art and celebrated it on its walls.

That first evening, after we had all unpacked and showered and changed, we went for dinner to this incredible restaurant where I had real fondue. One was a cheesy fondue, and the other was a kind of thick, meaty sauce, and you dipped bits of potatoes and meat and veggies into both pots. It was delicious, and such fun to eat, and there was wine and beer, and everyone drank and dunked and laughed and laughed.

The funny thing was that no one except Emira realized how clueless I was. I had read so much literature, knew so much of history and art and current affairs, that the giant holes in my experience went unnoticed or got written off because I was American. "Ah, she's an American," I'm sure they said to themselves. "Americans are ignorant by definition."

I was getting along well with everyone, but I noticed that if I spent any time with a particular person, Emira would come and whisk me away. She got very drunk and belligerent toward the end of the evening, and I became concerned. She was becoming possessive, and people looked at me with pity in their eyes, as if I was somehow responsible for her—which was exactly how I felt, because she was the reason I was there.

At one point during the evening, Kara and I sat together, and I finally got the scoop on Emira. Her father was an incredibly wealthy man in Saudi Arabia. She went to a boarding school in Switzerland with the wealthiest children on the planet. That's how all these people knew her. As teens, they had all flown around the world on their parents' private planes and thrown down $50,000 a night at clubs. It was an incredibly small, unbelievably tight-knit group of the world's most privileged people.

Kara told me that when Emira was twenty and still partying away, her father died. In Saudi Arabia, women couldn't inherit property, and her father had no sons—just a daughter, Emira. He had left no provisions for his wife and daughter, assuming his brother, who was to inherit his estate, would do the right thing and take care of his family. He did not. The week after her father died, her uncle kicked them out of their home and took away all their cars and houses. He bought them a tiny house in a poor part of the city and gave them just enough money to survive. Her mom was in her late sixties when everything was taken from her. She was uneducated, with no ability to protect herself and no legal recourse—a woman in a world ruled by men, in a country where women didn't count at all. My heart broke for Emira, and I told myself that I would be more patient and understanding with her. She had been to hell and back, and she had a good excuse for her manic behavior.

Kara told me that Emira turned to drugs when this happened. It was at that moment that I truly understood that Emira's energy was partly drug fueled, and that she was an addict. I ran into Emira a few years ago, and she told me that she recognized that she had had a drug problem and was working to overcome it. It gave me so much joy to know she was addressing this issue, because I do believe she has a good heart, and, even with all the craziness, she did really help me. I didn't know much about drugs then. I'd never met anyone who took them, and I didn't know what people on drugs looked like, or how a person found drugs or bought drugs. I didn't know that you smoke pot but snort cocaine and shoot up heroin. I was totally clueless.

Emira's limp was due to her driving high one night. When she crashed her car, everyone assumed she would die, but she had survived, with an injury that left her permanently disfigured. Apparently, I wasn't the only person Emira had taken under her wing. Kara told me that she tended to find wealthy women for whom she could open doors and provide entrée into the rarified circles of European society, and that she would live off them until she found the next person. She told me to be careful and to not give Emira too much money. Kara and I really connected that night, and I was hit with such a wave of gratitude toward this woman who had opened her home and her confidence to a total stranger and treated me as one of their own.

I considered Kara's warning, but I did feel a strong kinship to Emira and promised myself I would treat her with great respect and love.

What a tragedy to have everything torn from you by your own

uncle. It was religion once again forcing women to be subservient to men. Fundamentalists are all the same, using God as an excuse to keep women enslaved.

We went to a club after dinner, and I danced my heart out. It was my absolute first club, but of course they didn't know that, and it was much tamer and quieter than I had expected a club to be. The men all seemed to be in their fifties and sixties, and the women were a mix, a lot of younger women dancing with the older guys, and then women like Kara, in their fifties, dripping in diamonds, dancing the night away.

I'm a really good dancer, and so, put some music on and I don't feel uncomfortable or awkward at all. It's like sex. Sex and dancing are the two things in the world that have the power to still my mind. When I start dancing I let my body take over, and my constantly active mind shuts off. It's the exact same thing with sex: my mind is miraculously quiet. I also love the freedom of it, the fabulous, sensual movement. It had been forbidden for so long, and each sinuous turn felt like freedom. When I dance, I can move and no one will stop me; my body exulted.

When we finally got back that night, I fell into bed and slept like the dead. When I woke up in the middle of the night, it took me a moment to get my bearings. I thought there was a cat or a dog sleeping curled up at the foot of my bed. It was so dark, and the blackout shades didn't allow for any light. It took my eyes a moment to focus and realize it wasn't a cat or a dog; it was Emira! She was fast asleep, curled in a fetal position on the edge of my bed.

She was sleeping with me without actually sleeping with me. It felt like a huge invasion of my personal space, and I felt violated. She hadn't asked or knocked. She had snuck in while I was fast asleep and lay down on my bed. I was furious. Then I had a thought. What if she was in love with me? I badly wanted to be her friend, but I couldn't be any more than that. I didn't feel that way about her at all. And she knew I was straight. I could never be with anyone unless I wanted to be and was sexually attracted to them. I couldn't sleep with someone for any other reason. I had spent a lifetime sleeping with someone out of a sense of duty, and I had promised myself that the only people who would ever get to touch me again would be the ones I genuinely wanted.

I crept quietly to the bathroom, got dressed, and made my way out of the room without waking her. I didn't want to make a scene, and I had already started questioning myself. What if she had gone to my room by mistake? Her room was just one floor up. She had been so drunk last night. What if she didn't even realize it was my room and had just fallen into the first bed she had found? What if I was making a huge drama over nothing? I found a couch to sleep on and decided to play it by ear, to see how she acted the next day.

The next morning everyone was leaving, and Emira and I said our goodbyes as well, and she promised that she would do everything in her power to help me launch my brand. We made plans to keep in touch, and I flew home, my mind whirling with so many thoughts, so many experiences that I had no one to share with. I hadn't said a word about what happened with Emira. Who was I going to tell? My only "friend" was Samuel, and I didn't want to tell him anything. He would have freaked out and then given me a hard time the next time I wanted to spend time with these people. I decided I would simply process everything internally and try to learn from the experience. I was now part of a rarefied world, but I felt more alone than ever. I flew home and went straight upstate to Monsey. I had missed Aron and Miriam terribly and couldn't wait to see them again. Sheitel on. Long skirt on. All covered.

CHAPTER THIRTEEN

~

I cannot begin to explain the insanity of the next few weeks. The first group of shoes for Harrods arrived, and they were a disaster. All the heels were lopsided and some fell off. Most pairs were totally unwearable. New samples for February fashion week were starting to arrive, and they were beautiful, but unwearable as well. I had a serious problem on my hands. First, what was I going to tell Harrods, and second, how was I going to find another factory? Clearly, these idiots were incapable of making wearable shoes.

On top of that, I had ordered shoeboxes from India, and they arrived misshapen and discolored. The issue with the boxes was blamed on the shipping company. Luisa hounded me daily to pay for them, even though they were wholly unusable. I had no shoes and no boxes, and yet everyone was hounding me for payment. And they all had excuses. The shoe factory blamed it on the heel maker, the last maker, the mold maker—anyone but themselves. Trying to get to the bottom of who was actually responsible was like wading through quicksand. Sergio was absolutely zero help and just kept shrugging his shoulders and demanding payment.

No one was taking any responsibility, and I was overwhelmed and totally underprepared. I had no contracts, no means by which to hold anyone accountable. To say that every single one of those people took massive advantage of me would be a monumental understatement. I was such an easy target, and they'd played me. It was as simple as that. I wanted to scream and cry, and I had no one at all to share my frustrations with.

Samuel was totally useless. He was very busy with some huge deal that he and Ephrayim were working on. They had bought a house for the buyer from a major department store, their top client, as a bribe, so he would continue to order clothes from them. Samuel was happy to spend hours texting me about his thoughts, and the books he had read, but he didn't seem interested in helping the business. He simply put in more money every time there was a problem and told me to deal with it.

It was as though he genuinely did not care about losing money. I couldn't understand it. I told him that if he paid a little more attention to the business side of things and spent less time texting me about nonsense and trying to get me to confide in him, the company would be more successful, and his investment would be safe. But bizarrely, he didn't care. He told me repeatedly that it was the adventure he cared about, and the money was irrelevant. I realized that I desperately needed help on the business end of things, not to mention production, marketing, sales, and distribution. My shoes could be the most beautiful on earth, but if the structure of my company didn't improve, it wouldn't matter.

On top of all of this, I had the Emira situation to contend with. Every other day, she would call demanding money for her branding services. I couldn't wire it to her, because she had no bank account. She would only accept Western Union. She would demand a few hundred here, a few hundred there, and she would want it that very second. It didn't matter where I was or what I was doing.

I couldn't take the constant barrage of calls and the constant demands for money. I tried to send her a thousand dollars, hoping that if I sent a large sum, the requests would stop, but no such luck. At least four times a week I would have to find a Western Union, figure out what Western Union was closest to her in Europe, and send her money.

I discussed Emira's demands with Samuel, and we decided we had no choice. She had a whole plan for introducing my brand to the world, and so far, she had delivered on every promise she made. In addition to that, I had connected Kara Whyte to Samuel, and they were negotiating a deal. Samuel understood that Emira was crazy enough to put the kibosh on that deal if she got too upset. I felt both powerless and foolish running to wire her every time she commanded, but I had no choice.

At one point, I got so frustrated I told Samuel that I was done. No matter how great Emira's contacts and connections, never-ending stress wasn't worth it. Samuel freaked out and told me that from now on, he would go to Western Union. I happily gave Emira Samuel's number and prayed that she would leave me alone. Big, big mistake. I would pay so dearly for that mistake that it would almost destroy me.

At the same time, I was moving out of the WeWork on Madison Avenue and into a new WeWork office at Bryant Park, where I got much more space for less money, but I still needed actual business help desperately. Every time I brought the issue up, Samuel argued with me, claiming he didn't want to hire or pay a bookkeeper or a CEO. He told me that was his job. Of course, he wasn't doing his job, but I couldn't say that. I begged him to at least let me hire a sales-person and a PR firm so that we could have a strategy for the following season, and a real production person so that we could actually deliver the shoes that were ordered. He promised to consider it.

Eventually, there was no more delaying the inevitable. I had to tell Patricia Clark that I wasn't going to be able to deliver shoes to Harrods. Samuel wanted me to send the shoes we had and hope for the best. He said, better to send something, even severely flawed, than send nothing at all. I refused. In the end, I had her contact information, not Samuel, and so I did what I thought was right. I sent her a heartfelt email, crying as I wrote it. I told her the truth: that the factory I worked with had not managed to produce wearable shoes on time, and that I wasn't happy with the quality of the shoes that had arrived. I told her that I couldn't in good conscience send shoes to Harrods that were not of the highest quality, and that I was devastated at having to disappoint her. I hoped she would give me another chance for this spring season and allow me to produce a shoe that was as wearable as it was beautiful. I was crying uncontrollably when I sent it. I was so destroyed that I hadn't managed to get shoes produced that were wearable. I wanted to die. It was one of the most difficult moments of my new life

Her reply came the next day. It is still, to this day, one of the kindest and loveliest things anyone has ever done for me. She wrote me saying that these are the normal growing pains of any brand, and that she had known it was a possibility, since this was my first collection. She also told me that she believed in me and would be happy to come to see my new collection for spring/summer 2014, and would give me another shot at getting my shoes into Harrods. I must have read that email a thousand times. I couldn't believe it! This time I cried tears of joy. I had made the right decision. Telling her the truth had paid off. I was being torn asunder by all these people who wanted something from me, whether it was my time, my obedience, my money, or my attention. Thinking back to those days, I'm filled with pain. And yet here was Patricia giving me another chance, saving my life and the life of my company.

I also forced Samuel to allow me to hire a sales agent. I wouldn't be dissuaded. I also wanted a lawyer and a contract to secure my new hire, Stacy. Handshake deals were no longer working for me. I knew it was the Chasidic way, but it wasn't my way, or the way of the world, and I wanted a contract. I made such a fuss about it that he had no choice but to comply. He told me he would hire a lawyer friend of his to write the contract, and I was grateful. Of course, I didn't yet know enough to understand that there are many different types of lawyers. His lawyer friend, a genuinely lovely person with whom I am still in contact till this day, was a real estate lawyer and knew as much about fashion contracts and deals as I did. The contracts he wrote for our company, the first of many, caused innumerable issues, as certain protections common only in the fashion world were unfamiliar to him. I don't blame him at all. I know he tried his very best and charged a relatively small fee as a kindness.

We were now a two-woman show. Stacy, my salesperson, could

make line sheets and price out the shoes and help me deal with our current factory until I could find another one. I couldn't fill her in on everything, though. I thought if she knew how shaky the company really was, she would run for the hills, so I involved her in the things that were in her wheelhouse without sharing all the Emira and Samuel drama.

Now that my sales position had been filled, I needed to figure out a way to get my brand out there. I wanted to make a splash in March for F/W fashion week, and again with my 2014 collection at Paris Fashion Week in September. I also had to find a new factory to produce these shoes. The first factory still had my new samples as collateral and refused to release them unless I paid for the unusable shoes they had produced. It was tens of thousands of dollars in the garbage, but I had no choice. I couldn't miss another fashion week. I had Emira's and Kara's and Patricia's attention now. I had Samuel still believing in me and Stacy working for me. The shoes had to be shown, and that was that.

Every time I swore that I would never speak to Emira again, she would pull some rabbit out of her hat, and I would forgive her, because those rabbits were often amazing. The day that I hired Stacy, Emira called me and told me that I should meet a guy named Don, who, if he liked me, would introduce me to his partner, Pierre, and if they *both* liked me, they would introduce me to the owner of their event-planning firm named Alvaro, who was a thirty-year-old French billionaire (thanks to daddy's money), and a world-renowned "it" guy. Their event company threw massive parties, utilizing all of Alvaro's connections. If our meeting went well, they would throw my brand a party to launch my shoes to the world's fashion elite.

Before I met Don, Emira gave me specific instructions about what to say and what not to say. She told me not to be too eager or too serious. She said, "Wear jewelry, and make sure he knows you're rich and incredibly well funded. Talk about Ephrayim and Samuel." The list went on and on.

Don was tall, athletic, and Mediterranean-looking, with an aristocratic nose and wavy black hair. He had an equally beautiful girlfriend, who was quiet and very sinuous. She too had black hair, hers cascading down her back. They were so soigné. They didn't sit, they lounged, languorous and relaxed. They seemed so effortlessly cool and chic—a younger, wilder version of the people I had met with Kara.

We talked about art and history, and both Don and Pierre were very intelligent and worldly. Neither of the women spoke more than two sentences. They drank and smoked and consumed tiny morsels of food and just lounged. The guys did all the talking. And oh, the name dropping. They knew everyone intimately. Margherita Missoni, Charlotte Casiraghi. They did Burning Man. "What's Burning Man?" I longed to ask, but I waited to google it when I got home.

I made them laugh with stories of my misadventures in fashion, and refused point-blank to talk about my past except in the most general of terms, which apparently was the right thing to do, as I appeared mysterious. I was ungoogleable. I had no online presence at all, which, in this day and age, was unheard of. It made me seem unusual and exotic, and I could see that they liked it. It made me cool.

It was a magical evening, and I managed to mask my cluelessness with my knowledge, if that makes any sense. I had read so much and could speak intelligently about so many subjects that it covered up my total lack of experience in all those things that you couldn't learn from a book—what people call "street smarts." I had literally zero street smarts and massive holes in my pop-culture knowledge, but no one seemed to realize it.

I guess I passed the test, because the next day, I got a text from Don inviting me to Alvaro's table at the Foundation for AIDS Research (commonly known as amfAR) fundraiser at fashion week. I would meet Alvaro then, and if he liked me, they would take me on as a client and throw me a party for spring fashion week in Paris, which was just a month away. Of course, I didn't know then that parties like that are planned months in advance, and that it was unheard of to throw one at such short notice.

The amfAR event was two days later. I chose a dress with a slit high up the thigh, which made me feel like I was in a 1930s movie, elegant and mysterious. It was the most glamorous party I'd ever been to. There were famous actors and actresses, who I marveled at seeing up close. But I had a mission that night. I had to convince Alvaro that I was worth his time, and that he should take me on as a client. I knew nothing about him except that he was a charming and connected billionaire and he was someone who could help my brand.

I sat at their table, excited and nervous. I could see that they all thought that I was a very successful businesswoman. It was what I looked like, and I've learned that people generally aren't curious enough to look beyond the façade. Finally Alvaro arrived, all smiles and apologies for being so late. I liked him right away. He was so polite and unassuming. He didn't act as if he thought he was "all that." He was personable, relaxed, and very funny. I had a great time with all of them, and they treated me like part of their crew. I went home feeling like anything was possible.

The next morning, I woke up to Emira's repeated calls. She was ecstatic. Alvaro adored me and wanted to help. I would meet up with him to discuss fashion week in Paris as soon as possible, since there was no time to waste. It was a wonderful meeting, and Pierre, Alvaro, and Don offered to throw a massive launch event for me that all their friends would attend. They explained to me that usually these things took months of planning, but they felt confident that they could do it on short notice. They had a contract ready for me, and I said my CFO, Samuel, would have to look it over.

Meanwhile, Paris Fashion Week was only six weeks away, but I was starting to feel like I had a real brand. I had an event-planning company throwing me a party, I had a head of sales, and I had even hired an assistant—fresh out of college, very sweet and eager to please. Don, Alvaro, and Pierre booked the Shangri-La Hotel in Paris for the launch party and even convinced Aloe Blacc, who was one of my favorite singers, to perform. They had all put it together marvelously, and I was so excited.

I attended Lineapelle, the premier leather fair held in Milan, for the first time that February. Sergio took me around to all the leather suppliers, and I saw the most incredible array of new materials and magnificent colors that could be used for my next collection. There is no place like Italy when it comes to creativity and excellence in shoemaking, in my personal opinion. My imagination ran wild. It was glorious—my version of heaven. The smell of new leather, the riot of color, the innovative new materials that gave me even better ideas of how to make my shoes unique.

My experience with that first collection and Harrods made me realize that it wasn't enough to make my shoes luxurious and different with unique and innovative materials. I needed to invent a way to make high-heeled shoes comfortable.

I realized that as a woman, I couldn't design and sell anything that would hurt another woman. I was determined to make women's lives better, not worse. Our shoes would be luxurious *and* comfortable, a concept that was utterly foreign to high fashion at that time.

In fact, later on when I became creative director of La Perla, I was told not to use the word "comfort," as it had negative connotations in fashion. Fuck that! The whole concept of women suffering for beauty was old, archaic, and abominable. Fashion was being made for women without being made *for* women. No one cared what we felt like, only what we looked like. I thought that was crazy and set out to change it. I wanted to free women everywhere from suffering for beauty.

To me, choosing what you get to put on your body is one of the greatest freedoms there is. It is not something I take for granted. It took me years to give myself permission to wear what I wanted to wear as opposed to what I was brainwashed to believe God wanted me to wear. It is not an accident that, to this day, in countries where women are second-class citizens and are not free to own homes, drive cars, and divorce, they are also covered head to toe. A man created this concept to confine us, and to make us police ourselves by instilling in us this idea that it was godly to do so. That doesn't work for me, and so, to me, designing shoes that would be comfortable and sexy and feminine was a testament to freedom, and eradicating discomfort would make it all the more so. Freeing women from suffering for beauty seemed like exactly what I should be doing.

I ended up devising an arch that made wearing high-heeled shoes vastly more comfortable, and finding a way to make a deeper mold and embed antishock and cooling gel inside shoes. I called it Cloud 9 Technology, and I managed to get global patents pending by 2015. Nearly everything I dreamt up, I achieved. But that was a long way off.

I also made shoes out of the most unusual and unique materials. I had shoes made of all Murano-glass mosaics—a real, wearable glass slipper. Later on, I even convinced Swarovski to design a flat crystal, because I hated how the sharp prongs of traditionally shaped Swarovski crystals got caught on your stockings or scratched your ankle when you crossed your legs. After the Harrods situation, I made myself a promise that I would never again design anything uncomfortable. Everything I made needed to make women's lives better. Women wearing my designs would never have to choose between comfort and beauty.

At this point, I was still learning more about the actual construction of shoes. I discovered that the molds that most shoe brands use had been around for years. Often, designers for brands would simply buy an existing mold and change the upper part of the shoe and the decoration and color, which was cheaper and easier than starting from scratch. Making your own mold was time-consuming and massively expensive, so of course no brand bothered. Why should they? Women bought the uncomfortable shoes made with old molds that cost only four euros. To make your own mold could cost €40,000. And then you needed another mold for every two sizes. It was a huge investment and one that most brands did not feel the need to make.

I was determined to do it. I would figure out a way to design shoes differently, and then I would make my own molds. I planned to slowly build a collection of molds that I would be able to use again and again.

I knew it would be a massive uphill battle to make my nascent company a success, but it didn't occur to me that I would fail. I would rather have jumped off the Tappan Zee Bridge. It was success or death. Those were the stakes. Failure was unacceptable.

The following day, I took a flight to my second Paris Fashion Week, with four Louis Vuitton suitcases, ready to make a splash. What a world of difference six short months made. I now had people I knew in Paris, and although I wouldn't call all of them friends, at least I wasn't waiting alone in the George V lobby for someone to notice me. I even had a real showroom at the Shangri-La Hotel, the same hotel we'd secured for the launch party. Stacy came with me to set up the showroom and organize the shoes that had finally arrived. The plan was for Emira to visit the showroom daily, bringing a steady stream of people. That week she also introduced me to Fatima, her best friend, a cherubic-looking woman, who seemed so kind and helpful.

She told me which fashion parties I needed to attend, which clubs and bars I should be seen in. A few nights later, I went out to a club with some of my new friends. The food was wonderful, and the drinks were delicious and plentiful. I had never been properly drunk, not even once in my life, as the religious world is full of alcohol, so it was something I was accustomed to. I drank no more than usual that night—just enough to make me relaxed. I met this beautiful man who seemed to know a lot of the people I was with, and we drank and talked, and I enjoyed every moment I spent with him. That's all that I remember.

I must have fallen asleep, because when I woke up, feeling lost and woozy, I realized I was no longer in a club but in someone's apartment. My body felt like Jell-O, and I couldn't seem to command it. The guy was holding me up, basically carrying me. I couldn't understand how I'd gotten there, and I remember telling him that I wanted to go home; but he was leading me downstairs to his bedroom, and I didn't have the will to disagree. And then he was undressing me, and then I was in his bed, and then he was inside of me. At some point I fell back asleep and when I woke up, I felt horribly ashamed and embarrassed.

It took me a few minutes to even understand where I was, and when I did, I wanted to get out as soon as humanly possible. I got up and got dressed, but his alarm was on, and when I tried opening the door, it went off and woke him. He got up, clearly not pleased to be woken so abruptly, and let me out. I was trying really hard not to cry as pictures of the previous night swam through my head—horrible pictures that I couldn't really understand. I just wanted to go back to my hotel.

As awful as that night was, the worst part was yet to come. As I tried to make sense of that night, I thought back to every drink I had taken and tried to understand how I had ended up naked in some stranger's bed. Back then, I'd never heard of date-rape drugs. I didn't know there was something you could put in a person's drink that would let you do things to them that they were incapable of stopping. I didn't know you could be awake like that but not in control.

I went over it again and again in my mind and decided that it must have been my fault. I must have had too much to drink, although I hadn't drunk more than usual at all. But somehow it must have affected me differently, and apparently, drunk me had thought it was a good idea to go home with him. That must mean I liked him. It took me a few days, but I managed to convince myself that it had been my choice, and an excellent one, because he was a wonderful person and I liked him.

I was trying so hard to prove that version of events to myself that two days later, when he asked me out on a date, I agreed. We went to dinner, and he invited me back to his apartment, and I went willingly, telling myself that this proved that nothing had happened that night that I hadn't wanted to happen, and that he was worth my time. That night in bed, though, it felt as if I had never been with him before. I tried to recall what we had done the time before, and I remembered the actions, but I couldn't recall a single feeling or emotion. His body was totally new to me. It was awful, and the next time he asked me out, I very politely told him no. I chalked up the entire incident to a stupid decision on my part and let that be that.

It wasn't until many months later, when I was talking to a new friend named Cara and told her about the out-of-body experience that I'd had, that I finally understood what had happened. I told her that the entire incident felt like I was watching myself and trying to say no but not being able to, and then she told me about Rohypnol. I felt sick, and I was angriest with myself. How could I have pretended that it had been OK? I may have never heard about Rohypnol, but I knew myself. I knew I had felt wrong and not in control, and that I had heard myself saying no but been unable to stop it. I felt so revolted that I had gone back the second time consciously and willingly, all to prove to myself that he had been worth sleeping with—that it had been my decision all along.

I've learned so much these last few years, and I shake with anger at all that I missed, at all the years that have been stolen from me. That night taught me so many things about the world and about myself. I started to really listen to myself after Cara helped me to understand what happened that evening. I started to trust my instincts and my inner voice. The realization of what had occurred, and the way I had attempted to cover it up in my own mind, taught me a lot that I would never forget. It changed me.

I acknowledged my own deep insecurities, realizing I had left a world controlled by men only to join another world where their control was certainly less obvious but clearly still very powerful. I might have physically left, but I was still doubting myself constantly and assuming that men knew best. My body had fully left the religious world, but my mind and my heart had yet to internalize the change. I had been controlled by men for so many years that I still didn't fully trust myself. I am still a work in progress today. I've definitely come a long way, but I still find myself ignoring my inner voice sometimes when a man's voice is louder or claims more experience. I regret it every single time, and thankfully, those incidents now are few and far between. But all this realization came later, and it was hard won. Back then, I was still in a moment of transition, doing everything I could to survive and to make my brand a success.

Samuel decided he wanted to come to Paris as well. Our brand was going to launch in dramatic style, and he wanted to be there. Part of me was grateful that he was coming, as he would be able to help and deal with the constant barrage of requests for money that were now coming from Don as well as Emira. I was in over my head, and all those sharks knew it. Emira had somehow gotten control of one of my credit cards and Don another, and I was fast losing any sense of who was spending how much on what. And I was powerless to stop them, as they were still doing so much for my brand. So I was happy to have Samuel come and take control of the finances, but he was as much a hindrance as he was a help.

Emira was starting to freak me out. She would often start crying if I didn't spend enough time with her. She would scream obscenities at poor Stacy for no reason other than the fact I treated Stacy with respect and spent time with her. Emira didn't want anyone spending time with me unless the relationship was controlled by her. She would throw things around the room, as she tore into me and told me how ungrateful I was. And then, right when I couldn't bear another second, right when I would say, "Enough! Get out!" her fit would subside as quickly as it began, and she would run out to do some massive favor for me. I would feel bad and let her back in, and the cycle would start all over again. Emira was a force, and she did manage some extraordinary things. She got the owner of a boutique in Paris to come see my shoes, and she got Farfetch to make an order. She always knew someone who knew someone, so I knew I couldn't just cut her off. I was too loyal and too grateful, and I was constantly reminding myself of her terrible struggles, and that although she was clearly unstable, she had a good heart and was trying to help. I tried to be empathetic and patient. Emira brought dozens of people to the showroom, but one of them stood out. I remember exactly what I was wearing the first time I saw him—a short Miu Miu dress. I was so tired by the time she brought him around, and in classic Emira style, she had forgotten to tell me who he was or how she thought he could help me.

He was tall but not absurdly so—around six-foot-two, incredibly built, and wore his blond hair slicked ever so slightly back with a hint of a wave. He was good-looking, but I had met so many good-looking men in the last six months that I was starting to get a bit immune. Who was he? Why had she brought him? I couldn't for the life of me remember.

The first words I ever said to Lucas were "Who are you and how can you help me?" Literally. I had no time or energy left for subterfuge. And then Lucas smiled. Lucas's entire face changed when he smiled. It was the most breathtaking, earth-shatteringly glorious smile I had ever seen. It didn't just reach his eyes, it illuminated the room, filling it with life-sustaining warmth. It knocked me completely sideways. No one had ever looked at me like that, with admiration at my directness and appreciation of my appearance. His smile said so much. And then he laughed, and I think I fell for him that very second. His laugh was even more infectious than his smile.

It was such a deep and full laugh. Nothing held back. Complete and total pleasure. His appreciation burned me, left me feeling uncomfortable and hungry and wanting I didn't even know what. I told him about my vision, about eradicating discomfort and creating the first ever comfortable, luxurious, and sexy high-heeled shoe. I told him about my understanding of why people loved buying beautiful things, about our innate need to surround ourselves with and express ourselves through beauty, through art. I explained how, when we are feeling down, we can't afford a Renoir, so instead we buy a fabulous bag or a pair of stunning shoes or a glamorous dress, and that connection to beauty makes us feel better. To me fashion is wearable art, and I love how interactive it can be. Fashion melds the creativity of the designer and the beauty of the design with the

uniqueness of the woman wearing it. The same dress on two different women can look totally different, because a woman's character
and personality impact what she's wearing. Whereas a painting
might touch our innermost soul, our admiration doesn't impact the
painting in any way. In fashion, there is this bonding of artist and
wearer, and I simply love that.

I gave him my entire spiel, which I had now said a thousand
times, and he listened intently and hungrily. He asked intelligent
questions and listened with his whole body, leaning toward me, arms
open, soaking in my answers. I don't know how long we sat there
talking. I don't know who else was in the room. I don't remember
anything or anyone except for him.

It turned out that he was one of Emira's oldest friends. He had
gone to school with her and Fatima, and he had grown up as privileged and wealthy as she had. There wasn't a supermodel he hadn't
dated or a club he didn't know. We exchanged numbers that evening,
and half an hour after he left, he texted and asked me if I wanted to
go to a fashion party with him. I responded yes immediately. I was
ecstatic that he had texted me so quickly after meeting. He had just
turned thirty, so he was a cool thirteen years younger than me, but I
didn't care.

The club was horrible—loud and crowded. I felt like the odd one
out. Everyone else was so tall and young and perfect. Why had he
brought me here? To show me what I couldn't be? Who I wasn't?
Was this some kind of game? Some kind of joke? He introduced me
to his two impossibly good-looking friends and the women they
were with. One of his friends, Italian, also a billionaire's son, was so
tall and elegant and stunning. These Adonises who ruled the
world—I felt so massively out of place. His other friend was a fashion photographer, a giant blond Swede who looked like he had par-
tied for too many nights in his twenties. He looked dissolute and a
bit druggy, but still stunningly beautiful. And the women! Each one
was more beautiful than the next. They were all models, and they
were all so lovely to me. They asked me questions about myself, or
rather yelled questions at me, as it was impossible to hear anything,

and they all danced around with one another while I sat at the table they had gotten at the club and watched. Lucas never asked me to dance, and I never got up and danced myself. I was so upset and disappointed. It was official: I hated clubs. Partying wasn't my thing. Drinking the night away wasn't my thing. I just wanted to go back to the hotel. I stayed another half hour or so, and then finally I had had enough.

I was waiting in line to get my coat when Lucas found me. "Leaving without saying goodbye?" he asked. I didn't say a word, but my eyes said everything. Why bother bringing me if your plan was to ignore me completely? I took my coat and walked out into the night air.

He ran after me, and when he caught up with me, he said, "It would be rude to let you leave alone after I invited you. Please let me take you home." His eyes looked inside of me, or so it felt, and there was nothing I could do but agree, so I waited while he got his coat.

He was so amusing in the car, telling stories of how he and his crew grew up, and fashion weeks from years past. He walked me to the door of my hotel room, talking about the parties and cities he'd been to. I was genuinely fascinated by him, and I didn't want him to stop talking. His life and his upbringing were the opposite of my own in every imaginable way, and I wanted to hear more. I invited him in for a drink, and I meant just a drink. It didn't even occur to me to sleep with him. I just wanted him to keep talking, but of course he took it to mean I was asking him for more. He smiled gently and whispered in my ear, "Not yet," and said good night and left.

I was so embarrassed. Of course he would think that was what I meant. I would have thought the same in his position. In reality, I thought he was totally out of my league. I was humiliated, but what did it matter? I would consider this another lesson learned in the ways of the twenty-first century. I didn't have much time to dwell on my faux pas, as my launch was approaching. I was praying that Don and Pierre knew what they were doing, and that people would show up. I hoped we hadn't just wasted hundreds of thousands of dollars on an event that no one would attend.

CHAPTER FOURTEEN

The day before the party, I went shopping with Samuel to get him a suit and a fedora for the occasion. He couldn't go without a head covering but didn't want to wear his traditional Chasidic hat or a yarmulke either. He was in an excellent mood, and we went out to dinner afterward. When Samuel and I got back to the hotel, Emira was waiting for me in the lounge. She was furious that I had disappeared for the entire afternoon and evening without her permission. She raised her voice, and people began looking at us. The manager of the hotel tried to calm her down, but she slapped him in the face, and then two doormen came and each took one of her arms and walked her forcibly out of the hotel. I was afraid that they would kick me out as well, because she was my friend. But they had all known Emira for years at the George V, and as I found out later, they had been in this situation many times before.

I didn't sleep at all that night. I was awake when my phone exploded at 4:00 A.M. with more threats from Emira. She was going to make me pay for humiliating her. She would make sure no one came to my event. She would tell everyone I was an ungrateful bitch. She told me she could have me killed at her behest as easily as she could order a coffee, and that no one would ever find my body. The list of threats went on and on. I didn't respond, because there was nothing I could say. I had long ago learned that trying to reason with an unreasonable person got you nowhere fast.

The morning of the launch was a perfect March day in Paris. The air was crisp, the sun was out, and the city seemed full of promise and possibility. Everyone wanted a piece of me that morning, but I had to run to the Shangri-La to finalize the placement of the shoes around the space. I wanted it to be perfect. I was only going to have one shot at this.

I called Don and told him what had happened with Emira the night before, and he promised that he would take care of it. I honestly do not know what he did to this day; maybe he shamed her, or threatened that he'd tell Alvaro, but whatever he did or said to her worked. And when she came over later that afternoon she was all smiles, as if the night before had never happened. If she was going to be drama free, then I was going to roll with it and not start drama of my own. All that mattered was JH LLC. People could mess with my head, insult me, threaten me, do whatever they wanted. As long as they didn't harm my brand, my baby—my shot at freedom and independence—I was willing to forgive and forget. If you wanted me to spend time with you, hang out with you, then you had to somehow be connected to or helping my brand. It was simple and straightforward. I didn't have time to make friends and party the night away. I was here to launch my vision, and I wasn't going to ask permission or let anything or anyone stop me.

That evening started gloriously when I drove up to see the words "Julia Haart" emblazoned across the front of the Shangri-La. They reflected the glittering Eiffel Tower, which could be seen from the entrance to the hotel. And everyone who was anyone showed up, hundreds and hundreds of people. FashionTV interviewed me. *Vogue* did a story on me.

The buyers who had come to see my showroom were blown away. They decided I must have real money and real clout to throw something of this caliber and size and told me they would order my collection right then and there. People wandered the room admiring and praising the shoes. My heart felt ready to burst. My shoes were my self-expression, showing what was deep in my heart and soul to the world. It was the most frightening thing, letting them out into the world and hoping others would love them as much as I did. Every compliment made my eyes shine with joy and my heart fill till bursting.

And then Aloe Blacc got on stage and thanked me for having him. "Thank you to Julia Haart for making this evening possible," he said. And my eyes filled with tears to hear my name, the name I had invented, being called out by a famous crooner and someone whose music I adored. It was a massive moment for me. He was at a high point in his career, as 2013 had seen him release "Wake Me Up" and "The Man," and everyone was humming his songs. He was so kind and such a gentleman, and afterward, we went into a room on the side where photographers took photos of us together. It was the most perfect evening of my life.

Samuel was having the time of his life too. He had grown up as sheltered as me, and although he had long dealt with the JCPenneys and Kmarts of this world, Paris Fashion Week was a whole other level. That night, for the first time in his life, he wasn't in Ephrayim's shadow. I introduced him to everyone I knew, feeling grateful that he had believed in me when no one else had.

All evening, I was wondering if Lucas would appear, and what it would be like if he did—if he saw my triumph. I was so overwhelmed by the evening that I wasn't watching where I was going and ended up nearly careening into him. I managed to right myself, and there we were, staring at one another amid all those people. His smile killed me again, and he said something so quietly that I had to lean in to hear him. He complimented me on my designs, and on the turnout, and asked if he could bring a friend of his by the showroom the next day. She was a top model and would love to wear my shoes and post about them. I was excited by the potential exposure for my brand. I was totally fine with him bringing some stunning woman on his arm. I couldn't imagine us ever being together in that way; I just wanted to be near him, to know him better, to delve into who he was.

He was such a mythical creature to me, his life and experiences the total opposite of my own, and he seemed to embody, more than anyone I had met, all that I had missed growing up in my eighteenth-century shtetl far, far away from the modern world.

Over the next few days, because Biondini ordered my shoes, they also got into Galeries Lafayette and Farfetch. Every single buyer who came in to see the shoes later sent us an order.

Lucas returned to the showroom with his model friend, and she took a few pairs to wear to events and post about. But once she left, Lucas stayed. We talked for a long time, and he asked so many questions that I became adept at answering vaguely, because he listened and internalized and didn't take anything at face value. I had to watch myself around him. He was also very bossy, constantly telling me what to do. You shouldn't have said this to so and so. Don't you know how important she or he is? But I took it, because he didn't lie, he didn't prevaricate, and he seemed to genuinely give a shit. He would show up almost every day at the showroom, bringing someone new to wear my shoes. He was never flirty, and he didn't even give a hint that he cared about me at all, but he kept coming, day after day, and helping me in a thousand little ways.

He had a friend who offered to make a look book and a catalogue at half his usual rate. His other friend, a model, offered to wear the shoes for the shoot at half her rate. Another friend, who was buddies with Kanye West and owned an antique car showroom, offered to let us use his showroom and cars for the shoot. Lucas was everywhere helping with everything, and unlike Emira or Samuel, he asked for nothing in return. I paid the people he brought me, but he wouldn't take a dollar. The last time I asked him, he told me that if I asked him again, he would never speak to me, and he looked so serious that I took him at his word.

I started to learn more about Lucas. He was serious, and though he clearly was a party guy and every single club offered him the best table, he didn't party for a living. He had his own line of custom men's shirts that he produced in the UK. He worked and was serious, and he had such a beautiful, gentle way of speaking. Even when he was insulting you, he was doing it kindly. The way he said my name with his British accent, "Julia" rolling off his lips . . . Oh my God, I couldn't bear it. And he was so incredibly charming and polite, and his manners were impeccable.

We would go out to dinner with groups of people at the very hottest spots in Paris: Ferdi (where he could get a table, a true impossibility, in less than five minutes, no matter how packed they were), Matignon, Buddha-Bar and Costes, and Raspoutine. I was always astonished by his intuition on these evenings out. We would be sitting in a noisy restaurant, and I would look around for the pepper, and it would appear magically at my elbow, thanks to him. He spoke seven languages—perfectly, fluently—and had been everywhere and done everything before even turning twenty. He had been on safaris and deep dives and skiing in Courchevel. He played with the royals and was as comfortable in a palace as most people are in a Starbucks. He was suave and confident and always perfectly polite and charming, and every woman wanted him. I watched him as he took it as his due, so used to the attention, paying no one any heed, treating everyone courteously but flirting or paying special attention to no one. I also learned he slept around *a lot* but had sworn off having a girlfriend.

But in those two weeks following the night he dropped me off at my hotel, I hadn't spent a single moment alone with him. I would lie in bed, and the minute my eyes closed I would dream about him. My dreams were pathetically PG. I couldn't fathom ever sleeping with him. I was a forty-three-year-old mother of four. He was thirty and owned the planet. Why in the world would he ever want me? My dreams only took me as far as kissing. Plus, he hadn't even touched my hand.

A few nights after my party, I told Emira I wanted to take her out to thank her for the most wonderful fashion week of my life. After all, all these people who were now my friends—they had all come, every single one of them, thanks to her. Emira told me she would invite some important people, and she would choose the restaurant. She chose a place called Caviar Kaspia. It was the first time I'd ever heard of it, and although I knew caviar was expensive, I assumed it was just going to be me and Emira and one or two of her friends, so it wouldn't be too costly.

When I arrived that evening, I was taken aback to see a table set for twelve! At Caviar Kaspia, they only give out one menu with the prices listed. The other menus have the items but no prices. Perhaps they only do this when there are parties and they know one individual is paying. Since Emira had put the reservation under her name, they had given her the pricing menu. The food was ordered before I could even sit down and get my bearings. There were dozens of rounds of vodka, and the dish that Caviar Kaspia is truly famous for: their caviar in a twice-baked potato. There is probably no better dish on the planet than their caviar and potato. I literally moaned as I ate it and ignored everyone and everything around me as each magnificent morsel tantalized my tastebuds.

Reality came crashing down when they handed Emira the bill, which she very nonchalantly passed to me. It was for €12,000! For one meal! That was over $16,000. I almost passed out from sticker shock. There is no kosher place on the planet that could get you to that amount in one meal. Until that night, I hadn't known it was humanly possible to lay down that kind of money for food. Another first, though not a pleasant one. I felt physically ill paying that bill.

I had stayed for an extra week after fashion week, and the night before I was set to leave, Lucas and I had dinner with his close friends at Matignon. I was sitting next to him, and I whispered something in his ear, some silly nonsense. Afterward, I heard him say to his friend Oliver, in French, "My God, what am I going to do, Oliver? Even when she's had wine, her breath smells like heaven, and look at her. Do you see what I mean?" He didn't know this, but by then, my French was getting better, and although I couldn't speak it, I understood every single word he said. He likes me he likes me he likes me! I thought to myself, like a sixteen-year-old girl. And basically, I *was* a sixteen-year-old girl. I had still not had a real boyfriend. I'd never gone steady or to the prom. I had never once had a crush on a boy—until Lucas.

✦   ✦   ✦

I came home to New York with my mind filled with so many new emotions and experiences. I told Bat and Shlomo and Miriam what I could but left out all mention of Lucas. I told them about the party and the launch and showed them the FashionTV report, and they were so happy for me. We went out to a kosher restaurant to celebrate. Bat had become Aron's nanny. I was paying her $2,500 a month to watch him when he got home from school and make dinner and do homework with him while I was away. It was also time to celebrate Purim, a holiday I had grown to love since I had become more modern. Purim is the Jewish version of Halloween but backward. In Halloween, kids go trick or treating and ask for candy. On Purim, kids go from house to house and give candy and gift baskets. The emphasis is on giving and not on taking, but the end result is still the same: every kid gets lots of candy.

The holiday of Purim celebrates the story of Queen Esther, a Jewish woman who was married off to the non-Jewish king Achashverosh against her will and who stopped the evil Haman, the king's trusted right-hand man, from annihilating the Jewish people. The story went that Achashverosh married Esther not realizing that she was Jewish, and when Haman convinced the king to kill all the Jews, Esther risked her life and revealed her true identity to the king in order to get him to overturn the decree. Haman was summarily executed, on the same tree he had prepared to hang Esther's uncle (and the leader of the Jews at that time), a man named Mordechai.

So, on Purim, we dress up in costumes and pretend to be who we are not in honor of Esther's revealing her true self, which she had kept hidden. Men have a mitzvah to get drunk, "ad delo yadah," which means "until they can't tell the difference" (as in, between Haman and Mordechai). This was to teach us that the line between good and evil is paper thin, and that sometimes good masquerades as evil and vice versa. It was also a time to give gifts and show love and generosity as a thank-you to God by imitating His generosity to us in allowing the decree to be lifted. There's much more to it than that, of course, but you get the gist. It's a very fun holiday if you're a kid or a man but not so much fun for women. Women have no mitzvah to get drunk. They end up spending the day cooking for the big Purim meal and cleaning up the vomit that the men leave behind because of their mitzvah. But I was determined this Purim would be different.

My kids and I love a costume, and we would get very creative with ours. I didn't have time to cook, so one of my friends invited us to her house for the meal. I hadn't seen or spoken to any of those people in a long time, and I knew everyone in the community was talking about me.

On top of this, after a year away in Israel, Batsheva was back living in Monsey, and she told me about all the people who stopped her in the street or in the grocery to ask questions about me. "I heard your mom isn't well," they would say. "It must be so hard for you." Or "You poor dears. It must be so difficult to see your mother go off the derech. Is there anything we can do? I know of this and this rabbi who is an expert at helping women with issues."

Batsheva hated it and blamed me for all this "sympathy" she was receiving—and rightfully so. Everywhere she went, my former friends and neighbors would quiz her about my activities and whereabouts. "Does she still live at home?" was the question most often asked, and my kids always said yes.

"She travels a lot and sometimes has to sleep in the city because of work, but she still lives at home," they would say. In all honestly, every week was different, and it depended on where I was and what I was doing. But one thing was for sure: if I was in the country, I was upstate for Shabbos.

Despite the invitation, in the end I chickened out and sent the kids and Yosef to the Purim meal without me. I said I didn't feel well and stayed in bed until they returned. I just couldn't face everyone. I couldn't stomach the pitying glances and snide remarks. I was already so stressed, and I didn't have the bandwidth to deal with fake sympathy and judgment.

My company was starting to generate income, and I was able to help Bat pay for the apartment she shared with Ben so they would both be free to go to school. I wanted them both to go to college. Batsheva took me up on my offer, as she'd decided she wanted to be a fashion designer, specializing in accessories. She was going to FIT (Fashion Institute of Technology), and I was ecstatic. She was following in her mother's footsteps but doing it her own way.

It was bittersweet, though, because she was still a bit cold to me. Our relationship was improving, albeit slowly, and although she was still covering her hair and thought I was crazy for being so untznius and leaving the Torah, she was genuinely happy to see *me* happy. She was also appreciative that I was giving her so much money.

I started in on designing shoes for the September fashion show. Lucas introduced me to a pair of new production guys with factories in Italy and Serbia, who did shoes for Prada and Gucci, and I was hoping to convince them to take me on. If I couldn't find the right factory to produce my designs, I would have the same problem as before. I had five months, and I needed a solution ASAP.

My new favorite hotel in New York was the Chatwal, where I would spend much of the next few years, off and on. While I was there, I would print out pictures I had gathered over the previous months, reams and reams of inspiration shots, and lay them all over the floor and arrange them into piles and start drawing, turning each pile into a shoe. I would take the color from this flower, add it to a pattern from this painting and a curve from this chair, and voilà, a shoe was born. I allowed no interruptions when I was designing. I would lock myself away for three days at a time and draw and draw, until I was ready to share the sketches of my new collection.

Then it was April and Pesach. For my entire life, Pesach had meant hundreds and hundreds of hours of scrubbing everything, and then days of cooking and preparing. I used to feed more than a hundred people over the holiday. This year, I just didn't have time, and besides, who was speaking to me anyway? There was no one to invite. I also hadn't stepped foot into a shul since the day I left, and I still refused to do so. It seemed the height of ridiculousness. Why pray in a way I no longer believed in, in a building that symbolized my oppression? It was so much easier this way, and I marveled at all the drama of my old life, when I had worried about impressing the other women in the community and spent hundreds of hours cooking dishes to please others.

Although I didn't fully participate in the holiday, I made sure the kids had fun. Yosef and I managed to never be alone together or actually have to say anything to one another. He would make comments about the rashas, the evil ones who God didn't save when he took the Jews out of Egypt, and remind us that those who didn't follow God's ways now wouldn't be allowed to live during the time of the Messiah and wouldn't be resurrected. I knew he was aiming all those comments in my direction, but I didn't give a shit and said something about taking my chances.

While I was in New York City, Luisa from WeWork introduced me to a friend of hers named Tina, who said she would connect me to a film production company. The idea was floated that I could design shoes as a tie-in for a new movie about Grace Kelly, *Grace of Monaco*, that Nicole Kidman was starring in, and they would display them at the launch party. Some of the actresses from the movie would wear the shoes, and JH LLC would be part of the after-party at the premiere in Cannes, during the Cannes film festival. I was thrilled, as this would be next-level exposure for the brand.

The deal was coming together, and it was decided that I would be going to Cannes, and Samuel would as well. Tina would come to help with the film deal and the after-party, and Fatima would come to work as my assistant and help get me into all the important parties. Tina also promised to deliver an article in *Interview* about me and my shoes. Tina and Luisa hated Fatima and Emira. They all fought constantly about who would get to tell me what to do and where to go, and who would get paid for what. I paid each of them, Tina and Luisa and Fatima and Emira, to do different things, and I tried as hard as I could to keep the peace.

When Pesach was over, it was back to Italy to test new ways to structure a comfortable pair of heels. We threw out thousands of ideas, and it was while we were talking and experimenting that I realized that the way to change the shoe was to change the arch. It was so simple, really, once you realized it. Now we had to test it, so Lucas's connections took on an even greater significance.

I went to Paris the last week of April, staying there until I flew to Cannes. This time, I needed a really large hotel room, because I was planning on spending the time between meetings working on my designs, which would involve cutting and banging and drawing and creating. I decided to stay in a suite at La Réserve, and I felt like a real Parisian. It's not a traditional hotel, as it just has suites. Someone comes to clean each day, and to bring you breakfast and croissants, but that's it. I would go across the street to the café and watch Parisians walking by, feeling like I was one of them.

And then there was Lucas. We had started texting often, but it was mostly shoe related. I had recently found out that he no longer had a dollar to his name, and I liked him all the more for it. His story was, in a way, like Emira's. He had grown up crazy rich, the kind of rich where you spend $100,000 over a weekend to party in Ibiza. It was his British grandfather who made all the money. But by the time Lucas was in his late twenties, their fortune had completely disappeared. He was from a rather prominent, fabulously wealthy British family that, in his grandfather's time, owned factories all over the UK.

When I met Lucas, he was thirty, and his family had sold all their fancy villas and homes. They lived in the one property that was left, outside London, in a sort of shabby splendor. By then, Lucas had gone from spending $100,000 in one weekend to spending $30,000 a year. He spent a lot of time in Paris, due to his growing fashion business, but lived very simply and discreetly.

Emira had told me the lowdown on Lucas spitefully, thinking it would turn me away from him, because, of course, she was jealous. She couldn't have been more wrong. I thought his experience made him more impressive. Whereas Emira had turned to drugs when her world fell apart, Lucas had stood up and tried to make do. He had two businesses, which weren't exactly successful yet, and I knew full well how difficult a startup was. He was working his ass off, and he never complained about what he had lost. Emira also told me that he hadn't had a girlfriend since he was twenty-six. When his family lost all their money, he promised himself that he wouldn't get serious about anyone again until he had his own money and could treat a woman the way he thought she should be treated.

Everything made so much sense then: Why he liked me against his will. Why he was polite without ever being anything more. Why he spent time with me but never touched me. He had drawn a line for himself that he wouldn't cross: he wouldn't get serious about someone until he was successful. I had been so mystified by his behavior, and Emira, in an attempt to drive us apart, had answered all my questions without my having to ask.

I had never cared about money, or been with someone for money, and so to me, it made no difference. Plus, I was going to be wealthy myself. I didn't need a man to give me money. Once I understood this, I realized I had a way to create a beneficial situation for everyone. I could hire him to do what he had already been doing for me as a favor. I would pay him a salary, and give him a fancy title so as not to offend him. I hoped he would accept the offer.

In Paris, Emira and Fatima introduced me to another young billionaire, Geoff, whose family was heavily involved and well connected in fashion and art. He had started a men's wellness brand and was going to have a huge showroom in Cannes, and Emira thought that we might be able to do something together. He was forty-five minutes late to our first dinner. I was getting very fed up and about to leave when he finally arrived, extremely apologetic. It was obvious that he had just woken up, but for all I knew, he had arrived from a different time zone that day. I was cold to him that evening, because I didn't buy his excuse and I was annoyed that I had waited for so long.

The following night I went out with Lucas, but again, not alone. I met some more of his friends and some of his employees. We went to this amazing sushi place off Avenue Montaigne called Orient Extrême, which is still one of my favorite sushi restaurants in Paris. I loved spending time with him, but I wanted more. I wanted time alone.

He had accepted my job offer, which made me very happy but caused a lot of internal drama. Samuel wasn't pleased, because he realized I was getting attached to Lucas. Emira didn't like it because she wanted me all to herself. Tina and Luisa didn't like it because he wasn't one of them and was therefore someone who they couldn't control. Lucas fit no one's agenda but my own. He was smart enough to see the dynamic, so we agreed he would work as a contractor for six months and we would see how it went.

I also knew most successful fashion brands have two people in a relationship at the helm, because you need a massive amount of understanding and trust between business and creative in the fashion world. There are hundreds of examples: Dior, Dolce & Gabbana, Roberto Cavalli, Valentino, Hervé Léger. All were led by lovers or married couples. Not that I had any relationship with Lucas, but I certainly wanted to.

I went out with Geoff, and Fatima again the following night, and Geoff took us to a two-Michelin-star restaurant with a fantastic wine cellar. We wandered around the cellar and had a perfect meal. That night, he was so attentive and gentlemanly that I forgave his earlier faux pas. He offered to share his showroom in Cannes with me at a very minimal cost. I thought it was a hugely generous offer, which solved the problem of where and how I would be showing there, so I was thrilled. We shook hands that night, and I decided that he was a good man and could be a real friend.

The next night, Lucas invited me and his friend Alex to go to Ferdi. He knew I was leaving for Cannes the following morning. I wore the absolute sexiest dress I owned, and I must say, I looked fabulous. That night, dinner was bittersweet. I wanted to cherish every moment, but I was so sad to leave him. I had grown so accustomed to the sound of his voice, to my name flowing off his lips. I had been so cold until he woke me up, and I basked in the warmth of his smile, of his presence. I had never longed for anyone before. I had never felt so drawn, body and soul, to a single human being. It wasn't at all like Victor or Brian or my one-night stand; it was so much more. I was drawn to the sound of his voice. I wanted to know him, to help him, to understand him. And yes, all I wanted was one kiss. One kiss to quell this horrible curiosity that plagued me.

The dinner ended a little past 11:00 P.M., and Lucas said he would take me back to the hotel in a taxi—always the gentleman. It was the first time since I had arrived that we had been alone together (if you don't count the taxi driver). The taxi made a sharp turn, and our bodies collided in the car. He held on to me, his face so close to mine that I felt his breath on my skin. And then he kissed me. Nothing in my life had ever prepared me for that.

I had dreamt of this moment for months now, and here it was, except it exceeded everything I had imagined. Then his tongue traveled to a spot between my neck and my shoulder that I had never even noticed, and he ran his lips over the spot, back and forth and back and forth, until I was moaning with desire and shaking desperately with need. It was clearly a move that he had learned from years of experience and hundreds of women's necks, but I didn't care. I was very grateful to whichever former lover had taught him this trick. I'd never felt anything like it in my life. We only stopped kissing when the driver harrumphed and we both realized that we had been sitting, parked, for quite some time.

Lucas paid the driver, scooped me up, and carried me inside. Somehow, we were in my bed and his body was on top of mine and he was undressing me while still fully clothed. And then he seemed to wake up and realize where he was and what he was doing. There was real anguish on his face, and his eyes seemed to hold the weight of the world.

"I can't do this, Julia," he told me, the pain clear in every syllable. "You are too important to me. You matter. This isn't some casual fuck for me, but I cannot be your boyfriend. I swore to myself that I wouldn't get serious about a woman until I was financially successful, and we both know I'm not there yet." He was so real, so earnest in that moment. He was trying to do the right thing, trying to be a gentleman.

He looked so torn and worried, and I saw such pain in his eyes, and I wanted to respect his decision, but what came out of my mouth instead was a moan, nothing more, as my body writhed with need. And that was that. This desire was just too strong to be ignored. He moaned himself and threw off his clothes, and then he was on top of me and we were both naked, touching each other for the first time. He was enormous, and his body was the most beautiful I had ever seen. I wanted him inside of me so badly that I couldn't bear it. I guided him in, body arching in pleasure, screaming his name when I felt him deep inside of me. He was so huge that every time he thrust, it felt as if my entire body was being filled. I had never in my life felt anything so pleasurable.

He made love to me for hours, and I came again and again and again. I thought I was going to have a heart attack. He would stack them, one on top of the other, so when I was done with one orgasm, another would burst. When he finally couldn't hold it in anymore, he came, and I could see that the strength of it had surprised him. We cradled each other and fell asleep, and then sometime later he woke up, and I felt him entering me again, and it was even better the second time. He had been so pleased with my eruptions. He'd never been with a woman who squirted before, and by the time we were done, there wasn't a single spot on the bed that wasn't soaking. I don't think we slept more than an hour. I had never felt anything so magical or so perfect in my entire life. We got up, making love one last time, and then I had to shower and pack.

I didn't want to leave. At that moment, I didn't care about anything. I just wanted to stay here, in this bed, and make love to this man. I didn't know what it had been for him, but for me, it had been the most incredible experience of my life. He had touched my soul. My heart was filled with emotion. That night with him was something totally different from the other great sex I had had. Our night mattered to me. *He* mattered to me. I was shocked by the depth of my emotions, and a bit shattered.

We said goodbye, and it was awful. I had this strong, horrible feeling that this would be our first and last time together. He was such a proud man, and I had more money than him, and I could see that it killed him. He didn't want to fall for me. He hadn't wanted to fall for anyone, but it hadn't mattered. I had wanted him, and here he was. But I thought that the second I left, his sense and sensibility would take over, and I would never feel him inside of me again.

Flying to Cannes that day, I had never felt more miserable, despite everything I had been through. I was crazy about Lucas, and there was no future for us. Whether he knew it or not, I was thirteen years his senior, and one day he would want to be a father. Though of course I hadn't told anyone, right before I left the community, I made sure I could never get pregnant again. Rather than having my tubes tied, I had a device called Essure implanted, a procedure that is irreversible. I was told there was a way in which your tubes could be untied, and that seemed like too much of a risk at the time. I wanted to be utterly and irrevocably done with having babies. My childbearing days were over. But Lucas deserved a real life and a real family. A wife his own age. I tried to imagine what his future held for him, tried to picture his wife and his family and his children. Tears streamed down my face when I thought about what could never be.

I arrived in Cannes looking like hell. I made up some story about Yosef upsetting me to Samuel, who had flown there separately, because I certainly wasn't going to tell him about Lucas. Samuel already didn't trust Lucas and hated how much time I spent with the guy he called the "good-looking British fucker."

That night, after Emira, Fatima, Tina, and Samuel left my room, I got in the tub, filled it up, and just cried and cried till I thought my heart would break. I cried for what could never be with Lucas, but more than anything, I cried for my lost years, for the experiences I would never have, for the moments that had been stolen from me. I had never imagined what it would be like to be young and married to someone I chose, to someone I loved. To be pregnant with a child born from love and passion. I had never truly thought about what it would have been like to be married to someone who made my heart soar when I saw him.

You can't miss what you've never felt. When I left the community, I was so excited to try sex, so excited to enjoy the physical aspect, that the emotional part never even occurred to me. I didn't know that such a thing was possible, but that night, imagining Lucas with some lovely young woman, and their growing family, made me realize that I had never had that. I would never be young again. I had lost forty years, twenty-four of them with someone I didn't love. I would never have the joy of having a child with a man I truly loved, body and soul. I had been robbed of the chance, and I would never get it back, and I cried, tears of sorrow and loss streaming down my face, soaking me. My body shook with the pain of it. I got into bed and wept and wept, my heart breaking, the realization of all I had missed and could never regain hitting me with such power that I wanted to die and stop this horrible pain. Why had I been shown what it felt like to be with someone you care about, just to have it snatched away? It was unbearable. I lay there, no more tears left, staring at the ceiling, shaking with grief.

The phone buzzed around 1:00 A.M. It was Lucas. Apparently, I wasn't the only one whose life had been irrevocably altered. He had felt it too. His soft, gentle voice over the phone said the words I wanted to hear so badly. "I can't stop thinking about you," he whispered into my ear. "That was the most incredible night of my life." And I could tell that he meant it. We talked for hours, and I fell asleep to the sound of his voice, binding us closer and closer together.

CHAPTER FIFTEEN

I woke up and realized that I needed to focus—I was in Cannes. Lucas's and my feelings needed to be set aside. I had a company to run and a lot of marketing to do. I was at the Hôtel du Cap-Eden-Roc, which Emira and Fatima had told me was the *only* place to stay for the Cannes film festival. It was stunning, and I had gotten a small suite with a magnificent view. There were famous people everywhere you looked, and although technically it was a good thirty-to-forty-five-minute drive from where all the Cannes activities were taking place, it was definitely a very chic address. amfAR threw their party there that year, which made life very easy for me, as that was one of the events I would be attending.

It was very Mediterranean in feeling, and the stone façade, the greenery, the fragrant flowers all added to the sense of beauty and wonder that I felt. I'd never been to the French Riviera. I was charmed by the elegance and opulence of it all. Everyone was beautiful. Lean men with slicked-back hair and $15,000 Tom Ford suits attended the galas. Women, skin gleaming, wearing Missoni, with hats perfectly perched on hair that was effortlessly piled up in regal disregard. These people made looking cool seem effortless.

Everyone was tall and slim and young and glorious. I felt like an imposter. An interloper. But I had no time for introspection. The next two weeks were critical for my company. I understood that I had to be my own PR machine, and so I set out to do just that. I wanted my shoes gracing the feet of the most discerning clientele. I wanted actresses and queens to wear them. I wanted everyone to wear them. A recurring dream I had, night after night, was of walking along a street in Manhattan, and looking down, and seeing that every woman was wearing my shoes. I would wake up, energy renewed, eyes determined, completely confident in my ability to make my dreams turn into reality. Cannes was going to bring my shoes into the spotlight. I was going to make sure of it, whatever it took.

That first year at Cannes was quite an overwhelming experience. I was juggling a thousand balls while surrounded by sycophants and users. I'd only been in the outside world for a year and a half, and now the firsts were coming in such rapid succession that I could barely keep my head above water.

I'd never been to Cannes, never been to a movie premiere, never been to a film after-party. I was engulfed in new experiences, all of them epic in scope and mind-blowingly different from the world I had just left behind.

I went first to see the showroom I was sharing with Geoff, where he was showing his new men's wellness collection. It was in a huge suite in the Hôtel Martinez in Cannes proper. He had taken one room for himself and the adjoining suite for the showroom. I split the cost of his PR person with him, so that she could push my shoes as well as his products.

I went from event to event wearing my own shoes, trying to speak to as many people as possible, always talking about my nascent brand. We gifted shoes to actresses and models in the hope that they would post pictures of themselves wearing them on social media. Often, they did, and it filled my heart with joy to see these extraordinary women with their feet ensconced in my creations. It made all the madness worth it, and madness there was.

Emira was constantly getting high (I recognized the signs by this time) and was always getting kicked out of one place or another. She was a thorn in my side. She would knock on my door at bizarre hours of the night and sit outside crying piteously until I let her in.

One night, at the entrance to the restaurant where a dinner for the jewelry brand De Grisogono was being held, she waited with me for Geoff. When he finally arrived, Emira was furious. "You fucking garbage human," she screamed at him, spittle flying, hands waving frantically. "We waited for you and waited for you! You humiliated us! I'm going to kill you and your family and I'm going to tell everyone to never buy anything from you!" The threats came fast and furious, and she wasn't yelling, she was screaming like a banshee, her voice climbing octaves with each sentence. I wanted to sink through the floor and disappear. It was horrible.

Given that reception, Geoff of course decided to ditch the dinner, and Emira also left, so I ended up sitting with a lovely group of people from Mexico who made me feel instantly comfortable. I used the opportunity to talk about and show my shoes, and that evening I managed to get seven orders. I was never not selling.

On one hand, I was living my dream—sharing my designs, meeting some of the world's most famous actors and actresses, and living a glamorous lifestyle. On the other hand, everything I had built was at risk of collapsing at any given moment because of the people I employed. Tina and Luisa were always complaining about Fatima and Emira, claiming they were taking advantage of me. Fatima and Emira detested Luisa and Tina, and were also trying to prove to me that the two others were using me for money and a good time. The sad thing is, I thought they were each totally wrong about the other when the reality was that they were both right.

All of them were taking advantage of me. The one thing that I didn't worry about, as I trusted Samuel to take care of it, was the finances of the company. All bills went to him, and he was the one negotiating things with Luisa, Fatima, etc. My oh my, was that a mistake!

I kept no record of how much money I paid them, and I never asked for invoices or receipts. They would say, "Julia, I paid two thousand dollars for such and such, can you please pay me back?" And I would give them the money, no questions asked, without getting a paid receipt, or any kind of formal acknowledgment that the payment was made. I wonder how often they made expenses up, knowing I wouldn't question anything and that I trusted them. My lack of keeping proper documentation in those early days in the outside world would still harm me for years and years to come.

In addition to all that, I also had Samuel himself to contend with. As usual, Samuel refused to focus on the business, or even care about the fact that we were spending hundreds of thousands of dollars to be there and that we should take every opportunity to utilize the time properly. All he wanted was to go out to dinner and have long, rambling philosophical discussions. If he wasn't in the room with me, he sent me thousands of texts and harangued me incessantly if I didn't respond instantaneously. My attempts to reason with him, to focus him on the business that we were building, failed miserably. He kept on telling me he didn't care about the money, he was there for the experience, and he was jealous of every single second that I spent with anyone else.

I wish I knew how to describe and encapsulate what my emotional state was like then. It was a constant roller coaster of feelings. Looking back, I don't know how I managed to keep sane amidst it all. Perhaps I wasn't actually sane. I think I was so driven and determined and so laser focused on success, that sanity wasn't really top of my list. Whatever was going to come my way, I was going to deal with it, one step at a time, one foot in front of the other, never allowing myself the luxury of feeling or acting overwhelmed. I had to keep it together. I had no choice. I couldn't fail. I felt death's call on the other side of failure. It was death or success. Nothing else.

And to top it all off, I had to pretend that I belonged, that going to Cannes and meeting elegant billionaires and actresses and the world's most famous producers was a normal Monday for me. Inside, I felt like a six-year-old dressing up in her mommy's clothing. On the outside, I tried to exude a sense of confidence that I was far from feeling.

I was out one night when this really cute guy came over to me and started a conversation. I recognized him right away, as I had recently watched one of his movies. Here I was, a Monsey mom of four, chilling with Jason Statham. He even asked me, "Would you ever date a guy like me?" I thought that was such a gentlemanly way of asking someone out, as it implied that he didn't think he was all that, and it was one of the few times in my life that I blushed. I replied honestly, saying, "I sort of have a boyfriend, I think," which made him chuckle. I invited him to the *Grace of Monaco* after-party at Bungalow 8, and we said goodbye.

Finally, the night of the after-party arrived. I had designed a special gold-coin shoe in the colors of the Monaco flag, just for the occasion. Geoff's PR woman was there, and she did an excellent job of taking me around and introducing me to actors and actresses and others she deemed important. Rosario Dawson was effusive in her praise of my shoes, which were scattered—by design, of course—all over the party. Adrian Grenier and I were photographed together, and James McAvoy sat at my table with Rosario Dawson, and we all chatted and laughed. Around 1:00 A.M., Jason Statham even showed up. He complimented my collection, and we danced. Here I was— Talia Hendler, religious Monsey housewife turned Julia Haart, fashion designer—dancing with some of the most famous people in the world. Rosario and Jason and James were all planning on going to an after-after-party, but I declined because it was already almost 4:00 A.M. and I had meetings to take in a few hours. I wasn't here to party, after all; I was here to sell shoes.

The next morning, Tina ran into my hotel room, very excited. "You made it onto Page Six! It's official! You've made it!" I had no idea what she was talking about. I had made it onto page six? Wouldn't page one have been better? I asked her, "What is so important about the sixth page?" Tina couldn't stop laughing and then explained that Page Six was a gossip column and that I was mentioned there "dancing the night away" with Jason Statham. It was incredible, and I wasn't even worried about Yosef seeing it, because there was literally no way that he would know what Page Six was—just like I hadn't known until a few minutes prior.

Then there was an article in *Interview* magazine. When I read

what they had written, I thought to myself, Now we are really getting somewhere. My favorite line was when they said that my shoes
were "already the favorite of A-list stars and royalty." Just a year ago,
I was in upstate New York making kugel, and now royalty were
wearing my shoes.

I even got invited to an event on Roberto Cavalli's yacht. I was
very excited, as I'd never been on a yacht before. It seemed so utterly
glamorous. When I showed up, however, his staff wanted me to take
off my shoes and put on disposable slippers that they had for everyone who came onboard. No one had warned me that on a yacht
you're not allowed to wear regular shoes. I once wore my high-heels
to give birth! I took off my shoes for no one, and here I was in a long-
ass gown, being told to take my five-and-a-half-inch heels off. My
gown was now ridiculously long on me, and I was a good ten inches
shorter than everyone else. I felt like the ugly duckling. I found a
place to sit on the yacht, so at least it wouldn't be so obvious that my
dress was unceremoniously dragging behind me.

I sat there that evening, depressing thoughts swirling in my mind,
as people laughed and danced and twirled around me in joyous
abandon.

I knew I was the only person who really cared about JH LLC. I
knew, deep inside, that everyone was "helping" me for an ulterior
motive. I had paid for everyone's hotel rooms, their food, and their
company. I was paying Fatima around €50,000 for helping me on the
trip, and of course Emira used me like an ATM and everyone wined
and dined on my dime, but there was nothing I could do about it.
Samuel told me it was the way of the world and I believed him. I felt
the cost of it deeply. I had no one. I knew that I was really alone. No
one to lean on, no real person to call friend. Samuel's constant ha-
ranguing and bottomless demand for my attention were incredibly
stressful and draining, but he was my cross and I had to bear him.
That's how deeply I felt my responsibility to him.

Something about that night made me feel how much time I had
lost, how much making up I had to do. I was still the outsider looking in.

Whereas at Bungalow 8 I'd felt at home, here in this magnificent yacht, the realization of all I had lost and all that I had to make up for came crashing down. The party at Bungalow 8 was about my shoes and my fledgling company. I was fearless when it came to my company, and I could go on for hours talking about the innovations and the unique materials we were using. But here, all alone on this yacht, I felt so left out. I knew no one and no one knew me, and it felt like the odds stacked against me were completely insurmountable.

A part of me felt that that was the way it would always be. I had no idea whether I would ever find my place. But I refused to give up. Even if I was going to be alone the rest of my life, at least I would leave my mark. I wanted to create beautiful things. I wanted to show the world what I was capable of, even if I could never fully be a part of it.

I was being torn asunder by the various factions of hangers-on that surrounded me, while struggling and fighting to keep my brand alive. While I was there, we'd gotten even more exciting news: Lady Gaga had seen my shoes and was going to wear them to a performance in Las Vegas. The invitation to the performance featured a drawing of her wearing *my* shoes. I was breathless with joy. For a moment, all this madness and craziness, the constant upheavals and the roller coaster of emotions, felt worth it. Lady Gaga was wearing my shoes! It felt like things were happening.

I was headed back to Paris for the weekend, as on Monday I would be off to Saint-Tropez, where Kara had a villa that she'd invited me to. I would be seeing Lucas again in Paris. By the time my flight landed, I was shaking with a mix of fear and excitement. What if the second time we were together wasn't as magical as the first? What if, after seeing me again, he changed his mind?

He was waiting for me in my hotel room. I opened the door, and he enveloped me in his arms. I don't remember if we even spoke; we ended up naked within moments of my arrival. I wouldn't have believed it was possible, but it was better than the first time. This time he really took his time with me, and we made love the whole night. I never wanted to leave that room or that bed. I wanted to forget everything else and just stay there, wrapped in his arms, the warm glow of multiple orgasms suffusing my body with a sense of utter well-being. I'd never felt anything like it. We talked and made love and ate, luxuriating in our togetherness. It was pure magic.

For those two days, we didn't leave the hotel room. I decided I deserved a two-day break from the world after everything that had transpired in Cannes, and I knew that the week in Saint-Tropez would be me selling, selling, selling all over again and having to be "on."

With Lucas, I didn't have to be anything or anyone but myself. I didn't tell him about my life or my past—not fully, at least—and he still thought I was thirty-five, but we spoke of everything else. I shared my dreams, and he shared his. He was struggling to build his businesses, but he was determined to make them a success and take care of his parents. When our two days were up, I packed and said goodbye, holding on to him for dear life, as if he were just a figment of my imagination, and if I let go, he would disappear into thin air.

I'd accepted Kara's invitation to Saint-Tropez because I knew that she knew exactly the type of people who would be able to appreciate and hopefully boost my shoes. I stayed at Kara's villa, which was as stunning as her chalet in Courchevel. She has such exquisite taste and was an incredible hostess. There was no Emira this time, so I managed to enjoy myself getting to know her crowd, going to dinners and house parties, and riding on yachts—with proper footwear this time.

One night, one of Kara's closest friends, a guy who owned an international chain of stores, was having a birthday party and she brought me along. Kara and I wandered around as she introduced me, but as usual, during the cocktail part of the evening, I felt like the odd woman out. I sat down on a couch, hoping that the dinner would start soon and we would all be seated at a table. I smiled at the women sitting next to me, both looking barely legal and barely dressed. Suddenly Kara ran over, a look of horror on her face. She grabbed me and pulled me off the couch.

"Darling, that's the prostitute couch. You don't want to sit there," she informed me.

I marveled again at this strange world that I was now part of, but I kept my thoughts on the matter to myself.

The next day we went on her friend's yacht. I had now learned about the no-shoes rule and made sure to bring a pair of platforms (a mere three-inch heel instead of my usual five) with a rubber sole that's allowed on yachts. I wore a short dress to avoid the problem I had on the Cavalli yacht. Slowly but surely, I was learning.

I flew back to Paris for just one night. Lucas and I spent another perfect evening together, and I woke up to him staring at me. He looked at me, as I was still wiping the sleep from my eyes, and said, "I love you." I sat up, body shaking, heart overflowing with joy, and told him that I was in love with him as well. We had barely been together a month, but the intensity of our feelings overwhelmed us both. For the first time in my life, I was in love.

Then I flew back to New York. I didn't know it was possible to feel this good, and all I wanted was to be in Lucas's arms again, but nothing was going to deter me from making JH a success. I had also been gone almost a month, and I really missed the kids. When I went back to Monsey, Aron slept in my bed with me, and I lay there listening to the sound of his breathing, marveling at how strange and surreal my life had become.

Back in New York, I was looking more closely at how the business was operating, and I started noticing things I didn't like. Samuel had been pretty good about paying bills on time, and he was constantly telling me that he'd put in $500,000 here and a million here. He told me not to worry about the finances at all, and it was all under control. Since I was designing everything myself, selling everything myself, producing everything myself, and operating as my own PR, the fact that he was dealing with the finances was fine with me; I simply didn't have time for it.

But now that I was back, people started contacting me and telling me that they hadn't been paid. I started getting messages from random people: the person who had printed invitations for the Bungalow 8 party, the person who had designed my showroom; there were bills large and small that I had been told had been paid but clearly hadn't been. I would call Samuel and ask him when the money was coming, and he would hem and haw and say it was coming "tomorrow." We would end up talking for hours, and the same thing would happen the next day. He started sending the money more slowly, in dribs and drabs, and then we were always late in paying people. He told me not to worry, that it was a temporary setback, and I believed him. I figured that all I could do was keep working hard and hoping for the best. In the end, I found out he had a lot less money than he had said, as a deal he was counting on fell through.

When we met later that week, he went on a giant diatribe about how little time I was spending with him and how frequently I traveled. "Samuel," I told him, "my eight-year-old son gives me less grief about my constant travel. He understands I'm trying to build us a better future. You are a grown man, and you're kvetching because I spend every waking moment working for JH LLC and trying to make it a success? You should be so grateful that I'm so committed and driven."

It was a miserable few days. He threatened to withdraw from my company if I didn't spend more time with him; I refused to give in to his blackmail and told him that if he wanted to leave the company, he should just do so, but I was going to continue to focus on making it a success, and I wasn't going to let anyone deter me.

I had an even more serious problem to contend with, however. Miranda Lambert had worn a pair of my cowboy boots on an interview with 60 Minutes, which should have been a triumph but was instead a disaster, because the heel had broken as she was walking off the stage.

My shoes were beautiful, but they were still badly made. I had gotten rid of my original factory but had yet to find a replacement. Lucas came to the rescue, finding two brothers named Reggiano who owned factories in Italy and in Serbia and who produced shoes for Gucci and Prada. I made an appointment to meet them in Rome, and off I went again to try and solve the production problem. Lucas planned to join me in Rome and help me negotiate with the brothers. This time, I wanted a contract.

I hadn't been to Rome since the internment camp when I was three years old. My life had taken so many strange twists, and now here I was, a modern woman living in a modern world, heading to Rome with her new non-Jewish, British boyfriend to solve the production problems of my own company. It seemed impossible.

I arrived at the airport just before Lucas. Coming off an international flight, I felt grimy and smelly, and I didn't even have deodorant. I tried finding a place in the airport that sold it but to no avail. I did find perfume, and so I bought it, hoping the scent would mask any BO. When he walked toward me, my knees actually buckled, and then I ran headlong into his arms. I thought, This must be what love feels like. We kissed all the way to the hotel and made love the second we were alone.

I had booked a room at the Hotel de Russie, which is a perfect place for lovers. It's old but incredibly well kept, and there is a garden in the center that looks like what I imagined the Secret Garden looked like when I read the children's book.

We had flown in on a Saturday so we could have the rest of the weekend to ourselves. By this point, I was flying on Saturday without giving a second thought to Shabbos. There were too many unhappy memories tied to it, too many days sitting around being unable to do anything or go anywhere, staring at the walls. The first time I flew on Shabbos, I was quite scared, thinking Hashem could crash the plane to punish me, but then I looked around and comforted myself with the thought that Hashem wouldn't kill all these innocent people just to get rid of me. And so, afraid but determined, I flew on a Saturday. By now I felt no guilt, sometimes forgetting it was Shabbos altogether. I felt so proud that I was no longer afraid.

We woke up Sunday morning, and after making love, we were both ravenously hungry. We decided to be decadent and order breakfast in bed. I showered, and when I came out of the bathroom, breakfast was on two trays and Lucas was sitting in bed, munching on a piece of bacon. It smelled heavenly. The one thing I still hadn't done since I'd left my community was to eat pork. That morning, at peace with the world, I looked longingly at the crisp, fragrant slices. Lucas watched me watch him. "This is stupid," he said. "What do you think is going to happen if you eat a piece of bacon?" By then, Lucas knew part of my story. He knew that I had been married before and had lived in a religious community, but nothing more. He was the only person in my new life I had told. I didn't want to lie to him (except about my age, but it is every woman's right to lie about her age).

He and that bacon both looked so delicious that I decided, "Fuck it, give me a piece." I devoured his bacon and we immediately ordered more. That morning it felt like the last remnant of my past life had finally left me. I realized I was no longer afraid, that all the brainwashing and indoctrination was finally out of my system. I promised myself that this perfect morning in Rome would be one I never forgot.

Because I hadn't been there since I was a little girl, Lucas decided we should be very touristy and go to all the different ancient ruins. We started walking, and we hadn't gone two feet when my phone rang. It was Samuel. His tone was very accusatory. "Who are you with?" he demanded.

"I'm with Lucas," I replied. "Why are you asking, and how is it any of your business who I spend my weekend with?"

"Oh, so you don't have time to spend with me, but you have a free Sunday for Lucas," he whined. I explained to him that Lucas was introducing me to the two guys who would hopefully produce our next collection, and that I had purposefully come a day early, as I wanted to see the sights in Rome. It in no way distracted me from my focus, and how I spent my Sunday was none of his business.

"You don't own me," I told him. "Anyway, how did you know I was with someone? When you called, I could tell you already knew the answer to that question." It turned out that Emira had found out Lucas was coming through one of Lucas's friends and had immediately informed Samuel. Emira and Fatima both thought Samuel was fantastically wealthy, and they chose him over me. They figured they could be his spies, and that he would pay them extra for the service. Did I mention connecting Emira and Samuel would almost destroy me? Well, this was just the very beginning.

When I left my community, I left being made to feel bad and guilty for who I was and what I wanted to do. He had no right to question who I slept with or spent my weekend with. Even I deserved a day off on a weekend.

He was screaming so loudly on the phone that I finally just hung up, and we continued on our way. It didn't end there. The entire day, he sent me reams of texts, filling screen upon screen. I was ungrateful, I didn't care about him, and I was a bad friend. He again threatened to remove funding from my company, and even though the fear in my heart that he would really do it was very strong, I refused to be cowed. I'd had enough of men telling me what to do. I would find another investor. I would do whatever it took to keep JH LLC alive, but on my own terms and in my own way. The whole purpose of the brand was freedom, and I would allow no one to enslave me. After ignoring his deluge of texts, I finally picked up the phone to set the record straight.

I told him in no uncertain terms that I wasn't his wife or his lover, and I never would be.

"Being my partner doesn't mean you own me! Stop spying on me!" I yelled at him. That call solidified my determination to find more partners. Between his always paying late, his inattention to the business he was responsible for, even though not a single dollar left the company without his approval, and his insane obsession with me, it was overwhelming. Later that evening, around eleven, he started sending apology texts. I decided I wouldn't allow anyone to ruin my day.

I put all the Samuel madness aside and went to see the Colosseum and the Pantheon with Lucas. We walked through the city holding hands, stopping every so often for a deep, long kiss. We sat in a café in Piazza Navona, and while we were munching on prosciutto and some incredibly delicious Italian cheeses, Fatima called. She had a possible Middle Eastern buyer for the shoes, which was exciting because the Middle East is a very important market for luxury brands. We spoke for about fifteen minutes, and when I hung up the phone, I was ecstatic. But when I looked up, Lucas's face was stone cold, and his eyes angry.

"What's wrong, my love?" I asked.

"You're sitting here with me at lunch, in the most romantic place in the world, and you have to take a phone call from Fatima? Couldn't it have waited till tomorrow?" he demanded. I have to say that I didn't take that well. Frankly, I got really upset. First, however, I tried to reason with him.

"Lucas, you know where I come from. You know what's happened to me. You must understand that I am a workaholic, and that I will always be working. And if you're not comfortable with that, then you're not comfortable with me. I love every moment we spend together, but I will not apologize for working. Ever." That didn't go over well, and he said, "Well, if Fatima is so important to you, then go spend the day with Fatima!" And he stormed off, leaving me sitting alone in the piazza.

My perfect man wasn't so perfect after all. If he couldn't comprehend that my company was my lifeline and my path to freedom, if he couldn't understand why I was always working and that I always would be, then how could we possibly be together? I was so disappointed in him. Our perfect Sunday had been ruined, just because I took one business call.

I decided to continue exploring Rome without him. I wasn't giving in to his temper tantrum and I certainly wasn't chasing him. I went to the Capitoline Museums and marveled at all the beauty and art that I saw. It soothed my soul, and I took hundreds of photos—inspirations for my next collection. All I wanted was to see as much as possible of this incredible world that I had been kept from, and to be a successful businesswoman. I wanted to try everything, taste everything, see everything. And wherever I went and whatever I saw inspired a shoe, a color, a new idea.

Two hours flew by, and Lucas called. He was apologetic. He told me he understood and wouldn't bug me about how much I worked ever again. I told him it was OK. Slow to anger and quick to forgive. That's who I am and how I live.

We met back at the hotel, and—equilibrium restored, arms intertwined—walked to the Trevi Fountain, kissing as we went. I remembered seeing the fountain in *Roman Holiday* with Audrey Hepburn, and now here I was, standing next to the fountain of love, walking in the same footsteps as Audrey herself.

Throngs of people surrounded the fountain, and we stood there, me in front, him behind me, encircling me with his arms, and I had never felt so safe and so at peace. Then I felt his hand reaching under my miniskirt, and before I knew what was happening, he was inside me! I had never been so shocked in my life. We stood there amid the multitude of people with him pressed so tightly against me that no one around us had any idea what was going on. I tried to be quiet so as not to give us away. It was crazy. I came and then he came, and we stood there clasped together, and then down went my skirt, and we looked at each other, delighted. It had been such a mad, crazy thing to do.

The next morning, I met with the two brothers that Lucas had found, and we hit it off right away. They were both incredibly good-looking Italians. They worked together, lived right next to one another, and were both very charming. They were tall and dark haired. One was in his fifties but was really fit and looked patrician and elegant. The younger brother looked a bit dissipated. I could see he drank a lot, but he was so funny and entertaining, and when it came to shoes, their vast knowledge filled me with relief and confidence.

I managed to convince them to take a chance on me. They wouldn't make much money from my company in the beginning, but if the shoes were good and sales took off, they would make real money then. They could clearly see the determination in my eyes, and the fact that I had had so many orders my first season out boded well for the brand. According to the brothers, I needed a much larger order of shoes to do the production in Serbia, so we decided to use a factory in Italy called Calzatura Classici. We had a deal, and we signed a very bare-bones contract, which didn't do too much to protect me. But at least we had something in writing.

I had to leave Rome the next morning and would meet with the brothers again in a month. I would have to use the samples from the original factory for the showroom in Paris in September, as there was no way for a new factory to remake the samples in time for fashion week. But the new factory we picked would do the eventual production, which was the most important part.

Back to Monsey I went, to spend a few days with Aron and Miriam. I always told them about all the places I'd been, and the interesting people I'd met. I showed them hundreds of pictures and even started a new custom: in every city I went to, I would buy Aron magnets and a snow globe with that city's name. I wanted to show him that wherever I went, I was always thinking about him. He's got hundreds of snow globes now, and a special bookcase to hold them all. We would sit there together, him picking up one globe or another, and I would tell him about the city and the people and everything I had done (edited, of course). He loved hearing the stories, and somehow, even though he was so young, he understood that my decisions would lead us to a better life.

As my world opened up, so did Miriam's. Now she was going to a much less fundamentalist school. It was still all-girls, and it recognized Shabbos and kosher, and there was no talking to boys and all the rest, but the school had a soccer team and a basketball team. She loved being able to play sports, even if her classmates were snobby and didn't welcome her with open arms. She even got press because she won a soccer trophy. I was so proud. We have the photo till this day! She looks gloriously happy.

Batsheva and Binyamin were living in Monsey, and we were slowly rebuilding our relationship. Bat was still Aron's nanny, because if I left Aron's care to Yosef, he would be eating pizza or macaroni and cheese out of a box every night. There is a double standard that exists in people's perception, even in the outside world today. For a man to travel for business is perfectly normal and wonderful, and if he's a "good provider," then he is lauded and praised. The small amount of time he spends with his kids is always met with *oohs* and *ahhs*, and everyone praises him for being such a wonderful dad. The wife who stays at home is expected to cook and clean and take care of the house and make wholesome meals for the family and take care of homework and everything else. No one *oohs* and *ahhs* over her taking care of the kids. It's her duty and her responsibility, so what's to praise?

However, if a woman travels for business, she is a bad mother and shirking her familial duty. Do you know how many times I've heard "I feel so bad for your kids that you're always traveling?" Yosef was gone for a year and a half, only coming back on weekends, when I had three babies in the house alone, and no one raised an eyebrow. No one commented or told him he was being a bad parent. No one praised me for raising them alone. For a year and a half, I was basically a single parent.

No one expected Yosef to take care of Aron or make healthy meals or do homework. All the comments he got started with "Poor Yosef" or "Poor Aron." Although I was bringing in money and working tirelessly to create a better world for myself and my family, all I got was grief. When will this double standard end? I will not apologize for anything. I did all that I did to have freedom for myself and my children, and I succeeded beyond my wildest expectations. If it weren't for me, my kids' lives today would be small and still trapped behind those ghetto walls. They would be poor, as they would never have gotten college degrees, and they would have baby after baby until they were old and gray. Their world is open and wonderful, and they've traveled all over the globe with me. Now they understand why I did what I did. Now they appreciate all the sacrifices I've made and the mad crazy journey that I took alone. Miriam is at Stanford University, Shlomo will graduate from Columbia University, and Bat is getting her degree at FIT. Everything that they are experiencing is because I left and built us a life.

My second day back, I went into the city to meet with a PR person we were hiring. The plan was for us to set up two showrooms, one in New York City and one in Paris. Tina and Luisa and this PR girl would set up the one in the States, and Lucas and Fatima would set up the one in Paris. Lucas found a fabulous art gallery to use, and I came up with the idea to display the shoes as if they were paintings, surrounded by frames. The showroom in New York was a lot simpler, a hotel room with pedestals where the shoes would be displayed. I knew New York was mostly for press and not buyers, and I was really focused on selling, so we chose to spend less in New York and more in Paris, where all the buyers would be during fashion week.

The following weekend I went to the Hamptons for the very first time. I was always networking, always selling, always on. Samuel, of course, hated the idea, as he wanted me to just stay in the city and hang with him and spend the day talking about anything other than work. It was now abundantly clear that he didn't care at all about the company. It was a nightmare, and I constantly felt torn. On one hand, I felt a huge debt of gratitude to him for continuing to invest in the company and believing in me, but on the other, the emotional price I had to pay was a massive one. There wasn't a single day that he would leave me alone in peace. If we didn't speak at least twice a day, he would get furious with me and call me until I picked up. He would send the money, always late, always after a thousand texts in which I had to beg him for every dollar.

As if Samuel's constant harassment weren't enough, Lucas had begun to show a very jealous side to his personality. He would text me all hours of the day, ostensibly to say "I love you," but if I didn't respond right away, he would get very upset and accuse me of being with some guy. He was constantly quizzing me on who I met and where I went, and I would literally write him a schedule of my day so that he would know where I was at all times. I look back at it now and wonder how and why I put up with that. The answer, unfortunately, is rather pathetic. I had left my community behind, but somewhere deep inside of me, I was still accustomed to men ruling me and telling me what to do. I had lived under a man's rule for so long, so accustomed to getting permission for everything, that I was almost comfortable with it. It was familiar. It was the only kind of relationship I knew. I excused his behavior and indulged him and constantly told him where I was. He wasn't happy about my going to the Hamptons either.

Now, if Samuel and Lucas weren't enough, Emira chose that weekend to call me hundreds of times asking me to go to a Western Union and send her cash. I tried to explain to her that I was in the Hamptons and there was no Western Union anywhere. It was Shabbos, so Samuel wasn't taking her calls either, and she let me have the brunt of her anger. She threatened to tell all the buyers in Paris that my shoes were badly made. She told me that she would send people to physically hurt me if she didn't get her money. She chose the wrong day. Coming on top of all the pressure from Lucas and Samuel, it was just too much. My whole body trembled as I told her, "Emira, I don't ever want to speak to you again." Even though I was genuinely afraid of her and the harm she could cause my brand, I was done with her. I called Fatima, desperate for her intervention, and begged her to please control her best friend so she wouldn't harm my brand. I write these words and remember that horrible sense of fear that was ever present those first few years. I don't even recognize that woman.

I was really a child, newly born into the twenty-first century, and I was so easily frightened. Everything scared me. Everyone who threatened me caused me to panic. I was in a state of perpetual fear, and they could smell it on me. I was constantly being threatened—by Samuel, by Emira—and it caused me so many sleepless nights. I hadn't built up my courage yet, hadn't fully come into myself. I was still testing the waters and trying to swim, and I was swimming with predatory sharks who sensed my weakness and used it to control me.

Today, when someone threatens me, I am no longer afraid. Those who try to take what's mine or betray me learn the hard way that I can be as cruel and unforgiving to my enemies as I am loyal and generous to my friends. Nowadays, my enemies may win a battle once in a while, but they will never win the war, because I am more stubborn, more driven, and more determined than all of them combined. The wheels of justice may move slowly, but I have learned that they do move. I am a patient planner, and I will never allow anyone's jealousy or dishonesty to keep me from my mission.

I may have been panicked and afraid, but nothing could dampen my excitement to begin designing my new spring/summer collection. It had wedge sandals with hammered gold on the back that were incredibly comfortable, and even the super-skinny high heels felt good to wear. I was still petrified that the heels would fall off, as had happened on several of the prototypes, but I consoled myself with the fact that this factory wouldn't be producing the shoes going forward, and I would never have to see them again.

I wanted to have all my drawings ready before Lineapelle this year so I could choose the materials for the shoes that I'd designed. It was my absolute favorite part of my new life. I planned to lock myself in my hotel suite that now doubled as an office for two days and do nothing but draw. We had begun having all our meetings there, and having guests over, as it was vastly nicer than our WeWork office. It had a conference room that could seat at least twelve people, and a living room, and in the very back, a bedroom that I slept in. It allowed me to utilize every waking minute to design. I canceled all meetings so I could concentrate and draw.

Samuel kept begging to come visit and "see the shoes," but I told him he couldn't come until I was finished. Tuesday late afternoon, he showed up unannounced and wouldn't leave. When I couldn't take another minute, I told him, as politely as possible, that I needed to get back to work, and that it was time for him to go. He stood up, and I thought he was walking out, but instead, he lunged for me and tried to kiss me. I avoided his embrace, putting the couch between us, and screamed, "Get out of my suite, you fucking asshole!" I was shaking, livid with anger and rage.

"What's the big deal? It won't hurt you to kiss me. It will make me happy, and it doesn't cost you anything," he said. I ran out of the living room of the suite, straight to the bedroom, and locked my door.

That night, he texted again asking to kiss me, and again asking why I wouldn't grant him this tiny request when he had invested so much money and time in JH LLC. I had come so far to be free—free from men telling me what to do, free to choose who I would love. And here was this man, a man from my old world, a man who I had thought of as my friend, a man who I had pitied and tried to help, trying to force me into a sexual relationship.

Because I was still in a transition phase from old world to new, I answered him and tried to reason with him and explain why his request was wrong. Today, I would never have spoken to someone who tried to force himself upon me. Then I explained that all I had done was for freedom, and his trying to force me to kiss him was a negation of everything I had worked so hard to achieve. I told him that just because he had invested in my company, he hadn't purchased my love or affection. I begged him to accept just being my friend and told him that friendship lasted so much longer than any affair.

His response broke my heart. He said that he had done so much for me, and that I was a horrible, ungrateful person who couldn't even manage to give something so simple as a kiss. He accused me of being selfish and, as usual, threatened to pull his funding if I didn't agree to his request. At that point, I was so angry that I refused to pick up the phone and speak with him for several days.

Samuel wrote another one of his rambling apologies the following week, and of course, being me, I accepted and continued to treat him as a friend. I was obligated to him, so I felt I couldn't be anything but forgiving and kind. It is only with several years of experience behind me that I realize that he was very adept at playing on my gratitude and my kindness. He used my sense of obligation in a dangerous, passive-aggressive way. He was a master manipulator with years of practice, and I was a child, barely two years old in the outside world.

Samples of the shoes from the new factory were starting to arrive, and they were stunning. There were heels made of metal in the shape of the Chrysler Building and heels made of multicolored Plexiglas. I loved every single pair. And then it was back to Paris, where my shoes had finally arrived and were in Galeries Lafayette. I walked around the store and couldn't believe that my shoes were there among the Chanels and the Guccis. I sat down in a chair and burst out crying, right there in the middle of the store. A kind woman came over to see if I was all right, and I told her they were happy tears. She looked at me quizzically, and you could see her thinking, Ah, these Americans, completely crazy. Little did she know how far I had come, and what a moment this was for me.

Lucas and I had gotten into a crazy kind of rhythm. He would do something really controlling, I would break up with him, he would call and apologize, and we would get back together. By that point, we were breaking up every two weeks or so. We fought and made up and fought and made up, repeatedly.

Once, after a party, I was on the phone with him as my Uber arrived, and I told him I'd call him the second I got to my room. He mapped the distance and time it would take me to get from the club to my hotel, and when I didn't call him when Google told him I should be there, he texted and accused me of hooking up with some guy and not going home at all. That was taking it one step too far. We had hit traffic, and the Uber ride took longer than expected. He was accusing me of sleeping with some guy because of traffic?

I broke up with him yet again, but he was so apologetic and loving the next day, explaining that his jealousy stemmed from his feelings of being unworthy of me. My heart melted and I took him back. It went on like this week after week, month after month. Looking back at my relationships with Samuel and Lucas, I realize that I was still in an in-between state. Lucas had elements of my new world—he was non-Jewish, sexy, younger—as well as my old world, because he was domineering, jealous, and controlling. Both had enough of the familiar that I think they were a bridge I needed to cross before I fully integrated into this century.

Lucas and I were back on my last weekend in France before I had to go home, and he invited me to go with him to Normandy. A friend of his was getting married, and he thought it would be a great getaway for us. I'd never been properly invited to a non-Jewish wedding before (at the one in Florence I was an interloper), and I didn't know what a full goyish wedding was like.

Heading to Normandy, we were both in a very happy mood, as there had been no drama for the last few days. That weekend was another deluge of firsts, some of them more pleasant than others. Many of Lucas's friends were there, so for the first time, I didn't feel like the odd one out, as I had met them all many times now and really adored them. We stayed in a hotel near a beautiful lake, and of course the first thing we did was try out the mattress. That evening, when we were at the welcoming party, we heard two of his friends talking about how some couple in the hotel must have been having a lot of fun in the afternoon, as they'd made so much noise. Lucas and I looked at one another and burst out laughing.

His friends owned a crumbling castle in Normandy, like something out of an eighteenth-century novel. The place itself was stunning, all ancient paintings of long-dead relatives and beautiful artwork and sculptures everywhere you looked. The carpets were completely threadbare, and the couches had all seen better days. It looked so authentic and ancient and unforced. They were who they were, and this was their estate, and they weren't apologizing for it. I loved the ancient elegance of it all. You could see it had once been grand. The gardens had crumbling columns that gave the entire place a truly historic air.

Friday night was the rehearsal dinner. The food was out of this world, one course following another in glorious procession. Lucas's friends had made a video for the groom, full of a lifetime of partying and growing up together. Their childhoods were so different from mine. In the video, they skied and scuba'd and danced and had constant adventures. Their lives looked impossibly perfect. I watched that video holding back tears, wondering what my life would have been like, what my childhood could have been like, if we had never become frum—if I hadn't been locked away. The audience laughed and applauded, and it was such a convivial, warm atmosphere that I couldn't stay sad for long. I'm here now, I told myself. That's all that matters. From Monsey to Normandy. My life was expanding every single day.

After the dinner, the entire wedding party trouped to a club to dance the night away. Lucas had warned me that a friend of his, Mark, was very adept at getting people drunk and I should stay away from him.

Of course, the minute you tell me not to do something, I immediately want to do it. Besides, I thought to myself, I never get drunk. So when Mark offered me a special drink, I accepted with alacrity and downed the fiery brown liquid in a single shot. It tasted a bit like scotch, but to this day I'm not 100 percent sure what kind of hard alcohol it was.

One drink followed another, and the next thing I remembered, I was somehow in a gold cage on a stage in the club, dancing my heart out. I don't remember going onstage or getting into the cage, but somewhere in the middle of the dancing, my sanity slightly returned and I jumped out, purple from embarrassment. Lucas was too amused to be upset. He couldn't stop laughing and saying "I told you so." I've got to admit it: I should have listened to him, because the next thing that occurred while I was drunk was going to cost me dearly.

I was still drunk when we got to the hotel. I was lying in bed when a wave of absolute panic engulfed me. I was convinced that someone had tried to break into my phone and iPad to steal all my designs. Still completely drunk, I went and changed every single password on every device I owned; my phone, my iPad, and my computer. Once I'd done it, I promptly fell asleep.

I woke up the next morning and couldn't open my iPhone. Strange, I thought to myself. I tried my iPad. Same problem. No dice. And then it came back to me. Changing my passwords. Everything. I couldn't remember the drunk password I'd come up with for love or money. I tried everything I could think of. I kept getting locked out and having to wait hours to try again. I had nothing on the cloud at the time, as I was very private and paranoid that somehow Yosef would be able to see what I was up to. I backed up everything religiously onto my computer. The only problem was that I had changed the password on the computer as well. I was devastated and panicked. I was hoping that Apple would be able to fix it, but no luck. I lost hundreds upon hundreds of drawings and designs, all disappearing in an instant. I was beside myself.

The thing is, I wasn't so paranoid after all. Someone *had* been sneaking into my phone and looking at my texts and WhatsApp messages and emails. It wasn't someone trying to steal my designs, though; it was Lucas, checking up on me and making sure I wasn't secretly having an affair. And I finally caught him doing it.

A few weeks after we'd left Normandy, I walked out of the bathroom and there he was, with my phone in his hand, scrolling through my messages, reading everything. "What the actual fuck, Lucas?" I asked, clearly angry. "Why are you *going through my phone?*"

For a moment, I could see him considering his options. Should he apologize and admit what he did or deny and say it just happened to be open and it rang, or something stupid like that? He shrugged his shoulders casually, appearing unconcerned, and said, "Choose a better password next time." That was it. But did I break up with him? Did I behave like a modern, self-reliant woman and tell him to go fuck himself? No, I did not. I was still transitioning, so conditioned to letting men control me. So, I let it go.

CHAPTER SIXTEEN

Thinking about the month after Normandy, to this day, fills me with so much anger and fury. It was the most difficult month of my new life, and I paid a very heavy price. During fashion week, our showroom in New York City was a huge success. Editors from *Glamour*, *Vogue*, *Elle*, *Harper's Bazaar*, and *Women's Wear Daily* all came. As usual, I slept in the city during the week but went back up to Monsey and spent Shabbos with the family—and then it was off to Paris. I was staying in Le Bristol, because it was on the same block as our showroom, which was stunning. It featured all my latest creations framed as if they were works of art. We had dozens of appointments lined up and we had great hopes of selling a lot of shoes.

Day after day we showed shoes to clients that Fatima brought in. Many were from the Middle East, and they seemed to love my shoes. One of the clients ordered several hundred pairs, totaling $3 million. My company was saved! That order alone would see us through the next months, and the down payment would be a godsend. I called Samuel, beside myself with joy.

I was surprised when, instead of responding with excitement about the new orders, he asked me if I was still sleeping with Lucas. "Emira and Fatima both told me you're still seeing him," he accused me. "So?" I replied. "What does that have to do with anything, and how is it your business? Haven't you apologized enough times about getting involved in my personal life? We've just had our second fashion week and we've sold millions of dollars in shoes! Your money and your faith in me have been redeemed, and our company is going to prosper and grow! Can't you focus on being my partner, and the business?"

His response chilled me to the bone. He made it crystal clear that he didn't want me as a partner or a friend. He wanted me sexually, and since I continued to refuse him, he decided to destroy the company I had so lovingly built. It was horrible. His rage at my being with Lucas obliterated whatever tenuous hold he had on decency. He knew how much the company meant to me. He knew it was my chance at freedom and independence, and he wanted to wound me, to destroy me.

I was both petrified and devastated at the same time. I felt afraid that everything I had worked for would fall apart, and I had no one to turn to. Everything I had suffered, all the uncertainty, the madness, it would all be for nothing if my company was destroyed by jealousy and the need to possess me. The realization almost broke me.

Samuel started by calling Fatima and telling her that he could no longer pay her because I had used the money on myself. It was a lie, of course, but it didn't matter. She was furious. Within two days, every single order Fatima had brought in was canceled. One after another, her clients called to rescind their orders because they "heard that we had no money to make the shoes." I was inconsolable. I had come so close. We had over $3 million in orders. And now, because of one man's jealous rage, he had not only lost all of his money—he had taken down our company.

I wanted to die. You cannot fathom the depths of my despair. I was heartbroken. I cried like I hadn't cried since I had left the community. I felt the same anguish and hopelessness that I had felt trapped in my old world. I really wanted to die. What was the point of it all? If I lost Julia Haart, what would I be? Who would I be?

Fatima called me day and night. She sent people to my hotel room to try and force me to pay her. But I couldn't do anything, because Samuel controlled the money. I begged her to let me work on it and tried to explain that if she kept bad-mouthing JH, the company would have to close, and she would never get paid. I think that finally sank in, but it was too late. The damage had been done.

I realized then that Fatima and Emira were two sides of the same coin. Emira's belligerence and obsessions were there, open, and obvious for all to see. You couldn't spend time in her company without soon understanding that there was something wrong. Fatima, however, was, in her own way, more dangerous. She came across as such a helpful, kind woman, and I adored her in the beginning. She always seemed so calm and rational. But her true nature, her vindictiveness and cruelty, were only apparent after a long time. She hid her dark nature well.

She came to my suite in Paris and told me that she finally believed me that Samuel had lied because of his jealousy over Lucas. I was so pathetically grateful. I believed we could put this behind us and told her that I would take care of her payment. Although in reality she had not brought me a single sale, as they all remained canceled. All that work and effort for nothing, and I still paid her. When she left, however, I was relieved, as her constant threats had worn me down and I was petrified of her.

I had no one to talk to and no one to confide in. Fatima had tried to wreck my relationship with Lucas and his friends. She sent a picture of my passport to all my new Parisian friends, which clearly showed I was eight years older than I had said. They were so convinced that I was thirty-seven that they thought it was quite pathetic for Fatima to forge a passport just to fuck with me. They literally laughed at her sad attempt to discredit me. My boyfriend's best friend, this guy named Parth, was the first one to call me and tell me what Fatima had done. He said, "She should have picked a more believable age. Had she chosen thirty-nine, maybe we would have believed her, but forty-five? That's too absurd. It's too obvious that you're not forty-five." Years later, when I told the truth about my age, they never gave me a hard time. They were so understanding and kind that it made me treasure their friendship all the more.

She did manage to drive a wedge between me and Lucas. He wasn't speaking to me, as Fatima had told him that I'd had a one-night stand, which was something he hadn't known. "I cannot be with a woman who has had a one-night stand," he told me. This from a guy who had slept with pretty much every woman we ever ran into. "There is one rule for men and one rule for women," he instructed me. "A man can sleep around and that's fine, but I don't want to be with a woman who's had a one-night stand. You're supposed to be pure," he continued.

Can you believe this shit? And again, instead of telling him to go fuck himself, I did what I had done with Samuel. I tried to appease and explain. I am so embarrassed of the woman I was then. It was over forty years of conditioning that I had to overcome. Forty years of being told that I was always wrong and the man was always right. I had spent forty years apologizing. I might have left my physical world behind, but it still had a strong grasp on my psyche. I had brought a lot of that world with me.

I'm sure anyone who knows me now will read this and find it impossible to believe. Now, when someone attacks me, instead of being frightened, I get angry and then I get even. I will treat you with respect until the moment you harm me. People always mistake my kindness for weakness. They soon learn just how wrong they are. I don't ever give up or give in, and the more someone tries to extort or harm me, the harder I work to bring them down. Now you mess with me at your own peril.

I used to want everyone to like me. I used to want to please everyone. And yes, it's still something I battle with to this day, with one major difference. Nowadays, I'm as proud of my enemies as I am of my friends. When your enemies are liars and thieves, abusers and sexual predators, then you've done something right. I have become comfortable with being uncomfortable. I no longer shirk from a fight. I look forward to it. Every time I win, it makes me stronger and more able to handle the next attack that comes my way. And I know now that the more successful I become, the more enemies I will attract, as criminals think you're an open target, and they want to take what you have. I've accepted that. I still want to please and help those I love and care about. I'm still very loyal and loving to those who are loyal to me. I'm just not afraid anymore. You threaten me, I won't threaten you back. I will annihilate you. Period. No threats, just action. That is now. Back then, however, I was still a newborn babe, afraid of my own shadow, and they all knew it.

For two weeks I didn't speak to Samuel at all. He had done the one thing that I couldn't forgive. He had destroyed my chance at freedom. He was dead to me. Finally, after I couldn't take his constant calling any longer, I answered the phone. He had never admitted what he had said to Fatima, but Fatima had shown me the texts between them after she "forgave" me. So I picked up the phone and told Samuel that the first step in our reconciliation was that he had to admit that he had purposefully destroyed our company. He did. He finally admitted his actions. And I couldn't bear it. The betrayal was too much, too horrible. I told him I never wanted to see or speak with him again. And then, still there in Paris, trying to pick up the pieces, I decided that I wouldn't give up. I couldn't. Success or death. The one thing I had going for me was a huge order from Galeries Lafayette Dubai. It proved that people loved my shoes. I decided to try to use that order to go and find other investors.

I flew back to New York feeling the most alone I'd ever felt since I left my world behind. No Lucas, no business partner, no Fatima, and no Emira. I understood that I could trust none of them. I'm embarrassed to say that I sobbed pathetically all the way home on the plane. I couldn't stop. I had been through so much and had succeeded, to have it snatched away in an instant of jealousy. And Lucas, when I needed him the most, when I was at my lowest, had abandoned me and accused me of being a whore for having a one-night stand. My heart might have been broken, but my spirit refused to give up.

I came home determined to find more capital. The difficulty with finding new investors was that I still knew so few people, and none of them were people I felt comfortable asking to invest. I couldn't ask my new billionaire friends, as they assumed I was already successful, and I couldn't expose the truth. I racked my brain trying to think of who to ask.

Now, I know this is gonna sound funny, but the only person I could think of was a doctor named David Liebergall. He was related to Yosef and was irreligious and living in Rockland County in a secular neighborhood. He and I had become friends, and he was the only person from my old community who knew about my old life *and* my new one. I decided to screw up the courage to ask him, determined I would tell him the truth about everything.

We met in Nyack for a drink, and I had prepared a thirty-page presentation about JH LLC.

The evening went smooth as silk. He really listened, and he got it. He understood how revolutionary it was to meld comfort and luxury and was intrigued by the idea of women having both. He told me he would take my business plan to his wife and his brother and get back to me. He was respectful and excited and incredibly supportive.

The next day, he and his wife came to see the shoes so she could try them on and see how comfortable they were. They both loved the shoes and were excited by the venture. They clearly saw the potential and agreed to invest. They saved my life. If that wasn't enough, he also mentioned that he had a brother, Jon, who was well versed in startups and finance, and that this was something he might want to invest in as well. I met with Jon, and sure enough, he was excited about the brand too. You have no idea how much courage their approbation gave me. It was exactly the shot in the arm that I needed. Their support, when I needed it most, was lifesaving not only in the financial sense but in the mental one as well. To this day, I consider them among my dearest friends.

It took me six months—until I fully trusted them and saw how much they loved the company—before I felt comfortable asking them for advice and letting them in on all the crazy that was my life. I wish I had done it sooner; I could have saved myself months of misery, but I had already been so badly burned by the people I trusted that now it was difficult for me to trust anyone.

By this time, I had hired my own lawyer and was emphatic about contracts. I am now so versed in legal business contracts that I could probably write them myself. It is much easier to learn from others' mistakes, and so, dear reader, I beg that you learn from mine. Always demand a contract.

Those weeks in New York City not only gave me renewed strength, but I also read the third book that would have such a powerful impact on my life. It answered a question that had been tormenting me ever since I left my community. It wasn't some ancient tome, but rather a delightfully insightful book called *How We Got to Now*, by Steven Johnson. The focus of the book was "six innovations that made the modern world." What made such an impact on my life, however, was his use of a theory called "the adjacent possible," which, in addition to explaining how the human mind works and its deficiencies, defines why breakthroughs often occur in clusters (which is truly a fascinating phenomenon). Think about it: when Alexander Graham Bell was inventing the telephone, so was Marconi in Italy. When Edison was working on electricity, so was Tesla. According to the theoretical biologist Stuart Kauffman, as explained by Steven Johnson,

> That's because ideas are fundamentally networks of other ideas. We take the tools and metaphors and concepts and scientific understanding of our time, and we remix them into something new. But if you don't have the right building blocks, you can't make the breakthrough, however brilliant you might be. The smartest mind in the world couldn't invent a refrigerator in the middle of the seventeenth century. It simply wasn't part of the adjacent possible at that moment.

What this basically means is that our minds are incapable of imagining something too far removed from, not adjacent to, our current possible. No one in the eleventh century could invent a television, because first so many other things had to be invented, electricity, photography, etc. When a concept or an idea is too far removed from the world we live in and understand, it is impossible for us to grasp and comprehend it. That's why inventions often occur in clusters, because once something *is* adjacent to our current possible, many people can imagine the evolution of it, and therefore can be working on the same thing at the same time without ever having met or communicated with one another.

Now, you are probably reading all of this and wondering why this would have such an enormous impact on me and how this could alleviate any burden or pain that I carried.

The question that had caused me so many sleepless nights was a simple one. I couldn't understand the dichotomy between the beauty behind the concepts of my religion and the ugliness of the practices. We were taught so many beautiful character traits and modes of behavior. Be kind to others, live for something greater than yourself, be more focused on your responsibilities than your rights, just to name a few. My world believed in kindness, in humility, in charity. How could such extraordinarily beautiful concepts create a world and laws that kept women and men enslaved, forced into certain roles based purely on their biology?

How could a religion so conceptually beautiful force women to stay married to abusive men? How could it force us to make ourselves less than in order to not inconvenience men? There is even a law in the Gemara (which thankfully is not practiced today) that if a man raped a woman, he was forced to marry her. Can you imagine being forced to marry your rapist? This enormous contradiction between the beautiful concepts of Judaism and the horrible practices that had kept me imprisoned my entire life tormented me. I needed to understand how this was possible.

When I read the theory of the adjacent possible, everything fell into place. It gave me such peace, and eradicated the last vestiges of rage I felt at what had been stolen from me, as it proved what I'd believed in my heart all along: that there was no intent to harm in my religion. That these laws, when originally written, weren't there to torment us. I'm sure you're still wondering how this theory addresses this conundrum.

Let's assume for a moment, and accept as a given, that there was some kind of interaction between mankind and some Divine Power or Alternate Being or whatever. This took place after the exodus of the Jews from their slave masters in Egypt, which occurred, according to historic data, in addition to the beliefs of the three largest monotheistic religions, somewhere between the thirteenth and twelfth century B.C.E., in the time of the rule of one of the Ramses in Egypt. According to the Torah, or what Christians refer to as the Old Testament and also accept as truth, God came to the Jews on Mount Sinai after their escape from Egypt, and gave them the Bible and the Ten Commandments. My entire life, I was taught that the reason Judaism is the "true" religion is because three million people witnessed God's word, as all the Jews who had left Egypt heard God's word, whereas in Christianity and Islam, it had just been one man, Christ or Mohammed, depending on what faith you practice. The reality, however, is that the Bible itself states that Moshe went up to the heavens and brought back the Ten Commandments and the Torah.

The Torah itself says that once they heard the word of God, the Israelites were frightened that they would die and so they asked Moshe to go and get the rest of the Torah from Hashem and he could teach it to them. They only heard the first two commandments: "I am Hashem, your God" and "Don't have any gods besides me."

The Torah also says, "All the people witnessed the thunder and lightning, the blare of the horn and the mountain smoking; and when the people saw it, they fell back and stood at a distance. 'You speak to us,' they said to Moses, 'and we will obey; but let not God speak to us, lest we die.'" Later on, it adds, "I stood between the LORD and you at that time to convey the LORD's words to you, for you were afraid of the fire and did not go up the mountain." There isn't a single rebbe or Torah scholar who can pretend that we heard all the oral Torah ourselves and that God directed us about kosher and tznius Himself. Even in the Bible it says that Moshe got the rest of the laws from God and then transmitted them to the rest of the Jews.

So, just like in all the other religions, it was one man telling the rest of the Jews what God's word was.

The reality is, all that the three million Jews supposedly heard was the law of monotheism, or at the very most, the very moral dictates that make up the Ten Commandments.

And then a guy supposedly went up to heaven and God taught him the rest of the laws, some which were written into the Bible (Torah) and most of which were oral (and later became part of the Talmud), and he came back down and taught it to the rest of the Jewish people. So, just as in Christianity and in Islam, it's one guy telling the rest of the world what God said.

And now let's look at the time period in which this godly manifestation occurred. At the time, women living alone truly were in danger. Between marauders, soldiers, and the like, a woman on her own was unheard of in that part of the world, no matter who you worshipped. Hiding a woman in the tent was a practicality, as it was considered perfectly normal to rape and pillage when you conquered a town or village. A woman pregnant and alone, even if she was a victim of rape, with a baby? She would have been utterly shunned and probably forced into prostitution, before dying of hunger. When the laws regarding the roles of men and women were written into the Torah, the world at that time treated women abysmally. Without a man, they had no protection, no rights. It was the norm at the time for men to do the heavy labor, as it was often physically intense, or to be hunters, etc. Having children was necessary for survival. The more children you had, the more people were there to help support the family, carry on the family name, help with the farm, raise arms when necessary. When these laws were written, the idea that women could live on their own without danger, be masters of their own destiny, control large fortunes and companies, be CEOs, was so far removed from their adjacent possible as to be utterly and completely unimaginable.

Think of how morality has changed since those days. Slavery was the norm. Poor people were considered to be cursed by God. People believed that kings were chosen by God. LGBTQ+ people were arrested for being true to themselves.

When you think about it, these people had to take these esoteric concepts and figure out a way to translate these concepts into laws that seemed perfectly normal and were considered both moral and ethical in their time, but in our time are tortuous and destructive.

The adjacent possible answered everything! It was humans being humans, translating and inferring according to what their world looked like. The problem is, that be it fundamentalist Judaism, fundamentalist Christianity, or fundamentalist Islam, they are still sticking to those self-same rules that in today's world don't protect, but rather inhibit and prohibit and cause untold pain to millions all over the world. That's why the concepts are so beautiful . . . because it is the concepts themselves that are eternal. Mankind's original interpretation of those concepts, from several thousands of years ago, in a world so radically different from our own, no longer make sense. The idea that changing any laws in the Gemara is akin to going against God is absurd and inaccurate. There are many examples of laws, customs, and practices that are in the Mishna and Gemara that we no longer follow. One example is the law requiring a rapist to marry the woman he raped. There are also all sorts of medical laws and practices that we are told to ignore as medical advancements make it clear that the advice found in the Mishna and Talmud relating to health is incorrect. It says "nishtanu hativ'im," which means "their nature has changed," and therefore we do not follow the medical advice in the Talmud or Mishna. So, basically, we no longer have to practice the things rabbis decided are literally impossible to defend. This serves as a very clear precedent and gives me hope that if enough women stand up and demand that the laws of divorce and tznius change, they will. If we all stand together and make it clear that forcing people into specific roles because of their biology is no longer justifiable, that a woman isn't responsible for a man's thoughts and that a man is perfectly capable of controlling himself, then those laws can also go the way of archaic interpretations of beautiful eternal concepts. It is possible. I believe it with all my heart and soul and will continue to have faith in the innate goodness of mankind.

If God came to us now, I guarantee you that no single religion would consider being LGBTQ+ wrong.

This understanding gave me such inner calm and peace I cannot even begin to describe it to you. Of course, these are my thoughts and my thoughts alone. I make no claim to have the answers, but I hope these thoughts can help others try to make peace with what was taken from them.

I also spent a lot of time with my kids. Even though we spoke on the phone every day while I was gone, it still wasn't the same as seeing their faces. I looked into their eyes and remembered again why I was doing this. Miriam's life wasn't going to be anything like mine, I promised myself. And Aron, fearless and funny and incredibly smart, didn't deserve the same education that poor Shlomo had gotten. I was going to make it better for all of us or I would die trying.

Batsheva and I were continuing to repair our relationship. It still wasn't as close as it had been, but every single day I felt us getting a little closer. She was at FIT, and her sheitel kept moving farther and farther back on her head. She was slowly growing up and realizing that I might not have been so crazy after all. She didn't understand my journey yet, but I could see acceptance beginning to form in her eyes, and that gave me great hope for the future.

It took years before my and Bat's relationship was fully healed. We spoke about that first year, 2013, only several years later in 2017, and she told me how hurt and alone she had felt. I had gone against every precept that I had taught her, and even more surprising for a woman like me, whose main focus had always been her family and children, I wasn't as available as I had been her entire life.

It was a very emotional conversation, as I told her, for the first time, what I was going through back then, and how unwell I was. I explained that I was close to committing suicide, and if I hadn't left and lost myself in my work, I would have died, and she wouldn't have had a mother at all. Those first six months after I left, I was a mess. It was work and focus and single-minded determination that kept me from totally losing my mind. I couldn't be there for her that first year, mainly those first six months, because I was barely keeping it together myself. I knew that to be there for her for the rest of my life I had to fix myself first, or I would be no use to anyone. Now we are finally as close as we once were and speak as often as we used to.

She understands what I did, and why I did it, and she has forgiven me. Her wig has come off. She wears pants and lives a free life with all the world's beauty and possibility before her. She now resides in a world of yes. But it took years of patience and love to get her to forgive me for what she saw as abandonment those first years but was, in fact, a desperate attempt to save myself.

At some point that fall, Lucas and I made up. We just couldn't keep our hands off each other. It was a mad addiction that we felt. We both knew deep inside somewhere that this wasn't love but intense desire, but we couldn't bring ourselves to give it up.

And then, in November, my younger sister Naomi's son was being bar mitzvahed. It was the first major family event that occurred since I left, and despite everything, there was no way I wasn't attending—though I was really nervous. I brought my sheitel, as my extended family still had no idea that I was irreligious. All they knew was that I had left Yosef, but they were all sure that I'd go back any day. They knew that I had started a shoe company, but they thought I was crazy already, so my opening a business seemed perfectly in sync with my being so weird. It didn't occur to them that I was no longer keeping Shabbos. So, to honor my parents, I decided I would wear the hated sheitel once again.

However, when push came to shove and it was time to get dressed and put on the sheitel, I just couldn't do it. I tried. I really did. I managed to put on a tznius dress that I had bought just for the occasion. But when I put the sheitel on my head, I ran to the bathroom and threw up. I couldn't go back to being that woman. I wanted to burn it, not wear it. It felt like lead on my head.

And so I went, sans sheitel, to the last family event that I was ever invited to. Naomi now has eight or nine children. I'm not even sure, as she doesn't speak to me, but I was never invited to a family function again. I don't blame her. It must have been embarrassing to have to explain to her fundamentalist neighbors about her non-sheitel-wearing sister. I'm sure she was just worried for her children's shidduchim. Having an off-the-derech sibling could completely derail a match. It raised too many uncomfortable questions. What mental disorder, which could be hereditary, would cause a forty-year-old woman to leave everything she knew behind? So I don't blame her for not ever inviting me back.

By December, although I was still panicked constantly—feeling the world could crash down around me at any moment—I knew our company had survived. Between Jon's and David's money and the small percentage payment from Galeries Lafayette Dubai, I had somehow managed it. I now had two employees working for me, a bookkeeper, and an intern straight out of college.

I even got a call from Paris from one of the shop owners who had canceled their order. They had reconsidered and now wanted to see some shoes. In addition to that stroke of luck, I met a makeup artist in Paris named Isabela, who did a lot of the shows and was really good friends with the top models. According to Lucas, she was very well connected, and her close friend worked for a powerful business-man in Hong Kong. Lucas's idea was that I would meet with both of them, and for a fee on profits, they would introduce me to this busi-nessman who could get me into all the department stores in Hong Kong and Shanghai. Things were happening once again.

I flew back to Paris to meet with everyone a few days before Christmas. It was perfect, as Lucas had invited me to spend Christ-mas at his family house in the English countryside. I would go to Paris for the meetings, then go to Lucas's house for Christmas, and then to Israel, where Shlomo was studying, to be with him for New Year's, and then back to New York City. I was worried about how brainwashed Shlomo was becoming, and I wanted to spend as much time with him as I could.

The Paris meetings had mixed results. The Parisian shop owner turned out to be a hoax perpetrated by Fatima, just to mess with me and try to get more money. But the second meeting, with Isabela and her friend Jean Louis, who lived in London and Hong Kong, went fantastically well. They loved the shoes and immediately saw poten-tial in my brand. Jean Louis promised to come with me to Hong

Kong and set up a meeting with his boss, Matthew Yang. Asia was a huge market, and I had been dying to get into it, and here, it seemed, was my opportunity to do just that. Matthew was a huge deal in Hong Kong. He worked for a global investing company, which owned a popular record label, and he knew everyone. He also owned a restaurant and ran a society whose mission was to help bring western culture and brands to the East. He was the perfect person to meet.

On a total high, I went to Lucas's country house the day before Christmas. It was the first Christmas that I had ever celebrated. Their place was something out of a fairy tale. It had turrets and fireplaces and all these nooks and crannies. And I fell in love with his parents instantly. His mother was incredibly beautiful, tall and lithe and graceful, and she spoke with a soft, gentle air. She was enchanting. And Lucas's dad was a plump British country gentleman. He was articulate, funny, and charming, and they both treated me like family. I was the only woman Lucas had ever brought home, so they knew it must be serious between us.

His grandmother lived in the house too, and she was such a spirited, lively woman. I don't think I understood a word she was saying, but she had a fantastic laugh, and every time I looked at her, smiling and so cheerful, it made me feel welcome.

I had bought a stunning cashmere scarf, hat, and gloves for his mother, and an expensive bottle of scotch for his dad. I bought Lucas a blue cashmere sweater that perfectly matched his eyes. I didn't want to arrive empty handed.

His mother was a religious Christian, and I worried about how she would treat me, this Russian Jewish woman, but I shouldn't have had any concerns at all. She was friendly and warm, and made me feel instantaneously welcome. Lucas had also made sure to have all my favorite foods: frozen grapes, bananas, and Special K. We made love the night we arrived, and I had never felt closer to him.

On Christmas Eve, everyone went to Mass except me. I explained that I didn't believe in any organized religion, and it would seem hypocritical to go. No one even raised an eyebrow. They all accepted me exactly as I was.

When Lucas got home that night, I could see that something was wrong, and for the first time in our relationship, he didn't want to have sex. I begged him to tell me what was troubling him, and finally, after much pleading, he told me that he regretted bringing me here. Not even his friends had ever been to his family's place in the country. He had kept it hidden from everyone because it wasn't glamorous or fancy. "You know too much about me now," he explained. "I don't like it. I have no secrets left from you. It's making me feel weak." All I could think was how easily pride destroys everything.

"I love your house," I told him. "It's perfect and charming and beautiful and I can imagine no place where I'd rather be than right here, right now, with you." (Yes, I was that dopey and romantic. You should have read our texts. I promise they would make you blush.) "And your parents! I wish my parents were like yours," I told him. But nothing I said mattered. For the first time in our relationship, he turned his back to me when he fell asleep.

The next morning, we opened Christmas presents under the tree. They all loved the gifts I had brought. His mother had bought Lucas many gifts: Loro Piana cashmere sweaters, Dior jeans, and handmade shirts with his initials sewn on. Money was certainly not plentiful, and yet here they were, buying him the most expensive clothes on earth. But he accepted all the gifts as his due. I learned a lot about him that day. I saw that his parents' lives revolved around him, and that he had been brought up to think that his needs and desires were all that mattered. They had taught him the most beautiful manners and educated him in incredible ways, but their spoiling him had caused real damage. He was a little boy who was used to being the center of attention. Always. An only child born to older parents. He had been their miracle baby, and he was still their entire world. They both openly worshipped him.

He opened my gift and put on the sweater, and he looked so deliciously good.

Then it was my turn to open his gift. He had gotten me a key chain. I was devastated.

It was not the fact that it was cheap and small. It was the fact that it was obvious that so little thought had gone into it. I had been to dozens of stores to find just the right color sweater that would match his eyes. He bought me something you buy for family members when you're out of town and you forgot a gift, so you buy it from the airport giftshop. There was no loving message, no note. Had he just written me a card and given me nothing, I would have swooned. But a key chain? Really?

I tried to be cheerful, because we were going to eat Christmas dinner, which I'd never had before. I told myself that I was being silly, and that a key chain was a lovely present, and that I should be grateful just to be here. They had a family tradition of watching a horror movie together on Christmas, so after dinner we munched on chestnuts and watched *The Babadook*. I tried to pretend all was well between me and Lucas, even though I knew it wasn't.

I flew to see Shlomo, wondering if my relationship with Lucas was finally over. I wasn't ready for it to be done. My desire for him was still so strong. I asked him what he would be doing for New Year's while I was spending it with Shlomo, and he told me that he would be spending it alone, as he needed to come up with a plan to help his parents financially. He was worried about them and wanted to take care of them, as they were getting older. My heart melted again at this, and I decided I'd again misjudged him.

Shlomo and I had a great time on New Year's. I took him and three of his friends to Tel Aviv, and we wandered the streets and went to bars, as the legal drinking age in Israel is eighteen. We danced and laughed, and I felt hope that if he was here with me, in Tel Aviv, he wasn't as indoctrinated as I thought. Of course, they all wore black hats and white shirts and black pants, the uniform of the very yeshivishe, and they were spending New Year's with their friend's mom, which no normal eighteen-year-old would ever do, but it was still something. It became obvious that I was the coolest person they knew, and they were happy to dance and drink and let off a little steam. I brought them back to the yeshiva in the wee hours of the morning, and the others snuck in while Shlomo and I went back to the hotel, where I had booked us a suite.

I was a bit hurt that Lucas hadn't texted me a Happy New Year message, but I excused it, thinking he was busy planning his business. I take my work too seriously to ever fault anyone for working overtime, even on New Year's. It made me feel proud of him. And then someone sent me a picture of him partying in London.

The next morning he sent me loving messages, telling me he had been "dragged" to a party by his friends. He didn't, however, apologize for not texting me at midnight. It was pathetic, but I could not help myself: I told him, "I forgive you, and I'm not upset." But I didn't mean it, and I didn't believe him. If I had told him I was working and then gone off to party without telling him and without wishing him Happy New Year, he would never have forgiven me. The double standard was too much. We broke up again, but it would not last long. I was trapped in a cycle with him, and I could not figure out how to break it.

I flew back home to wonderful news. Matthew Yang had loved my designs when Jean Louis had shown them, and he was willing to meet with me. And if things went well, he would help me get them into his department stores.

I had many things to do prior to the meeting, though. I needed all my new samples to be finished and sent to Hong Kong prior to my arrival. I had to beg the new factory we were working with in Civitanova Marche to get them done in time. They were a vast improvement on the first factory, but the shoes still weren't the quality that I needed. But it would have to do for now. I had recently discovered that the only factories the Reggiano brothers actually owned were in Serbia. My brand was too small to make orders big enough to be produced there, so what they had done in Italy, essentially, was to act as brokers and find me a factory to work with until I was large enough to be of use to them. I ended up paying both the brothers and the factory. They swore up and down that the samples would be ready and waiting for me when I arrived in Hong Kong. I prayed that they were right, and I had no choice but to trust them. And then there was Samuel to contend with. He begged me to go with him to a mediator so we could "iron out our differences." I agreed, on one condition: that if I went, he would never again bother me. He agreed, and the next day, we went to the office of a lawyer who was a friend of Samuel's. This lawyer would act as our mediator. I spoke first, describing everything that had happened. Samuel vehemently denied it all, even though he had admitted it to me that day on the phone in Paris. I was livid. How could he lie, after all he had done to me? I thanked the lawyer for his time and left the room, sure that I would never see Samuel again.

I tried to put Samuel behind me and remind myself that, despite his best efforts, JH LLC was still alive, even if we were barely scraping by. We'd had no choice but to pay for the current shoe production up front, and this was causing a terrible cash flow issue that kept me up at night We kept having to front hundreds of thousands of dollars that we just didn't have. The money Jon and David Liebergall had put in was quickly spent on rent, production, molds, and samples. We were creating new molds, making them with a different angle and shape so that the pressure points would be evenly distributed across your entire foot as opposed to all the pressure and the weight of your body resting on your toes and the ball of your foot. The result was spectacular, but until I was able to build up enough molds to be able to constantly reuse them, it was also massively expensive. I was barely keeping us above water, but I just wouldn't give up. Any small business owner will understand exactly what I'm talking about. The only thing keeping us afloat was my sheer perseverance and an intense desire to succeed. Despite all this, I was hopeful about Hong Kong. The meeting could help my company go further than it ever had.

And then I received an email from a psychiatrist, who wrote me that Samuel was a patient of his, and that for his mental health and stability, he needed me to come to his office. The letter said Samuel had finally acknowledged what he did wrong and wanted to apologize and take full responsibility for his actions. He asked me to please come, as Samuel was now aware that he was unstable and was working hard with medication to change his life. I was torn. On the one hand, I never wanted to see Samuel again. On the other, there was my debt of gratitude to him for having believed in me in the first place. As usual, my empathy won, and I decided to agree to meet with the doctor and Samuel.

It had now been months since I last saw him, and the Samuel who sat in the doctor's office was a Samuel I didn't recognize. He appeared truly contrite and was actually crying. With the doctor sitting there, Samuel told me, "I'm so sorry that I denied what I did. You're right. I destroyed the company because of my jealousy. You have never led me on and have always been a great friend to me, and I couldn't help myself. I couldn't admit what I had done, even to myself, and so I denied it all. I'm so sorry, Julia."

He looked so repentant, so miserable. He was getting help, taking responsibility for his actions. And he went on: "If you forgive me, I will focus solely on the business and helping it grow. I will give you back all my shares, every single share I own of the company, because I destroyed it, and I will work hard to earn them back. Please forgive me and give me one last chance."

He was offering me full ownership of the company. Yes, he had put in millions of dollars, but then, he had cost the company millions of dollars in lost orders. This time, I desperately wanted to believe him. I knew that people were capable of change; look how much I had changed over the last few years.

"I forgive you," I told him. "I will give you one more chance, but if you ever do anything like that again, or try to force me to have any kind of sexual relationship, or try and be anything other than my partner and friend, you and I will be finished forever. No excuse, no apology will cut it next time," I said. "This is it." He started to cry again, and I left the office feeling hopeful that he had really changed, and that I would have a partner whom I could one day rely upon. I flew to Hong Kong with hope in my heart. Everything, my company's future, rested in the hands of a total stranger named Matthew.

CHAPTER SEVENTEEN

I was instantly obsessed with Hong Kong. What a city! It was frenetic, youthful, and pulsing with promise and possibility. I wandered, wide-eyed, through narrow streets filled with exotic scents and sights. My favorite part of the city was the fascinating melding of the old and the new. There were hundreds of buildings going up all over the city, construction everywhere you turned. And the scaffolding on all these magnificent steel high-rises? Bamboo! I'd never seen anything like it: the ancient being used to create the modern.

I walked around the food markets and saw dead ducks hanging by their feet. I tasted snake soup and chicken knuckles. I wanted to immerse myself in that world. It reminded me of Manhattan in so many ways—the thrumming energy, the feeling of possibility in the air, the fabulous shops. There were so many malls, so many stores. Everywhere I went, people were carrying shopping bags of goods. Wait till they're buying my shoes, I told myself. Hong Kong needs Julia Haart shoes, I decided, and I was going to make it happen one way or another.

My shoes finally arrived the morning of my meeting with Matthew, with only hours to spare. The day of the meeting, I wore a very chic blue dress with a zipper down the front—professional and feminine at the same time. I arrived at Matthew Yang's office schlepping a giant rolling suitcase that held my entire spring collection. I wanted him to touch the shoes, see the extraordinary materials with his own eyes, and understand the difference between the shape of my arch and everyone else's. It was one thing to talk about them; it was another thing for someone to hold them and see them.

Matthew was a very chic and handsome man. He was perfectly attired, and everything about him said "elegant." He was, however, extremely cold when I walked through the door of his office. The first words out of his mouth, even before saying hello, were "You have five minutes. I'm in a rush, so make it quick." Five minutes? I flew halfway around the world and paid an inordinate amount of money for five minutes of his time? I nearly gave up then and there. I mean, what could I do with five minutes? But I couldn't give up. That was not an option. So instead of launching into my prepared spiel, I started taking my shoes out of the suitcase and placing them on the meeting table.

Then something wonderful happened. Some women who were working in the office started peeking in to see the shoes. Within minutes, we were surrounded by women admiring the designs and trying the shoes on and discussing how comfortable they were. I still hadn't said more than two words. I had let the product do all the talking.

My five minutes turned into three hours, and that turned into an invitation to dinner with Matthew and his wife. He loved the shoes, the brand, and the concept, and it looked like he was going to help me. After our meeting, I ran back to the hotel, floating on hope, changed for dinner, and went to meet him and his wife.

I adored his wife. She had a wicked sense of humor, and she gave as good as she got, which I loved. Matthew made some comment about how much she was eating, and she turned and patted his belly and told him to watch his own plate. It was hilarious.

And then, as we were finishing the last of our desserts, Matthew looked at me and said the words that would forever change my life. "I'm going to help you get into the department stores here, but that may take a year or so, as there is quite a process, and they'll probably want to try a small order first," he told me. "However, I have a more immediate idea that I think will be even better for your business than getting a few shoes into a department store. I am on the board of La Perla, the lingerie brand, and the owner, a man named Silvio Scaglia, is trying to turn the lingerie brand into a full fashion brand," he explained. My heart was beating so loudly by this point, I was surprised that people from the other table couldn't hear it.

"La Perla hired a famous shoe designer to create some La Perla shoes," he continued, "but they're not selling at all, as people keep complaining that they're uncomfortable. Your shoes are exquisite, and more importantly, I spoke to the women at the office who were wearing them while we were meeting, and they couldn't stop talking about how comfortable your shoes are."

Hearing him praise my shoes and talk about the world's largest lingerie brand in one sentence was almost too much for me. I wanted to reach across the table and hug them both. But I just sat there, barely daring to breathe lest I break the spell, and waited for him to continue. "I think your shoes will be a perfect fit, excuse the pun, for La Perla. They're beautiful, high-end, and uniquely comfortable. If you're interested, google some La Perla images and draw an entire shoe collection as if you were already working for LP, and then, if I like your drawings and designs, I will introduce you, and we can show the owner your shoes and your designs for LP, and we can take it from there," he said.

It took me a second to gather my words and say, "Matthew, I don't know what to say. This is an incredible opportunity, and I totally agree with you that I should focus on this rather than getting into a department store." With some trepidation, I asked the most burning question in my mind. "How many stores and points of sale does La Perla have?" I asked.

"One hundred twenty-seven" was his succinct and glorious reply. I was so excited that my skin was tingling. My shoes could be in 127 stores all over the world! My imagination conjured up beautiful images of women of every ethnicity in every country, in every city, wearing my shoes. I was so excited I felt like I was going to burst. I couldn't wait to tell Lucas and David and Jon and even Samuel. With everything stacked against me, I had managed to keep the company alive, and now here we were, about to be in hundreds of stores.

It didn't occur to me that I would fail. I was going to design the most stunning shoes that anyone had ever seen. I was going to knock the socks off both Matthew and the owner of La Perla. I was going to blow their minds, and then the world would really know Julia Haart.

I felt, for the very first time since the day I'd left, that success was truly within my grasp. This wasn't just a single order of $3 million. This was serious global distribution. This would literally put us on the map.

The second I was back in my hotel room, I called Lucas. He answered immediately, and I said, "Lucas, you'll never believe it. Matthew, the guy that I met with, sits on the board of La Perla, and they're making shoes now, and he thinks that we can do some kind of co-branding deal to make Julia Haart shoes for La Perla! Do you know what this means? Can you believe it? Lucas! My company is saved . . . Julia Haart shoes are going to be all over the world!"

"Why are you back so late?" he asked. "Who has a business meeting that ends at 10:00 P.M.?"

"What? What do you mean?" I asked. "He and his wife took me out for dinner after we met in his office. That's why I am back so late. Didn't you hear what I said? He's gonna give me a chance to make shoes for La Perla! They've got a hundred twenty-seven points of sale all over the world!" I was so excited. I couldn't understand why he wasn't celebrating with me.

"Bullshit," was his response. "I don't believe you. You weren't having dinner with his wife. You were fucking him to get him to help you. He doesn't give a shit about your shoes. You fucked him, and now he's obsessed with you, and that's why he's gonna introduce you to La Perla."

It was so wrong. So patently untrue and hurtful. It shook me to the core. He had unjustly accused me of something that was utterly against the very foundation of my being, for no reason other than that I was a woman. Didn't he understand that I had left my world precisely to never have to fake anything again? Didn't he understand that my whole life was about freedom? What kind of freedom would it be if I had to pretend to be attracted to someone to get ahead? What kind of freedom would it be if I had to sell my body in order to sell my shoes? Did he understand nothing about what mattered to me, who I was?

I wish this was the only time that accusation has been leveled at me. I wish that the world treated women the same way they treat men. I would love to see someone accuse a guy of sleeping his way to the top. Do you know how many times I've heard those words? Forget the fact that I worked twenty-hour days. Forget the fact that I ate and slept JH LLC. Forget the fact that I had literally stood my life on its head to change my future and the futures of my children. Forget that I had done it alone. Forget the fact that my designs were loved wherever they were seen. All of that counted for nothing. I must have slept my way to success. Had I been that kind of person, I would have slept with Samuel or Ephrayim eons ago. It would have saved me so much trauma.

I didn't make the mistake I had made before of trying to defend myself and convince him that he was wrong. I was done. I hung up the phone. He had ruined this amazing moment for me. He had accused me of something that was against the very core of my being. It killed me. I never wanted to see or speak to him again.

I knew, however, that I would weaken if I saw him. And so I did something that I would tell others never to do. I broke up with him through a series of text messages, right before I boarded my sixteen-hour flight back home. I knew that he wouldn't be able to reach me and change my mind for nearly a day. I told him that I never wanted to see him again, and this time, I stuck to it. I said goodbye to Lucas, and a chapter of my life closed behind me. I was starting to learn to stand up for myself. But I still had a very, very long way to go. If I could get a deal with La Perla, my company wouldn't be a major risk for anyone, and it would be so much easier to attract investors. So when I got back to New York, I started to do just that. Luisa, Samuel, Jon, and David all set about trying to help me as well. Luisa came through first. She told me that she had this close producer friend in Hollywood who could bring in money as well as get celebrities to wear my shoes. She said he'd even been an early investor in some famous fashion brand. I told her to set up a meeting.

I was staying at the Bryant Park Hotel, and I was set to meet the producer downstairs in the bar at 7:00 P.M. I was sitting there, materials in hand, excited to do my pitch. My excitement waned when seven turned to eight, which turned to nine, without a text or a call.

I called Luisa, who said he probably got stuck in filming or something, and he likely wasn't allowed to have his phone on the set. She seemed so confident that again I questioned myself and decided I should still give him a chance. It was 10:30 P.M. and I was already in pajamas in my room when the front desk called from downstairs and told me that a man named Brad was here to see me.

I thought about telling the concierge that I was now unavailable, as it was three and a half hours after our meeting was supposed to take place and I was already in bed. But then I became afraid that Luisa would get angry at me for being so picky, so I hurriedly got dressed and ran downstairs to meet him.

He was a mountain of a man. His shirt was untucked, and his eyes frightened me. He was clearly high and drunk. But he was effusive in his apology. "Today is my birthday," he explained. "My friends threw a surprise party for me. Sorry I'm so late, but they got me super drunk and so I didn't see the time and here I am." He looked so apologetic, and a surprise birthday party did seem like a legit excuse, so I decided to give him a chance.

I shut off the voice in my head that said he was bad news and told myself that I still didn't understand the ways of the world, and that this is probably what famous Hollywood people are like. Of course, now that I know very famous producers and directors in Hollywood, not one of them is like that. They always arrive within fifteen minutes of the meeting time, and if they're ever held up, they immediately text. Good people are good people, no matter what their profession or how successful they are. Remember that.

That night Brad painted quite an enticing picture. He told me that if he liked the business plan, and if I really did manage to get the La Perla contract, he would invest $5 million in two tranches: $2 million first, and then if I hit my goals, the next $3 million. I was thrilled. That would mean no more panicking about cash flow. I would be able to hire a production manager, a CEO, a product manager, salespeople, and more. I would have the money I needed to really make the business grow. I called Luisa and thanked her profusely for setting this up.

Samuel was over the moon and told me that he would take care of the contract, as I didn't have time. I, meanwhile, got busy designing the best collection I possibly could for La Perla. I used the colors from the runway collection that they had recently shown in Paris, working to create shoes that meshed perfectly with their creative director's clothing designs. (At the time, I had no clue that they had gone through four creative directors in the last four years, and that the owner's concept of making LP into a full-fashion brand was constantly hitting snags.)

Meanwhile, Samuel negotiated with Brad that while the contract was being drafted, Brad would loan us $150,000 so that I could produce the next set of sample shoes. I was grateful to Samuel for taking this on. He hadn't bothered me at all in the last month and had been professional and courteous and focused on the business. I spoke to Brad very infrequently, and Samuel told me that part of the deal with Brad was that Luisa would become the CEO of the company and handle finances. I thought this was genius. I trusted her, as she had been running her own company (successfully, I thought) for years. She had helped me in the past, and I counted her a very dear friend. I was grateful that she was going to stop running her own business to come run mine. My mind told me it was suspicious, but I was still doubting myself, still so naïve. As I later learned, she was happy to give up her business because it was failing, and she knew my business was on the way up.

Back then, I was just grateful to be able to focus on the creative side and have someone taking care of the nitty-gritty. I was happy to be left in the dark. I just wanted to design. I didn't want to be bogged down in business minutiae. That's another thing I've learned now: I love the business aspect of my companies and brands. I oversee everything. I am particularly proud of it. I am as comfortable with a spreadsheet as I am with a sketch pad.

Every time I win, it makes me stronger and more able to handle the next attack that comes my way. Now I listen to my own voice. I trust my instincts, and so far, ever since I have truly begun to believe in myself and my capabilities, it has not once steered me wrong. Everything I have achieved is due to the difficult lessons I learned those first few years in the outside world. Everything I've built with my own two hands (and plenty of miracles) is thanks to the painful lessons I learned. I wish the road had been less difficult. I wish I was done paying the price for my lack of faith and judgment back then. But I am who I am today thanks to the traumas I suffered. With everything that was going on, it was still imperative for me to stay focused and not lose sight on my goal.

During the day I was busy designing and creating, and in the evening, I would make the drive up to Monsey so that I could be with Miriam and Aron. Aron was getting older now, and we spent every available second together. He would fall asleep on my bed every night, and then I would carry him back to his room, and in the morning he would come and snuggle with me, and then we would get breakfast together. It was so special to be able to spend those hours with him. I carefully counted every second of my day so that all I was doing was designing and being with my kids.

I was spending very little time in the WeWork office, but on a Monday, I happened to go in. When I got there, it was clear that Samuel and Luisa weren't expecting me. There was a brown paper bag on a table in front of them, and out of curiosity, I reached out to see what was inside. You should have seen their faces. "Why do we have a bag full of money?" I asked.

"Oh, we needed money over the weekend, and of course the bank wasn't open, so Brad kindly sent over some cash that he had lying around at home," Luisa answered, as if it were perfectly normal to have this much cash around your house.

"How much is in there?" I asked.

"Just ten thousand dollars. Nothing major," Luisa said. It seemed so odd to me, and they were both behaving strangely, but I had so much to do, and if they were fine with it, then I guess I would have to be fine with it as well.

February was here, and we were doing another showroom in Paris. This time, we had hired a friend of Jean Louis's (the guy who introduced me to Matthew) to run the showroom. We had to pay for the space, and for the shoes from the factory, but the money still wasn't coming. Brad would send $5,000 here, $2,000 here—always ten days late, and always in some very shady way. Then one day I got a call from my bookkeeper telling me that Luisa had come into the office while I was gone and said she was her boss now, and Julia's boss too.

You can imagine how well that went over with me. I worked for no one. I was my own boss. The whole purpose of this company was freedom. I wasn't relinquishing control to anyone. She was supposed to *help* me by becoming CEO, not control me.

I was getting a lot of grief from Jean Louis and the factory and the Reggiano brothers. And Luisa's plan was now becoming clear: ingratiate herself to me, make me trust her, get me to put my company in her hands, and then it was all hers. She who controls the money controls the company. Remember that.

I told Samuel we needed to immediately get Brad and Luisa out of our lives and out of our company. Samuel promised he would take care of it, and again, I believed him.

My plan was to pay Luisa and Brad back every penny they'd lent the company in order to be free of them. That created its own set of problems, as we were short on cash, and Jean Louis and Isabela in Paris were demanding payment too. They threatened to call Matthew and kill the deal with La Perla. I was petrified. Isabela even sent me messages saying that her cousin, who was about to get out of prison, would come and beat me up if I didn't pay that very day. I knew all of this wasn't normal at all, and that if I didn't fix it and get rid of these people, I was going to regret it for the rest of my life.

I was so close to succeeding. I could taste it. La Perla was everything. And in addition to that, Galeries Lafayette Dubai was creating an entire new floor devoted to shoes. They made a massive order, and the CEO even told me that they loved my designs so much that Julia Haart shoes would be the first shoes people saw when they entered the shoe floor.

I was calling everyone I knew to see if I could get $300,000 as soon as possible. I needed these people out of my life. I needed to pay them back, as well as pay my employees and the factory. And then I found an investor in the most unexpected place: a frum laundry-service owner whose business I frequented back in my past life. His name was Yankie Gold. He was very kind and not fundamentalist in his beliefs, even though he had long payos and was Chasidishe. We had become friends. I think that was why he was willing to take a chance on me.

I called Samuel, jubilant. I had the money to get these people out of our lives. And this time, I had learned the power of a contract. I told Samuel not to pay Brad and Luisa back a cent until we had something signed that acknowledged we paid them back every dollar, and that we had concluded our business amicably. I left it all in Samuel's hands, as I was busy running the showroom, making sales, and finalizing the designs for La Perla. I had found the money. All he needed to do was to get Luisa and Brad to sign a piece of paper stating that we had paid them back, and then he needed to pay them. When I saw the wiring confirmation that the money came through, I felt free again.

But when I asked to see the contracts they'd signed before we paid them, Samuel hemmed and hawed and then admitted that he hadn't actually given them a contract. We had paid them over $150,000 without a single piece of paper—no proof of our deal.

"Don't worry, Julia," Samuel told me. "Luisa and I came to an understanding. We've paid them back. They're totally happy, and we have parted ways on good terms. You don't need a contract."

Of course, within two weeks, Brad started demanding we give him an extra $50,000 as interest—on a four-week loan. Now, I know that's illegal, and it's called usury. But back then, I had no clue that they couldn't demand it. And of course, what did they threaten? That they would reach out to Matthew and tell him that my business had no money and was disorganized.

My days and nights were filled with a dizzying mix of intense fear, constant threats, lack of funds, and hope for the future. I, who have always had difficulty sleeping, stopped sleeping altogether. I was so afraid. I felt so alone. Jon and David Liebergall promised that when I got back from Paris, they would help me find a really good CFO and CEO, and that they would help me get real money to run the business. I was so grateful for their help but too afraid to tell them about all the threats I was receiving from Brad and Luisa and Isabela and Jean Louis. I thought they'd get nervous and run for the hills. I know now that I misjudged them, as when I did finally tell them everything about Samuel—who ended up stealing company funds, trying to use the company to avoid paying taxes on his other businesses, and gambling with company money that I needed to pay salaries—they were incredibly helpful and supportive in kicking him out of Julia Haart. But back in February 2015, I still didn't fully trust them. They were too new.

While all of this was happening, I had finally found a really good head of production, and he had introduced me to several incredible factories in Padova, where Tom Ford and Dior and many others produce their shoes. It had taken me two years to finally get production and the factories right, but I'd done it. For the first time, my shoes were not only beautiful and comfortable but also well made and built to last. No heels would break on these.

The past weeks had been the stuff of nightmares, but now the biggest moment of my life had arrived. I was set to go to Tokyo to meet Silvio Scaglia, the owner of La Perla. If he liked my designs we would do a co-branding deal, and Julia Haart would be saved.

+ + +

I didn't sleep a wink on the plane. I was surviving on pure stubbornness and adrenaline. I kept telling myself, I can't fail, I can't fail. I was so close. I was constantly being threatened and begging people to leave me alone. And at the same time, I was heading toward the biggest opportunity of my life, and I had no one to lean on. I had only myself. But I was going to succeed. End of story.

I landed in Tokyo, and a few hours later, I was supposed to meet Silvio and Matthew. Then it hit me. I had left my computer in Paris. I ran to an Apple store and bought myself a laptop, which of course had Japanese instructions, but I managed to switch the settings to English and access the cloud (which I'd started using after my drunk debacle), and the presentation was there. I arrived at the meeting with minutes to spare.

I walked into that meeting a jumble of nerves, but I hid it well. Matthew told me afterward that he was so impressed with how composed and confident I was. Fake it till you make it is my mantra. I faked being confident until I finally internalized it.

Despite everything, I came to that meeting dressed to the nines, acting cool as a cucumber. I was so professional that the two of them, Silvio and Matthew, didn't even ask me about the financial viability of my company. That's how perfect my armor was. That's why what you wear and how you comport yourself matter so much. I learned that watching my father make deals in our laundry room with presidents of foreign countries. The face you show the world is the face people will accept.

However, the meeting did not begin auspiciously. I had googled Silvio, and I didn't like what I'd found. He had melded technology with business and finance. That part was extremely impressive. What made me very wary of him was what he did after he sold his company, Fastweb, to Swisscom. He bought a lingerie brand and a modeling agency. Based on that fact alone, I assumed he was a total player.

Then, when I walked into the meeting, the first thing Silvio told me was that the current person designing shoes for La Perla was a close personal friend of his. Well, thanks, I thought to myself. What's the point of my designing a whole collection for your company and flying all the way to Tokyo if you were just gonna tell me that the guy currently making your shoes is your best friend?

Silvio looked so ominous sitting there, and I already thought he was an asshole, so my heart dropped to my knees, and for a second, I thought about walking right out without saying one more word. I had my computer with me, and my usual suitcase of shoes to show, and I just wanted to turn and run.

I threw that idea out of my mind immediately, though. He could be besties with the other shoe designer. He had agreed to meet with me, and I was going to make the most of it. Matthew looked at me and smiled for encouragement, and off I went. The minute I started talking about the altered arch of my shoes, the precious materials, the idea that a woman shouldn't have to suffer for beauty, I could see that I'd caught their attention.

The meeting lasted forty-five minutes, and Silvio asked some excellent questions about production capabilities and speed. And even though neither of us broke a smile the entire meeting, I walked out of there feeling hopeful. Yes, I would have felt better had they given me more time, but I told myself that forty-five minutes was a long time and hoped for the best. I thought that he had clearly liked the shoe designs I had drawn to match La Perla's last collection. He had even asked to keep them. I took this as a good sign. I waited impatiently for Matthew to call me and give me some feedback. He finally called much later that evening and simply said he thought it went well, but with Silvio you never knew.

The next morning I had to fly back to New York. I had come for one purpose only—to give my brand a chance to survive—and I'd done the best I could. The rest was up to God, or whatever you wanted to call it.

After touching down, I turned on my phone with great trepidation. My hands were shaking. Would the words there be the end? Did Silvio think I was rude? Had I been too tough? Too cold? What if he had sent my designs to his team and they hated them? What if *he* hated what I drew?

I saw Matthew Yang's name on my screen. Four text messages. Oh God. I put off looking at them. It was too much. I couldn't bear to have failed. Finally, my curiosity overcame my fear. The first text from Matthew read, "When can you come to Bologna to meet the new creative director? Silvio really loved the designs, and so did the head of marketing at La Perla. If you can get along with the CD, you're going to have yourself a deal."

I dropped my phone. I stood there, baggage swirling all around me, the sounds and smells of the airport fading into the background, my heart pounding in my ears. I had done it. There were no ifs in my mind anymore. This was going to happen.

I'd been alive, in the outside world, in the current century, for a little over two years. My shoe company, basically as old as I was, was going to not only survive but thrive. We'd made it, my brand and me. We had withstood threats, anger, criminals, heartbreak, and mistakes. I had left everything I'd known behind. I had embarked on a spectacularly mad and impossible journey, and now, I had made it. It had all been worth it.

The next month was filled with contract negotiations as well as threats from all sides, and a continued lack of funding, but none of it mattered. They didn't defeat me. I may have been alone and afraid, but I'd survived. I had beaten them all. I hadn't let anyone or anything stand in my way. I had defied all of them, all the voices telling me that I was just a woman, that my only purpose in life was to make children and be subservient to men. I had defied tradition, religion, and my "determined" place in life to make my own way.

A few years later, Samuel and Luisa and Brad tried to damage me by threatening to accuse me publicly of not paying invoices that we all knew I'd paid. I fought them long and hard, and eventually I proved them wrong. Back then, I was fighting for my life alone, without knowledge, experience, or help. Today there isn't a shred left of the frightened little girl that I was.

I had chosen freedom, and then I had fought for it. That April I walked into La Perla, contract in hand, to design my first shoe collection for the world's most famous lingerie brand. Little did I know that one thing would lead to another quickly. Designing shoes would turn into designing bags, which turned into "Julia, can you help with the lingerie designs? With the clothing designs?" Within one year of walking into La Perla and three years after I had left the eighteenth century behind, I became creative director of the world's most luxurious lingerie brand.

When I first became creative director of La Perla, I was given media training and guidelines about what to say and what not to say, etc., when I was being interviewed by the press. As usual, I showed up to the media training session wearing a low-cut top and a very mini miniskirt. The instructor, who by the way became a great friend of mine and is someone I adore, told me that if I wanted to be taken seriously and become respected, I could not wear low-cut tops and miniskirts. You should have seen my face. I explained, very politely and calmly, my stance on this matter. I told them I would wear whatever made me happy, and that people would learn to respect me anyway. To me, real feminism is what I call feminine feminism. You don't need to pretend to be a man to be respected. You don't need to dress like a man to be taken seriously. Enjoy being a woman. Luxuriate in your curves. And stand up and claim that boardroom. True freedom is being yourself—not having to hide your curves, your personality, your opinions.

I don't care if I'm inappropriate. I don't give anyone the right to tell me what is and what is not appropriate. I spent the first forty years of my life trying to be appropriate, and let me tell you: not only did I suck at it, I hated it. Every religion's or society's definition of what is and what is not appropriate is different. In the religious world, voicing an opinion at the dinner table was inappropriate. In the secular world, wearing a miniskirt to a business meeting is inappropriate. Too fucking bad. I should not have to worry about what inappropriate thoughts a man has when he sees my décolleté. It's not my problem. You're a grown-ass man! Take responsibility for your own thoughts and actions. This whole appropriateness thing is something I feel very strongly about. We are so conditioned to be polite, to not offend, that we spend years of our lives miserable and unhappy rather than offend someone's sensibility regarding what is proper and appropriate. It was inappropriate for women to work outside their homes a hundred years ago. Appropriateness is just another form of slavery—conditioning to get women to police themselves, to limit themselves, because they are so afraid of being deemed inappropriate. Stop worrying about it, ladies. To borrow the title of a book by Laurel Thatcher Ulrich, "Well-behaved women seldom make history." Fuck appropriateness, make history instead.

Seven years after leaving my world behind, I feel closer to a higher power, call it God or whatever other name you want to, than I ever did when I was religious. My rebirth, since the day I left, has been a string of miracles. It's also been bigger, crazier, faster, and luckier than I ever imagined. But not always easier.

Today, I feel that there are two parts of me. I am both forty-nine and seven years old. Part of me is a strong, experienced woman. I feel as old as Methuselah and as wise as Euripides. It is impossible to scare me or weaken my resolve. The other part of me is still so young. I have so much to do and accomplish, so much still to see and experience and learn. Freedom has been the single driving force of my life. It has been my raison d'être, the desire that no one could extinguish. Every choice I have made, every step, has been taken with that desire in mind. Free. Free. Free. Freedom is my mantra, my protection against fear and loneliness. It is what defines me and sustains me.

I appreciate every sunrise, relish the briny, salty taste of every oyster. I take nothing for granted. I am a proud, feminine feminist for whom every success, every obstacle is another step toward my goal of true freedom, toward helping other women achieve the same. I am old and young, free of the prison that restrained me, collecting firsts, and trying to live life to the fullest. And I'm just getting started.

NOTES

13 **unkosher food is toxic:** Rif on Babylonian Talmud, Tractate Yoma, 39; see also Mesilat Yesharim, chapter 11.

13 **There is this concept of a "tinok shenishbah":** Babylonian Talmud, Tractate Shabbat, 68a–b.

14 **the ba'al teshuva has a much harder road:** For a complementary view, see Babylonian Talmud, Tractate Berachot, 34b.

15 **In his introduction to the Mishna:** Maimonides, Introduction to the Mishneh, 17:41.

17 **which shoe to put on first (the right shoe):** Shulchan Aruch, Orach Chaim, 2:4.

20 **never being special or exceptional in any way:** See generally Babylonian Talmud, Tractate Bava Metzi'a, 87a, and Rashi (Abraham told the angels that Sarah was in the tent, because she is not seen, she was "modest"); Mishneh Torah, Marriage, 13:11 (stating "it is a disgrace for a woman to always go out to the street, and a husband should prevent his wife from being outside and not allow her to go out more than once or twice per month," and quoting Psalms 45:14, "Kol kevuda bas melech penima" ["All the honor of the king's daughter is inside"]).

21 **should only be seen by her husband:** Babylonian Talmud, Tractate Berachot, 24a.

22 **the wine becomes unkosher instantaneously:** Shulchan Aruch, Yoreh De'ah, Siman 123, 124:8; Halachot Gedolot, Siman 60 (Warsaw, 1874), p. 252.

23 **dancing was prohibited in front of men:** Ben Ish Chai, Year One (Jerusalem, 1898) p. 103; Shoftim 18.

23 **repent your sins on Yom Kippur:** Mishneh Torah, Repentance 2:7.

23 **tip the scales of judgment in your favor:** Babylonian Talmud, Tractate Rosh Hashanah, 16a.

24 **Friday night sundown to Saturday night sundown:** Mishneh Torah, Shabbat, 11:9–17 and 23:12; Shulchan Aruch, Orach Chaim, Siman 340.

24 **you're not allowed to even hold a pen:** Kitzur Shulchan Aruch, 88:5.

24 **called it cow's milk:** Babylonian Talmud, Tractate Avoda Zara, 35b; see also Shulchan Aruch, Yoreh De'ah 115:1.

25 **the community we were moving to didn't have dogs:** There are different reasons for this: For one, it is impermissible to lift animals on Shabbos. See Shulchan Aruch, Orach Chaim, 308:40. Second, having a dog in one's home prevents poor people and guests from entering one's home. See Rashi and Chidushei Agadot on Babylonian Talmud, Tractate Shabbat, 35a.

27 **the prevailing religious issue of that time:** For a complementary view, see Rabbi Aryeh Leifert, "The Role of Messianism in the Development of Hasidism," *Milin Havivin Journal*: 2, https://library.yctorah.org /files/2016/09/The-Role-of-Messianism-in-the-Development-of -Hasidism.pdf.

28 **not to be seen by anyone other than her husband:** Babylonian Talmud, Tractate Ketubot, 72a.

28 **aren't allowed to study Talmud is exactly the same:** See generally Babylonian Talmud, Tractate Sota, 21b.

28 **Why does a woman need to study the Talmud?:** For a complementary view, see Babylonian Talmud, Tractate Sota, 21b; see also Jerusalem Talmud, Sota 3:4.

34 **three times a day in shul (synagogue) like men:** Mishnah, Kiddushin 1:7.

35 **skirt to her legs by impaling herself:** Isaac Leib Peretz, *The Three Gifts* (London, 1946).

37 **for all eternity, even after death:** Exodus 12:15, 12:19 (Hebrew Bible).

39 **"nashim daytan kalos":** Babylonian Talmud, Tractate Kiddushin, 80b; Tractate Shabbat, 33b.

40 **"Thanks for not making me a woman":** Shulchan Aruch, Orach Chaim, 46:4.

40 **that women don't have:** Abudarham (Lisbon, 1489), Weekday Prayers, Morning Blessings, 29.

40 **with additional commandments:** Abudarham (Lisbon, 1489), Third Gate, Blessings on Commandments, 28.

43 **"Aishes Chayil mi Yimtzah":** Proverbs 31:10.

51 **"ve gilu bir'ada":** Psalms 2:11.

52 **"reached a very high spiritual level":** Mesilat Yesharim (Amsterdam, 1740), chapter 10.

79 **not to become a Talmudic scholar:** For a complementary view, see Babylonian Talmud, Tractate Sota, 21b; see also Jerusalem Talmud, Sota 3:4, and Babylonian Talmud, Tractate Ketubot, 59b.

80 **She ended up committing suicide:** Rashi on Babylonian Talmud, Tractate Avoda Zara, 18b.

87 **only be alone with one another:** Shulchan Aruch, Even Ha'Ezer, Siman 22.

98 **"with the elders of the land":** Proverbs 31:10–31.

104 **menstruating and thus impure:** See generally Leviticus 15:19–24; see also Babylonian Talmud, Tractate Niddah, and Maimonides, Mishneh Torah, Those Who Defile Bed or Seat.

104 **he's not allowed to touch her *at all*:** Leviticus 18:19 and 20:18; Shulchan Aruch, Yoreh De'ah, 195:1–2.

104 **pass her the salt:** Shulchan Aruch, Yoreh De'ah, 195:2.

105 **there is no blood:** Shulchan Aruch, Yoreh De'ah, Siman 196.

105 **seven clean consecutive days:** Shulchan Aruch, Yoreh De'ah, 196:4, 196:10.

105 **go to the mikvah:** Shulchan Aruch, Yoreh De'ah, Siman 197.

105 **a sort of deep square:** Shulchan Aruch, Yoreh De'ah, Siman 201.

105 **your child is considered "ruined":** Mishneh Torah, Forbidden Intercourse, 15:1.

105 **Not a single extraneous anything:** Shulchan Aruch, Yoreh De'ah, Siman 198.

106 **your whole body:** Shulchan Aruch, Yoreh De'ah, 199:3.

106 **night of the mikvah:** Shulchan Aruch, Yoreh De'ah, Siman 197.

107 **"Don't talk to a woman a lot":** Pirkei Avot, 1:5.

107 **"your help against you":** Genesis 2:18.

107 **make any blessings:** Babylonian Talmud, Tractate Shabbat, 10b; Shulchan Aruch, Orach Chaim, 84:1.

111 **to have righteous children:** Midrash Rabba, Deuteronomy 20:11.

111 **dip into again to achieve purity:** Shulchan Aruch, Yoreh De'ah, Siman 196.

112 **"please his wife first":** Babylonian Talmud, Tractate Niddah, 31a.

114   **supposed to be more readily answered:** Sefer Nit'ei Gavriel (Jerusalem, 1998), Nisuin vol. 1, chapter 18, FN 13.

114   **like a mini–Yom Kippur:** Babylonian Talmud, Tractate Yevamot, 63b; Jerusalem Talmud, Bikurim 3:3.

114   **nor even a sip of water:** Shulchan Aruch, Even Ha'Ezer, 61:1.

114   **first time in the yichud room:** Ibid.

115   **marrying Leah instead of Rachel:** Genesis 29:20–25.

125   **including your hair:** Babylonian Talmud, Tractate Yoma, 47a.

128   **she who goes out:** Rashi on Genesis 34:1.

128   **untold disaster followed:** Genesis 34.

135   **learn Torah all night long:** Magen Avraham on Shulchan Aruch, Orach Chaim, 494:1.

135   **came to visit its holy sites:** Pirkei Avot 5:5.

142   **get any naughty ideas:** Rashi on Genesis 12:14.

143   **(daughter of Israel) should behave:** Demanding sex is considered "shameless." See Babylonian Talmud, Tractate Nedarim, 20b; Mishneh Torah, Forbidden Intercourse, 21:13.

152   **outside of your home on Shabbos:** Shulchan Aruch, Orach Chaim, Siman 346.

152   **confines of the religious community:** Ibid.

152   **utilize the leniency of an eiruv:** For a complementary view, see Igros Moshe, Orach Chaim, vol. 1 (New York, 1959), pp. 138–140.

152   **You aren't allowed to use electricity:** Chazon Ish, Orach Chaim 50:9, and others.

155   **have a goyish English name:** For a complementary view, see Midrash Rabba, Numbers 13:20.

158   **husband refuses to grant a "get":** Mishneh Torah, Divorce 13:29.

158   **A man can divorce a woman for any reason whatsoever:** Mishneh Torah, Divorce 1:1.

158   **acceptable as reasons for divorce:** Babylonian Talmud, Tractate Gittin, 90a.

158   *under any circumstances* **without his approval:** Mishneh Torah, Divorce 1:2.

163   **the ones who seemed nice:** For a complementary view, see Rashi on Genesis 32:7.

165   **that mitzvah is *only* for men:** See generally Babylonian Talmud, Tractate Ketubot 64b.

167   **allowed to break the yom tov:** See generally Babylonian Talmud,

Tractate Sanhedrin, 74a, and specifically Shulchan Aruch, Orach Chaim, 328:17.

186 **without having first recited kiddush:** Shulchan Aruch, Orach Chaim, 271:4.

188 **going to the Egyptians' teatrot (theaters):** Yalkut Shimoni on Torah, Remez 162:11.

188 **"storm winds that will uproot them":** Meshech Chochma (Riga, 1927) on Leviticus 26:44.

193 **outside of the succah:** Shulchan Aruch, Orach Chaim, 639:2.

193 **supposed to sleep in there:** Babylonian Talmud, Tractate Sukah, 28a.

197 **a body must be buried immediately:** Babylonian Talmud, Tractate Sanhedrin, 46a.

199 **went back up to heaven, purified:** For a complementary view, see Derech Hashem (Jerusalem, 1914), part 2, chapter 3, letter 10.

204 **take some form of birth control:** Babylonian Talmud, Tractate Yevamot, 12b.

204 **be fruitful and multiply:** Babylonian Talmud, Tractate Yevamot, 61b.

208 **you could try nonkosher food:** Sifra and Rashi on Leviticus 20:26.

208 **controlling your desire is in and of itself a mitzvah:** For a complementary view, see Pirkei Avot, 4:1.

214 **great scholar that he was:** Babylonian Talmud, Tractate Ketubot, 62b–63a.

226 **"stopped him from committing adultery":** Babylonian Talmud, Tractate Sota, 36b.

236 **this was a sin:** Babylonian Talmud, Tractate Yevamot, 12b.

243 **say your sin out loud:** Mishneh Torah, Repentance, 2:5.

244 **"Death and life are in the hands of the tongue":** Proverbs 18:21.

253 **they left him in peace:** 1 Samuel 21:10–15.

265 **to exterminate the Jewish race:** Rav Avigdor Miller, *Rejoice O Youth: Rational Approaches to God's Existence and the Torah's Divine Origin* (Brooklyn, 1962), p. 136.

265 **Haskalah movement:** See generally Meshech Chochma on Leviticus 26:44; and article by Rav Elazar Menachem Shach, *Yated Ne'eman*, December 29, 1990, reproduced in *Chai Be'emuna* by Rabbi Yaakov Israel Lugasi, vol. 2 (ed. Jerusalem, 2014).

266 **proof of our chosen-ness:** Discourse by Rabbi Yitzchok Hutner in *The Jewish Observer* 12, no. 8 (October 1977): p. 9, https://agudah.org/wp-content/uploads/2016/10/JO1977-V12-No8.pdf.

266 **cornerstones of my belief system:** Rav Avigdor Miller, *Awake My Glory* (Brooklyn, 1980), p. 146, and *Rejoice O Youth*, pp. 144–147, 349–351. For a complementary view, see *A Divine Madness: Rabbi Avigdor Miller's Defense of Hashem in the Matter of the Holocaust* (Monsey, NY, 2000).

269 **"Meetoch shelo leshmah bah leshmah":** Babylonian Talmud, Tractate Pesachim, 50b.

327 **as in, between Haman and Mordechai:** Babylonian Talmud, Tractate Megila, 7b.

327 **show love and generosity:** Esther 9:22.

328 **Women have no mitzvah to get drunk:** See generally Babylonian Talmud, Tractate Ketubot, 64b.

371 **the Bible and the Ten Commandments:** Exodus 20:2–17; Deuteronomy 5:6–21.

371 **They only heard the first two commandments:** Rabbeinu Behaye on Exodus 20:1.

371 **"lest we die":** Exodus 20:15–16 (JPS).

371 **"not go up the mountain":** Deuteronomy 5:5 (JPS).

373 **marry the woman he raped:** Deuteronomy 22:28–29.

373 **Mishna and Talmud relating to health is incorrect:** Kessef Mishneh on Mishneh Torah, 4:18; Tosafot on Tractate Mo'ed Katan, 11a; Tosafot on Tractate Yoma, 77b.

ABOUT THE AUTHOR

JULIA HAART is the CEO, co-owner, and chief creative officer of Elite World Group. She is guiding the company to expand the definition of a "model" while growing the company's digital footprint and transforming it into a talent media network. She is incorporating new and creative talent, improving client services, and giving a fresh new voice to EWG's clients. Julia was previously the creative director of La Perla, the luxury Italian intimates brand. She launched her career as a designer with her namesake shoe collection. Julia is the star of the Netflix docuseries *My Unorthodox Life*. She lives in Manhattan.